# Degrammaticalization

# Degrammaticalization

MURIEL NORDE

OXFORD
UNIVERSITY PRESS

OXFORD
UNIVERSITY PRESS

Great Clarendon Street, Oxford OX2 6DP

Oxford University Press is a department of the University of Oxford.
It furthers the University's objective of excellence in research, scholarship,
and education by publishing worldwide in

Oxford New York

Auckland Cape Town Dar es Salaam Hong Kong Karachi
Kuala Lumpur Madrid Melbourne Mexico City Nairobi
New Delhi Shanghai Taipei Toronto

With offices in

Argentina Austria Brazil Chile Czech Republic France Greece
Guatemala Hungary Italy Japan South Korea Poland Portugal
Singapore Switzerland Thailand Turkey Ukraine Vietnam

Oxford is a registered trade mark of Oxford University Press
in the UK and in certain other countries

Published in the United States
by Oxford University Press Inc., New York



Reprinted 2010



ISBN 978-0-19-920793-0

Printed in the United Kingdom by
Lightning Source UK Ltd., Milton Keynes

# Contents


*Acknowledgments* ix
*List of Tables* xi
*Abbreviations* xiii
*List of Swedish sources referred to in the text* xvii

1 Introduction
1.1 Downs and ups in the history of degrammaticalization 1
1.2 Aims and outline 2
1.3 Preliminary definitions and observations 5
1.3.1 Grammaticalization 5
1.3.2 Degrammaticalization 8
1.3.3 Lexicalization 9
1.3.4 Areas of overlap 11
1.3.5 Diachronic gradualness and synchronic gradience 16
1.3.6 Reanalysis and analogy 18
1.4 Controversial types of grammaticalization 20
1.4.1 'Secondary' grammaticalization 20
1.4.2 Pragmaticalization 21
1.4.3 Clause combining 23
1.5 Context and constructions 26
1.6 Methodological issues 29
1.6.1 Processes versus results 29
1.6.2 Grammaticalization as a 'theory' 33
1.6.3 Changes and correspondences 35
1.6.4 Reconstruction as evidence 36
1.6.5 Case study: Romance MENTE 41
1.7 Summary 46

2 Unidirectionality 48
2.1 Introduction 48
2.2 Conceptualizations of language change 54
2.2.1 Clines 54
2.2.2 Cycles 55
2.3 Irreversibility 58

2.4 Non-directional change: lateral shifts 61
2.5 Alternative sources of grammatical markers 64
2.6 Allegedly irreversible changes 66
2.6.1 Desemanticization 67
2.6.2 Decategorialization 72
2.6.3 Univerbation 77
2.6.4 Phonological attrition 83
2.6.5 Subjectification 85
2.6.6 Summary 89
2.7 Explaining directional tendencies 90
2.7.1 Usage-based approaches 90
2.7.2 A psycholinguistic approach 93
2.7.3 Generative approaches 94
2.7.4 Other formal explanations 100
2.8 Summary 103

3 Defining degrammaticalization 106
3.1 Introduction 106
3.2 Regrammaticalization and antigrammaticalization 107
3.3 Terminological proliferation and confusion 109
3.3.1 Loss of grammatical meaning 110
3.3.2 Mirror image reversal 111
3.3.3 Lexicalization of function words and affixes 112
3.3.4 Euphemism 114
3.3.5 Adaptation and exaptation 115
3.3.6 Replacement 118
3.4 A generic definition 120
3.5 Classifying degrammaticalization 123
3.5.1 Lehmann's parameters 124
3.5.2 Some notes on the parameter of structural scope 126
3.5.3 Parameters of degrammaticalization 130
3.5.4 Andersen's levels of observation 132
3.5.5 Three types of degrammaticalization 133
3.6 Summary 134

4 Degrammation 135
4.1 Introduction 135
4.2 From modal auxiliary to lexical verb 136
4.3 Bulgarian *nešto*: from indefinite pronoun to noun 'thing' 143
4.4 Welsh *eiddo*: from possessive pronoun to noun 'property' 145

4.5 Middle Welsh *yn ol*: from preposition to Modern Welsh full verb *nôl* 'to fetch' 148

5 Deinflectionalization 152

5.1 Introduction 152
5.2 Classifying bound morphemes 152
5.2.1 Inflectional versus derivational affixes 153
5.2.2 Inflectional affixes versus clitics 157
5.2.3 Continua 159
5.3 The s-genitive (English and Mainland Scandinavian) 160
5.3.1 Introduction 160
5.3.2 The s-genitive in Swedish 162
5.3.3 The s-genitive in English 172
5.3.4 Alternative analyses 175
5.4 Swedish *-er*: from case suffix to nominalization suffix 179
5.5 Swedish *-on*: from number suffix to 'berry-name suffix' 181
5.6 From inflection to derivation in Kwaza quotative constructions 183

6 Debonding 186

6.1 Introduction 186
6.2 Replacement and retraction 188
6.3 Infinitival markers 190
6.3.1 English 190
6.3.2 Scandinavian 193
6.4 Japanese connectives 199
6.5 Old Estonian emphatic *ep* and interrogative *es*: from clitic to free particle 201
6.6 Irish *muid*: from verb suffix to pronoun 204
6.7 Northern Saami *haga*: from case suffix to postposition 207
6.8 Deaffixation in the Hup verbal compound 210
6.9 Dutch/Frisian/German *tig*/*tich*/*zig*: from suffix to quantifier 213
6.10 Northern Swedish *bö-*: from prefix to lexical verb 220
6.11 English *-ish*: from suffix to free morpheme 223
6.12 Tura LÁ: from bound to free derivational marker 225

7 Conclusions 228

7.1 Lehmann's parameters revisited 228
7.2 Defining characteristics of the three types of degrammaticalization 231

7.3 Mechanisms and motivating forces 233
7.4 Outlook 237

*References* 239
*Author Index* 259
*Subject Index* 263

# *Acknowledgments*

This book grew out of a paper I presented at a workshop organized by the Grammaticalization Network of the University of Copenhagen, in May 2003. I have presented it since on many occasions, and while I developed my ideas, adding ever more examples along the way, it became evident that this was a subject of monographic proportions which would take me years to complete. I owe a huge debt to all the people who have helped me shape and reshape my views during the process, or who encouraged me to pursue my work.

First and foremost, thanks are due to Laurel Brinton, Olga Fischer, Elizabeth Traugott, and David Willis, for their detailed reports on the penultimate draft or the book proposal. Their innumerable suggestions for improvement and constructive criticism cleansed the manuscript of quite a few misrepresentations and inscrutable arguments, thus making this book a far better one than it would have been otherwise.

I am also grateful to a number of other colleagues for their willingness to discuss specific theoretical points with me, or for generously sharing their native and/or expert knowledge of the languages which provided the data for this book. They are Ante Aikio, Henning Andersen, Jóhanna Barðdal, Anders Bay, Heike Behrens, Aidan Doyle, Pattie Epps, Külli Habicht, Cornelius Hasselblatt, Bernd Heine, Tette Hofstra, Peter Houtzagers, Dmitri Idiatov, Bob de Jonge, Sebastian Kürschner, Stefanie Kuzmack, Thérèse Leinonen, Thérèse Lindström-Tiedemann, Mark Louden, Ferdinand von Mengden, Helle Metslang, Heiko Narrog, Karl Pajusalu, Harm Pinkster, Liefke Reitsma, Henrik Rosenkvist, Mara van Schaik-Radulescu, Hindrik Sijens, Katerina Stathi, Freek van de Velde, Gunther de Vogelaer, Hein van der Voort, Jussi Ylikoski, and Jan-Wouter Zwart. Needless to say, none of the abovementioned necessarily agree with all the points raised in this book, and all ritual disclaimers about being responsible for one's own errors apply.

This book could not have been written without financial support from NWO, the Netherlands Organization for Scientific Research (grant no. 365-70-016), which is gratefully acknowledged. I also wish to thank John Davey at OUP, who never failed to find the right words of encouragement.

Last but not least I am greatly indebted to my extended family for all their love and support, and for childcare when deadlines brought me to the verge of despair. My deepest gratitude goes to the people who are my life and my home: to my husband Peter for patiently playing shuffleboard and board games during all those weekends when mum was glued to her computer screen, and to our daughters Mara and Erin, the loveliest people I know, for their unswerving and contagious belief that writing books must be the best pastime ever.

# *List of Tables*


1.1. Levels of synchronic variation and diachronic change 17
1.2. Pronouns and verbal endings in Buryat Mongolian 37
2.1. Kala Lagau Ya case and tense-aspect markers 62
2.2. Strong neuter nouns in Old Swedish 65
2.3. The development of the Romance inflectional future 78
2.4. Some weak preterite paradigms in Germanic 80
2.5. The indicative preterite of PGmc **dōn* 'to do' 81
3.1. Lehmann's parameters 124
3.2. Lehmann's parameters in primary and secondary grammaticalization 127
4.1. Parameter analysis of Pennsylvania German *wotte* 141
4.2. Parameter analysis of Chinese *děi* 143
4.3. Parameter analysis of Bulgarian *nešto* 145
4.4. Paradigm of the possessive pronoun in Welsh 146
4.5. Parameter analysis of Welsh *eiddo* 148
4.6. Parameter analysis of Welsh *nôl* 150
5.1. Diachronic characteristics of derivation and inflection 156
5.2. (Changes in) the morphological status of *-s*, *∼s*, and *=s* 170
5.3. Parameter analysis of the Swedish s-genitive 171
5.4. Parameter analysis of Swedish *-er* 181
5.5. Parameter analysis of Swedish *-on* 182
5.6. Parameter analysis of Kwaza *-nĩ* 185
6.1. Parameter analysis of English infinitival *to* 192
6.2. Parameter analysis of Norwegian infinitival *å* 198
6.3. Parameter analysis of Japanese connectives 201
6.4. Parameter analysis of Estonian *ep* and *es* 203
6.5. Synthetic and analytic verbal paradigms in Early Modern Irish 204
6.6. Parameter analysis of Irish *muid* 206
6.7. Parameter analysis of Northern Saami *haga* 209

6.8. Parameter analysis of Hup *hɔ̃* and *yæ̃h* 213
6.9. Parameter analysis of *tig* 219
6.10. Parameter analysis of Northern Swedish *bö* 222
6.11. Parameter analysis of *ish* 224
6.12. Parameter analysis of Tura LÁ 227

# *Abbreviations*

Abbreviations used in glosses

| | |
|---|---|
| 1, 2, 3 | first, second, third person |
| ABL | ablative |
| ACC | accusative |
| ADJ | adjective |
| ADV | adverb |
| CAU | causative |
| CAUS | causational |
| CL | classifier |
| COMM | common gender |
| COMIT | comitative |
| COP | copula |
| CSO | cosubordinating mood |
| DAT | dative |
| DEC | declarative |
| DEF | definite |
| DEP | dependent |
| DIM | diminutive |
| DYNM | dynamic |
| EMP | emphasis marker |
| ERG | ergative |
| EXH | exhortative |
| FEM | feminine |
| FOC | focalizer |
| FRUST | frustrative |
| FUT | future |
| FUT.CNTR | future contrast |
| GEN | genitive |
| ~GEN | phrase-marking genitive |
| =GEN | enclitic genitive |

| | |
|---|---|
| GER | gerund |
| IMP | imperative |
| INCH | inchoative |
| IND | indicative |
| INDEF | indefinite |
| INF | infinitive |
| INFR | inferred evidential |
| INT | interrogative |
| INTS | intensifier |
| ITG | intangible |
| L | grammatical low tone |
| MASC | masculine |
| NEG | negative |
| NEUT | neuter |
| NOM | nominative |
| NOML | nominalizer |
| NONVIS | nonvisual |
| OBJ | object |
| OBL | oblique |
| PART | particle |
| PASS | passive |
| PERF | perfect |
| PL | plural |
| PM | predicative marker |
| POSS | possessive |
| PRD | predicate marker |
| PRES | present |
| PRET | preterite |
| PROG | progressive |
| PRT | particle |
| PTCP | participle |
| SBJ | subject |
| SG | singular |
| SUBJ | subjunctive |

| | |
|---|---|
| TAM | tense-aspect-modality |
| TEL | telic |
| TM | terminal marker |
| TOP | topic marker |
| TR | transposer |

Other abbreviations

| | |
|---|---|
| Adj | adjective |
| Adv | adverb |
| C | Complementizer |
| Conj | conjunction |
| CP | complementizer phrase |
| DP | Determiner Phrase |
| Du | Dutch |
| EMoNw | Early Modern Norwegian |
| EMoSw | Early Modern Swedish |
| Gm | German |
| Goth | Gothic |
| IP | Inflectional Phrase |
| Lat | Latin |
| MHG | Middle High German |
| MiSw | Middle Swedish |
| ModE | Modern English |
| MoDu | Modern Dutch |
| MoNw | Modern Norwegian |
| MoSw | Modern Swedish |
| N | noun |
| NP | noun phrase |
| OE | Old English |
| OHG | Old High German |
| OSw | Old Swedish |
| OT | Optimality Theory |
| PGmc | Proto-Germanic |
| PIE | Proto-Indo-European |
| PP | prepositional phrase |

| | |
|---|---|
| Pro | Pronoun |
| V | verb |
| $V_{fin}$ | finite verb |
| $V_{infin}$ | infinite verb |
| VLat | Vulgar Latin |
| VP | verb phrase |

# *List of Swedish sources referred to in the text*

### *Old Swedish*

**Bur:** *Codex Bureanus.* In George Stephens (ed.), *Ett forn-svenskt legendarium* (=*Svenska Fornskriftsällskapets Samlingar* 8, 9, 12, 17, 18, 28). 1847–1858.

**Vidh:** *Vidhemsprästens anteckningar.* In H. S. Collin and C. J. Schlyter (eds.), *Corpus iuris Sueo-Gotorum antiqui I.* 1827.

### *Middle Swedish*

**Bild:** *Codex Bildstenianus.* In George Stephens (ed.), *Ett forn-svenskt legendarium.* (=*Svenska Fornskriftsällskapets Samlingar* 8, 9, 12, 17, 18, 28). 1847–1858.

**Bir:** *Heliga Birgittas uppenbarelser,* 1, ed. G. E. Klemming. (=*Svenska Fornskriftsällskapets Samlingar* 29). 1858.

**Did:** *Didrikssagan* ed. G. O. Hylthén-Cavallius. 1850–1854.

### *Early Modern Swedish*

**Gyll:** *Carl Carlsson Gyllenhielm's Egenhändige anteckningar rörande tiden 1597–1601,* ed. J. A. Almquist. (=*Historiska handlingar* 20). 1905.

**Petri:** *En Swensk Cröneka af Olavus Petri,* ed. Jöran Sahlgren. (=*Samlade Skrifter af Olavus Petri* 4). 1917.

Electronic versions of these texts can be found at www.nordlund.lu.se/Fornsvenska/Fsv%20Folder/index.html.

# 1

# Introduction

## 1.1 Downs and ups in the history of degrammaticalization

This is a book about degrammaticalization, the ugly duckling of grammaticalization studies. Whereas grammaticalization has firmly established itself as a most thriving topic within historical linguistics, boasting a veritable flow of papers and monographs, a lexicon (Heine and Kuteva 2002), and its own international conference, degrammaticalization is, and always has been, the subject of much controversy. With the revival of interest in grammaticalization in the 1980s, linguists initially believed that grammaticalization was a unidirectional process from lexicon to grammar, and that changes in the opposite direction were impossible. Nevertheless a term for this supposedly non-existent phenomenon was coined, in Lehmann's foundational grammaticalization monograph:

> Various authors . . . have claimed that grammaticalization is unidirectional; that is, an irreversible process . . . there is no **degrammaticalization**. (Lehmann 1995 [1982]: 16, emphasis original)

An interesting, if unintended, result of Lehmann's introduction of the term has been that people actually started to look for, and found, examples of it. But the relative infrequency of degrammaticalization changes, as opposed to grammaticalization changes, prompted many authors to ignore them at first. Indeed, in some of the major works on grammaticalization, for instance in the writings of Bernd Heine, degrammaticalization is dismissed as 'statistically insignificant' (cf. e.g. Heine, Claudi, and Hünnemeyer 1991: 4f.; Kuteva 2001: 110; Heine and Kuteva 2002: 11), or simply 'the result of an inadequate analysis' (Heine, Claudi and Hünnemeyer 1991: 5).

Others however were early to recognize the existence of degrammaticalization as a separate type of change which should be included in a theory of grammaticalization. Ramat (1992: 553), for instance, suggests that: 'The question we have to deal with is therefore, why is it that grammaticalization and degrammaticalization coexist in natural languages?' Also Traugott and Heine (1991: 7), in their discussion of counterdirectional evidence in Greenberg (1991) and Campbell (1991), note that the examples provided by Greenberg and Campbell 'test the boundaries of what may be considered bona fide cases of grammaticalization'. Similarly, Hopper and Traugott (1993: 126) assert that: 'Extensive though the evidence of unidirectionality is, it cannot be regarded as an absolute principle. Some counterexamples do exist. Their existence, and their relative infrequency, in fact help define our notion of what prototypical grammaticalization is.'[1]

In the years that followed, an ever-increasing body of evidence was presented, and the strongest version of the unidirectionality hypothesis ('there is no degrammaticalization') appears to have been abandoned in almost all current theorizing. At present, the general consensus appears to be that 'a presumed absolute universal had to be weakened to a statistical universal' (Haspelmath 2004: 23). Traugott (2001: 1) similarly defines grammaticalization as a 'hypothesis about a robust tendency'. Thus, over a period of twenty-odd years, degrammaticalization has come to be increasingly recognized as an independent type of change, which is one giant leap for a phenomenon that its inventor believed to be non-existent.

## 1.2 Aims and outline

Ever since the first presentations of degrammaticalization case studies, these have played a prominent role in discussions about the unidirectionality hypothesis. This hypothesis is illustrated by Hopper and Traugott's (2003: 7) famous 'cline of grammaticality' in (1):

(1) content item > grammatical word > clitic > inflectional affix

The '>' symbols in (1) signify the unidirectionality of lexicon-to-grammar change. Thus, there is only left-to-right movement along this cline. For instance, a content item may develop into a grammatical word, and subsequently acquire increasingly specialized grammatical functions (accompanied by increasing bondedness), but not vice versa. Changes in the opposite direction (e.g. from affix to clitic or from grammatical word to content item) obviously challenge the universalness of this cline, and hence the very existence of degrammaticalization has weakened unidirectionality from an absolute to a statistical universal, as we have seen in the previous section. On the other hand, it is also clear that grammaticalization changes are attested far more frequently than 'counterdirectional' degrammaticalization changes. The first aim of this book will therefore be to explore the concept of unidirectionality. What is unidirectionality a property of? Is it observed on

[1] See also Hopper and Traugott (2003: 132) for a similar statement.

all linguistic levels (semantics, pragmatics, morphology, syntax, phonology)? How can directional preferences be explained? These questions will be addressed in Chapter 2 of this book.

My second aim will be to define and classify degrammaticalization. For although there is general agreement that degrammaticalization *exists*, there is very little, if any, agreement on what it entails, and which changes count as valid examples of it. The term 'degrammaticalization' has been used to refer to a number of different phenomena, some entirely unrelated. This has had the unfortunate effect that every book or article on degrammaticalization has to start with discussing this terminological medley and providing its own definition. In Chapter 3, I will therefore start by reviewing earlier definitions of degrammaticalization, after which I will present my own, which is more restricted than most. But it will be seen that this definition still leaves us with a set of changes that may be quite different from one another, which makes it obvious that they require further sorting. This issue has been put on the grammaticalizationist's agenda by van der Auwera, who writes that:

> I have argued that two decades of relatively intensive research on grammaticalization have shown that degrammaticalization exists . . . and that it should be studied in its own right, and not as a quirky, accidental exception to grammaticalization. One of the tasks on the agenda is to compare the properties of grammaticalization and degrammaticalization. Another one is to classify all types of degrammaticalization. (van der Auwera 2002: 25f.)

To my mind, this can only be achieved by contrasting these cases in a systematic way. This has not been done before – papers on degrammaticalization usually focus on the details of a single case (or at best a few related cases), or they concern themselves with a mere enumeration of cases. A systematic comparison of differences and similarities (on different levels of linguistic observation) will facilitate the classification of degrammaticalization. This classification is based on Lehmann's 'parameters of grammaticalization' (Lehmann 1995 [1982]: 122ff.), as well as on recent work by Andersen (2005, 2006, 2008). It will be seen that, among the cases that have been presented as degrammaticalization and that meet the definition of degrammaticalization as defined in this work (see Chapter 3), three distinct types can be distinguished, which I will term 'degrammation', 'deinflectionalization', and 'debonding' respectively.

Degrammation is a change whereby a function word is reanalysed as a content item, often as a result of pragmatic inferencing, as in the following example from Welsh (Willis 2007: 294, 297):

(2) a.

| | | | | | | | |
|---|---|---|---|---|---|---|---|
| Yna | yd | aeth | y | gweisson | ***yn ol*** | y | varch |
| then | PART | went | the | lads | after | his | horse |

| | | | | |
|---|---|---|---|---|
| a | 'e | arueu | y | Arthur |
| and | his | weapons | for | Arthur |

'Then the lads went after / went to fetch his horse and his weapons for Arthur'

b.

| | | | | | |
|---|---|---|---|---|---|
| **Nolwch** | y | Brenin | i | 'w | examnio |
| fetch-2PL.IMP | the | King | to | 3MASC.SG | examine-INF |

'Fetch the king to be cross-examined'

In (2a), the phrase *yn ol*, originally an adposition, is ambiguous between 'after' and 'fetch'. This ambiguity led to the reinterpretation of *yn ol* as a verb. Verbal *yn ol* was subsequently reduced to *nôl*, and appears in unambiguous contexts such as (2b). Degrammation is rare, but of particular interest because some of the changes typically associated with increasing grammaticalization (pragmatic inferencing, phonological reduction), are witnessed here in the course of increasing degrammaticalization. Chapter 4 discusses this type of change in more detail.

Deinflectionalization, likewise rare, occurs when an inflectional affix becomes less bound, while at the same time gaining in semantic or functional substance. The best-known example of this kind of change is the s-genitive, which is found in English and Mainland Scandinavian (Norde 2006a: 205):

(3) a.

| | | | |
|---|---|---|---|
| ens | riks | mans | hws |
| a-MASC.SG.GEN | rich-MASC.SG.GEN | man-MASC.SG.GEN | house |

Old Swedish

b.

| | | | |
|---|---|---|---|
| en | rik | mans | hus |
| [a | rich | man]'s | house |

Modern Swedish

'a rich man's house'

When the Old Swedish inflectional genitive and the Modern Swedish enclitic genitive are contrasted, a number of changes can be observed to have occurred. One is an increase in syntactic scope – the inflectional genitive only took scope over a single word (e.g. a noun or an adjective) and hence had to be repeated on every element in a full NP as in (3a), whereas the Modern Swedish enclitic genitive takes scope over the entire NP and hence needs to be realized only once, as in (3b). A second change was the development of determiner function – Old Swedish genitival attributes did not make their head NP definite, but Modern Swedish equivalents do. Examples of deinflectionalization will be discussed in Chapter 5.

The most common type of degrammaticalization, finally, also involves bound morphemes (inflectional or derivational affixes, or clitics). These become free morphemes, as in the well-known case of the Irish 1PL verbal suffix which developed into an independent pronoun *muid*, meaning 'we' (Doyle 2002: 68):

(4) a. molfa-**maid** — Early Modern Irish
praise.FUT-1PL

b. molfaid **muid** — Contemporary Connemara Irish
praise.FUT we
'we will praise'

This type of change forms the subject of Chapter 6. Chapter 7 draws conclusions from the previous chapters and provides an outlook for further research.

In the remaining sections of this chapter, I will discuss the theoretical preliminaries of this study.

## 1.3 Preliminary definitions and observations

### 1.3.1 *Grammaticalization*

Because of the very composition of the term 'degrammaticalization', i.e. as a derivation of the term 'grammaticalization', any definition of the former is in a sense derived from the latter. In this section I will provide a brief survey of some of the standard definitions of grammaticalization – a more fine-grained discussion of the primitive changes involved in grammaticalization will be discussed in the next chapter.

As is well known, the term 'grammaticalization' was coined by Meillet in 1912,[2] for one of the two processes to create new grammatical forms (the other being analogy, see section 1.3.6). Meillet (1926 [1912]: 131) defined this process as 'l'attribution du caractère grammaticale à un mot jadis autonome', or, in other words, as 'le passage de mots autonomes au rôle d'agents grammaticaux'. Further on in his seminal paper Meillet (p. 133) writes: 'la "grammaticalisation" de certains mots crée des formes neuves, introduit des

[2] Although the term was coined by Meillet, the phenomenon itself had been noted much earlier, e.g. by von der Gabelentz (1901: 255): 'Was heute Affixe sind, das waren einst selbständige Wörter, die nachmals durch mechanische und seelische Vorgänge in dienende Stellung hinabgedrückt wurden.' According to Heine, Claudi, and Hünnemeyer (1991: 5ff.), the study of what is now called grammaticalization can even be traced back to the eighteenth century.

catégories qui n'avaient pas d'expression linguistique, transforme l'ensemble du système'. Thus Meillet was not only the first to use the term grammaticalization, he was also the first to see the interwovenness of grammaticalization and the grammar as a whole.

A little more than fifty years later, Kuryłowicz published his famous bipartite definition:

(5) Grammaticalization consists in the increase of the range of a morpheme advancing from a lexical to a grammatical or from a grammatical to a more grammatical status. (Kuryłowicz 1975 [1965]: 52)

The significance of this definition lies in Kuryłowicz's observation that grammaticalization does not merely involve a change from a lexical item to a function word, but that there may be subsequent changes when the gram[3] becomes 'more grammatical'. I will review the notions of 'grammatical' and 'more grammatical' in section 1.4.1. A few more recent definitions of grammaticalization are given below:

(6) With the term 'grammaticalization' we refer essentially to an evolution whereby linguistic units lose in semantic complexity, pragmatic significance, syntactic freedom, and phonetic substance, respectively. (Heine and Reh 1984: 15)

(7) For us it is a two-pronged branch of linguistics: (i) a research framework for studying the relationships between lexical, constructional and grammatical material in language, diachronically and synchronically, both in particular languages and cross-linguistically, and (ii) a term referring to the change whereby lexical items and constructions come in certain linguistic contexts to serve grammatical functions and, once grammaticalized, continue to develop new grammatical functions. (Hopper and Traugott 2003: 18)

(8) Grammaticalization of a linguistic sign is a process in which it loses in autonomy by becoming more subject to constraints of the linguistic system. (Lehmann 2004: 155)

(9) A grammaticalization is a diachronic change by which the parts of a constructional schema come to have stronger internal dependencies. (Haspelmath 2004: 26)

[3] The term 'gram' (short for 'grammatical morpheme') is adopted from Bybee, Perkins, and Pagliuca (1994: 2) to cover all sorts of grammatical morphemes (e.g. function words, particles, clitics, affixes), including phrasal grammatical items such as auxiliary *be going to.*

From the definitions above it becomes evident that grammaticalization involves changes on several levels (Heine and Reh 1984; Lehmann 1995 [1982]; see Croft 2000: 157 for a convenient summary). A prototypical example of grammaticalization is English *to be going to*, exemplified in (10) (Fischer and Rosenbach 2000: 3):

(10) a. I am going (to Haarlem) to visit my aunt
b. I am going to marry (tomorrow)
c. I am going to like it
d. It is going to rain
e. I am going to go there for sure
f. I'm gonna go

In example (10a), *go* functions as a lexical verb, with directional meaning. In contexts where *going to* and the infinitive are adjacent, *going to* developed a temporal meaning (as in (10b)) by means of pragmatic inferencing: if one is going somewhere with a certain purpose, this event is inherently going to take place in the future. Once this new sense had developed, *to be going to* started to appear in contexts where a purposive meaning is no longer possible, as in (10c), from where it became further generalized still. As a future auxiliary, it can even be reduced to *gonna* (example (10f); note that this is not possible with *go* as a fully lexical verb: **I'm gonna Haarlem*).

The development of *to be going to* into a future auxiliary reveals a number of prototypical characteristics of grammaticalization. First, it involves changes on several linguistic levels: phonological (*going to*>*gonna*); morphosyntactic (only the participial construction *to be going to* develops a future meaning, and its syntactic position is more fixed than that of lexical *go*), and functional (*to be going to* comes to be used in a larger number of – non-directional – contexts). Secondly, it shows that grammaticalization has both a diachronic and a synchronic dimension. The constructions in (10) form a diachronic chain, which is reflected by synchronic variation, a phenomenon for which Hopper (1991: 22) introduced the term 'layering'. Finally, the development of *go* into a future marker is found in a number of other languages as well (e.g. *gaan* in Dutch, *aller* in French; for more examples see Heine and Kuteva 2002: 161ff.). This cross-linguistic replication is said to be indicative of regular tendencies in semantic change (see further 2.6.1).

Other typical examples of grammaticalization include the rise of locative adpositions out of body-part nouns (e.g. Danish *bag* 'back' > 'behind'), the development of the numeral 'one' into an indefinite article (e.g. English *a*(*n*)), or the change from a noun meaning 'man' into an indefinite pronoun (e.g. Latin *homo* > French *on*). An extensive survey of grammaticalization changes from languages all over the world is provided by Heine and Kuteva (2002).

Apart from such transitions from lexical word to function word, much more elaborate chains of changes have been attested, of which the French inflectional future (ultimately from a Latin verb *habere* 'to have') is best known. Such chains will be discussed in more detail in Chapter 2.

### 1.3.2 *Degrammaticalization*

For the past two decades, the term 'degrammaticalization' has been used to refer to an impressive range of phenomena, some of them entirely unrelated. This definitional pandemonium will be discussed in Chapter 3. In this section, I will present my working definition of degrammaticalization, without providing an exhaustive list of subtypes and changes involved, since these will also be discussed in Chapter 3. For now, I will expand on the definition I have proposed earlier (Norde 2001a, 2002), which is based on Hopper and Traugott's (2003: 7) 'cline of grammaticality' in (1), repeated here for convenience as (11). Even though it will be seen in section 2.2.1 that the cline is not uncontroversial, and not a sufficient diagnostic, it makes a good starting point for further analysis.

(11) content item > grammatical word > clitic > inflectional affix (> ø)[4]

On the basis of (11), degrammaticalization will be provisionally defined as a single shift from right to left on this cline. Three important properties of degrammaticalization need to be mentioned at this point. First, there are no examples of degrammaticalization 'all the way up the cline' – a degrammaticalization chain from suffix all the way to lexical item has not been attested. Two types of degrammaticalization (degrammation and deinflectionalization) involve a single shift to one point further to the left on the cline of grammaticality. In the third type (debonding), a gram may also 'jump over' an intermediate stage.

Secondly, Haspelmath's (1999a: 1064) observation that 'in grammaticalization the identity of the construction and the element's place within it are always preserved' is relevant for degrammaticalization changes as well. Degrammaticalization changes are thus shifts from affix to clitic or from clitic to grammatical word, within an ambiguous context which allows for reanalysis. A shift from

[4] The zero stage does not officially form part of Hopper and Traugott's cline, but it has been added here because loss (of form and/or function) is considered to be the end product of grammaticalization (Hopper and Traugott 2003: 172ff.). The question of whether loss is really the only option for maximally grammaticalized morphemes (i.e. inflectional endings) is discussed in Norde (2002).

grammatical word to content item will also qualify as degrammaticalization if the constructional identity of the degrammaticalized item is preserved (at least initially). Changes into content items where function words or bound morphemes are 'taken out of their context', as it were, will be considered lexicalization, not degrammaticalization (cf. section 1.3.3). These include 'upgradings' from minor to major word classes (*pros and cons, to up, to down*), and from derivational affix to hypernym nouns (*isms, ologies*).

Thirdly, degrammaticalization must result in a novel gram, that is, when grams can be shown to continue a less grammatical function that had always been around, however marginalized, the change will not qualify as a case of degrammaticalization. An example of this kind of change, which has been termed 'retraction' in Haspelmath (2004: 33ff.), is the history of English *man*. Originally this was a noun, but in Old English it had also grammaticalized into an indefinite pronoun 'one' (cf. German *man*) and at one period the pronoun had even become more frequent than the noun. Later on, however, pronominal *man* became obsolete and in present-day English, *man* is only used as a noun. According to Newmeyer (1998: 273) this is a counterexample to unidirectionality, but Haspelmath correctly rejects it as such, because the non-grammaticalized *man* had never disappeared from the language. Another case of retraction will be discussed in section 3.4.

### 1.3.3 *Lexicalization*

When it comes to definitional proliferation, the one term to beat 'degrammaticalization' is 'lexicalization' (see Brinton and Traugott 2005 for the most extensive survey to date). In the first place, definitions of lexicalization are dependent on one's concept of the lexicon (see Brinton and Traugott 2005: 9ff.), for example whether one regards lexical items as unanalysable wholes (the holistic approach) or as consisting of minimal components of meaning (the componential approach). In the latter approach, the lexical item *boy* is viewed as consisting of the components +HUMAN, −ADULT, +MALE, which are seen as 'innate properties of the mind that determine the way in which the world is conceived' (Brinton and Traugott 2005: 10).

Another important distinction is that between lexical and grammatical categories, where 'lexical' can mean (i) belonging to the inventory, or (ii) having a specific, concrete meaning (Brinton and Traugott 2005: 11, quoting Lehmann 2002: 14); and 'grammatical' can refer to (i) conforming to the rules of grammar, or (ii) having an abstract, structural, or functional meaning (Brinton and Traugott 2005: 11). In the functional-typological approach taken by Brinton and Traugott, there is no strict boundary between lexical and grammatical categories. They correctly observe (p. 18) that a continuum model fits better with historical change, which is generally gradual in the sense that it occurs in a series of (very) small steps.

In their research survey of lexicalization, Brinton and Traugott (2005: 32ff.) identify three broad definitions of lexicalization:

(i) *Ordinary processes of word formation.* Traditionally, little or no distinction is made between lexicalization and routine processes of word formation, including compounding (*blackboard*), derivation (ranging from purely semantic such as *un-* in *unhappy* to forms with grammatical meaning, such as agentive *-er* in *swimmer*), conversion (category shift, e.g. from N to V (*to calendar*) or from Conj to N (*ifs*)), clipping (*phone* < *telephone*), ellipsis (*pub* < *public house*), blending (*bit* < *b(inary)* + *(dig)it*), back formation (*enthuse* < *enthusiasm*), acronyms (*scuba* < *s(elf) c(ontaining) u(nderwater) b(reathing) a(pparatus)*), loan translations (Gm *einmütig* 'one-minded' < Lat *unanimus*), coinage (*hobbit*) and metalinguistic citation (*There are two e's in my name*).

(ii) *Processes of fusion resulting in a decrease in compositionality.* Lexicalization as fusion involves a complex structure becoming simpler, with or without (considerable) semantic change. Examples of such structural simplification are the development from syntagm to lexeme, or univerbation (*mother-in-law*), or from complex to simple lexeme (*lord* < OE *hlaf* 'loaf' + *weard* 'guardian'). The latter type may also give rise to derivational morphemes such as adjectival *-ly* (from OE *līċ* 'body'). Fusion may be followed by coalescence, the loss of phonological segments, which may result in the loss of morpheme boundaries. English examples are *hussy* (< OE *hus* 'house' + *wif* 'wife') or *awake* (< OE *on* + *wacan*) (Brinton and Traugott 2005: 54). In Brinton and Traugott's work, only this type is considered lexicalization.

(iii) *Processes of separation resulting in an increase in autonomy.* Lexicalization as separation concerns the emancipation of bound morphemes into free morphemes (Brinton and Traugott 2005: 57ff.). Usually, this amounts to the abbreviation of a word, in which part of it is 'clipped off' (hence their term 'clippings'), as in the examples in (12):

(12) a. *ade* 'fruit juice' (< *lemonade, orangeade*)
*ism* 'doctrine, theory, practice' (< *fascism, socialism, communism*)
*ology* 'subject of study' (< *zoology, sociology*)
*onomy* 'area of knowledge' (< *economy*)
*ocracy* 'form of rule or influence' (*aristocracy, bureaucracy*)
*itis* 'sickness' (< *appendicitis, bronchitis*)
*burger* (< *hamburger*)
*hood* (< *neighbourhood*)

b. *bi* (< *bi-sexual*)
*ex* (< *ex-husband, ex-wife*)
*teen* (< *teenager*)

An important difference between (i) and (iii) on the one hand and (ii) on the other hand is that the former are instantaneous, whereas the latter are gradual in the sense that they comprise a series of small changes (see Hopper and Traugott 2003: 134 for a similar point). Many authors (e.g. Lehmann 2002, Brinton and Traugott 2005) have therefore chosen to restrict the term to processes of fusion:

(13) Lexicalization involves a holistic access to a unit, a renunciation of its internal analysis. (Lehmann 2002: 13)[5]

(14) Lexicalization is the change whereby in certain linguistic contexts speakers use a syntactic construction or word formation as a new contentful form with formal and semantic properties that are not completely derivable or predictable from the constituents of the construction or the word formation pattern. Over time there may be further loss of internal constituency and the item may become more lexical. (Brinton and Traugott 2005: 96)

In the present work, however, the term lexicalization will be used in a broader sense, to include most changes mentioned in (i)–(iii) above, with the exception of productive and regular word formation processes such as derivation (both of the *un-* and *-er* type mentioned under (i)).[6] The reason for this is that changes such as clippings and conversions result in new lexemes, the meaning of which is not fully predictable from the (part of the) word from which they evolved, nor from the nature of the word formation process that formed them. For instance, conversions from adverb to verb do not form a regular process of word formation, because (i) not all adverbs can be converted (e.g. *up* and *down* can, but *left* or *ahead* cannot), and (ii) the meaning of the verb may be idiosyncratic (as with *to down* 'to finish (a drink)'). I will return to the lexicalization of function words (conversion) and affixes (clipping) in section 3.3.3.

### 1.3.4 *Areas of overlap*

There are many parallels between grammaticalization and lexicalization, which does not always makes it easy to assess how a given change ought to be

[5] Note that this definition is more restricted than an earlier one by the same author: 'alles, was eine Einheit ins Lexicon zieht, ist Lexikalisierung' (Lehmann 1989: 15).

[6] Note however that such items may be lexicalized at a later stage, e.g. when the affix fuses with its stem and is no longer recognized as a separate morpheme (e.g. the former nominalization suffix in *length* (<PGmc *-*iþō*).

characterized. Words or phrases that are superficially similar can nevertheless be the result of different processes. This may be illustrated by composite predicates in English, which may be either lexicalized or grammaticalized (Trousdale, in prep.). Predicates such as *lay hold of* or *curry favour with* are lexicalized, since they are non-productive and idiomatic and lack syntactic variability (*he laid hold of the rope – *hold was laid of the rope by him*), but others such as *take a bath/shower/walk/rest/drink* etc. are grammaticalized, because the pattern is very productive, with the verb developing an aspectual function.

The primary reason why grammaticalization is not always easily distinguishable from lexicalization is that they have a number of characteristics in common, such as fusion, coalescence, or demotivation (see Brinton and Traugott 2005: 110 for a list). As a consequence, changes involving one or more of these common characteristics have been treated as either grammaticalization or lexicalization. This can be observed, for example, in cases involving univerbation such as *today* (<OE *to* + *dæge* 'at day-DAT') or German *heuer* (< OHG *hiu jaru* 'this year-DAT'; Brinton and Traugott 2005: 63), or epistemic adverbs such as *maybe* or Swedish *kanske* (< *kan ske* 'can happen'; Norde 2007).[7] Lehmann (2002: 15) characterizes the main difference between grammaticalization and lexicalization as follows:

> Both are reduction processes (cf. Lehmann 1989), but in a different sense. Grammaticalization reduces the autonomy of a unit, shifting it to a lower, more strictly regulated grammatical level... Lexicalization reduces the inner structure of a unit, shifting it into the inventory.

In a particularly lucid contribution to the delineation of the terms 'grammaticalization' and 'lexicalization', Himmelmann (2004: 21) identifies two common metaphors: the 'box metaphor', according to which the lexicon and the grammar are two separate boxes which items can be moved into or out of, and the 'process metaphor', which implies that lexicalization and grammaticalization are orthogonal (i.e. completely independent) processes which may affect lexical items or grammatical constructions, possibly following similar developmental paths.

Himmelmann notes a number of problems with the box metaphor. Most importantly, this metaphor depends heavily on one's definition of the lexicon,[8] in particular whether or not this includes grammatical items (function words, inflections) or derivational affixes and word formation rules. When

[7] Brinton and Traugott themselves regard these cases as lexicalization (p. 100).

[8] Himmelmann restricts his treatment of the lexicon to 'the grammarian's lexicon', i.e. 'every form-meaning pairing which cannot be derived by productive rules' (Himmelmann 2004: 23) – the 'lexicographer's lexicon' and the 'mental lexicon' are not relevant to the discussion in his view.

grammar and lexicon are not consistently defined, Himmelmann argues, the box metaphor becomes problematic.

Himmelmann goes on to observe (p. 36) that '[t]he major commonality [between lexicalization and grammaticalization] is that the two processes have a common point of origin, i.e. the spontaneous and productive combination of lexical items in discourse'. They differ in the subsequent steps: in lexicalization (when this comprises univerbation or fossilization of phrases such as *großer Wurf* 'big success'), two elements form a unit whereby the syntagmatic context may or may not change, and the semantic-pragmatic change is non-directional. That is, lexicalization may involve both generalization (*großer Wurf*) and narrowing, as in *Hochzeit* 'wedding', from OHG *diu hōha gezît* 'high time' which could be used to refer to all kinds of festivities (Himmelmann 2004: 36). In grammaticalization on the other hand, an element combines with a class of other elements, the syntagmatic context is usually expanded, and the semantic-pragmatic change is unidirectional (from more specific to more abstract).

Fischer (2008: 352) suggests that lexicalization operates on the token level, whereas grammaticalization takes place at the type/token level. As a consequence, Fischer argues that a development which only affects a particular token (e.g. Old English *þa hwile þe* 'that time that' > Modern English *while*) is 'much closer to lexicalization than grammaticalization'. A 'true' case of grammaticalization, in her view, would be the development of Romance adverbs in MENTE where the suffix developed out of the ablative singular of the Latin noun *mens* 'mind' (see section 1.6.5). Here the change is not only from lexical item to suffix, but also affects a type, i.e. the class of adjectives to which MENTE was suffixed. Although Fischer is right that lexicalization always concerns tokens, the claim that grammaticalization must always affect types I find less appealing, because it would effectively eliminate many changes from lexeme to grammatical word as valid instances of grammaticalization. It is not quite clear why, for example, the rise of prepositions out of individual lexemes or phrases (such as *pending* or *on top of*), which are tokens, are less prototypical instances of grammaticalization than e.g. the rise of a declensional class of definite articles out of a declensional class of demonstrative pronouns, which are types. In terms of Lehmann's parameters (see section 3.5.1) they are very similar, and considering the first as ('closer to') lexicalization obscures this fact.

A particularly problematic area of overlap between grammaticalization and lexicalization is derivation. Several authors (most recently Brinton and Traugott 2005) have aimed to tackle this problem, but thus far without completely satisfying results. In a nutshell, the problem is this: when derivational affixes arise (typically from compound members) several processes can be observed which are generally held to be characteristic of grammaticalization: bleaching (see section 2.6.1), decategorialization (2.6.2), morphologization (2.6.3), and phonological reduction (2.6.4). And indeed, the rise of derivational affixes has been termed grammaticalization in a number of works (e.g. Anttila 1989: 150; Lehmann 1989: 17; Heine, Claudi, and Hünnemeyer 1991: 96; Ramat 1992: 558; Giacalone Ramat 1998: 120; Giacalone Ramat and Hopper 1998: 2).

On the other hand, derivational affixes are a productive means to create new lexemes, and derived forms can be seen as instances of lexicalization, depending on definition (see section 1.3.3). In the definition of lexicalization as word formation, all derived words are instances of lexicalization. But in the definition of lexicalization as fusion, too, derived forms qualify as lexicalization, when they have become idiomaticized (e.g. English adjectives in *-ly* such as *lovely, lively, friendly*). A complicating factor, furthermore, is that there is no clear-cut boundary between inflection (mostly associated with grammaticalization) and derivation (mostly associated with lexicalization), which makes the classification of particular suffixes even more problematic (see section 5.2.1 for a discussion of the inflection–derivation interface). Thus, the further development of adjectival *-ly* into an adverbial affix (*quickly, legally, extremely*) is sometimes considered grammaticalization, even by authors who regard derivation as lexicalization, because it is seen as movement towards inflectional status (e.g. in Brinton and Traugott 2005: 132ff.).

One additional reason for the problematic status of derivation is, I think, that it is not always clear whether the term refers to the derivational suffix per se (e.g. *-wise*), the derived form as a whole (e.g. *clockwise*), the word formation process (*clock* > *clockwise*) or the historical development of the suffix (from OE *wíse* 'manner').[9] For instance, Brinton and Traugott (2005) regard the derived forms as a whole as lexicalization, and the word formation process as preceding lexicalization. It is unclear, however, how they view the suffix and its historical development itself (Norde, forthcoming). According to their own chart of typical properties of grammaticalization and/or lexicalization (p. 110), (the development of) a derivational suffix has positive scores for all grammaticalization characteristics with the exception of subjectification.[10] For example, they are semantically bleached, decategorialized (i.e. they lose morphosyntactic characteristics such as inflection), become fused and (often) phonologically reduced.

[9] See Himmelmann (2004) for a similar point.

[10] The properties that grammaticalization and lexicalization have in common are: gradualness; unidirectionality; fusion; coalescence; demotivation; metaphorization/metonymization. The properties that are characteristic of grammaticalization but not of lexicalization are: decategorialization; bleaching; subjectification; productivity; frequency; typological generality.

And crucially, like grammaticalized items, but unlike lexicalized items, they are often productive and frequent. Accordingly, Brinton and Traugott regard word-class-changing derivational morphemes as grammaticalized morphemes, whereas other derivational morphemes are mentioned as instances of lexicalization (e.g. pp. 97, 98), but it is not quite clear on the basis of what criteria derivational affixes are classified as either lexicalization or grammaticalization.

If, however, we do make a clear distinction between the derivational affix, the word formation process, and the derived form, I propose to consider the affix as the result of grammaticalization, and the derived form as either the result of regular word formation or (subsequent) lexicalization (when the meaning of the derived form is no longer predictable from its component parts). Thus, when Himmelmann (2004: 28) asks whether derivation is an instance of grammaticalization, lexicalization, or possibly 'a process *sui generis*, i.e. neither lexicalization nor grammaticalization', I would say that it is a process *sui generis* only in the sense that it is *both* lexicalization and grammaticalization.

This is also the position adopted by Douglas Lightfoot (2005: 594), after his detailed analysis of the historical development of the German suffix *-heit*. This suffix derives from an Old High German (OHG)[11] noun *heit/heid*, which covers a wide range of meanings ('way, nature, appearance, property, characteristic, person, position, rank, honor'). An example containing *heid* as a noun is given in (15) (from the OHG *Isidor*, *c.* 790–800):

(15) oh in dhem dhrim **heidim** scal man ziuuaare eina
but in the three persons one shall indeed one
gotnissa beodan
deity proclaim
'but in the three persons (i.e. the Holy Trinity) one shall indeed proclaim one deity'

Apart from these independent uses, *heit/heid* is attested in compounds such as *magadheit* 'position, rank of a young girl'. From such compounds, the step towards derivation is a relatively minor one. Thus, a word such as *uuízentheit* ('knowing'-*heit*) is ambivalent between a compound meaning 'knowing person' and a derivation meaning 'knowledge, consciousness'. In the course of the OHG period, derivational *-heit* becomes increasingly frequent, at the expense of *heit* as a compound member, and by the Middle High German (MHG)[12] period, the latter usage had largely disappeared. By this time, *-heit*

[11] The Old High German period lasted approximately from 750 to 1050.
[12] The Middle High German period lasted approximately from 1050 to 1350.

had also started to replace older derivational suffixes with a similar function, such as *-ī* and *-ida.*

Lightfoot (603ff.) goes on to characterize the development of derivational *-heit* as having properties of both lexicalization and grammaticalization: lexicalization, because it derives new lexemes, and grammaticalization because it entails loss of autonomy at several levels.

A final observation as regards the relation between lexicalization and grammaticalization is that they may be subsequent stages in a chain of events. Thus, lexicalization may feed grammaticalization, as in German *aufgrund* 'on the basis of' (Lehmann 2004: 169). First, the phrase *auf Grund* loses its internal structure and becomes a single word which has to be stored in the lexicon (lexicalization). Subsequently, *aufgrund* loses its nominal properties and becomes a preposition (grammaticalization).[13]

By contrast, grammaticalization may also feed lexicalization (Moreno Cabrera 1998: 218ff.). Consider for example Latin present participles in *-ens*, which had grammaticalized into modifiers of a noun (thus shifting from a PROCESS meaning to a QUALITY meaning), but which at a later stage started to function as nominalizers to form agentive nouns, e.g. Spanish *calmante* 'sedative' (from *calmar* 'to soothe') or *viajante* 'salesman' (< *viajar* 'to travel'). Most of these nouns can no longer be used as adjectives and are listed as full-fledged nouns in dictionaries. Note also that in the example *viajante* the noun has acquired an idiosyncratic meaning (i.e. one not directly derivable from the meaning of the verb), which is typical of lexicalization.

### 1.3.5 *Diachronic gradualness and synchronic gradience*

In the functional-typological approach which prevails in most grammaticalization theorizing, language change is typically regarded as gradual. For instance, in Brinton and Traugott's (2005: 6) or Hopper and Traugott's (2003: 49) framework, a change typically looks like (16):

(16) A > {A / B} > (B)

The cline in (16) acknowledges that change is not the abrupt substitution of one structure by another, but always involves variation, with older and newer forms coexisting side by side. This synchronic reflection of gradual change has been termed 'gradience' (Traugott and Trousdale 2008).

Brinton and Traugott (2005) distinguish between gradualness of change and gradualness of frequency. Gradualness of change is evidenced by am-

[13] For more examples of lexicalization feeding grammaticalization see Rostila (2004).

biguous constructions in historical sources: 'textual evidence suggests that many changes involve periods of relative indeterminacy in which it is not clear whether the older or the newer usage is in evidence; in other words, the steps may be tentative at first. Indeed, the first steps may never result in change, in the sense of acceptance by a community of speakers.' (Brinton and Traugott 2005: 26). For example, most instances of *be going to* in sixteenth and seventeenth century texts in the Helsinki corpus are ambivalent between motion verb and future auxiliary. Gradualness of frequency signifies the generally slow pace at which changes spread in the language system. In the case of *be going to*, it refers to the fact that this construction increasingly co-occurs with verbs or subjects which are incompatible with the original meaning of motion of the verb *to go* (Brinton and Traugott 2005: 30; see also Bybee 2003 for a detailed account of the role of frequency).

The most radical expression of gradualness in grammatical change is, undoubtedly, Hopper's concept of 'emergent grammar':

> Because grammar is always emergent but never present, it could be said that it never exists as such, but is always coming into being. There is, in other words, no 'grammar', but only grammaticalization – movements towards structure... It goes without saying that many phenomena which we would agree to call grammatical are relatively stable and uniform. That is not in dispute. The point again is that any decision to limit the domain of grammar to just those phenomena which are relatively fixed and stable seems arbitrary. (Hopper 1987: 148)

Gradualness has not only been considered typical of grammaticalization, but also of lexicalization. In Brinton and Traugott's (2005: 94, 102) integrated approach to grammaticalization and lexicalization, three levels of increasing grammaticality and three levels of increasing lexicality are identified, as a property of both synchronic variation, and of diachronic change (see Table 1.1).

TABLE 1.1. Brinton and Traugott's (2005: 94, 102) levels of synchronic variation and diachronic change

| Level of grammaticality | | Level of lexicality | |
|---|---|---|---|
| G1 | periphrases (*be going to*) | L1 | partially fixed phrases (*lose sight of*) |
| G2 | semi-bound forms, such as function words and clitics (*must, 'll*) | L2 | complex semi-idiosyncratic forms (*unhappy, desktop*) |
| G3 | affixes (both inflectional and derivational) | L3 | simplexes and unanalysable idiosyncratic forms (*desk, over-the-hill*) |

The conception of gradualness contrasts sharply with the generative approach, which conceives of first-language acquisition as the only locus of language change, which makes change inherently abrupt. I will return to this issue in section 2.7.3.

### 1.3.6 *Reanalysis and analogy*

1.3.6.1 *Reanalysis* Most current theorizing identifies two central mechanisms in grammaticalization: reanalysis and analogy (see e.g. Hopper and Traugott 2003: 39ff., Brinton and Traugott 2005: 7). In some works (e.g. Harris and Campbell 1995, Hopper and Traugott 2003), reanalysis is regarded as the most important one, 'because it is a prerequisite for the implementation of the change through analogy' (Hopper and Traugott 2003: 39).[14] Reanalysis, in the classical definition by Langacker (1977: 58) involves a 'change in the structure of an expression or class of expressions that does not involve any immediate or intrinsic modification of its surface manifestation'. (See Harris and Campbell 1995: 61 for a similar definition). Brinton and Traugott (2005: 7) distinguish three subtypes:[15]

(17) a. change in constituency (syntactic or morphological rebracketing)
b. change in category labels (e.g. main verb > auxiliary)
c. boundary loss (e.g. *be going to* > *gonna*)

All these three types have been observed to occur in grammatical change. Syntactic rebracketing and category reanalysis are typically found when a lexical item is reanalysed as a function word, as in example (18), where the former noun *back* comes to form a constituent with *of* when it is reanalysed as a preposition (Hopper and Traugott 2003: 51).

(18) a. [[back] of the barn] >
b. [back of [the barn]]

Boundary loss is more typical of later stages in a grammaticalization chain, for example when the grammaticalized function word subsequently fuses with a preceding or following word (as in the *gonna* example).

[14] Note however that this view is not uncontroversial – see e.g. Haspelmath (1998) for an argument why grammaticalization need not involve reanalysis.

[15] Langacker (1977: 64ff.) uses a more theory-dependent classification, which distinguishes two basic types: 'resegmentation' (with three subtypes: 'boundary loss', 'boundary creation', 'boundary shift') and 'syntactic/semantic reformulation', which is reanalysis in the more abstract sense of rules, semantic and syntactic categories, or semantic or syntactic configurations (e.g. tree structures). In this view, reformulation usually goes hand in hand with boundary changes, but not necessarily so (Langacker 1977: 79).

1.3.6.2 *Analogy* The second main mechanism in grammaticalization is analogy. Unlike reanalysis, analogy is overt, indeed, 'in many cases [it is] the prime evidence for speakers of a language (and also for linguists!) that a change has taken place' (Hopper and Traugott 2003: 64). There are many types of analogy (see e.g. Hock and Joseph 1996 for a lucid review), a discussion of which falls outside of the scope of this monograph, but some examples will be given, because these are also attested in degrammaticalization. Among the relatively systematic types of analogy, the most important ones are 'levelling' and 'four-part analogy' (Hock and Joseph 1996: 154ff.). Levelling is the reduction or elimination of morphophonological variation. For instance, the *s* ~ *r* alternation in some Germanic strong verb paradigms (introduced by Verner's law) has been levelled in most Germanic languages. Thus OE *ċēosan* ~ *coren* has been levelled to Modern English *choose* ~ *chosen*, whereas in German (archaic) *küren* ~ *gekoren* *r* has been generalized (Hock and Joseph 1996: 156).[16] In four-part analogy, or proportional analogy, a pattern (e.g. an inflectional one) is changed on the model of another one, which may be schematized as follows (Hock and Joseph 1996: 160f.):

(19) a : a'
b : X (> b')

Four-part analogy is responsible for the loss of some irregular plurals in English such as *kine* (the plural of *cow*), but it is by no means deterministic, because many irregular plurals have been retained (*foot* ~ *feet*/**foots* etc.). Also, the model pattern need not be the least marked one. For instance, many vernaculars of English have replaced *bring* ~ *brought* ~ *brought* by *bring* ~ *brang* ~ *brung* (on the model of e.g. *sing* ~ *sang* ~ *sung*), instead of by the unmarked weak conjugation (*bring* ~ **bringed* ~ **bringed*).

Some researchers consider analogy to be primary in grammaticalization (see in particular Kiparsky 2005 and Fischer 2007, 2008). Fischer (2008: 350) for instance argues that 'analogy should be seen as both a *mechanism* and a *cause*... By means of analogy we may change structures and the contents of paradigmatic sets, but it is also analogy that causes the learner to build up more abstract types or schemas. In other words in this learning model analogy is the primary force (and not reanalysis)'.

The discussion of which force is primary in grammaticalization is one which I will not pursue here. For degrammaticalization, it appears to be the case that sometimes analogy comes first (e.g. in the degrammaticalization

[16] Dutch has retained the *s* ~ *r* alternation in some verbs, e.g. *verliezen* 'to lose' ~ *verloren* 'lost' (but not in *kiezen* ~ *gekozen* 'choose, chosen').

of Irish 1PL *-muid* > free pronoun *muid*, see example (4) above), whereas in other cases it is reanalysis (e.g. in the degrammaticalization of Welsh *yn ol* 'after' > *nôl* 'to fetch': see example (2)). I will return to this issue in Chapter 7.

## 1.4 Controversial types of grammaticalization

### 1.4.1 *'Secondary' grammaticalization*

Lehmann (1995: 9ff.), points out that the term grammaticalization, though now so well established that it would seem undesirable to replace it, is 'unfortunate in several respects'. Literally, it indicates that an element becomes grammatical, in other words, it only refers to a change whereby lexical items become function words, and it does not cover the subsequent stages of increasing abstractness and bondedness.

Some authors have been arguing that those later stages should not be subsumed under grammaticalization at all. To them (e.g. Detges and Waltereit 2002: 188; Von Mengden 2008) only the first part of Kuryłowicz's definition (see (5) above) refers to grammaticalization proper. On this view, subsequent changes (cliticization, affixation) are merely examples of increasing bondedness which may or may not follow a shift from lexeme to grammatical word.[17] In some cases, this observation is correct. For example, cliticized *'m* has become bound and is syntactically more restricted[18] than its unreduced equivalent *am*, but there is no change in meaning. In other cases however, changes on other levels can be observed as well. One of the textbook examples of grammaticalization, the Norwegian inflectional passive in *-s(t)*,[19] is a case in point. This suffix ultimately derives from a 3SG reflexive pronoun, which not only became increasingly bound (ending up as an inflectional suffix), but went through several changes in grammatical meaning as well, following the well-known path REFLEXIVE > ANTICAUSATIVE > PASSIVE (cf. Heine and Kuteva 2002: 44; for details of the development in Scandinavian languages see

[17] Von Mengden (2008) proposes a far more complex model where grammaticalization is but one of a series of interconnected processes, which von Mengden considers 'modules' of grammatical change. In this model, grammaticalization is primarily seen as a change in function or meaning, with other changes (e.g. reanalysis, phonological attrition) as separate modules. Whether there exist deterministic relationships between some of the modules and whether modules are (ir)reversible are matters still to be explored. Like Lehmann's parameters of grammaticalization (see section 3.5.1) this modular approach has the advantage of identifying primitive changes in grammaticalization and the relations between them.

[18] For instance, *'m* cannot be used in comparisons (*he's younger than I am* / **I'm*, or in elliptical answers (*Who's in charge? I am* / **I'm*).

[19] Equivalent suffixes are found in the other Scandinavian languages.

Enger 2002, 2003; Faarlund 2005). In other words, cliticization (and subsequent affixation) of grams need not be a mere morphological change, but may continue a chain of semantic changes that began when a lexeme grammaticalized into a grammatical word.

In any event, it is useful to distinguish between the two main stages reflected in Kuryłowicz's definition. For these two stages, Traugott (2002: 26f.) proposes the terms 'primary grammaticalization' ('the development in specific morphosyntactic contexts of constructions and lexical categories into functional categories'), and 'secondary grammaticalization' ('the development of morphophonemic "texture" associated with the categories in question').[20] Secondary grammaticalization in Traugott's view, then, pertains to the degree of morphological bondedness, phonological reduction, and semantic bleaching, but the term has also been used to refer to advanced grammaticalization of tense or aspect markers (Kranich 2008, in prep.).

Traugott observes that the two subtypes of grammaticalization are 'linked in ways still to be understood, but in general we can say that changes of type B are later than, or at least start at the same time as changes of type A, *and crucially not before them*' (Traugott 2002: 27f.; emphasis mine). Since 'primary' and 'secondary' stages may form part of the same chain I see no reason to consider only the former as 'grammaticalization', as suggested by Detges and Waltereit. Also where degrammaticalization is concerned, I will distinguish between primary and secondary degrammaticalization (see Chapter 3).

### 1.4.2 *Pragmaticalization*

More controversial than secondary grammaticalization, in my view, is the development of discourse markers, sometimes termed 'pragmaticalization' (see e.g. Traugott 1982; Traugott 1997a; Tabor and Traugott 1998; Brinton 1996; Wischer 2000; Traugott and Dasher 2002: 152ff.; Visconti 2004; Brinton and Traugott 2005: 136ff.). Historical sources for discourse markers include SUBJECT + VERB matrix clauses (*I say, you know*), imperatives (*look'ee*), adverbial or relative clauses (*as it seems*), and adverbial prepositional phrases (*indeed*) (Brinton and Traugott 2005: 137). These cases are often considered grammaticalization because they exhibit some typical characteristics such as divergence, layering, decategorialization, morphologization, and phonological reduction. This is illustrated by the development of English *look*

[20] The term 'secondary grammaticalization' was introduced by Givón (1991: 305) in a slightly different sense than the one adopted by Traugott, namely to denote the advancement of one grammatical category to another. For example, nominative case markers seldom grammaticalize directly, but derive typically from genitive or ergative case markers.

(*you*) in examples (20a–c) (from Brinton 2001, quoted here from Brinton and Traugott 2005: 138). Brinton and Traugott argue that in (20a), *lok* is an imperative matrix clause meaning 'attend to'; in (20b), from Shakespeare's *Romeo and Juliet, look you* is a parenthetical and has been desemanticized, now functioning as a pragmatic instruction ('be careful'); (20c) shows fusion and further subjectification, conveying the speaker's impatient attitude:

(20) a. But **lok** thou dele nought withl [*c.*1386]
but look you deal not therewith
'see to it that you do not deal with it'

b. **Look you**, she loved her kinsman Tybalt dearly, / And so did I [1594–1596]

c. **Look'ee** Serjeant, no Coaxing, Wheedling, d'ye see [1706]

However, discourse markers differ from other cases of grammaticalization in several ways, listed in (21) (Brinton and Traugott 2005: 138f.; Ocampo 2006: 316f.):

(21) a. They show scope increase instead of scope reduction.
b. They show an increase in syntactic freedom instead of syntactic fixation.
c. They do not belong to categories traditionally considered 'grammatical'.
d. They do not become part of a paradigm.
e. They do not become rule-governed (i.e. there is no obligatorification, cf. section 3.5.1).
f. They do not fuse with another constituent.[21]

An evaluation of the differences and similarities between pragmaticalization and (other types of) grammaticalization has given rise to several strategies. The first is to consider the development of discourse markers as a process entirely separate from grammaticalization, which is the position taken in Aijmer (1997), and Ocampo (2006). Another option is to consider pragmaticalization as one of two subtypes of grammaticalization, as proposed in Wischer (2000) who distinguishes between 'Grammaticalization I' (movement towards morphology) and 'Grammaticalization II' (movement towards

[21] This may seem to contradict Brinton and Traugott's claim with respect to example (20c) that discourse markers do exhibit fusion. But the kind of fusion attested in *look'ee* differs crucially from the kind attested in grammaticalization, where the grammaticalizing item fuses with a constituent it governs, e.g. when a future auxiliary fuses with the main verb to form an inflectional future. *Look'ee*, then, is a mere case of univerbation commonly found in the lexicalization of phrases (*forget-me-not, no-show*, etc.).

discourse).[22] A third strategy is to consider (some of) the changes in (21) as non-characteristic for grammaticalization. As far as I know, this has only been attempted for scope changes ((21a)). See for instance Brinton and Traugott (2005: 138 and references there to previous works of these authors), who argue that 'the notion of scope reduction has been challenged in grammaticalization generally'.

But even if we were to accept that scope is no parameter of grammaticalization, we are still left with a substantial number of parameters in which pragmaticalization differs from grammaticalization. Another argument against considering pragmaticalization as (a type of) grammaticalization is that discourse and grammar form the opposites of Givón's (1979: 209) cline:

(22) discourse > syntax > morphology > morphophonemics > zero

A final note of interest is that pragmaticalization does not appear to be unidirectional, as Ocampo (2006: 317) convincingly argues. Citing a study by Mithun (1988) of co-ordinating conjunctions in a wide variety of languages, including languages for which some historical records are available (e.g. Mohawk), Ocampo provides several examples of conjunctions that derive from discourse markers. To conclude, movement towards discourse is genuinely different from movement towards grammar, and the two are therefore best kept separate.

### 1.4.3 *Clause combining*

The rise of complementizers has frequently been cited as an instance of grammaticalization. Cross-linguistically, complementizers typically develop out of demonstratives (Heine and Kuteva 2002: 106f.), as in the German example in (23) (Diewald 1997: 12), or from adverbs, as in the Finnish example in (24) (Anttila 1989: 151):[23]

| | | | | | | | |
|---|---|---|---|---|---|---|---|
| (23) | a. Ich | weiß | **das:** | Er | kommt. | | (pronoun) |
| | I | know | that: | He | comes. | | |
| | b. Ich | weiß, | **daß** | er | kommt. | | (complementizer) |
| | I | know | that | he | comes. | | |
| (24) | a. Minä | luulen | **että.** | Sinä | tulet. | | (adverb) |
| | I | think | thus. | You | come. | | |

[22] These terms are not to be confused with primary and secondary grammaticalization discussed in the previous section.

[23] See Cristofaro (1998) for additional examples of the grammaticalization of subordinators.

| | | | | | |
|---|---|---|---|---|---|
| b. Minä | luulen, | **että** | sinä | tulet | (complementizer) |
| I | think | that | you | come. | |

The aim of this section is to show that the development of complementizers may not be the prototypical example of grammaticalization as it has often been held to be, but first I will outline how clause combining is usually treated in current theorizing.

In Hopper and Traugott (2003: 175ff.), the development of complementizers illustrated in (23) and (24) is considered an example of grammaticalization across clauses along the cline of clause combining:

| | | | | | |
|---|---|---|---|---|---|
| (25) | parataxis | > | hypotaxis | > | subordination |
| | −dependent | | +dependent | | +dependent |
| | −embedded | | −embedded | | +embedded |

Hopper and Traugott (2003: 177) define the three 'cluster points' on the cline of clause combining in the following way:

(a) Parataxis: 'relative independence, except as constrained by the pragmatics of "making sense" and relevance'.
(b) Hypotaxis: 'interdependency, in which there is a nucleus, and one or more clauses which cannot stand by themselves, and are therefore relatively dependent. However, they are typically not wholly included within any constituent of the nucleus'.
(c) Subordination: 'complete dependency, in which a margin is wholly included within a constituent of the nucleus'.

The three types of clause combining are exemplified in (26) below. Example (26a) is a paratactic construction, in which the two fully independent clauses are in juxtaposition, and the semantic relationship between them is one of inference only. In (26b), on the other hand, the adverbial clause *Before leaving Krishnapur* cannot stand on its own, and is hence dependent, but it is not fully embedded, because the two clauses can be reversed in order (*The collector took a strange decision before leaving Krishnapur*). Also semantically, the hypotactic clause is less dependent than a subordinate clause, for instance because it denotes its own event: thus, in (26b), the *Before leaving Krishnapur* can only be replaced by an adverbial clause which presents an event as an entity, e.g. *before his departure*, but not by a mere temporal adverbial such as *before noon*. In (26c), finally, the clause *That the Titanic sank* is both dependent on the matrix and embedded in it. Both syntactically and semantically, it functions as a constituent – in (26c), it functions as the subject of the matrix.

(26) a. Fort Sumter has been fired on. My regiment leaves at dawn. [parataxis]

b. Before leaving Krishnapur, the Collector took a strange decision. [hypotaxis]

c. That the Titanic sank was unexpected. [subordination]

The difference between parataxis, hypotaxis, and subordination is one of gradience, and the line between the last two cluster points on the cline is particularly hard to draw, both synchronically and diachronically. Historical data may be ambiguous, as is illustrated by example (27) (from the *Anglo-Saxon chronicle*, ms. A):[24]

(27)

| | | | | | | |
|---|---|---|---|---|---|---|
| Ða | on | morgenne | gehierdun | **þæt** | þæs | cyninges |
| when/then | in | morning | heard-PL | this | that-GEN | king-GEN |
| þegnas | þe | him | beæftan | wærun | **þæt** | se | cyning |
| thanes | who | him | behind | were | that | the | king |
| ofslægen | wæs, | þa | ridon | hie | þider | |
| slain | was | then | rode | they | thither | |

'Then in the morning the king's thanes heard this (these thanes had been left behind): that the king had been slain. Then they rode up there.'

According to Hopper and Traugott (2003: 191) the first *þæt* in the above example is a pronoun anticipating the second *þæt*. The clause introduced by the second *þæt* is not embedded, yet it is 'already something more than merely paratactic', and therefore the *þæt*+*þæt*-construction is best analysed as hypotactic. According to them, the equivalent of (26c), with a *þæt*-clause functioning as a subject, is not yet unequivocally attested. In present-day English, the grammaticalization of *that*-clauses has not yet run its full course, because there are still some constraints on the occurrence of *that*-clauses as subjects (**Did that John showed up please you?*).

The view that the development of *that*-clauses is an instance of grammaticalization is however contested by Fischer (2008: 358ff.). According to her, the loss of the double *þæt*-construction may well be the result of the change from SOV to SVO in Middle English, because in SVO sentences first and second *that* would follow each other directly, which would not only produce an awkward repetition (*I want that, that you come with me*), but it is also unnecessary for processing reasons (which was one of the reasons why, Fischer suggests, the first *þæt* occurs in sentence (27)).[25] Another reason

[24] The glosses have been slightly modified to clarify the construction of this sentence.

[25] An argument in favour of this view is that a double 'that' is still possible in SOV languages such as Dutch:

why Fischer regards clause combining as atypical is that it does not show common grammaticalization characteristics such as semantic bleaching or decategorialization.

I agree with Fischer that clause combining is too different from other types of grammaticalization to be subsumed under it, but I do not share her view (p. 360) that the shift from demonstrative *that* to complementizer *that* is no grammaticalization either, since this does involve primitive changes such as bleaching and reduction (unlike demonstrative *that*, complementizer *that* can no longer be stressed).[26] Clause combining (or its opposite, but it is hard to see what that might be) is not relevant in the degrammaticalization changes discussed in this work, and I will therefore leave the discussion at this.

## 1.5 Context and constructions

Much work from the first decade of the twenty-first century has emphasized the importance of context in grammaticalization (e.g. Heine 2002; Diewald 2002, 2006; Bybee 2003; Traugott 2003; Haspelmath 2004; Himmelmann 2004; Lehmann 2004; Brinton and Traugott 2005: 24ff.; for a slightly earlier account see Hopper 1998). Himmelmann (2004: 31), for instance, observes that 'major diagnostics' for grammaticalization (bleaching, morphologization, phonological reduction) focus on the grammaticalizing element. But according to him (ibid.) 'the unit to which grammaticization properly applies are *constructions*, not isolated lexical items' (emphasis original). The context that needs to be considered ranges from the NP level (e.g. in the case of the grammaticalization of articles) to the clause level (e.g. in the case of the grammaticalization of adpositions) to the discourse level (in the case of the grammaticalization of clause linkers). Croft (2000: 162) explains the neglect of context in the early days of grammaticalization studies as follows: 'Of course, it is precisely the specific, especially invariant, morphemes associated with the construction that are interpreted by the interlocutors as encoding the meaning characteristically associated with the construction as a whole... It is this fact that gives the impression that grammaticalization is a process affecting individual morphemes (and the lexemes they are derived from).' For example, in the case of English *be going to*, it is *going to* that is reduced (to *gonna*), because it is

(i) Ik heb **dat** steeds gezegd **dat** ik dat nog doen moet
I have that always said that I that still do must
'I have always said that I still have to do that'

[26] The shift from demonstrative to complementizer *is* problematic for the notorious parameter of scope, but that is another matter (see section 3.5.2).

the most characteristic (and invariant) element of this construction, but it is only reduced in this context, not in others.

The role of context has been formalized in papers by Heine (2002) and Diewald (2002, 2006). In the following I will briefly discuss Heine's model, which distinguishes four stages in a grammaticalization process.[27] In Heine's model, the meaning of a construction changes in three subsequent steps. Point of departure is the initial stage, at which there was only the original meaning. At the second stage, the 'bridging context', a new meaning (the 'target meaning') has arisen as a result of pragmatic inferencing. At the third stage, the 'switch context', the original meaning of the construction (the 'source meaning') has disappeared. At the fourth and final stage, the target meaning becomes conventionalized and is no longer restricted to the context in which it initially appeared. One of Heine's own examples will be used to illustrate these stages. This example concerns the German temporal adverb *dabei* (Heine 2002: 91ff.), which developed the additional function of concessive marker. The four relevant stages are illustrated in (28).

(28) I. Karl geht schlafen; **dabei** trägt er einen Schlafanzug.
Karl goes sleep thereby wears he a pyjama
'Karl is going to bed; (at that occasion) he is wearing pyjamas.'

II. Karl geht schlafen; **dabei** ist er gar nicht müde
Karl goes sleep thereby he is at.all not tired
'Karl is going to bed; still, he is not tired at all' [target meaning]
'Karl is going to bed; at that time he is not tired at all' [source meaning]

III. Karl geht schlafen; **dabei** geht er um diese Zeit nie schlafen
Karl goes sleep; thereby goes he at this time never sleep
'Karl is going to bed; although he never goes to bed at this time'

IV. Karl geht schlafen; **dabei** war er eben noch überhaupt nicht müde
Karl goes sleep; thereby was he just still at.all not tired
'Karl is going to bed; although a moment ago he was not tired at all'

[27] Heine's stages are primarily semantically based, while Diewald also takes morphosyntactic properties of the contexts into account. Therefore, the stages Diewald distinguishes cannot be mapped onto Heine's stages in a 1:1 fashion (Diewald 2002: 117), but that discussion falls outside the scope of this work.

At Stage I in (28) above, *dabei* is most likely to receive a temporal interpretation (of simultaneity), and it can occur both clause-initially and after the finite verb (*er trägt dabei einen Schlafanzug*). At Stage II, the *dabei*-clause denotes a contrast, contradicting common experience (one does not normally go to bed when one is not tired yet), and could be paraphrased by a concessive clause such as *obwohl er gar nicht müde ist* 'although he is not tired at all'. Stage II is a bridging context in that the temporal meaning (the source meaning) is still possible, if less plausible than the concessive meaning (the target meaning). At Stage III however, the temporal interpretation is ruled out, and the construction has 'switched' to the concessive meaning. At both Stage II and Stage III, *dabei* has become fixed in clause-initial position. At Stage IV, finally, the concessive sense is no longer context-dependent (as it was at the preceding two stages): it can now be used in clauses in which simultaneity is explicitly ruled out by the adverbial *eben noch* 'a moment ago'.

A more recent approach to the role of context in grammaticalization is the integration of grammaticalization studies and construction grammar (see Traugott 2007, 2008; Trousdale 2008a; Trousdale, in prep., and references there). Below are two definitions of 'construction' in two of the main textbooks on construction grammar – a fairly narrow one (Goldberg 1995:4) in (29), and a more recent one by the same author (Goldberg 2006:5) in (30). The latter is obviously less restrictive in that it includes fully compositional patterns, as long as they are sufficiently frequent.[28]

(29) C is a CONSTRUCTION $\text{iff}_{\text{def}}$ C is a form-meaning pair $<F_i, S_i>$ such that some aspect of $F_i$ or some aspect of $S_i$ is not strictly predictable from C's component parts or from other previously established constructions.

(30) Any linguistic pattern is recognized as a construction as long as some aspect of its form or function is not strictly predictable from its component parts or from other constructions recognized to exist. In addition, patterns are stored as constructions even if they are fully predictable as long as they occur with sufficient frequency.

The main questions are, at present, 'whether a construction is simply the context for grammaticalization, or whether constructions themselves may be subject to grammaticalization' (Trousdale, in prep.). Constructions, by the way, can be 'of any size from morpheme to complex sentence' (Traugott 2007: 525).

[28] Trousdale (in prep.) makes the interesting observation that Goldberg's 1995 definition is more typical of lexicalized constructions, whereas her 2006 definition is more typical of grammaticalized constructions.

A construction grammar approach to grammaticalization emphasizes that grammaticalization is a change in form as much as it is a change in meaning.[29] This, of course, is not a revolutionary view, but construction grammar offers a means of formalizing grammaticalization changes that is potentially more adequate than generative grammar, because the latter cannot really cope with directional tendencies or layering (see section 2.7.3), whereas these can easily be accounted for in construction grammar terms (Trousdale, in prep.). Publications on this line of research started to appear only shortly before this monograph was finished, but to me it seems a most promising new direction for grammaticalization studies. In section 5.3.4, I will provide an example of how a construction-based approach and a morpheme-based approach can offer different perspectives on one and the same change.

## 1.6 Methodological issues

### 1.6.1 *Processes versus results*

Some authors, in particular Fischer (2000), Joseph (2001, 2003, 2004) and Newmeyer (1998, 2001), have argued that grammaticalization is not a separate process of change. According to Newmeyer (1998: 232), the term 'process' should refer to 'a distinct phenomenon requiring an inherent set of explanatory devices', but in the case of grammaticalization changes, '[t]he term "process" is often used informally to mean nothing more than "phenomenon to be explained"'. Instead, Newmeyer (1998: 235) characterizes grammaticalization as 'essentially an epiphenomenal result of *independent* historical developments each of which falls out of some independent theory.' Since semantic change, phonetic reduction, and reanalysis, Newmeyer argues, may occur independently from one another, there is no reason to assume a separate dynamic force (i.e. grammaticalization) when these changes happen to co-occur. For the same reason, he argues, there is no need for a 'grammaticalization theory'.

In his discussion of some stock examples of grammaticalization (among them the well-known development of the Greek future marker *tha*, ultimately from a full verb *thélo:* 'want') Joseph (2001, 2003, 2004), too, argues that this change can be fully explained within the framework of 'traditional' historical linguistics, and that grammaticalization is at best 'just a label given to a

[29] Nevertheless, some approaches to grammaticalization regard it as primarily semantically-pragmatically motivated. See Fischer (2008: 340) for a convenient overview.

particular type of outcome of independently needed mechanisms of change' (Joseph 2004: 51).

Fischer (2000: 151, 152) similarly argues:

> One of the problems I have with the way grammaticalization has been dealt with in the literature is that the mechanistic side of it has been overemphasised, with the result, I think, that the mechanism has become too powerful as an explanatory tool or as a description of a diachronic process of linguistic change... Although I would agree... that reanalysis and analogy, or metonymic and metaphorical processes, are important in language change... I still cannot see that there is room for a separate or 'independent' process of grammaticalisation. Where most linguists see a unidirectional process from concrete to abstract, a process that cannot be cut up into segments, I can only see a more or less accidental concurrence.

In a more recent paper Fischer (2008: 337) maintains that 'the notion of grammaticalization can be useful as a heuristic device to discover changes that have taken place in language and to understand why changes often follow similar pathways', but that it is 'incorrect to elevate grammaticalization to some higher status, to some independent mechanism of change'.[30]

This line of criticism is rejected by Haspelmath (1999a: 1062), and Heine and Kuteva (2002: 2f.). According to the latter, 'the main task of grammaticalization theory is to explain why grammatical forms and constructions are structured the way they are, and these four mechanisms [see (31) below], as opposed to many other conceivable mechanisms, have been found to be relevant to achieve such explanations'.

(31) The principal mechanisms involved in grammaticalization (Heine and Kuteva 2002: 2):

1. Desemanticization or semantic bleaching – loss of (concrete) meaning
2. Extension or context generalization – use in new contexts
3. Decategorialization – loss of morphosyntactic properties (e.g. inflection)
4. Erosion or phonetic reduction – loss of phonetic substance

The mechanisms in (31) are clearly interrelated according to Heine and Kuteva (2002: 3f.). The initial stage of grammaticalization involves context-induced reinterpretation of concrete items as abstract items. Such reinterpretations can often be described as metaphorical extensions, for example when a body-part

[30] Instead, Fischer (2008: 338) argues that grammaticalization is essentially derived from more fundamental, cognitive principles which are at work in both language change and language acquisition. This is a novel and interesting approach, but one that cannot be discussed in detail in the present work.

noun such as 'back' is used to denote a spatial concept 'behind'. Semantic bleaching is thus the result of the transition from concrete meaning to abstract, grammatical meaning. Once such forms have acquired grammatical meaning, they are subject to decategorialization and phonetic reduction (because grammatical forms are usually unstressed). In other words, even though the four mechanisms in (31) have been observed to occur independently, they are not independent of one another in grammaticalization. In a pertinent comment on *Linguist List*, Dahl (1996) puts it this way:

> This to me seems like saying that since love and sex can occur without each other, they are totally different phenomena. For [Newmeyer's] argument [in an earlier posting, against grammaticalization as a process] to go through, he would have to show not only that the processes can occur independently but also that they are unrelated even in the well-documented cases when they show up together. What some of us have claimed is that the things that happen in grammaticalization do so in an orderly fashion which not only predicts what changes can occur but also puts constraints on what synchronic grammatical systems are found.

Heine (2003b: 579) also acknowledges the criticism by Newmeyer and Campbell that the changes involved are not unique to grammaticalization, but he points out that 'jointly they are responsible for grammaticalization taking place', and thus, that 'they can be said to constitute different components of one and the same process'.

To sum up the discussion thus far, I think that the arguments brought forward by Heine, Kuteva, and Dahl are sufficiently convincing to allow grammaticalization to be regarded as a process with a dynamics of its own. Nevertheless, three caveats are in order. First, acknowledging that grammaticalization is a process is not tantamount to saying that grammaticalization is a 'driving force'. To my mind, Bybee, Perkins, and Pagliuca (1994: 298) hit the nail on the head when they write that 'The processes that lead to grammaticalization occur in language use for their own sakes; *it just happens that their cumulative effect is the development of grammar*' (emphasis mine).

Secondly (and this has frequently been stressed in grammaticalization literature), there is nothing deterministic about grammaticalization (see e.g. Traugott 2001). In other words, grammaticalization is a process in the sense that it involves a series of subsequent steps that occur in a certain order, as we have seen above, but not in the sense that each step inevitably leads to the next (this lack of inevitability was Newmeyer's (1998: 251) main argument for rejecting the view of grammaticalization as a 'distinct process'). Traugott (2001: 3) puts it this way: 'Changes do not have to occur. They also do not have to go to completion, in other words, they do not have to move all the way down a cline, or even continue down it once they start out on it.'[31] In addition, grammaticalization need not involve change at the level of phonology (at least not initially). For instance, there is no difference in pronunciation between the participle *considering* (*We are considering going to Denmark*) and its grammaticalized form as a conjunction (*Considering her age she is still quite active*). In fact, it may take ages before a grammaticalized form is phonetically reduced, if this happens at all. The Modern Swedish preposition *bland* 'among', for example, which grammaticalized over half a millennium ago from a (now obsolete) noun *bland* 'blend' (Norde 2000), shows no signs of reduction to the present day.

Finally, and perhaps most importantly: saying that grammaticalization is a process does not imply that there are universal pathways of grammaticalization. Heine and Kuteva's *World Lexicon of Grammaticalization* (2002) may seem a veritable treasure-trove of cross-linguistically similar grammaticalization changes, but it has to be noted that many of the cases quoted in this work have not been studied in sufficient detail to substantiate claims about such universal pathways. In languages with little or no written histories this has of course not been possible, but even some of the pet examples from well-documented Indo-European languages do not stand up to scrutiny. Enger (2002, 2003), for example, has shown that the well-known development of the Proto-Scandinavian reflexive pronoun **sik* (3SG.ACC) into a verbal suffix -*s(t)* with passive meaning in the modern Mainland Scandinavian languages, was not a simple development from free form to clitic to suffix, as is generally assumed (e.g. Hopper and Traugott 2003: 159ff.). Enger convincingly argues that many Old Norse *st*-verbs are to be considered derived forms rather than inflected ones, which implies an unusual pathway, namely free form > clitic > derivational suffix > inflectional suffix.

Another case in point is the Modern Finnish conjunction *kun*, which has both temporal and causal meaning. On the basis of this homonymy alone, Traugott and König (1991: 197) and Heine and Kuteva (2002: 291, quoting Traugott and König) conclude that the causal meaning was inferred from the temporal one. From a recent paper on this conjunction however (Herlin and Kotilainen 2004), in which the authors did examine the history of *kun*, it becomes evident that the state of affairs in Modern Finnish is not at all the result of an internal development following a universal semantic pathway, but the result of standardization, influenced by cognates from Indo-European

[31] Traugott's first point, that changes need not occur, is beautifully depicted in the following quote from Kuryłowicz (1966: 174, cited in Lass 1997: 302): 'Il en est comme de l'eau de pluie qui doit prendre un chemin prévu (gouttères, égouts, conduits) *une fois qu'il pleut*. Mais la pluie n'est pas une nécessité.'

languages. The causal meaning may very well have developed from the one-time comparative and similaritive functions of *kun* or its usage as an emphatic particle. The comparative and similaritive meanings were restricted to the conjunction *kuin*, originally a variant form of *kun*. In addition, *kun* was assigned contrastive meaning. Thus an artificial distinction between *kun* and *kuin* was introduced by nineteenth-century Finnish language reformers, inspired by the same distinctions in Indo-European languages (primarily Swedish).[32]

What these three examples (and the list could easily be expanded)[33] show is that even in grammaticalization studies people tend to base their analyses on results (a superficial comparison of initial and final states) rather than on a detailed examination of the change itself. It is therefore more appropriate to speak of *tendencies* than of 'universal pathways', 'laws', or 'principles' (Traugott 2001: 1; Joseph 2003: 486f.; Fischer, Norde, and Perridon 2004: 13; see also section 1.6.3).

For degrammaticalization, finally, no one would wish to claim that there exist universal pathways, because degrammaticalization changes are rare and mostly unique to a single language. It is not even clear indeed whether degrammaticalization is a process. I will return to this issue in Chapter 7.[34]

### 1.6.2 *Grammaticalization as a 'theory'*

The study of grammaticalization has frequently been referred to as 'grammaticalization theory' (Newmeyer 1998: 234ff. and references there), which according to Newmeyer (1998: 240) merely reflects 'carelessness of usage'. In what is probably the most vehement critique of grammaticalization to date, Janda (2005: 47) puts it as follows:

> The fervency of grammaticalization 'theorists' makes grammaticalization studies feel almost like a religion, while criticisms by perceived outsiders provoke reactions suggesting that critics are heretics... he [i.e. Richard Janda] should, for the record, state: Grammaticalization phenomena exist, and occur frequently, but all valid

[32] Compare Swedish *medan* 'while' (both temporal and contrastive), *än* 'than' (comparative), and *som* (similaritive).

[33] See for instance Detges (2004) and Tsangalides (2004).

[34] This being said, I will continue to use phrases such as 'X degrammaticalizes' or 'Y is a degrammaticalization', assuming that most (if not all) readers will understand that these are metaphors for hopelessly tiresome formulations such as 'X is the result of changes brought about by (unintentional) actions of language users.' When I use formulations such as 'changing morphemes', or 'changing constructions', by no means do I imply that language is conceived of as having a ' "trans-individual, trans-generational", (near-)immortal "life of its own" ' (Janda 2001: 290), entirely beyond the control of language users (see Newmeyer 1998: 239 for remarks similar to Janda's).

generalizations concerning them result from the interaction of other, primary linguistic elements, because grammaticalization is not a (single) thing, but the outcome of other processes, and so grammaticalization is neither ubiquitous nor monolithic... Many alchemists made non-optimal use of scholarly time due to distraction by the notion 'philosopher's stone'; grammaticalization 'theorists' have an equivalent obsession: fixed grammaticalization 'path(way)s'/ 'chains' as putative guarantees for accurate reconstruction.

Janda surely exaggerates, but I agree that the use of the term 'theory' may lead to confusion, for instance in Heine (2003b), who states both (32) and (33):

(32) Grammaticalization theory is neither a theory of language nor of language change; its goal is to describe grammaticalization, that is, the way grammatical forms develop through space and time, and to explain why they are structured the way they are. (Heine 2003b: 575)

(33) As observed earlier, grammaticalization theory is a theory to the extent that it offers an explanatory account of how and why grammatical categories arise and develop. (Heine 2003b: 578)

Haspelmath (2004: 23) finds the criticism that grammaticalization is not a theory 'partially justified', since it is not a 'theory in the sense of a well-defined system of interconnected falsifiable hypotheses'. He also notes that grammaticalization researchers do not subscribe to a single monolithic theory, but that they try to understand and explain large classes of similar semantic and morphosyntactic changes. Therefore, Haspelmath argues, the term 'theorizing about grammaticalization' would perhaps be more appropriate.

To conclude: although grammaticalization is not a theory, its merits as a descriptive framework, I think, are beyond dispute. What is more, the relevance of grammaticalization studies is not confined to the description of grammaticalization phenomena itself. For instance, it may feed other branches in linguistics, such as evolutionary linguistics, as is evidenced by the following quote from Tomasello (2003: 13f.):

Generative grammarians believe that the human species evolved a genetically based universal grammar common to all peoples and that the variability in modern languages is basically on the surface only... The alternative is the usage-based view, in which there is no need to posit a specific genetic adaptation for grammar because processes of grammaticalization and syntactization can actually create grammatical structures out of concrete utterances – and grammaticalization and syntactization are cultural-historical processes, not biological ones. Thus, it is a historical fact that the specific items and constructions of a given language are not invented all at once, but rather they emerge, evolve, and accumulate modifications over historical time as human beings use them with one another and adapt them to changing communicative circumstances.

In section 2.7.3, I will return to the advantages of a usage-based approach over a generative approach to grammar change.

### 1.6.3 *Changes and correspondences*

If I drive from Edinburgh to London, make some stops for petrol, and take a brief trip east on the way to visit a friend in Cambridge, I can still be said (from the point of view of 'the accomplishment', or juxtaposition of initial and final states) to 'have driven from Edinburgh to London'. How I got there is another (kind of) story... We seem usually to be thinking of macro-stories when we talk about 'change'; but the micro-stories are of enormous theoretical importance as well. (Lass 1997: 288)

The above quote nicely illustrates an important distinction in historical linguistics, namely the distinction between, in Andersen's (2001: 228) terms, 'diachronic correspondences', and 'changes'. A diachronic correspondence is the 'relation between homologous elements... belonging to two chronologically separate synchronic states in a linguistic tradition'. Andersen makes a point similar to Lass's when he notes that language historians often speak of 'changes' when what they mean are diachronic correspondences, which are not changes, but the results of change. 'True' changes, on the other hand, are 'the historical events in a linguistic tradition by which practices of speaking vary over time'. Changes can be observed when they occur (though they often go unnoticed by members of a speech community) and they are reflected in synchronic variation or diachronic correspondences. The problem with much work on grammaticalization is that the distinction between changes and correspondences is not always observed:

To some extent, a basic problem here, as I see it, is that either by working from synchronic data and drawing even well-reasoned historical inferences (i.e., making a claim of grammaticalization based on internal reconstruction) or by comparing two stages somewhat distant in time and trying to infer what the pathways from one stage to the other were, one is falling into the trap discussed by Andersen... of confounding a diachronic correspondence with an actual innovation or change. While this is not a problem that is restricted to grammaticalization studies, it is a real one, and, speaking just impressionistically here, it is one that proponents of grammaticalization, with its appeal to universally applicable pathways of change that in essence do the work of historical investigation for one, seem rather prone to fall victim to. (Joseph 2004: 52)

Janda and Joseph (2003: 13) even propose a three-way distinction: 'diachronic correspondence (juxtaposing two potentially non-adjacent times) versus *innovation* (initiated by an individual person at one particular time) versus *change* (requiring adoption, over time, by all – or at least much – of a group).' Although it is unquestionably true that these three are essentially different phenomena, it is not always easy, to put it mildly, to distinguish the latter two in diachronic linguistics. In most cases it is indeed impossible to detect innovation, since new features are generally not recorded until they have spread to other members of a speech community. (Who, for instance, was the first speaker of English to use the reduced variant *gonna* instead of *going to*?) I will therefore take 'change' to comprise both innovation and spread.

An additional problem with complex phenomena such as grammaticalization and degrammaticalization is that they typically involve 'micro-stories' (in Lass's terminology) on several linguistic levels (semantic-pragmatic, morphosyntactic, phonological). In the remainder of this work, I will therefore use the term *composite change* to refer to grammaticalization and degrammaticalization changes, and *primitive change* to refer to a change at one linguistic level. A composite change, then, always involves several primitive changes. In Chapter 3, I will outline a classificational model to distinguish primitive changes in degrammaticalization, in order to avoid the 'correspondence trap'.

This implies that, wherever possible, historical evidence of primitive changes must be provided. This is not standard practice, as noted by Joseph (2004: 47), who accuses much work on grammaticalization of being 'ahistorical, not giving due consideration to the full range of information about the steps in a particular development and attempting to work out the history of various phenomena from synchrony alone'. This caveat obviously holds for languages with little or no written histories, but even for abundantly documented languages such as Greek or the Romance languages. As an example of such avoidable oversimplification I will discuss one of the pet examples in grammaticalization studies, which can be paraphrased as 'the development of the Romance suffix *-ment(e)* from the ablative singular of the Latin noun *mens* "mind"' in section 1.6.5.

### 1.6.4 *Reconstruction as evidence*

For languages without written histories, changes can only be reconstructed. A clear example of reconstruction in grammaticalization studies is the case of person-number endings on the verb in Buryat Mongolian (cited in Hopper and Traugott 2003: 141, based on Comrie 1980), which bear a striking resemblance to pronouns with corresponding person and number, as is shown in Table 1.2.

Such reconstructions are very common in theorizing about grammaticalization, but they have been heavily criticized, in particular for their potential

TABLE 1.2. Pronouns and verbal endings in Buryat Mongolian (Hopper and Traugott 2003: 141)

| | Pronoun | Verbal ending |
|---|---|---|
| 1SG | *bi* | *-b* |
| 2SG | *ši* | *-š* |
| 1PL | *bide* | *-bdi* |
| 2PL | *ta* | *-t* |

circularity. Newmeyer (1998: 279ff.), for instance, points out that it is inadmissible to use reconstructed pathways as 'evidence' for universal pathways, which subsequently serve as the basis for further reconstruction. According to Janda (2005: 46), reconstruction forces the linguist 'to understand the data-rich present based on the lacunar past'. And for once, Lehmann (2004: 156) appears to agree with grammaticalization critics when he writes: 'Such cases of diachronic variation where [an earlier form] is reconstructed do not count as historical evidence either.'

One obvious problem with reconstruction is the possibility of false friends in grammar. Possessive constructions in Norwegian are a good example of this. Among the various ways of expressing possession two constructions are superficially similar (Fiva 1987: 42):

| | | | | | | | |
|---|---|---|---|---|---|---|---|
| (34) a. | den | gamle | mannen | med | skjeggets | | hus |
| | [the | old | man-DEF | with | beard-DEF]=GEN | | house[35] |
| b. | den | gamle | mannen | med | skjegget | **sitt** | hus |
| | the | old | man-DEF | with | beard-DEF | POSS | house |

'the house of the old man with the beard'

Example (34a) represents the s-genitive (see section 5.3), example (34b) contains a so-called resumptive possessive pronoun (Norde 1997: 55ff.). Even though there are distributional differences between these two constructions (Venås 1989; Torp 1992; Norde 1997: 79ff.), there are some striking similarities: Norwegian resumptive possessive pronoun constructions are confined to animate possessors and the s-genitive has a strong preference for animate possessors as well; both can occur in group genitive constructions (see section 5.3), as exemplified in (34). In addition, it is phonologically plausible that *-s* is a reduced variant of the resumptive possessive pronoun (*sin* for non-neuter possessees; *sitt* for neuter possessees). Geographically,

[35] On the notation <=GEN> see section 5.3.2.

they are in complementary distribution, but this is not necessarily a problem for reconstructing the s-genitive as a reduced variant of the pronoun, if one assumes that the pronoun was cliticized and phonologically reduced in some dialects but not in others. In effect, such a reconstruction has been suggested by some Norwegian scholars (Fiva 1987; Lødrup 1989). In the absence of historical evidence, this would be as reasonable a scenario as the Buryat Mongolian case exemplified in Table 1.2, but for Norwegian, there *is* historical evidence, showing (i) that the (enclitic) s-genitive is not a reduced pronoun, but a direct continuation of the former inflectional genitive suffix *-s* (see Trosterud 2001: 176ff. and references there), and (ii) that the s-genitive predates the *sin*-possessive, which was most probably borrowed from Middle Low German (Nesse 2002: 170ff.). For these reasons, a reconstruction *sin/sitt* > *-s* can be safely dismissed.

In the remainder of this section, I will discuss some additional pitfalls, with particular reference to the reconstruction of morpheme order. This type of reconstruction is inspired by Givón's slogan 'Today's morphology is yesterday's syntax' (Givón 1971: 413).[36]

Attractive though this slogan may be, it is by no means exceptionless. First, it does not apply to strongly isolating languages, which 'typically do not allow yesterday's syntax to become today's morphology' (Ansaldo and Lim 2004: 345; cf. also Bybee, Perkins and Pagliuca 1994: 118).[37] Secondly, speakers may reanalyse the relative ordering in sequences of morphemes, especially during language acquisition (Comrie 1980; Bybee 1985a: 30ff). The well-documented example of the morphologization of Spanish unstressed object pronouns (Enrique-Arias 2005) is a case in point. Whereas in Old Spanish unstressed pronouns (deriving from Latin pronouns or demonstratives) could be cliticized to a variety of hosts (verbs, complementizers, negation markers, and NP's), their position and distribution have become far more restricted in Modern Spanish, where they occur before finite verb forms and after non-finite verb forms, as illustrated in (35) (the asterisked examples were still possible in Old Spanish). On the basis of this, some linguists have proposed

[36] Actually, Givón's slogan was inspired by an aphorism which according to Givón was uttered by Lao Tse, who, on being informed that Chinese was an isolating language, reportedly remarked: 'Weep not, my children, for today's syntax is tomorrow's morphology' (Givón 1971: 413n.). As slogans go, Givón's has often been paraphrased. Thus Ramat (1992: 557) asserts that 'today's grammar may become tomorrow's lexicon', while Janda (1995: 119) suggests that: 'sometimes, "Today's morphology is tomorrow's syntax"'.

[37] This does not mean however that grammaticalization does not occur in these languages. Even though reduction at the morphological level is prohibited because of discrete syllable boundaries and phonotactic constraints, reduction can be observed in vowel quality and suprasegmental features such as duration (see Ansaldo and Lim 2004 for interesting examples).

to treat the pronouns not as clitics, but as inflectional agreement markers on the verb (Enrique-Arias 2005: 68 and references there).

(35) a. Juan **lo** hizo / *hízo-**lo**
John it did / did-it
'John did it'

b. Juan vino para hacer-**lo** / ***lo** hacer
John came to do-it / it do
'John came to do it'

In this diachronic study of the morphologization of unstressed pronouns to finite verb forms, Enrique-Arias (2005) showed that these word orders are not merely reflections of earlier syntactic patterns. Rather, the position of the pronoun is primarily determined by two factors: (a) the frequency of syntactic contexts in which either Pro-$V_{fin}$ or $V_{fin}$-Pro prevails,[38] and (b) prosody. Thus, since the syntactic contexts in which Pro-$V_{fin}$ were more common throughout the history of Spanish, this order became standard in Modern Spanish, even in contexts where the pronoun originally followed the verb. And both Pro-$V_{fin}$ and $V_{infin}$-Pro are consistent with the most natural prosodic pattern in Spanish. What the Spanish case shows, as Enrique-Arias convincingly argues, is that word order typology is not a very reliable tool in morphological reconstruction. For a proper understanding of contemporary morphological patterns a detailed historical analysis of individual languages is indispensable.

Morpheme order is also determined by the relevance of the category expressed by the bound morpheme to the stem (Bybee 1985a).The relevance of a category correlates with the amount of semantic change it generates – the more relevant a category is to nouns or verbs, the more it will affect the semantics of a noun or verb. In her survey of the relevance of morphological categories to the verb in fifty genetically and areally unrelated languages, Bybee found that mood, person, number, and aspect were most often expressed inflectionally on the verb (in 64%, 56%, 54%, and 52% of the languages in her sample respectively). According to her study, the most common type of inflectional system was one that included mood and either tense or aspect or both (Bybee 1985a: 24). And when it was possible to establish the order of morphemes,[39] she found that aspect markers were

[38] In his study, Enrique-Arias (2005: 69) distinguished thirteen syntactic contexts. Of these, four types were predominantly $V_{fin}$-Pro (e.g. after vocatives), six allowed both $V_{fin}$-Pro and Pro-$V_{fin}$ (e.g. after adverbials or PPs), and three were exclusively Pro-$V_{fin}$ (e.g. subordinate clauses).

[39] In the following cases the relative order of morphemes could not be established: (i) cases of portmanteau expression (particularly common were morphemes which simultaneously expressed tense and aspect, or mood and person); (ii) cases where morphemes appeared on different sides of the

closer to the stem than tense, mood, and person markers, tense markers occurred closer to the stem than both mood markers and person markers, and mood markers were closer to the stem than person markers (Bybee 1985a: 25f.). In the majority of cases, morphological ordering reflects syntactic ordering where, according to Bybee's relevance principle, there is a clear relation between the degree of semantic relevance of (for example) modals or auxiliaries to the main verb, and their proximity to that verb. However, Bybee also notes that 'we cannot assume that morphology is only fossilized syntax and stop at that'.

A final factor which complicates the reconstruction of morpheme order is the phenomenon of 'trapped morphology', where inflections are either re-ordered (Haspelmath 1993; Faarlund 2005: 66f., 71n.) or lost (Harris and Faarlund 2006). Haspelmath discusses a number of cases in various languages where inflections that have become wedged between their stem and another bound morpheme are 'externalized'. This happens, for instance, when a clitic (which may later become an affix itself) is added to the inflected stem, as in the pre-classical Latin forms of the emphatic pronoun, where a postfix *-pse* was added to inflected forms of a demonstrative (as attested in MASC.SG.ACC *eum-pse*, FEM.SG.NOM *ea-pse*, FEM.SG.ACC *eam-pse*). In classical Latin, the inflections have become externalized (compare MASC.SG.ACC *ipsum*, FEM.SG.NOM *ipsa*, FEM.SG.ACC *ipsam*), probably with an intermediate stage of 'hybrid' forms, i.e. forms with both internal and external inflection (attested examples are MASC.SG.ACC *eum-ps-um*, FEM.SG.NOM *ea-ps-a*, FEM.SG.ACC *eam-ps-am*) (Haspelmath 1993: 283f.). According to Haspelmath (1993: 291ff.) such changes are motivated by independent principles such as the 'inflection-outside-derivation principle', which states that '[a] morphologically complex word is preferred if its inflectional affixes are further away from the root than its derivational affixes'.[40]

Among the examples discussed by Harris and Faarlund (2006) are the loss of case inflection in definite nouns in the Mainland Scandinavian languages (e.g. Old Norse *hest-s=in-s* [horse-GEN=DEF-GEN] > Norwegian *hest-en=s* [horse-DEF=GEN] 'the horse's', and the loss of the ergative case marker in definite nouns in Georgian (e.g. **saxl-n=man* [house-ERG=DEF.ERG] > *saxl-man* 'the house' [ergative]). For all examples discussed in their paper, Harris and Faarlund conclude that the change must be morphological in nature,

verbal stem; (iii) cases where morphemes were mutually exclusive. Where one category was expressed inflectionally and one as a modification of the stem (e.g. by reduplication or vowel change), the latter was considered closer to the stem (Bybee 1985a: 25).

[40] Note that such preference principles are not 'hard' constraints, for otherwise the rise of forms with derivation outside would be blocked in the first place (Haspelmath 1993: 304).

because there was no plausible phonological explanation for the loss of the trapped morphemes, and because entire morphemes are targeted (which need not be the case in 'ordinary' phonological erosion).

### 1.6.5 *Case study: Romance* MENTE

Some stock examples of grammaticalization are so commonly quoted in grammaticalization studies that they appear to have become part of the linguistic collective memory. More often than not, they are quoted without references, since everybody has at least a vague notion of their development. Thus they start to lead a life of their own, figuring prominently in grammaticalization studies, and few people seem to be bothered about the details of development, let alone the question of whether these really are such straightforward examples as tradition has it.

In order to illustrate some of the methodological issues discussed in the previous sections, I will now turn to the history of the Romance suffix MENTE. The purpose of these sections will be to show that what may seem a clear-cut case of grammaticalization may in fact be far more complex once the historical details are considered, which has serious implications for too sweeping universalistic claims.

The development of *mente*, the ablative form of the Latin noun *mens* (GEN *mentis*), into an adverbial suffix in all Romance languages except Romanian is one of the most quoted examples of grammaticalization of a derivational suffix (Hoenigswald 1966: 44; Hopper and Traugott 1993: 131; 2003: 141f.; Lehmann 1995: 87; Giacalone Ramat 1998: 120). Examples from contemporary Romance languages are French *heureusement* 'fortunately', Portuguese *cruamente* 'cruelly', Spanish *distintamente* 'distinctly', Italian *raramente* 'rarely', Occitan and Catalan *bellamen(t)* 'beautifully', and Sardinian *finalmenti(s)* 'finally'. In some older Romance languages, as well as a few minor contemporary ones, we also find forms in *-m(i)entre*, e.g. Old Spanish *solamientre* 'only' or Lombard *longamentre* 'long' (Bauer 2003: 440). Because of this formal variation, the abstract notation MENTE will be used to refer to the morpheme in general when no particular language or dialect is being discussed.

The lexical origin of the suffix is reflected both by the feminine form[41] of the preceding adjective (*mens* was a feminine noun), and by stress patterns in some of the adverbs, e.g. Spanish *fácilmente* 'easily'(Bauer 2003: 440).[42] Although the

[41] That is, when the adjective belongs to a declension which distinguishes between masculine and feminine in the ablative singular.

[42] If this had been a lexical unity, only the penultimate syllable would have been stressed, as in other Spanish adverbs, e.g. *lentamente* 'slowly' (Bauer 2003: 440f.).

history of this suffix has been studied in great detail (see for instance Karlsson 1981; Detges 1998; Hummel 2000; Bauer 2003), some questions concerning its actual development remain, which makes MENTE less of a copybook example of grammaticalization. In this section, I will discuss three major problems regarding the grammaticalization of MENTE, namely (i) that the actual development from Latin to Romance is not known in much detail, (ii) that the morphological status of MENTE in some Romance languages is not quite clear, and (iii) that distributional differences in the contemporary Romance languages are usually ignored when MENTE is quoted as an instance of grammaticalization.

(i) *The development from Latin to Romance is not known in much detail.* The development from Latin ablative *mente* to Romance MENTE was far more complex than it is generally presented in grammaticalization literature. The construction with *mente* was just one type of phrasal adverbials in Classical Latin using the ablatives of nouns referring to one's mental state.[43] It is traditionally illustrated by the following passage from Ovid's *Metamorphoses* XIII:

(36) consolor socios ut longi taedia belli
encourage-1SG allies-ACC so.that long-GEN boredoms-ACC war-GEN
**mente** ferant **placida**
mind-ABL bear-SUBJ.3.PL quiet-ABL
'I encourage our allies so that they may bear the boredom of the long war with a quiet mind'

In example (36), the adverbial denotes a specific state of mind, but the meaning 'mind' gradually gave way to 'manner', by means of metonymic transitions along the following lines (for details of this development see Detges 1998):

(37) 'mental state of the participant in the event' > 'way in which the event is perceived' > 'manner in which the event takes place'

Such metonymic inferencing is typical of the first stage in grammaticalization (Hopper and Traugott 2003: 87ff.). Once the new meaning 'manner' had been established, *mente* could also be combined with adjectives that did not express AGENT or EXPERIENCER attitudes. In the course of time, adverbials with *mente* replaced a number of adverbs formed with the classical Latin adverbial suffixes *-e* and *-iter* (Elcock 1960: 159).

[43] Other adverbials of this kind involved the nouns *pectus* 'breast; spirit', *cor* 'heart', *animus* 'soul, mind': *laetanti pectore* 'with rejoicing breast' → 'joyfully', *immiti corde* 'with a rude heart' → 'harshly', *studioso animo* 'with a zealous mind' → 'eagerly' (cf. Karlsson 1981: 42f.). Note, however, that *pectore* and *corde* are predominantly found in poetry, for instance in the writings of Catullus, and *studioso animo* is used by Catullus as well (Harm Pinkster, p.c.).

What is crucial in the development of MENTE, however, is that it, in Bauer's words (2003: 447), 'does not represent a straight line', because it is not always clear whether or not the [Adj-SG.FEM.ABL + *mente*] combination functions as an adverb. In her study of the *Vulgata* bible (translated into common – as opposed to literary, Ciceronian – Latin around AD 400), Bauer (2003: 447ff.) found that unambiguous adverbial Adj-N constructions involving ablative *animo* 'mind' were far more common than their *mente* equivalents, from which she concludes (p. 450) that 'nothing seems to indicate that that *mente* was going to be the adverbial suffix in Romance'. This raises the question of why *mente* developed into a suffix but not *animo*, which is not only much more frequent but also more consistently adverbial (p. 450).[44]

Another controversial issue concerns the origin of the construction. Lausberg (1972: 100) assumes that the generalization of *mente* adverbs originates in the spoken language, but this is disputed by Hummel (2000: 464), who points out that *mente* adverbs are frequently attested in legal and religious (Christian) texts. What is more, such formations as *prona mente* 'pronely' or *devota mente* 'devoutly' are not particularly colloquial. A final argument in favour of written (Church) Latin as the primary source of the spread of the *mente* adverbs is that the adverbs are not found in Romania, where Latin was not in use as the main liturgical language (Hummel 2000: 465). Hummel (pp. 465ff.) furthermore observes that *mente* adverbs as modifiers of verbs are relatively rare in contemporary spoken Romance languages. The most common strategy to derive verb-modifying adverbs from adjectives was zero conversion (*rápido* 'fast (ADJ)'>*rápido* 'fast (ADV)'). But *mente* adverbs frequently occur as sentence adverbs (Spanish *naturalmente* 'naturally') and modifiers of adjectives (Spanish *totalmente innecesario* 'totally unnecessary').[45] Hummel hypothesizes (p. 466) that it was in these contexts that the concrete meaning 'mind' disappeared and *mente* spread to other

[44] Harm Pinkster (p.c.), however, points out that it is difficult to draw conclusions from the relative frequencies of *animo* and *mente*, because they may be different translations for different Greek or Hebrew words.

[45] Hummel (pp. 467f.) explains these distributional differences as follows: when an adverb modifies a verb (as in *Mirar rápido al coche* 'look quickly at the car', it is evident from the position of *rápido* that it is an adverb modifying a verb, so it need not be marked by means of an adverbial suffix. When the adverb modifies an adjective, on the other hand, the addition of the *mente*-suffix (e.g. *altamente importante* 'highly important') makes clear that the construction is Adv+Adj, not Adj+Adj. Finally, when a sentence adverb is required, zero-conversion is impossible, because in that case the interpretation would be adjectival, as the following French examples show:

(i) Curieux, il ne l' a pas fait
curious-MASC he NEG it has NEG done
'(although he was) curious, he did not do it'

adjectives. This spread may have been facilitated by the fact that *mente*-adverbs could be used as intensifiers, a type of adverbs particularly subject to renewal (Lorenz 2002; Hopper and Traugott 2003: 122). According to Harm Pinkster (p.c.), however, the debate about the origins of *mente* adverbs in Latin is still far from settled. If there really were a distributional difference between colloquial and liturgical language, one should be able to find such differences, for example in the writings of Saint Augustine (354–430), who wrote both sermons for the common people, and scholarly works such as *De civitate dei*, but to date such research has not been carried out.

(ii) *The morphological status of* MENTE *in some Romance languages is not quite clear.* MENTE is usually considered a suffix, but this analysis is by no means unproblematic for all manifestations of MENTE. For example, for Spanish *-mente* Torner (2005) discusses three competing morphological analyses: it is either considered as the second member of a compound, as a derivational suffix, or as a phrasal suffix. I will briefly mention arguments in favour of each position.

A first argument in favour of the view that *-mente* is a compounding element, is the fact that it can be deleted in co-ordinations:[46]

(38) Lo hice rápida y cuidosamente[47]
it did-1SG quick and carefully
'I did it quickly and carefully'

Suffixes (including derivational ones) cannot take scope over a phrase in Spanish, but compounding elements can. Another argument for the compounding analysis is the intonational pattern of *-mente* adverbs: like some compounds, but unlike derivational affixes, *-mente* receives secondary stress.

(ii) Curieuse, elle ne l' a pas fait
curious-FEM she NEG it has NEG done
'(although she was) curious, she did not do it'

(iii) Curieusement, il ne l'a pas fait
'Curiously, he did not do it'

[46] Deletion of MENTE in co-ordinations is also attested in other Romance languages (Karlsson 1981: 58ff., 101ff., 121ff.; Bauer 2003: 441). In some older Romance languages, it was even possible to attach the suffix to the first of two co-ordinated adverbs (Elcock 1960: 158; Karlsson 1981: 121f.) as in Old Italian *cominci il detto suo pianamente e soave* 'he begins his speech slowly and smoothly' (Karlsson 1981: 122).

[47] Spanish *-mente* may also be deleted in disjunctive co-ordinations (*directa o indirectamente* 'directly or indirectly') and in comparative constructions: *Lo han resuelto tanto técnica como teóricamente* 'They have solved it both technically and theoretically' (Torner 2005: 117).

The view that *-mente* is a derivational suffix is probably more widespread. First, the word-internal relation (both syntactic and semantic) between *-mente* and the preceding adjective is similar to derived words, but not to compounds. For example, *-mente* selects a particular grammatical category (adjectives) as its base, as do derivational suffixes. Secondly, *-mente* changes the grammatical category (from adjective to adverb), a characteristic typical of derivational morphemes (cf. section 5.2.1), and finally, *-mente* is quite productive, whereas Spanish compounds are usually subject to a number of restrictions.

Torner (2005) himself proposes to treat Spanish *-mente* as a phrasal affix, because of its hybrid behaviour between free word and bound morpheme. But this analysis is not without problems either, primarily because phrasal affixes usually share their affixal properties with inflectional affixes and their phrasal characteristics with clitics. However, there is neither synchronic nor diachronic evidence which suggests that *-mente* is developing into a clitic, or ever was one at some point in its history. Also, *-mente* has no clitic prosody (it has tonic accent, which is very unusual for Spanish clitics).

In my view, Spanish *-mente* is most appropriately analysed as a derivational suffix which has not fully grammaticalized (yet), with constructions such as (38) as vestiges of an earlier compound stage.

(iii) *Distributional differences in the contemporary Romance languages are usually ignored when* MENTE *is quoted as an instance of grammaticalization.* MENTE is often simplistically referred to as '*the* Romance suffix', but this characterization is incorrect for three reasons. To begin with, the suffix is not Pan-Romance, for it is not found in Romanian – the handful of examples in that language are borrowings (Bauer 2003: 439). Secondly, as we have seen above, the suffix comes in various forms, a fact which is not always acknowledged. Thirdly and more importantly, various stages of development are attested in different languages, which suggests that the suffix did not develop at a similar pace in all Romance languages. The change seems more or less completed in Old French texts from the eighth century onwards, with MENTE adverbs generally written as one word. In other languages, by contrast (Spanish, Portuguese), the change has not yet run its full course up to the present day (see Karlsson 1981 for extensive treatment). Also, the original noun (*mens* and its successors) has disappeared as an independent lexeme in some languages (e.g. French), but not in others (e.g. Italian: *imparare a mente* 'to learn by heart' (Bauer 2003: 446); Spanish *lo tendré en mente* 'I'll keep it in mind' (Bob de Jonge, p.c.)). Thus, the development of MENTE has to be studied for each language separately – for what is true for one Romance language, may not be true for another. And finally, in some languages

(Spanish, southern Italian dialects) there has been no continuous development from Latin *mente* to the suffix at all, because the form -*mente* was a loan (Karlsson 1981: 100, 124; Joseph 2004: 54; Torner 2005: 139). In Spanish, for instance, -*mente* was borrowed (probably from Aragonese or Catalan, or even French; Karlsson 1981: 99ff.), replacing the native forms -*mientr*(*e*) and -*mient*(*e*) from the first half of the thirteenth century onwards.

To conclude, the development of Romance MENTE is usually treated as a simple change whereas in fact it is a correspondence (all details of the change are not yet known). First, its history is extremely complex and a number of loose ends still need to be investigated. Secondly, the subsequent developments in the individual Romance languages may differ considerably, and may even be discontinuous (as in Spanish, where the form -*mente* was borrowed to replace earlier -*mientr*(*e*) and -*mient*(*e*)). Due to these divergent developments the suffixes have also grammaticalized to various degrees, another reason to refrain from bracketing them together. All MENTE suffixes are best characterized as a morpheme which is located at some point on the cline of lexicality (see section 2.2.1), their exact position depending on the language of which they form part.

## 1.7 Summary

In this first chapter, I have outlined the theoretical foundations of degrammaticalization research. Degrammaticalization cannot be studied in isolation – it is intrinsically linked to two other major types of grammar change, grammaticalization and lexicalization, sharing some properties with both, but also differing from both in crucial respects. All three involve some form of reanalysis, and analogy can be observed to be at work in both grammaticalization and degrammaticalization. Both grammaticalization and degrammaticalization (and some forms of lexicalization too) are gradual in the sense that they encompass a series of small steps, which may take centuries to complete. In addition, it is increasingly recognized that both grammaticalization and degrammaticalization (but not necessarily lexicalization) are changes in context. Where earlier research was primarily morpheme-based, recent construction-based approaches have proved useful to provide complementary evidence.

For grammaticalization, there is evidence that intermediate steps occur in a certain order (with pragmatic-semantic change occurring first), which makes it seem appropriate to speak of a grammaticalization process. However, in spite of all the attested regularity in grammaticalization, it is not appropriate to speak of universal pathways, because there is still considerable variation in the nature of changes involved. The absence of such universal pathways also implies that linguistic reconstruction has to be treated with much caution. Furthermore, there is as yet no general consensus on what counts as a valid example of grammaticalization. Grammaticalization across clauses, and particularly pragmaticalization, still form the subject of some controversy.

We have also seen that there are two subtypes of grammaticalization, termed 'primary grammaticalization' (lexeme>grammatical word) and 'secondary grammaticalization' (bonding, usually accompanied by further semantic and phonological reduction). These types may form a chain of events, but need not do so. There is nothing deterministic about primary grammaticalization in the sense that it should be followed by secondary grammaticalization. In later chapters, it will be argued that primary and secondary degrammaticalization exist as well.

A final observation on grammaticalization, lexicalization, and degrammaticalization is that all three are composite changes, comprising primitive changes on several linguistic levels. Identifying these primitive changes is crucial, if one wishes to discuss change and not mere correspondences. In what ways grammaticalization, degrammaticalization, and lexicalization differ as to the directionality and the nature of these changes, is a matter that remains to be addressed. Directionality of change will be explored in Chapter 2, and a model to classify types of degrammaticalization using primitive changes as criteria will be outlined in Chapter 3.

# 2

# Unidirectionality

## 2.1 Introduction

In his widely acclaimed novel *Time's Arrow* (1991), Martin Amis relates the life of a Nazi doctor in reverse chronology, from death to birth. It is a gripping and gruesome story, in which the reversal of the entire story-line, and indeed every single event in it (babies return to their mothers' wombs, romantic relationships start with combat and end in infatuation), leaves the reader completely disoriented, as the following two passages from the book demonstrate:

> Maybe Tod is considering Vietnam. Vietnam might do him good. The gibbering hippies and spaced-out fatsoes who go there, they come back looking all clean and sane and fine... (p. 68)
>
> I'm on a train now, heading south at evening. The American Atlantic moves past me. All business is concluded. I don't know where we're going: our ticket, dispensed with a contemptuous flick by the station trashcan, bears the name of our starting-point, not our destination. (p. 90)

Why do these scenes strike us as grotesquely counter-natural? Presumably because humans possess a subjective sense of the direction of time which, as Hawking (1996 [1988]: 151ff.) lucidly explains, is essentially due to the second law of thermodynamics, which says that in any closed system disorder always increases with time. This is illustrated by his example of a cup falling off a table and breaking into pieces on the floor. If one were to take a film of this, one could easily tell whether the film was being run forward (cup breaking into pieces) or backward (pieces gathering and jumping back onto the table to form a whole cup). This law determines the 'psychological arrow of time' of human beings, but the law itself does not distinguish between past and future.[1]

[1] For an insightful discussion of the relevance of this law to linguistics the reader is referred to Lass (1997: 290ff.). For a particularly entertaining illustration of how the 'forces of destruction' create grammar, read Deutscher's (2005: 144ff.) imaginary dialogue between a young academic and members of the Royal Society for the Protection of the English Language, who are appalled by the idea that grammar originates in what they consider the very decay of language.

In language change, too, an 'arrow of time' seems intuitively plausible. To give a fairly straightforward example, we expect words to erode over time, particularly so when they are used with great frequency. The reverse, words progressively gaining in phonological substance, would seem much less likely to occur. Grammaticalization is also generally considered to be unidirectional, progressing from the lexical to the grammatical pole on the cline of grammaticality. Indeed, unidirectionality 'is generally held to be a bedrock principle in grammaticalization' (Joseph 2005: 3). As such, it has been cherished by grammaticalizationists as a valuable tool in reconstruction, as well as attacked by grammaticalization critics as a trivial observation which follows naturally from the very definition of grammaticalization. Therefore, no account of either grammaticalization or degrammaticalization phenomena is complete without a discussion of the (non-)significance of unidirectionality.

Unidirectionality has been identified as both a principle and a hypothesis.[2] The unidirectionality principle entails that lexical items can become grammatical items, but never vice versa, and that further change affecting grammatical items always involves attrition: loss of semantic substance, of morphosyntactic properties, of morphological independence, and often of phonological substance too. Those who regard unidirectionality as a hypothesis, on the other hand, do allow for some counterdirectional change, i.e. an increase in semantic substance, morphosyntactic properties, etc., but note that these are extremely rare.

An important question presents itself at this point: what is unidirectionality a property *of*? In many works (e.g. Heine, Claudi, and Hünnemeyer 1991; Traugott and Heine 1991), unidirectionality is implicitly defined as an inherent characteristic of grammaticalization. But as critics of grammaticalization theorizing (see e.g. Campbell 2001; Janda 2001) have pointed out, unidirectionality cannot be used as an empirical hypothesis when it is built into the very definition of grammaticalization. For in that case, unidirectionality of grammaticalization is a tautology, and hence the claim that grammaticalization is unidirectional would be as meaningful as the claim that '"walking north" is unidirectional' (Janda 2001: 294). Following up on Janda, Joseph (2005: 4) writes that the relationship between grammaticalization and unidirectionality is 'void of any real interest.'

2 Compare Lass (2000: 216), who speaks of 'strong unidirectionality' ('all grammatical material is ultimately lexical in origin'), and 'weak unidirectionality', which is 'an inductive statement of commonly observed tendencies, pathways etc.'.

However, unidirectionality has also been defined as a constraint on grammatical change in general (Heine, Claudi, and Hünnemeyer 1991; Heine 1994 and 1997; Lehmann 1995 [1982]; Haspelmath 1999a and 2004). Heine (1997: 4), for example, writes: 'Grammatical change is unidirectional, leading from lexical to grammatical, and from grammatical to more grammatical, forms and structures.' Brinton and Traugott (2005: 25) similarly assert: 'Unidirectionality from lexicon or construction > grammar and not vice versa is a strong, empirical, and therefore interesting hypothesis.' This, of course, is a much stronger claim than the claim that unidirectionality is a property of grammaticalization, and one with serious consequences for linguistic reconstruction (see below).

Unidirectionality as a constraint on possible changes is tantamount to the claim that there is no degrammaticalization. As we have seen in the introduction, this claim originates with Lehmann (1995 [1982]: 16). Lehmann mentions three earlier works where it is allegedly argued that counterdirectional change is not attested: Givón (1975: 96), Langacker (1977: 103f.), and Vincent 1980: 56–60). However, of these authors only Vincent actually claims that grammatical change is unidirectional – the other two choose more careful formulations. Langacker (1977: 104) writes the following:

> I think the tendency toward signal simplicity[3] is an undeniable aspect of the evolution of natural language. Not only are all these kinds of change massively attested, but also they are largely unidirectional. Boundary loss is very common, for instance, but boundary creation is quite uncommon by comparison. Words are frequently incorporated as affixes, but affixes show no great tendency to break away and become independent words. Established locutions clearly show an overall trend towards erosion in their status rather than the opposite.

Givón (1975: 96), too, makes a much more modest claim: 'an opposite process than the one outlined above, i.e., a process of prepositions becoming *semantically enriched* until they turn into verbs, is at least in theory possible' (emphasis original).

Thus, Lehmann's claim about the non-existence of degrammaticalization is corroborated by earlier work from Vincent, but not by Langacker or Givón. Lehmann goes on to discuss a few cases that might qualify as degrammaticalization (mostly affixes that had become derivational or enclitic), but dismisses them all. Lehmann concludes that:

> no cogent examples of degrammaticalization have been found. This result is important because it allows us to recognize grammaticalization at the synchronic level.

[3] See section 2.2.2 for further discussion of this concept of Langacker's.

Given two variants which are related by the parameters of grammaticalization... *we can always tell which way the grammaticalization goes, or must have gone. The significance of this for the purposes of internal reconstruction is obvious.* (Lehmann 1995 [1982]: 19; emphasis mine)

This quote of Lehmann's reveals the principal appeal of a unidirectionality principle, which is its potential relevance to linguistic reconstruction (for similar claims see Vincent 1980: 59; Heine, Claudi, and Hünnemeyer 1991: 221; Heine 1994; Haspelmath 2004: 21f.).[4] In other words, a principle of unidirectionality would provide us with a universal with the explanatory power of a neogrammarian sound-law.

For unidirectionality can only be said to be relevant to reconstruction when this hypothesis is not about the unidirectionality of grammaticalization, but about the unidirectionality of change involving grammatical items in general, as correctly pointed out by Willis (2007: 272):

The only falsifiable claim is not that grammaticalization itself is unidirectional, but rather that grammaticalization exists in the absence of a parallel reverse phenomenon, degrammaticalization, which, if it were attested, would occur when items with a formerly exclusively grammatical function changed into items with a (more) lexical function.

Askedal (2008:49) similarly observes:

When no unidirectionality is assumed, there are no logical problems with considering degrammaticalization as the possible counterpart of grammaticalization. When, however, unidirectionality is considered a basic principle, degrammaticalization is evidently a contradiction in terms... If there is unidirectionality, there is no degrammaticalization... and if there is degrammaticalization, there can be no unidirectionality; but there may still be a strong preference for directionality in accordance with the cline. Stated in such terms, the (non-)existence of degrammaticalization is an entirely empirical issue.[5]

However, weakening unidirectionality from a universal to a statistical generalization would deprive us of a handy reconstructional tool, which may explain, in part, why degrammaticalization case studies have sometimes been received with remarkable hostility (Norde, in prep.). This, of course, raises the question of what would count as sufficient counterevidence to unidirectionality. The extreme view is: a single counterexample, as proposed by Newmeyer (1998: 263): 'I take any example of upgrading as sufficient to

[4] On grammaticalization and reconstruction see also section 1.6.4.

[5] It is not quite clear to me which kind of unidirectionality Haspelmath has in mind when he writes that '[t]he basic generalization of unidirectionality stands unchallenged as long as nobody shows that degrammaticalization is as common as grammaticalization' (Haspelmath 2004: 23).

refute unidirectionality.' To my mind, however, such a strong emphasis on counterexamples is the Achilles' heel of grammaticalization critics, as already pointed out by Heath (1998: 751). According to him, critics of grammaticalization theory tend to concentrate on counterexamples which show the reverse of grammaticalization examples (e.g. shifts from affix to clitic), and since these are few in number, they are bound to make little impact. Heath's concern is borne out by the following quote from Haspelmath (1999a: 1048):

> Although the evidence for the irreversibility of grammaticalization is very strong, some authors have given so much weight to the counterexamples as to effectively deny the general rule of unidirectionality... These authors seem to be skeptics with no particular theoretical axe to grind, and their reasons for skepticism are only as strong as their counterexamples.

My view on counterevidence is this: a single counterexample, or even a handful of them, would have no bearing on unidirectionality. But the evidence provided by degrammaticalization case studies is far more substantial, even to the extent that degrammaticalization is rapidly establishing itself as 'the exception that challenges the rule'. The inevitable consequence of all this is that grammaticalization is unfit as a tool in reconstruction,[6] unless it is used with extreme caution and the appropriate disclaimer. For if grammaticalization really were a universal of language change, and we were to find, in a language without a written history, a body-part noun meaning 'back' and an (almost) homophonous adposition meaning 'behind', we could be confident that the adposition derives from the noun. However, since the very existence of degrammaticalization implies that grammaticalization is *not* a universal of language change, we cannot be confident. Because we do have examples where the body-part noun is derived from the spatial expression, as in French *derrière* 'behind' or Dutch *achterste* 'most behind', both referring to a body part.

According to Joseph (2005: 4), the only sensible way to deal with this is to 'simply "bite the bullet" and accept that there can be movement involving grammatical elements both "up and down the cline", so that unidirectionality – or, better, movement in the direction of greater grammatical status – becomes a recognizable tendency in, but not an inviolable constraint on, grammatical change'. Luraghi (2005: 16) makes a similar point:

> [T]he idea of finding exceptionless principles in language change appeals to many linguists, who wish to give a more 'scientific' look to their discipline, because the

[6] In response to this, Joseph (2005: 4f.) raises the important point that it is perfectly possible to do historical linguistics without reconstruction: 'reconstruction is a nicety that arises out of the linguist's intellectual curiosity, but it is hardly an essential part of understanding language change per se'.

> existence of exceptionless laws makes linguistics closer to the hard sciences. The claim that, no matter what the data say, change is unidirectional reminds one of the Neogrammarians' attitude toward the *Ausnahmslosigkeit der Lautgesetze*... On the contrary, I think we should recognize that linguistics is a soft science and try to live with it. This means that we should be ready to admit that linguistic 'laws', such as unidirectionality, are at best tendencies. This more realistic attitude would prevent us from making too strong claims, while in the meantime providing us with better means to describe attested phenomena.

Haspelmath on the other hand states that linguistic theorizing cannot be bothered with too many details, at least not initially. On critics of unidirectionality he writes:

> In the writings of some of these linguists, one senses a frustration with theoreticians who make broad sweeping claims but do not back them up with solid and careful historical linguistic work. Clearly, once one starts asking larger questions, there is the danger that one pays less attention to the data and more attention to the ideas, but there is also the opposite danger of missing the generalizations and the big picture because one sees too many details. (Haspelmath 2004: 15)

To this, Luraghi (2005: 15) responds as follows:

> I don't think that one can ever see too many details, at least in considering language change: if a change is attested, it must be considered in one's theory of linguistic change. Indeed, the fact that some changes are less frequent than others is in itself a matter that should be explained, and I don't see what we gain by ignoring less frequent changes, and saying that change is unidirectional, rather than acknowledge that there are changes in both directions, but one is preferred.

Van Pottelberge (2005: 42) is also critical of Haspelmath's proposition:

> I agree with Haspelmath that we should try to understand language change, but I see no reason why this could only be done by looking for one strong universal (or one direction), rather than by trying to identify all types of changes and their directions.

To sum up the discussion thus far, I think it would be fair to dismiss unidirectionality as an absolute principle. But much as I agree with Joseph, Luraghi, and van Pottelberge, it is also evident that grammaticalization is far more frequent, and far more cross-linguistically regular, than is degrammaticalization (see further section 3.4). In other words, it cannot be denied that directional tendencies exist. This is an interesting observation, but one that is usually taken for granted, and few attempts have been made to account for it. As Haspelmath (1999a: 1049) put it: 'the most striking fact about previous explanations of unidirectionality is that there are so few of them'.

The purpose of this chapter, then, will be to review the concept of unidirectionality from several angles. I will start with some general discussion of conceptualizations of language change in section 2.2, and of types of 'reversal' in section 2.3. I will then consider changes that challenge the ubiquity of grammaticalization but are not degrammaticalization: lateral shifts (section 2.4), and alternative sources of grammatical markers (section 2.5). The subsequent sections deal with the question of what makes grammaticalization, and not degrammaticalization, the preferred direction in grammatical change. Is it because some, if not all, of its primitive changes are unidirectional as well? This has indeed been claimed for semantic, morphosyntactic, and phonological changes (cf. e.g. Hopper and Traugott 2003: 99ff.), and I will consider them in turn. In section 2.7, I will assess usage-based, psycholinguistic, generative, and (non-generative) formal explanations of directional tendencies.

## 2.2 Conceptualizations of language change

### 2.2.1 *Clines*

A basic concept within grammaticalization studies is the term 'cline', which was introduced to grammaticalization studies by Hopper and Traugott (1993: 6), as a means to illustrate the series of gradual transitions all the way from lexical item to inflectional affix. They define a cline historically as 'a natural pathway along which forms evolve, a kind of linguistic "slippery slope" which guides the development of forms.' By means of introduction they provide (1993: 7) two basic clines, the cline of grammaticality in (1), and the cline of lexicality in (2):

(1) content item > grammatical word > clitic > inflectional affix

(2) part of phrase > part of compound > derivational affix
a basket **full** (of eggs) > a cupful (of water) > hopeful[7]

Other clines discussed in Hopper and Traugott (1993) are the noun-to-affix cline (p. 107) in (3), the verb-to-affix cline (p. 108) in (4), and the cline of clause combining (p. 170) in (5):

(3) relational noun > secondary adposition > primary adposition > agglutinative case affix > fusional case affix

(4) full verb > (vector verb) > auxiliary > clitic > affix

(5) parataxis > hypotaxis > subordination

[7] The grammatical terms have been added by the present author. For some reason, Hopper and Traugott only provide the example with *full* to illustrate this cline.

When comparing these clines, it becomes immediately evident that they differ considerably in their level of abstraction. The cline of grammaticality pertains to the level of morphosyntactic bondedness, as does the cline of lexicality in the form it is given here (cf. footnote 7); the noun-to-affix cline and the verb-to-affix cline refer to the level of grammatical categories, and the cline of clause combining refers to the level of syntax. All these clines can be subsumed under the 'meta-cline' proposed much earlier by Givón (1979: 209):

(6) discourse > syntax > morphology > morphophonemics > zero

In the second edition of their handbook, Hopper and Traugott (2003: 6) present a slightly modified definition of the term 'cline'. Here, the slippery slope has disappeared, and instead Hopper and Traugott define a cline as 'a natural "pathway" along which forms evolve, a schema which models the development of forms'. With this neutral formulation they probably intended to bring their concept in line with the terms of others, such as 'path' (Bybee, Perkins, and Pagliuca 1994: 14), or 'grammaticalization chain' (Heine, Claudi, and Hünnemeyer 1991: 220ff.). A far more substantial change in the 2003 edition, however, is the disappearance of the cline of lexicality, possibly because Hopper and Traugott no longer regard the rise of derivational material as grammaticalization.[8]

The cline of grammaticality has been criticized for being an oversimplification, 'which blithely confuses content change and morphosyntactic change' (Andersen 2008: 15).[9] Nevertheless, the cline of grammaticality is of some use as a first criterion to select potential cases of degrammaticalization. For as we will see later on, a shift from right to left on this cline is attested in all types of degrammaticalization. This, of course, by no means implies that *all* movement (gradual or not) towards the lexical pole is a case of degrammaticalization (cf. Lightfoot 2005: 587), as I will argue in section 3.3.3.

### 2.2.2 *Cycles*

While a cline-based view of language change is essentially one-dimensional, a cycle-based view emphasizes that changes are often linked to other, simultaneous changes. With respect to grammaticalization, there are basically two kinds of cycles: (i) a primary / secondary grammaticalization cycle and (ii) cyclic reinforcement.

[8] Hopper and Traugott are however not consistent in this. Even in the 2003 edition, they frequently mention derivational suffixes as instances of grammaticalization.

[9] See section 3.5.4 for Andersen's own model, which does distinguish between different linguistic levels.

2.2.2.1 *The primary/secondary grammaticalization cycle* The primary/secondary grammaticalization cycle (see section 1.4.1 for discussion of the terms 'primary' and 'secondary') can be paraphrased as the loss of synthetic grammatical markers (typically inflectional affixes resulting from secondary grammaticalization), which tends to go hand in hand with the rise of new analytic markers with comparable function (primary grammaticalization). For instance, when inflectional case markers disappear, the grammatical relations they used to express often come to be encoded by 'periphrastic' constructions such as prepositional phrases (Heine, Claudi, and Hünnemeyer 1991: 120f.).[10]

In a usage-based view of language change, such cycles are traditionally seen as the interaction between speaker and hearer strategies. Langacker (1977), for example, identifies these strategies as 'signal simplicity' ('economy in regard to production of the physical speech signal', p. 102f.) and 'perceptual optimality' which 'pertains to the adequacy of sentences in their overt form to convey the desired information to the listener' (p. 105). On the interaction between these two Langacker writes:

> The tension between signal simplicity and perceptual optimality does not manifest itself basically as an ebb and flow in the erosion of established expressions; I have noted that the processes contributing to signal simplicity are largely unidirectional. Instead the central mechanism for achieving perceptual optimality in syntax is a process I will call 'periphrastic locution', which is simply the creation by ordinary or extraordinary means of periphrastic expressions to convey the desired sense. As these new locutions become established in a language, they too gradually fall prey to the processes leading toward signal simplicity, and the cycle begins again. (Langacker 1977: 105)

The term 'cycle' for this kind of change is potentially misleading, however, since it seems to suggest that analytic structures are direct descendants of the previous synthetic structures, as pointed out by Fleischman (1982: 103ff.) in her discussion of synthetic and analytic futures in the Romance languages. Instead, Fleischman argues, the alternation between synthetic and analytic patterns must be understood as consisting of two phases, which are clearly distinct from one another. In the analytic>synthetic phase, a periphrastic structure synthesizes, whereas in the synthetic>analytic phase, a new periphrastic structure arises. She also correctly notes that the synthetic and

[10] Often however, the relation between the fall of synthetic and the rise of analytic expressions is more complex than this. For instance, Old Swedish prepositional phrases that came to encode grammatical relations expressed by obsolescent case endings were often not 'purely' analytic since prepositions governed (a different) case as well, at least initially (Norde 2001b).

analytic phases concern the language as a whole – at some stage, a language may be predominantly synthetic or analytic, but not exclusively so, since the two processes go on simultaneously.

Another problem with the term 'cycle', discussed in Lass (1997: 111), is that it seems to suggest that the same change may happen over and over again, but this is not the case, since the complexity of change and the ever-increasing differentiation which results from it means that changes are generally not repeatable.[11]

An alternative term, proposed by von der Gabelentz (1901: 256), is the term 'spiral':

Die Affixe verschleifen sich, verschwinden am Ende spurlos; ihre Functionen [sic] aber oder ähnliche bleiben und drängen wieder nach Ausdruck. Diesen Ausdruck erhalten sie, nach der Methode der isolirenden [sic] Sprachen, durch Wortstellung oder verdeutlichende Wörter. Letztere unterliegen wiederum mit der Zeit dem Agglutinationsprozesse, dem Verschliffe und Schwunde, und derweile bereitet sich für das Verderbende neuer Ersazt vor: periphrastische Ausdrücke werden bevorzugt; ... immer gilt das Gleiche: die Entwickelungslinie [sic] krümmt sich zurück nach der Seite der Isolation, nicht in die alte Bahn, sondern in eine annähernd parallele. Darum vergleiche ich sie der Spirale.[12]

2.2.2.2 *Cyclic reinforcement* In the second type of cyclic change, a gram which has become phonetically and/or semantically weak is reinforced by another gram or a lexeme (Hopper and Traugott 2003: 65f., 117f.). The classic example of this type of change is the history of negation markers, which has come to be known as 'Jespersen's cycle' (after Jespersen 1917, 1924). Jespersen himself (1924: 335) describes this cycle as follows:

The general history of negative expressions in some of the best-known languages presents a curious fluctuation. The negative adverb is often weakly stressed, because some other word in the sentence has to receive a strong stress of contrast. But when the negative has become a mere proclitic syllable or even a single sound, it is felt to be too weak, and has to be strengthened by some additional word, and this in its turn may come to be felt as the negative proper, which then may be subject to the

[11] The only linguistic subsystem where 'exact repetitions' appear to be possible is phonology, but this is due to the relatively small inventory of phonemes (Lass 1997: 111).

[12] 'The affixes wear down, and disappear in the end without a trace; their functions however remain, and require to be expressed. As in isolating languages, these functions come to be expressed by word order or clarifying words. The latter are gradually subjected to processes of agglutination again, of attrition and deletion, and new replacements for the ailing [affixes] are recruited, preferably periphrastic expressions ... It is always the same thing: the line of development bends backwards to the point of isolation, not following the old track, but a parallel one. This is why I compare it to a spiral.'

same development as the original word. We have thus a constant interplay of weakening and strengthening...

The best-known case of this is probably the cyclic reinforcement of negation in French, for which Jespersen (ibid.) distinguishes the following stages:

Stage 1. Latin *ne dico* 'I do not say'. The negator *ne* was then reinforced by *oenum* (an older form of *unum* 'one thing'), yielding *non.*

Stage 2. Latin *non dico.* In Old French, *non* is then reduced to *nen* and later *ne.*

Stage 3. Old French *jeo ne di.* The negator *ne* then became reinforced once more, this time by a series of nouns (see also Hopper and Traugott 2003: 117), of which *pas* 'step' became most frequent.

Stage 3. French *je ne dis pas.* In spoken French, unstressed *ne* is often omitted.

Stage 4. Spoken French *je dis pas.*

Other examples of reinforcement include Latin *aliquis* 'someone', which was reinforced by *unus* 'one', yielding **aliqui-unu*, which became *alcuno* in Italian and *aucun* in French (Lehmann 1995 [1982]: 22); and the reinforcement of prepositions, e.g. French *avant* 'before' < Lat. *ab ante* 'from before'; *dans* 'in (side)' < Lat. *de intus* 'from within'; *derrière* 'behind' < Lat. *de retro* 'from the back'); *envers* 'against' < Lat. *in versus* 'in against' (Elcock 1960: 161f.), or Mainland Scandinavian *på* 'on' < *upp ā* 'up on' (Norde 2008). Like negation markers, reinforced prepositions may become subject to a series of subsequent reinforcements, as in PIE **in* > **en-tos* > Lat. *intus* 'inside' > *de intus* 'from within' > French *dans* 'in' > French *dedans* 'within' (Lehmann 1995 [1982]: 22).

## 2.3 Irreversibility

Unidirectionality is often treated as a synonym of 'irreversibility', e.g. in Haspelmath (1999a) and Lehmann (2004). The latter author puts it as follows: 'a unidirectional process is one whose converse does not exist' (Lehmann 2004: 178). But as with all the terms discussed in this chapter thus far, it is not always clear what is meant by 'reverse', or 'converse'. This issue is addressed in two recent papers (Haspelmath 2004 and Askedal 2008), which both argue that there are two kinds of reversal. Thus Askedal (2008: 49) writes:

When exceptions to unidirectionality are allowed for, one is faced with two logical possibilities that are not always kept apart in the literature. One is 'strict' or 'substantial degrammaticalization' in the form of 'etymological category reversal' (for short: 'etymological reversal'), in which case the source of some grammaticalized element at some point on the cline is restored... The other possibility is 'non-etymological category reversal' (for short: 'category reversal'), i.e., a backwards development that does not result in etymological restoration of the source of a grammaticalized element but is a purely categorial move, e.g. from affix or clitic to 'independent word'.

Haspelmath (2004: 28) makes a similar distinction between 'token reversal' (corresponding to Askedal's 'etymological reversal'), and 'type reversal' (corresponding to Askedal's 'category reversal'). As both authors correctly note, the first type is of little significance. A change of this kind would amount to the English past tense suffix *-ed* tracing back its steps to a verb **dōn* 'to do' (in its PGmc form) with exactly the same intermediate stages as the grammaticalization chain from (a preterite form of) **dōn* to *-ed*.[13] The occurrence of such an event is so fantastically unlikely that we may safely assume that it will never happen. Indeed, it would make as much sense to speak of degrammaticalization in this sense as it would to speak of 'de-ageing' (Dahl 1996), or of 'de-erosion' as a mountain-creating mechanism (Newmeyer 1998: 262).

It is not difficult to see why there are no token reversals: since grammaticalization typically involves loss of substance (semantic and phonological), and since we do not possess a memory for substance deleted by previous generations of speakers, we cannot possibly reintroduce them in a mirror-image fashion. An interesting example of this impossibility is given by Plank (2003 [2000]) in a paper on the relation between (de)grammaticalization and final devoicing in German, where he shows that the voiced/unvoiced alternation may disappear for good when lexical items grammaticalize to the point where they can no longer be inflected (the process known as 'decategorialization', see section 2.6.2). Consider the pronunciation of the inflections of the German noun *Weg* 'way' in (7), and its grammaticalized counterpart, the adverb *weg* 'away' in (8):

| | | | |
|---|---|---|---|
| (7) | SG.NOM/ACC | Weg | [veːk][14] |
| | SG.GEN | Weges | ['veː.gəs] |
| | SG.DAT | Wege | ['veː.gə] |
| | PL.NOM/GEN/ACC | Wege | ['veː.gə] |
| | PL.DAT | Wegen | ['veː.gən] |

[13] This change is discussed in section 2.6.3.

[14] On p. 173 of his paper, Plank gives the representation [vɛk], but it should be [veːk] (as elsewhere in the paper).

(8) a. Geh **weg**! [vɛk]
'Go away!'

b. Das Geld ist **weg**. [vɛk]
'The money is gone'

c. Er war so **weg** von ihr, dass er sie vom Fleck **weg** heiratete. [vɛk]
'He was so off (i.e. in raptures) about her that he married her from the spot off (i.e. on the spot)'

Syllable-final obstruents have undergone devoicing since Old or Early Middle High German, which explains the alternation between [g] and [k] in the inflections of the noun *Weg*. The adverb on the other hand, being indeclinable by definition, is always pronounced [vɛk].[15] This is also true for compounds such as *weg-laufen* ['vɛk.laʊfən] 'run away', where, following German syllabification rules, the obstruent could have passed the morpheme border so that it is no longer syllable-final and can hence become voiced again (* ['vɛ.glaʊfən]), but this does not happen. Apparently, then, speakers no longer associate the adverb *weg* with the noun *Weg*, which has underlying [g]. That the obstruent in the adverb *weg* has become reanalysed as invariably voiceless, becomes also evident when the adverb is recategorialized (see section 2.6.2) as an adjective:[16]

(9) das **weg**-e Geld
the gone-NEUT.SG.NOM.WEAK money
'the money that is gone'

The inflected adjective is pronounced ['vɛk̥ə], not ['vɛgə]. What this example shows is that once the indeclinable adverb *weg* had grammaticalized from the noun *Weg*, it lost the voiced/voiceless alternation in the final obstruent for good.[17] Even when it recategorialized into an adjective, the obstruent remained voiceless when it was followed by an inflection.

An example of token irreversibility on the semantic level is provided by Ziegeler's (2004) discussion of Mandarin Chinese *děi/dé*. Originally a main verb meaning 'to obtain', it is used as an epistemic modal verb in modern Mandarin, and, interestingly, as a main verb meaning 'to need'. Crucially,

[15] Note that the vowel changes too, but this alternation no longer forms part of present-day German phonology, and will hence be ignored in the remainder of this discussion.

[16] The usage of *weg* as an adjective is not possible in all variants of German. To my informants, it was jocular at best, if acceptable at all.

[17] In other cases of recategorialization, association with the lexical source must still have been possible, according to Plank (2003 [2000]: 184f.), because the obstruent can become voiced when the adverb, or predicative adjective, acquires inflection. Thus, inflected *genuge* 'enough' has a voiced obstruent (compare uninflected *genug*, with [k]), possibly by analogy with the verb *genügen* ([g]) 'to suffice'.

there has been no 'reversal', because the modal did not go back to a main verb meaning 'to obtain'.

Having established that token irreversibility is a non-issue, I will use the term 'irreversibility' as a shorthand for 'type irreversibility' in the remainder of this work, for example when referring to allegedly irreversible changes in the subsections of 2.6.[18] Irreversibility of desemanticization ('abstraction' of meaning) thus implies that there exists no resemanticization (i.e. an increase in semantic substance), irreversibility of decategorialization (loss of morphosyntactic properties) implies that there is no recategorialization (gain in morphosyntactic properties), and so on. I will be arguing that strict irreversibility is not to be found on any linguistic level. It will be seen that changes on all levels show strong directional preferences, yet none of them are unidirectional without exception.

## 2.4 Non-directional change: lateral shifts

That language change is not necessarily directional (be it from 'more' to 'less' grammatical or vice versa) is evidenced by so-called 'lateral' shifts, which are to be found on all grammatical levels. Obvious examples are zero derivations (Giacalone Ramat and Hopper 1998: 5) such as *to airbrush* (noun to verb) or *the rich and famous* (adjective to noun), but lateral shifts are also attested on the affixal level (Lehmann 1995 [1982]: 10).

Joseph (2005: 1f.) defines such shifts as:

> [A] change in the form of a grammatical affix that is not just a simple sound change... but does not alter the element's grammatical nature or status in terms of where it falls on the 'cline' of grammatical status (from word to affix). Thus after the change, the element in question is neither more nor less grammatical than before, so it is a 'movement', in that change has occurred, but one that goes 'laterally' on the cline, not up or down it.

According to Joseph, such changes must be quite numerous, because he has identified twelve of them in only one part of the Greek verbal system, ten of which are of a relatively recent date. These are changes such as Ancient Greek 2SG/3SG present nonactive *-sai/-tai* (< **-soi/*-toi*) under the influence of 1SG present nonactive *-mai*; or Modern Greek 1SG nonactive past *-muna* (<*-mun*), with *-a* added from 1SG active past. These changes are not, or not

[18] One of the very few people to claim type irreversibility for grammaticalization is Lehmann (2004). This is consistent with his own view (since his 1995 [1982] monograph) that degrammaticalization is (virtually) non-existent.

entirely, the result of regular sound change, but the result of analogical extensions. They are not exaptations in the sense of Lass (1990, 1997), (see section 3.3.5) either, because they are not 'junk' or 'marginal', and they do not acquire a new function.

Joseph (2004: 58) furthermore observes that unidirectionality in grammatical change can be interpreted in two ways:

(10) Two ways of interpreting unidirectionality (Joseph 2004; emphasis original)
  a. there exists *only* movement towards *greater* grammatical status
  b. there exists *no* movement towards *less* grammatical status

According to Joseph (2005: 5), (10b) is the weaker of the two, because it does not exclude lateral shifts (it merely says that an item cannot become less grammatical). If one adopts (10a), on the other hand, one cannot allow lateral shifts, because (10a) says that all change results in 'greater' grammatical status. Joseph goes on to discuss the relevance of lateral shifts to grammaticalization theorizing, concluding that they cannot be simply ignored because they are not grammaticalization, especially since they appear to be quite common. This prompts the rhetorical question of why 'one particular type of grammatical development [grammaticalization] should be the object of such intense interest, but not other types' (Joseph 2005: 6).

Yet another kind of lateral shift is the transference of case-marking morphemes to verbs, for example as tense/aspect markers. A striking example is from Kala Lagau Ya, an Australian language of the Western Torres Strait (Blake 2001: 180ff.). In this language, practically the whole system of case marking has been transferred to the system of tense/aspect marking on the verb; see Table 2.1 for matching morphemes. The shift is illustrated in example (11), where the marker *-pa* functions as a dative marker with nouns in (11a), and as an incompletive marker with a verb in (11b):

TABLE 2.1. Kala Lagau Ya case and tense/aspect markers (Blake 2001: 180)

| Marker | Case | Tense/aspect |
|---|---|---|
| *-n* | ergative<br>accusative[a] | completive |
| *-pa* | dative/allative | incompletive |
| *-pu* | comitative | habitual |
| *-ngu* | ablative | yesterday past |
| *-nu* | locative | immediate past |

[a] This morpheme functions as an ergative marker with nouns and as an accusative marker with pronouns.

(11) a. Nuy ay-**pa** amal-**pa**
he food-DAT mother-DAT
'He [went] for food for mother'

b. Ngoeba uzar-am-**pa**
1DUAL.INCLUSIVE go-DUAL-INCOMPLETIVE
'We two will go (are endeavouring to go)'

According to Blake, it is not surprising that local case markers come to express tense/aspect, since it is not uncommon for local expressions to extend to the domain of time (cf. the discussion of SPACE/TIME metaphors in section 2.6.1). In example (11a), the dative indicates activity directed towards a goal, and from there it is but a small conceptual step to the aspect marker in (11b), which signals an action not yet completed, but one which is clearly goal-oriented.

Other cases where it is not quite clear whether or not there has been a shift from 'less grammatical' to 'more grammatical' are discussed in Yap, Matthews, and Horie (2004). These cases concern a shift from pronominalizer to pragmatic (evidentiality) marker (which Yap et al. term 'stance') in three (unrelated) languages: Japanese, Mandarin Chinese, and Malay. Japanese *no* in (12) illustrates this shift (Yap, Matthews, and Horie 2004: 141f.):

(12) a. Taroo **no** hon
Taroo GEN book
'Taro's book'

b. Taroo **no**
Taroo PRONOMINAL
'Taro's'

c. Taroo-ga kat-ta **no** takakatta
Taroo-NOM buy-PAST (PRO)NOMINALIZER expensive-PAST
'the one Taroo bought was expensive'

d. asita wa hareru **no**
tomorrow TOP become-fine-weather STANCE
'(I assure you) the weather will be fine tomorrow'

In (12a), *no* functions as a genitive marker. When the possessee is elided, as in (12b), it acquires a pronominal function, which at a later stage has been extended to clausal constructions without a head noun. Subsequently, it came to function as a complementizer, which presents the nominalized sentence as a fact, and from there it developed into a stance marker, illustrated in (12d). All steps in this development are structurally and semantically contiguous, and they correspond nicely to Lyons's (1977) hierarchy of ontological entities.[19]

Mandarin *de* has a comparable range of functions, including possessive marker, relativizer, and nominalizer, as well as stance marker, but these functions developed in a different order (Yap, Matthews, and Horie 2004: 148ff.). *De* appears to originate in a noun meaning 'end', or 'bottom', from which it first developed demonstrative and lexical functions, followed by usages as a relativizer, and finally by pronominal functions. The genitive function however, is clearly a later development (in contrast to Japanese *no*). In Modern Mandarin, *de* can be used as a stance marker in a similar fashion to Japanese *no*. Malay (*em*)*punya*, finally, also serves genitive, pronominal, and stance-marking functions (Yap, Matthews, and Horie 2004: 151ff.), but here the development has been from a noun phrase[20] meaning 'ownership, lordship', etc., to a verb meaning 'to own', from where it grammaticalized into a genitive marker, and later to a nominalizing pronoun and finally to a stance marker. To sum up, Japanese *no*, Mandarin *de*, and Malay (*em*)*punya* have the same end-stage (stance marker) and very similar intermediate stages, but there is some variation in the ordering of these stages, which, according to Fischer, Norde, and Perridon (2004: 6), 'raises some doubts as to the universality of the direction of semantic change'. Yap, Matthews, and Horie themselves, however, argue that unidirectionality can be maintained for semantic change across ontological domains, but not for changes within one and the same domain. Since relative and genitive functions belong to the same ontological domain of first-order entities (cf. footnote 18), the relative order of these functions is not relevant to unidirectionality.

## 2.5 Alternative sources of grammatical markers

The emphasis on grammaticalization as the primary source of grams obscures the fact that these may also develop along different lines, for example as a result of morphological reanalysis (Haspelmath 1995). A clear example of the rise of a new suffix (and indeed of a new noun declension) is the development of the NEUT.PL suffix *-n* in Swedish (Norde 2001a: 241), as the result of reanalysis of the suffixed article.

Like all Scandinavian languages, Swedish possesses a suffix of definiteness, which ultimately derives from a demonstrative (Perridon 1989: 129ff.). This

[19] According to this hierarchy, a thing/animal/person is analysed as a first-order entity, an event as a second-order entity, and a proposition as a third-order entity (Yap, Matthews, and Horie 2004: 146).

[20] This NP consisted of a noun *empu* 'master' and a third person enclitic *-nya*.

Table 2.2. Strong neuter nouns in Old Swedish

| | | Indefinite | | Definite | |
|---|---|---|---|---|---|
| SG | NOM | *skip* | *äpli* | *skip-it* | *äpli-t* |
| | GEN | *skips* | *äplis* | *skips-ins* | *äplis-ins* |
| | DAT | *skip(i)* | *äpli* | *skipi-nu* | *äpli-nu* |
| | ACC | *skip* | *äpli* | *skip-it* | *äpli-t* |
| PL | NOM | *skip* | *äpli* | *skip-in* | *äpli-n* |
| | GEN | *skipa* | *äpla* | *skipa-nna* | *äpla-nna* |
| | DAT | *skipum* | *äplum* | *skipum-in* | *äplum-in* |
| | ACC | *skip* | *äpli* | *skip-in* | *äpli-n* |

pronoun, which in Proto-Scandinavian followed the noun, was first cliticized to the noun and is now generally considered inflectional. In Old Swedish, both the noun and the article were inflected (the so-called 'internal inflection'; see Norde 1997: 105ff.). In the paradigm of the strong neuter nouns, part of the suffix of definiteness was reanalysed as a plural suffix on the noun.

Originally, the indefinite plural suffix of Old Swedish strong neuter nouns[21] was *-ø*, and the definite plural suffix was *-(i)n*[22] (or the reduced form *-(e)n*), as in the inflection of *skip* 'ship' and *äpli* 'apple' in Table 2.2 (Wessén 1968: 102f., 119f.). In many variants of seventeenth-century Swedish, however, the definite form of the plural of strong neuter nouns ended in *-na* instead of older *-n*, probably under the influence of MASC.PL.DEF and FEM.PL.DEF forms, as *fisk-ar-**na*** 'the fishes', or *gat-or-**na*** 'the streets'.[23] With neuter nouns ending in a vowel, this resulted in NEUT.PL.DEF forms such as *äpple-na*. Subsequently, these forms were reanalysed as *äpplen-a*, yielding a NEUT.PL.INDEF *äpplen* (Wessén 1968: 200ff.). In this way, the strong neuter nouns acquired an overt distinction between the singular and the plural.

Heath (1998) discusses another type of gram-creating process, for which he coined the charming term 'hermit-crab restructurings'. Hermit crabs are crustaceans belonging to the Paguroidea family. They are soft-bodied, and to protect themselves they occupy shells left empty by (different species of) molluscs. The linguistic equivalent of a hermit crab is, in Heath's (1998: 734) words, 'a particular "method" of formal renewal of a grammatical affix that has undergone phonetic attrition to the point of being inadequately

[21] The term 'strong' inflection is traditionally used to refer to declensions with distinct inflections for genitive, dative, and accusative in the singular, as opposed to 'weak' declensions, which have the same endings for all non-nominative forms in the singular.

[22] The vowel *i* of the definite article was dropped when it was preceded by a vowel.

[23] By this time, the Old Swedish case system had largely disappeared (Norde 2001b).

perceptible or risking complete disappearance.' The obsolescent affix 'seizes' a phonetically more robust lexeme which bears some resemblance to the affix (e.g. sharing the same initial consonant). When a new generation of speakers reinterprets the lexeme as a grammatical marker, the erstwhile obsolescent affix has gained phonetic substance. The affix, and the category it expresses, is the hermit crab, and the lexeme which comes to express the affixal category is the mollusc shell. This scenario is crucially different from grammaticalization, because it presupposes that a lexeme moves into a grammatical function because of some phonetic association with an existing, but ailing morpheme. Heath argues that reconstructions of grammaticalization processes may be premature, because it cannot be ruled out that they have merged, in some way, with a morpheme that was already there. One of Heath's (1998: 744ff.) examples is the Germanic dental 'weak' preterite discussed in section 2.6.3. Heath argues that the dental suffix is not merely a grammaticalized PGmc auxiliary **dōn*, but (also) a reflex of participial *-*to*, which became replaced, in hermit-crab fashion, by the longer (inflected) forms of **dōn*. According to Heath (ibid.), '[a] more broadly based critique of grammaticalization theory should go beyond the tabulation of scattered counter examples and challenge the assumption that even the unassailable cases of compression work in a linear fashion alleged by the theory'. In such a view, grammaticalization theory would be severely challenged if it can be shown that grammaticalization is constrained by the grammar of a particular language, which selects grammaticalization candidates on the basis of formal similarity to existing grammatical material (e.g. affixes). This happens when 'an independent stem is seized upon by an affixal category in distress' (p. 752).

Although Heath's concept of 'hermit crabs' has undeniable appeal, the number of instances seems quite limited. Also, it is not quite true that grammaticalization only occurs for the purpose of repairing obsolescent grammatical categories. Recall that when Meillet coined the term in 1912, he wrote that 'la "grammaticalisation" de certains mots... introduit des catégories *qui n'avaient pas d'expression linguistique*' (Meillet 1926 [1912]: 133; emphasis mine). Definiteness, for example, was not expressed in Germanic or Romance languages before definite articles were developed from deictic pronouns.

## 2.6 Allegedly irreversible changes

As Fischer and Rosenbach note (2000: 19f.), '[u]nidirectionality is said to apply on all linguistic levels: the semantic (fully referential > bleached/ grammatical meaning; less subjective > more subjective), the syntactic (lexical > grammatical; less bound > more bound) and the phonological (full phonological form > reduced phonological form)'. In the following sections, I will examine the directionality of various primitive changes, in order to assess whether preferred directionalities in these changes can be held responsible for the preponderance of grammaticalization, which is a composite change. For this purpose, primitive changes need to be discussed in their own right, not necessarily as part of a (de)grammaticalization change.

### 2.6.1 *Desemanticization*

As regards semantic change, we have to 'abide by tendencies' (Lehmann 2004: 180), but these tendencies appear to be pretty strong. Metaphor, for instance, tends to be from concrete to abstract, the reverse is less common.[24] Semantic change in grammaticalization, too, is generally described in terms of 'abstraction', 'weakening', 'bleaching', or 'fading' (see Hopper and Traugott 2003: 94 and references there). In prosaic terms, grammaticalization involves the loss of concrete meanings, which can be observed for example when body-part nouns develop into spatial adpositions. Nevertheless, loss of lexical meaning in grammaticalization is not as straightforward as it may seem. Although it is probably uncontroversial that meanings fade over time, there may be an increase in semantic complexity at the very first stages of grammaticalization. In such incipient grammaticalization, there is not so much a loss of meaning (yet) but rather a shift in meaning, with the addition of (usually more abstract) connotations. Thus, when *to be going to* started to grammaticalize into a future auxiliary, the meaning of future prediction or intention was added by means of pragmatic inferencing. This process is termed 'pragmatic enrichment' by Hopper and Traugott (2003: 94).[25]

Heine, Claudi, and Hünnemeyer (1991: 48) propose the unidirectional cline in (13), of metaphorical[26] categories of increasing abstraction.

(13) person > object > activity > space > time > quality

[24] For metonymy, however, the picture is less clear. For instance, both *pars-pro-toto* (*three **heads** of cattle*) and *totum-pro-parte* (***France** won 5–4*) occur (Lehmann 2004: 180).

[25] Taking a slightly different perspective, Kuteva (2001: 35ff.) argues that incipient grammaticalization may involve the addition of semantic specificities, a mechanism which she terms 'specification', and which is not necessarily related to the semantics–pragmatics distinction.

[26] Following Haspelmath (1997b: 140 and references there) 'metaphor' will be defined as 'conceptualization of a target domain in terms of a source domain, keeping the profile constant'. Note also that Detges and Waltereit (2002: 168n.), as well as Hopper and Traugott (2003: 87ff.) and Brinton and Traugott (2005: 28f.), have suggested that the primary semantic process in grammaticalization is not metaphor, but metonymy, because grammatical material arises out of lexical material in specific contexts where speakers express one conceptual entity in terms of an adjacent conceptual entity. The synchronic result of this however, as Brinton and Traugott (2005: 28) concede, is often metaphorical, and I will therefore continue to speak of metaphors. (On the usage of the term metonymy in grammaticalization cf. also Heine 2002: 99n.)

One of the best-studied shifts on this cline is the shift from SPACE to TIME (see Haspelmath 1997b for an extensive treatment). It is a cross-linguistically common observation that temporal and spatial relations are expressed in similar ways, as the examples in (14)–(16) show (Haspelmath 1997b: 1). For languages where etymological information is available, it can be shown that, in the vast majority of cases, the temporal meaning is derived from the spatial meaning (Haspelmath 1997b: 20).

(14) a. The priest stood **before** the altar. (orientation)
b. St. Michael's day is **before** Christmas. (sequence)

(15) a. Pepito **is going to** the village to help his granny. (movement)
b. The rain **is going to help** the farmer. (future)

(16) a. We are still far from the **end** of the queue. (extreme part)
b. You will be tired at the **end** of the day. (last moments)

Cross-linguistic evidence suggests that people consistently conceive of the passing of time in the same ways as moving though space. According to Deutscher (2005: 135) '[t]he connection between space and time is so instinctive, and the metaphoric meaning so thoroughly naturalized in its new domain, that we need to make a considerable effort to register that even entirely different functional prepositions like "to", "from" or "in" could ever be used metaphorically.' Bybee, Perkins, and Pagliuca (1994: 25) similarly observe that '[i]f a subject is located spatially in an activity, it is unavoidable that that subject is also located temporally in that activity'.

Thus, the TIME > SPACE metaphor appears to be a convincing case of semantic unidirectionality. The converse development, i.e. the conceptualization of SPACE in terms of TIME, is said to be 'virtually unattested' (Haspelmath 1997b: 141).

Yet there is a possibility, quite common it seems, to use TIME > SPACE metaphors to express spatial notions in terms of temporal notions. In contemporary Western societies, where we 'live by the clock', space is not infrequently measured using time metaphors. This holds true, in particular, of vastness: when measuring distances between planets and stars, we speak of *light years*, i.e. the amount of time the light requires to travel that particular distance. Likewise, people flying from Amsterdam to New York usually do not have a clue about the number of miles they travel, so when asked about the distance between Amsterdam and New York, they will typically answer something like 'about six hours'.

Haspelmath (1997b: 141f.) does give a brief discussion of this kind of metaphor, but according to him, it is based on the phenomenon of 'abstract motion', which he defines as 'the construal of spatial configurations in terms of movement'. An obvious example is French *depuis* 'since' (from the preposition *de* 'from' and *puis* < VLat **postius* 'later'), which has acquired a spatial sense, as in *depuis le haut jusqu'en bas* 'from the bottom to the top'. This is the only case that Haspelmath (1997b: 142) accepts as a counterexample to the SPACE > TIME unidirectionality.

Other examples, such as the use of English *after* with spatial meaning, are dismissed as valid counterexamples by Haspelmath. He argues that in an example like *the poplar is after the oak* the speaker mentally travels a road, identifying a sequence of trees on the way, even though s/he is not actually moving physically. In this way, a temporal preposition 'seemingly comes to have a spatial use'. Haspelmath argues that *after* does not really have a spatial meaning, however, because it can be taken as a metonymical expression for 'The encounter with the poplar is after the encounter with the oak'. He then goes on to claim that the 'quasi-spatial' use of prepositions such as *after* never becomes conventionalized, so that they cannot be said to develop into truly spatial prepositions. It is however not quite clear to me why Haspelmath would allow for SPACE > TIME metaphors, but not for TIME > SPACE metaphors, when both seem to involve the same kind of conceptual mapping from one domain to another. One might as well claim that the use of *before* in example (14b) is 'quasi-temporal', because the speaker clearly envisages a timeline or calendar, in which St. Michael's Day is positioned before or above Christmas. As regards Haspelmath's argument of lack of conventionalization, this does not seem to hold for *after* at all, because there is evidence that *after* is starting to become conventionalized. Consider the examples in (17): (17a) can still be taken to be an instance of 'abstract motion', as Haspelmath would have it, but in (17b) it is less obvious that the speaker travels a mental road.[27]

(17) a. This camera is just after the North Street flyover. It is situated after the bend...
b. In CTEM the lens is situated after the specimen and is used to focus the beam directly onto the detector.[28]

[27] It does not seem to be the case that contemporary *after* continues the older (and original) spatial meaning, because this meaning had become obsolete before it was (re-)introduced in examples such as (17). The OED does list some spatial constructions involving *after*, but these are all expressions containing a verb of movement, e.g. *That merciless ghost that walks the sea After our ship for ever* (1816). *After* in constructions expressing rest appears to be a genuine innovation.

[28] The examples were excerpted on 2 July 2007, respectively from http://www.speedcamerasuk.com/database/YWY/ (a site to warn UK drivers of speed camera locations) and http://eprints.infodiv.unimelb.edu.au/archive/01057/01/findlay_thesis.pdf, a Melbourne PhD thesis on electron microscopy by Scott D. Findlay.

In sum, even though conventionalization of *after* as a spatial preposition may still be in its very early stages,[29] I see no a priori reason why it could not become fully conventionalized in the future. Consequently, this directional tendency is admittedly strong,[30] but it is by no means exceptionless. One might even speculate that, in societies which become increasingly time-oriented and travel distances continue to expand, the tendency to conceptualize SPACE in terms of TIME may become stronger.

In other domains as well, for example the development of conjunctions, semantic changes have been shown not to be irreversible. In his survey of the etymology of conjunctions in Germanic Braunmüller (1978: 113) notes that although a shift from TEMPORAL to either CAUSAL (see (18)) or CONDITIONAL (see (19)) is most frequently attested (cf. also Heine and Kuteva 2002: 328f.), a shift from CAUSAL to TEMPORAL (see (20)) may also occur.

(18) $\text{TEMPORAL}_{post}$ > CAUSAL: German *nachdem* 'after' > 'since'
Nachdem du schon einmal hier bist, kannst du mir beim Abwasch helfen.
'Since you are here, you may help me wash the dishes'

(19) $\text{TEMPORAL}_{simul}$ > CONDITIONAL: German *wenn* 'when' > 'if'
Wenn du kommst, kannst du bei uns mittagessen.
'If you come, you can have lunch with us'

(20) CAUSAL > $\text{TEMPORAL}_{simul}$: German *seit(dem)* 'since, because' > 'since that time'
Seit(dem) Peter im Krankenhaus ist, raucht er nicht mehr.
'Since Peter has been in hospital, he has stopped smoking'

Another study where counterdirectional semantic changes have been reported is Rosenkvist's (2004) detailed survey of the development of conditional subordinators in Swedish. Of the five subordinators studied here, two appear to have followed the path CONDITIONAL > INTERROGATIVE (instead of the regular INTERROGATIVE > CONDITIONAL; cf. Hopper and Traugott 2003: 186). Both subordinators, *om* and *ifall*, arose out of a complex series of changes. *Om* 'if; whether', derives from an Old Swedish preposition *um* 'around' (Rosenkvist 2004: 133ff.). This preposition could take an interrogative or conditional clause (introduced by the subordinator *æn*) as its complement. The sequence *um æn* was then reanalysed as a complex subordinator, after which *æn* was dropped. As a bare subordinator, *um* first

[29] A Google search of the strings 'is situated after' and 'is situated behind' on 2 July 2007 yielded 786 and 59,600 hits respectively. Admittedly this is not the most precise of empirical methods but it suffices to show that in this type of construction the preposition *behind* is (still) far more frequent than the preposition *after*.

[30] See section 2.7.2 for a psycholinguistic account of the SPACE > TIME preference.

appeared in conditional contexts only – in interrogative contexts it appears much later. Hence, interrogative *um* clearly did not develop into conditional *um*. What complicates this change further is that the meaning of *um* did not change directly from 'around' to 'if; whether'. Rather the conditional and interrogative meanings were transferred from *æn* to *um*, when *æn* was dropped. Rosenkvist's second example concerns Modern Swedish *ifall*, which derives from the Early Modern Swedish phrase *i fall* 'in case', which could be followed by a subordinate clause (introduced by *att* 'that', *om* 'if', or *där* 'where'). As in the case of Old Swedish *um æn*, *ifall* (now a single word) + the following subordinator were reanalysed as a complex subordinator, after which *att* / *om* / *där* were deleted. From the seventeenth century until the beginning of the twentieth century, *ifall* was restricted to conditional contexts, hence the interrogative usage is of a relatively recent date, and possibly the result of analogy (Rosenkvist 2004: 231).

The above examples unequivocally show that there exist no universal (i.e. exceptionless) semantic pathways of change, yet the number of counterexamples appears quite limited at present. Nevertheless, some counterevidence *does* exist, but attempts have been made to dismiss even this. For example, in her discussion of Chinese *dei/dé* which developed from an epistemic modal to a main verb meaning 'to need', Ziegeler (2004) makes an attempt to 'save' semantic unidirectionality. Presenting a conceptual network model of semantic change, Ziegeler (2004: 130f.) argues that 'a chain of contiguous meaning shifts can continue indefinitely throughout a network of family resemblances – this is permitted because of the constant motivation for metonymic shifts and increments of meaning to emerge in language use'. In networks of the kind proposed by Ziegeler, grammaticalization chains form only a small part of the entire network of metonymic links, and they may at any point split off to start a new chain, which may very well imply an increase in semantic substance. Crucial to Ziegeler's argumentation is that any movement from one link in the network to another is a direction in itself, and hence that there can be no counterdirectionality. Although such networks certainly have some advantages over one-dimensional chains or two-dimensional maps, in that they can account for multiple paths of developments, including split-offs and unexpected directions, I fail to see how they can be used to preserve unidirectionality at a semantic level,[31] because unidirectionality would be interesting precisely if it could be shown to hold for one-dimensional chains or two-dimensional maps. In conceptual networks where any movement appears to be possible, unidirectionality is

[31] Ziegeler does not deny that counterdirectionality is possible at other levels.

trivial. If anything, conceptual networks, which are inherently polydirectional, show that there is *no* unidirectionality.

### 2.6.2 *Decategorialization*

The term decategorialization refers to the (consequences of a) shift from one category to another, typically from a 'major' category (e.g. nouns or verbs) to a 'minor' category (e.g. prepositions or pronouns)[32] (Hopper and Traugott 2003: 106ff.).

From a functional perspective, decategorialization can be said to involve loss of discourse autonomy (Hopper 1991: 30). When nouns grammaticalize, they lose the ability to identify participants in discourse (example (21)), and when verbs grammaticalize, they lose the ability to report new events (example (22)):

(21) a. Our **thanks** were accepted by the major (referential)
b. **Thanks** to his generosity (grammaticalized, non-referential)

(22) a. They **saw** the Northern Lights (referential)
b. **Seeing** that you have declared bankruptcy, you can hardly make any new investments (grammaticalized, non-referential)

On the formal side, decategorialization entails the loss of morphosyntactic properties, such as inflections and/or the ability to take articles and modifiers. For instance, in the relational phrase *on top of*, the noun *top* cannot pluralize (example (23a)) nor can it take an article. The difference between referential *top* and relational *top* is illustrated in (23b–c). In (23b), *top* is referential and can be preceded by a definite article. But in (23c), without the definite article, *top* is a relational noun, and hence it need not refer to the upper part of the refrigerator. When the refrigerator is lying on its back, and something is resting on its door, we will still say that it is *on top of the refrigerator* (DeLancey 1994: 4).

(23) a. *On tops of all the houses
b. On the top of the refrigerator
c. On top of the refrigerator

Likewise, when full verbs grammaticalize into auxiliaries they may lose person endings (cf. English **he cans*, **he wills*) and become ungrammatical in certain contexts (e.g. certain temporal clauses such as English **Let's wait till she will join us* (Hopper and Traugott 2003: 111).

[32] According to Hopper (1991: 31) decategorialization, and hence grammaticalization, almost always concerns nouns or verbs.

There are several problems with the term 'decategorialization'. First, as argued by Ramat (2001: 398), it may be taken to mean 'loss of categorial status'. He therefore suggests the term 'transcategorization', but, as Brinton and Traugott (2005: 25) point out, this term includes 'lateral shifts' (see section 2.4) between major categories of the type *hand* (N) > *to hand* (V), and is hence not a synonym of decategorialization. I agree with Brinton and Traugott on this point, but the problem remains that 'decategorialization' suggests a 'demotion' from a major ('open') to a minor ('closed') category, but this is far from always the case. For instance, many subordinators derive from closed-class items such as pronouns (Cristofaro 1998: 82f.), and definite articles typically derive from demonstratives. In both cases, decategorialization goes hand in hand with a conversion from one minor category to another.

A second problem with the term is that decategorialization – i.e. the loss of morphosyntactic properties – need not involve a category shift at all. Consider, for example, the well-known semantic-pragmatic shift from deontic to epistemic modality, illustrated by German auxiliaries (Diewald 1997: 24ff.). When German modals have epistemic meaning, some forms may be precluded, e.g. the subjunctive forms of the verb *mögen* in (24c–d) and the preterite forms of the verb *wollen* in (25b) (Diewald 1997: 28).

(24) a. Sie mag darüber sehr verärgert sein
She may-PRES.IND about.that very angry be
'She may be very angry about that'

b. Sie mochte darüber sehr verärgert sein
She may-PRET.IND about.that very angry be
'She may have been very angry about that'

c. ?Sie möge darüber sehr verärgert sein
She may-PRES.SUBJ about.that very angry be

d. *Sie möchte darüber sehr verärgert sein
She may-PRET.SUBJ about.that very angry be

(25) a. Sie will im Büro gewesen sein
She will-PRES in.the-DAT office been have
'She has probably been in the office'

b. ?Sie wollte im Büro gewesen sein
She will-PRET in.the-DAT office been have

The point here is that the modal verbs *mögen* and *wollen* have clearly become restricted paradigmatically when they came to be used in epistemic constructions, yet there is no shift from one category to another. In other words, there is no decategorialization in this case in the literal sense, in spite of the fact that the shift from deontic modal to epistemic modal may be considered a case of increasing grammaticalization.

In spite of these problems I will retain the term decategorialization, but it will be restricted to the loss of morphosyntactic properties.

Let us now move on to the next question, which is whether there exists a reverse process, 'recategorialization', which should involve a gain in morphosyntactic properties such as inflection and the ability to be modified by (for example) articles (in the case of nouns) or modals (in the case of verbs). Plank (2003 [2000]: 177) discusses some examples of the transition from minor to major word class, which, according to him, is always abrupt, as opposed to the transition from major to minor word class, which is gradual. A well-known example of recategorialization from colloquial German is the development of uninflecting adverbs, particles, etc., which can only appear in predicative position, as full-fledged adjectives:

(26) a. Die Tür ist **zu**
the door is closed

b. die **zu(-n)e** Tür
the shut(-*n*)-FEM.SG.NOM.WEAK door[33]

The change in (26) amounts to lexicalization of a function word (see section 3.3.3), and is hence not an instance of degrammaticalization. This type of lexicalization is quite common in a language such as English, where all kinds of function words can be 'recruited' to serve as major word-class items. For instance, in (27a) a modal verb is used as a noun, in (27b) an adverb / verbal particle is used as a verb, and in (27c) adverbs / verbal particles are used as nouns.

(27) a. The white-trouser suit is a **must** this summer.
b. He **downed** a bottle of whisky like it was water.
c. The **ins** and **outs** of e-mail vulnerability.

But recategorialization can also be observed to occur in degrammaticalization, and then it is not abrupt, but gradual. This is most clearly evidenced by the degrammation changes discussed in Chapter 4. Function words which develop into members of a major word class acquire the morphosyntactic characteristics of that particular class. For instance, when Pennsylvania German modal *wotte* came to be used as a full verb, it gained, among other

[33] The -*n*- is an epenthetic consonant, which is typically required (or at least permitted) before a vowel-initial suffix with non-basic adjectives.

properties, a past participle form (example (28a)) and the possibility of being governed by an auxiliary (example (28b); Burridge 1995):

(28) a. Er hat **gewott** er kennt noch eens vun die Ebbel hawwe
He has wished he could again one of the apples have
'He wished he could have one more of the apples'

b. Ich muss **wotte** er brauch net lang Schmaetze hawwe
I must wish he need not long pain have
'I do wish, he didn't need to be in pain for long'

Finally, there is a type of gradual recategorialization which can be associated with neither grammaticalization nor degrammaticalization. This will be illustrated by the history of the suffix *-vis* in Swedish (Norde 2005). Like its English cognate *-wise* (*clockwise*), this originally adverbial suffix derives from a noun meaning 'manner'.[34] The suffix is still productive in Swedish and can be attached to various stems: adjectives (*lyckligtvis* 'luckily'), nouns (*delvis* 'partly'), and numerals (*tusenvis* 'by the thousands'). A quite recent development (the oldest known example is from 1797) is the usage of some words in *-vis*[35] as adjectives. When used as adjectives, the words in *-vis* have adjectival inflections, such as the neuter ending *-t* in (29b) and the plural ending *-a* in (29c). Interestingly, for some speakers the adjectivization has progressed to such an extent that they add an adverbial suffix *-t* to (re-)derive an adverb from the adjective, as exemplified in (29d):

(29) a. en gra**dvis** och mjuk övergång till euro (1998)
a gradual and soft transition to euro
'a gradual and soft transition to the euro'

b. ett fläck**vist** skydd (1997)
a-NEUT patch-wise-NEUT protection
'a patchy protection' (about sun cream)

c. steg**visa** reformer (1996)
stepwise-PL reforms

d. Fast slump**vist** vald är hon inte (1995)
Although chance-wise chosen is she not
'Although she has not been chosen at random'

[34] Some of the older *-vis* adverbs are native words, but most of them are loans from Low and High German (Hellquist 1980 [1922]: 1356).

[35] Only two subtypes of adverbs with a nominal base can be adjectivized: qualitative adverbs (*slumpvis* 'accidentally') and (more rarely) distributive adverbs (*droppvis* 'drop by drop') (Norde 2005: 240).

This is a case of category shift from adverb to adjective accompanied by the acquisition of (adjectival) inflection. In other words, in terms of an increase in morphosyntactic properties, it is a case of recategorialization (adjectives, unlike adverbs, are inflected for gender, number, and definiteness in Swedish). Crucially, however, neither grammaticalization nor degrammaticalization seems an accurate description of this process, because there is no semantic change and, in Swedish at least, adjectives cannot be said to be more or less grammatical than adverbs.[36] And it is not simply a case of lateral shift (see section 2.4) either, because it is abrupt, not gradual. For in cases of lateral shift, such as when the noun *cement* is used as a verb (*we cemented our friendship*), the noun is taken out of its context and comes to serve as a verb in verbal contexts instantly. But in the case of the *-vis* adjectives, a corpus-based analysis of Modern Swedish (Norde 2005) suggests that adjectivization is context-dependent.[37] Most examples of adjectivization were found in attributive position as modifiers of deverbal nouns. It seems likely, therefore, that adverbs first came to be adjectivized when the verbs they modified were nominalized. Compare example (30) below, which is very similar in content to example (29a) above.

(30) Övergången from den svenska kronan till den nya
Transition-DEF from the Swedish crown-DEF to the new
EMU-valutan sker gradvis och mjukt (1998)
EMU-currency happens gradually and softly
'The transition from the Swedish crown to the new EMU-currency proceeds gradually and softly'

To conclude, the terms decategorialization and recategorialization, as defined here, refer to the loss or gain of morphosyntactic properties such as inflection or the ability to select modifiers. It is not quite clear whether there is a preferred directionality. In primary grammaticalization we always find decategorialization, but recategorialization is commonly found as well, both in abrupt and gradual changes.

[36] Nevertheless, it is an interesting case, since a shift from manner adverb to adjective is held to be non-existent (Ramat 2001: 400 and references there).

[37] The data were drawn from the concordances at *Språkbanken* at the University of Gothenburg (http://spraakbanken.gu.se/konk/). The largest part of this corpus consists of newspaper text.

### 2.6.3 *Univerbation*

According to Andersen (1987) univerbation can be observed on three different levels: (i) the morphological level (loss of morpheme boundaries), (ii) the prosodic level (e.g. stress shifts), and (iii) the segmental level (phonological reduction).[38] Univerbation usually takes place at the morphological and the prosodic level, but not necessarily on the segmental level. For instance, in the Dutch compound *hogehoed* 'top hat' (from *hoge hoed* 'high hat') there is both morphological univerbation (as evidenced by, among other things, the fact that *hoge* can no longer be modified by an adverb: **een heel hogehoed* 'a very high hat'),[39] and prosodic univerbation, because only the last syllable is stressed (*hogehóed*), as opposed to the syntagm *hòge hóed* 'high hat', where the adjective *hoge* receives secondary stress. But in *hogehoed* there is no segmental univerbation – the compounding elements are still clearly recognizable and the compound is not infrequently spelled *hoge hoed* (van Bree 2004 [1990]: 159). An example of a compound where there has been segmental univerbation as well is Dutch *bongerd*, a literary variant of *boomgaard* 'orchard', which derives from *boom* 'tree' + *gaard* 'yard'. Segmental univerbation may proceed to the point where the compounding members are no longer distinguishable, as in Dutch *mes* 'knife', which derives from PGmc **mati-* 'food' + **sahsa-* 'cutting device' (van Bree 2004 [1990]: 158).

Examples of univerbation of an entire phrase are the Old Norse indefinite pronouns *nakkvarr* / *nǫkkurr* 'someone' and *nakkvat* / *nǫkkut* 'something' (Boer 1920: 181), which derive from the Proto-Scandinavian phrases **ne wait ek hwariʀ* 'not know I who' and **ne wait ek hvat* 'not know I what' respectively. Equivalents from other Indo-European languages are discussed by Haspelmath (1997a: 131),[40] who terms them 'dunno-indefinites', e.g. Middle High German *neizwer* 'somebody' (< *ne weiz wer* '(I) don't know who'), dialectal Bulgarian *na(m)koj* 'somebody' (< *ne znam koj* 'I don't know who') or Old Church Slavonic *někŭto* 'somebody' (< **ne vě kŭto* 'I don't know who'). According to Haspelmath (1997a: 132) it is not difficult to see why indefinite pronouns would arise out of 'I don't know' constructions. After all, indefinite pronouns are typically (if not always) used when the speaker does not know the identity of the person she or he is referring to. Syntactically, the 'I don't know' phrase must have been a wh-phrase

[38] In some works, the term 'coalescence' is used for univerbation at the segmental level, e.g. in Lehmann (1995 [1982]) or Brinton and Traugott (2005: 27f.).

[39] Compare the corresponding syntagm, where modification of the adjective is perfectly possible: *een heel hoge hoed* 'a very high hat'.

[40] Haspelmath (1997a: 131) incorrectly quotes this form as *nekkver*, and the reconstructed Proto-Germanic phrase contains a few typos as well. The correct forms are those in Boer (1920).

embedded in the matrix clause, as in (31a), a type of syntactic amalgam in the sense of Lakoff (1974).[41] Subsequently, this sentence is inserted in object position, as in (31b), the same position where the object form of a pronoun would appear. This makes them particularly prone to syntactic reanalysis, accompanied by univerbation and phonetic reduction (Haspelmath 1997a: 132):

(31) a. (She told him something$_i$.) I don't know what [it$_i$ was].
b. She told him I don't know what.

A special type of univerbation is morphologization, the rise of bound morphemes out of once independent words (Hopper and Traugott 2003: 140ff.). It is also known as 'secondary grammaticalization' (see section 1.4.1), because it reflects the final stages on the cline of grammaticality, repeated here in (32):

(32) content item > grammatical word > clitic > inflectional affix

As Hopper and Traugott (2003: 141) readily concede, not every instance of grammaticalization involves morphologization. As we have seen (in section 1.4.1), many cases of primary grammaticalization (e.g. auxiliaries or prepositions) show at present no signs of incipient secondary grammaticalization. As it happens, many cases of morphologization are (partially) based on reconstruction. This is even true of the pet example of a full grammaticalization chain, the Romance inflectional future (see e.g. Fleischman 1982; Vincent 1987; Pinkster 1987; Klausenburger 2000: 37ff., 71ff.; Roberts and Roussou 2003: 48ff.), though in this case, interestingly, it is not the first stage which is

TABLE 2.3. The development of the Romance inflectional future (from Lausberg 1972: 229ff.)

| | | Classical Latin | Vulgar Latin | Italian | French |
|---|---|---|---|---|---|
| SG | 1 | *cantare habeo* | **cantar'abeo*[a] | *canterò* | *chanterai* |
| | 2 | *cantare habes* | **cant'arabes* | *canterai* | *chanteras* |
| | 3 | *cantare habet* | **cant'arabet* | *canterà* | *chantera* |
| PL | 1 | *cantare habemus* | **cantara'bemus* | *canteremo* | *chanterons* |
| | 2 | *cantare habetis* | **cantara'betis* | *canterete* | *chanterez* |
| | 3 | *cantare habent* | **cant'arabunt* | *canteranno* | *chanteront* |

[a] ' indicates that the following syllable is stressed

[41] Lakoff defines a syntactic amalgam as 'a sentence which has within it chunks of lexical material that do not correspond to anything in the logical structure of the sentence' (Lakoff 1974: 321). Some examples are *Sammy's going to marry* ***guess who***; *Irving's gone* ***God knows where***; and, similar to Haspelmath's 'dunno-construction', *John invited* ***you'll never guess how many people*** *to his party.*

unattested in written sources (and hence needs to be reconstructed), but the middle stage.[42]

In most Romance languages, various periphrastic constructions gradually developed into new inflectional futures,[43] of which constructions involving an infinitive followed by present indicative forms of the verb *habere* 'to have' became the most common type (see e.g. Pinkster 1987 for diachronic details). Table 2.3 provides examples from Italian and French and its (reconstructed) predecessors.

An analogous development was the rise, in some Romance languages, of an inflectional conditional out of preterite and perfect tenses of the verb *habere* 'to have' (Lausberg 1972: 232). Thus, French *chanterais* 'I would sing', derives from Latin *cantare habebam* (sing-INF have-PRET.1SG), whereas its Italian equivalent *canterei* derives from *cantare habui* (sing-INF have-PERF.1SG).

Examples of *habere* + infinitive with a temporal (rather than modal) reading start to appear with some frequency in sources from the second century AD onwards, though more convincing examples are from a later date, for instance (33) (from the writings of Augustine (354–430)). In this example, a future reading is likely because *coli habent* is co-ordinated with the inflectional future *erunt* (Pinkster 1987: 206). Example (34) (from *Fredegar's Chronicle*) is traditionally given as the first instance of an inflectional future, but there is some uncertainty as to the exact date of the passage in which this sentence appears: it is dated 613, but may have been composed much later. The oldest uncontroversial examples are from the *Strasbourg Oaths* (843): *prindrai* 'I will take' and *salvarai* 'I will assist' (Fleischman 1982: 68).[44]

[42] The emergence of the synthetic future has been reconstructed as (i) a Western Romance innovation which spread to the other vernaculars, (ii) a parallel development in all Romance vernaculars, or (iii) a development during the last stage of Common Romance, i.e. before the split-off into individual vernaculars (Fleischman 1982: 68f.). The third scenario, which Fleischman sees as the 'preferred alternative' is the one adopted here.

[43] Latin also possessed an inflectional future (*cantabo* – *cantabas* – *cantabat* 'I – you – (s)he will sing' etc.) which continued to be used when *habere* developed into a future auxiliary (Pinkster 1987: 208). On the reasons for its eventual disappearance see Lausberg (1972: 226ff.), or Pinkster (1987: 210ff.).

[44] As was the case with the Romance suffix MENTE (see section 1.6.5), a sketchy description such as the one presented above does no justice to the complexity attested in contemporary Romance languages and dialects. To begin with, some languages did not develop inflectional futures from auxiliary HAVE (or lost them, cf. fn. 42) – Portuguese, for instance, still uses independent auxiliary forms (Lausberg 1972: 231). And secondly, there were several other verbs which came to be used as future auxiliaries in various Romance languages (Lausberg 1972: 228), but these developments cannot always be traced back to changes in Latin (Pinkster 1987). Romanian, for example, uses several periphrastic constructions (Daniliuc and Daniliuc 2000), involving the verbs *a avea* 'to have' or *a vrea* / *a voi* (both deriving from Lat. *velle* 'to want', though *velle* was not used as a future auxiliary in Latin; Pinkster 1987: 195). The *avea* future uses either inflected forms of the verb or (especially in colloquial Romanian) an invariant short form *o* + the conjunction *sa* + the present subjunctive, e.g. (eu) *am/o sa cânt* (I have that sing-SUBJ.1SG) 'I will sing'. The (now archaic) *voi* future is construed with the infinitive: *(eu) voi cânta* 'I will sing' (Mara van Schaik-Radulescu, p.c.).

(33) aliquando Christiani non erunt et
some.time Christians not be-FUT.IND.3PL and
idola rursus **coli** **habent**
idols again cultivate.INF.PASS have-PRES.IND.3SG
'Some day there will be no more Christians, and idols will be cultivated again'

(34) Iustinianus dicebat: 'Daras'
Iustinianus say-PRET.IND.3SG give-FUT.IND.2SG
'Iustinianus said: "You will give"'

Another example of morphologization is the so-called 'weak' preterite in Germanic (English *heard*, Dutch *hoorde*). As opposed to Germanic 'strong' verbs, in which the preterite is mostly formed by means of *ablaut*, i.e. vowel alternations in the stem (English *give – gave*; *ride – rode*, etc.), weak verb classes add a suffix to the verbal stem. Since the first consonant of this suffix is a dental (e.g. Goth *nasida* 'I saved', Goth *mahta* 'I could', Goth *kunþa* 'I could'; Tops 1978: 350) it is also known as the *dental suffix*. Some examples are given in Table 2.4.

The preterite suffixes are generally assumed to derive from the Proto-Germanic auxiliary **dōn* 'to do' (<PIE **dhē- / dhō-*), the preterite forms of which are given in Table 2.5. Thus Gothic *nasidēdum* 'we saved', for example, has been reconstructed to derive from a phrase meaning 'save did-3PL' (Bopp 1816: 151ff.; Boer 1918: 263; van Hamel 1923: 149; van Haeringen 1962: 47; Krahe and Meid 1969: 127f.).

TABLE 2.4. Some weak preterite paradigms in Germanic*

| | | PGmc[a] | Gothic | Old Icelandic | Old High German |
|---|---|---|---|---|---|
| SG | 1 | **salƀōðō*$^{n}$ | *nasida* | *talða* | *frumita* |
| | 2 | **salƀōðēz* | *nasidēs* | *talðir* | *frumitōs* |
| | 3 | **salƀōðē(þ)* | *nasida* | *talði* | *frumita* |
| DU[b] | 1 | **salƀōðēðu*$^{n}$ | *nasidēdu* | | |
| | 2 | **salƀōðēðuþ(i)z* | *nasidēduts* | | |
| PL | 1 | **salƀōðēðum(i)z* | *nasidēdum* | *tǫlðum* | *frumitum* |
| | 2 | **salƀōðēðuþ(i)* | *nasidēduþ* | *tǫlðuð* | *frumitut* |
| | 3 | **salƀōðēðun(þ)* | *nasidēdun* | *tǫlðu* | *frumitun* |

**salƀō-* 'to anoint'; *nasjan* 'to save'; *telja* 'to count'; *frummen* 'to support'.
[a] The PGmc reconstruction is from Ramat (1981: 172). Superscript $^{n}$ indicates an obsolescent nasal, deriving from PIE **m*.
[b] The dual forms have only been preserved in Gothic.

TABLE 2.5. The indicative preterite of PGmc **dōn* 'to do' (Ramat 1981: 177)

| | | | | | |
|---|---|---|---|---|---|
| SG | 1 | **deðōⁿ* | PL | 1 | **deðum* |
| | 2 | **deðēz* | | 2 | **deðuþ(i)* |
| | 3 | **deðē(þ)* | | 3 | **deðun(þ)* |

Although other explanations have been offered as well,[45] the DO-origin appears to be the most widely accepted scenario at present (Lahiri 2003 [2000]; Kiparsky 2003). Arguments in favour of this etymology are as follows. First, the reduplicating forms in the Gothic dual and plural are best explained as continuing preterite forms of **dōn*, because this is a reduplicating verb.[46] Secondly, as we have seen at the beginning of this section, it is not uncommon for auxiliary verbs to morphologize into verbal endings. And for the Germanic weak preterite the DO-origin is plausible because so-called DO-support is still attested in some varieties (e.g. in English and Eastern Dutch dialects). Finally, if a PGmc auxiliary were to morphologize, it would indeed become a suffix, because in Proto-Germanic (which was an SOV language) auxiliaries followed the main verb.[47]

In an interesting paper on morphologization from a phonological perspective, Lahiri (2003 [2000]: 71) gives the following definition: 'grammaticalisation seems to entail the reduction of a phonological word to a unit which then attaches to another phonological word: $[\text{WORD}]_\omega$ $[\text{WORD}]_\omega$ >

[45] For alternative explanations see Prokosch (1939: 195ff.) and references there, and especially the references in Tops (1974 and 1978). These proposals, however, fail to account for the Gothic dual and plural forms. And according to Tops (1978: 350) 'all other explanations of the long Gothic endings [e.g. the dual and plural] are so intricate and tortuous that they must be rejected.' Yet another proposal is Heath's (1998) 'hermit-crab' scenario, according to which the inflected forms of **dōn* replaced a dysfunctional 'preterite' involving predicative participles in **-to*. Extensive though the argumentation is, I am not quite convinced that participial **-to* came to function as a preterite, which is a prerequisite for the hermit-crab scenario (where a lexeme is recruited for a grammatical category with no sufficient phonetic substance of its own, see section 2.5).

[46] In the only surviving Gothic text (Wulfila's bible translation from the fourth century) a cognate verb of English *do* is not attested, but that this verb had reduplication in the preterite is evidenced by vestiges of reduplication in other (contemporary) Germanic languages, e.g. English *did* or Dutch *deed* 'did-SG' / *deden* 'did-PL'.

[47] Some loose ends remain however. Most problematic is that some of the forms must be traced back to PIE **-t-*, e.g. the Gothic forms in *-þ-* (via Grimm's Law). According to Tops (1978: 357), this can be explained by assuming that the auxiliary DO-forms were not attached to the infinitive, but to verbal nouns ending in **-ti* or **-tu* plus the perfect (not past) endings of **dōn*. The details of this proposal fall outside the scope of this paper, and in any event it does not challenge the position taken here that the weak preterite endings derive from an independent auxiliary.

[[WORD]$_\omega$CLITIC]$_\omega$ > [WORD AFFIX]$_\omega$. Hence grammaticalisation crucially involves phonological word... formation.'[48] In the final stage, when there is a single prosodic word, there are two possible structures (ibid.: 72):

(35) a. [ROOT + MORPHEME$_1$ + MORPHEME$_2$]$_\omega$
b. [[ROOT + MORPHEME$_1$] + MORPHEME$_2$]$_\omega$

In the (a) structure, the cliticized morpheme (e.g. an inflected auxiliary) is reinterpreted as two grammatical morphemes. In the (b) structure on the other hand, the base of the auxiliary is attached closer to the root, whereas the inflection is attached to the entire structure.

In her discussion of the Germanic dental preterite and the Bengali progressive and perfect (out of an auxiliary BE), Lahiri (2003 [2000]: 73) argues that the root of the auxiliary becomes a stem formative, whereas the inflection of the auxiliary becomes the inflection of the newly-formed verb. This of course is well known, but in grammaticalization studies changes in what will become a stem formative are often ignored (ibid.):

> The consequence of this claim for morphology is that the cline of grammaticalisation often assumed is not quite as simple as it seems. It is not that a phonological word is reduced both in form and in status to an affix which attaches to the nearest convenient phonological word. The grammaticalised word continues to be more than one morpheme, though with a reanalysed hierarchical structure.

Lahiri furthermore shows that one and the same lexeme can grammaticalize into different grams and, crucially, at different morphological levels. One of her examples concerns the colloquial Bengali[49] verb /ɑtʃʰ-/ 'to be', which has grammaticalized into both a progressive marker and a perfect marker. As a perfect marker, the auxiliary has become a clitic, as is shown in (36a), but as a progressive marker, it has become separated from the person affix, and reanalysed as a tense marker suffixed to the stem (where it underwent gemination following a Bengali phonological rule), as is shown in (36b).

(36) Grammaticalization of /ɑtʃʰ-/ in colloquial Bengali
a. Perfect: [[/ROOT + e/]$_\omega$ + [/tʃʰ-/ + person affix]$_{\text{clitic}}$]$_\omega$
b. Progressive: [[/ROOT + tʃtʃʰ-/] + [person affix]$_{\text{affix}}$]$_\omega$

What Lahiri's examples thus show is that there are no universal pathways in secondary grammaticalization, and that phonology may constrain morphologization.

[48] The notation $_\omega$ stands for prosodic word.
[49] The development in literary Bengali has been somewhat different, see Lahiri (2003 [2000]) for details.

In sum, the current body of evidence suggests that univerbation, or morphologization, is far more common than its reverse. Examples of bound morphemes 'detaching' themselves will be discussed in Chapters 5 and 6.

### 2.6.4 *Phonological attrition*

On 24 September 2007, the Dutch Scientific Council for Government Policy published a report entitled *Identificatie met Nederland* ('Identification with the Netherlands'). Upon presentation of the report, the Argentinian-born Crown princess Máxima delivered a speech, which sparked vehement protests by both politicians and the people, and the immensely popular princess suddenly found herself being criticized by even the most ardent of royalists. But what did Máxima actually say? These were her exact words, quoted from the official website of the royal family:[50]

> Zo'n zeven jaar geleden begon mijn zoektocht naar de Nederlandse identiteit... Het was een prachtige en rijke ervaring waarvoor ik enorm dankbaar ben. Maar '*de*' Nederlandse identiteit? Nee, die heb ik niet gevonden [italics mine].
>
> 'About seven years ago I started my quest for the Dutch identity... It has been a wonderful and rich experience, for which I am extremely grateful. But '*the*' Dutch identity? No, I have not found it.'

The crux of these words lies in the pronunciation of the word *de*: when unstressed, it is merely a definite article with non-neuter nouns, but when stressed, it gains a more specific meaning (analogous with English stressed *the*): 'the one and only, exclusive, unique' etc. When unstressed, the vowel in *de* is a schwa ([ə]), but when stressed, the vowel is [ɵ] (as in the Dutch word *put* 'pit'). The single quotes in the princess's speech indicate that *de* was stressed, and she clearly pronounced it that way, too. Thus, what she meant was that there exists no single and uniform Dutch identity, because no two Dutch people are the same, but immediately afterwards she was quoted as having said that there existed no Dutch identity at all (which would have been the correct interpretation if *de* had been unstressed). The difference in meaning is subtle, especially because it can only be perceived in the spoken language (and the single quotes were frequently omitted in written comments), and in hindsight, it might have been wiser to use a more explicit formulation. But still, much of the controversy could have been prevented with reference to the actual pronunciation of the word *de*, which almost all commentators failed to do.

[50] http://www.koninklijkhuis.nl/content.jsp?objectid=20871

What does this anecdote demonstrate? That public debate needs linguists, obviously, but the reason I relate it in this section is because it reflects an interesting counterdirectional example of phonetic strengthening, that is, an increase in phonetic substance of the definite article *de*. Further details of this particular case will be provided below, but first I will discuss phonological/ phonetic attrition and 'strengthening' in general.

As I wrote in the introduction to this chapter, words tend to erode in usage. 'Erosion' is a rather sloppy term, referring as it does to both the loss of segments (as in PIE **egom* > English *I*, which is a phonological change) and to phonetic reduction. The same goes for the term 'attrition', but I will retain that one since it forms part of Lehmann's parameters model discussed in Chapter 3. Attrition is a prototypical case of speaker economy (see 2.7.1), since reducing a word obviously reduces the effort required to produce it. Paradoxically, however, less-effort strategies may also give rise to the opposite, i.e. the addition of segments. Thus we find prothesis (Latin *schola* > French *école*) besides aphaeresis (loss of /h/ in French *homme*), epenthesis (Old English *ǣmtig* > Modern English *empty*) besides syncope (Dutch *weder* > *weer* 'weather'), and paragoge (Dutch *nieman* > *niemand* 'nobody') besides apocope (loss of /t/ in French *lit*). All of these processes have in common that they ease pronunciation, either by inserting segments (e.g. in awkward consonant clusters), or by deleting segments. Even though the general trend is one towards shortening, the opposite processes are by no means rare.

In the case of purely phonetic reduction (e.g. from full vowel to schwa in unstressed syllables) the reverse is far less common, but the princess's pronunciation of *de* is an example of it. In this particular case, stressing the article results in a vowel shift from [ə]) to [ɵ]. Although these vowels differ only marginally as to place of articulation, they do differ with respect to length (significantly shorter for [ə]), and roundedness ([ə] is unrounded when following an unrounded vowel; see Rietveld and Van Heuven 2001: 129ff. for phonetic details of Dutch vowels).

Basically, there are two kinds of strengthening. One is so-called spelling pronunciation, that is, the reintroduction of segments that had been lost in the spoken language but retained in the written language, such as (formal) Dutch final [n] in words like *lopen* 'walk' or *huizen* 'houses'. The other one is more interesting, because it goes hand in hand with an increase in semantic substance, such as Dutch *de* quoted above. The difference between these two kinds is illustrated in (37): the Dutch neuter pronoun *het* is usually pronounced [ət], as in (37a), but the spelling pronunciation [hɛt], as in (37a′), is not infrequently heard. However, there is no difference in meaning between

(37a) and (37a′), and in neither case is the pronoun stressed. A difference in meaning arises first when the pronoun receives main stress, and thus becomes a euphemistic expression for 'sex', as in (37b):

(37) a. Ik wil **het** niet horen [ət]
a′. Ik wil **het** niet horen [hɛt]
I want it not hear
'I do not want to hear it'

b. Heb je **het** al met hem gedaan? [ˈhɛt]
Have you it already with him done?
'Have you slept with him already?'

To conclude, phonological/phonetic reduction is not irreversible, since strengthening has also been observed to occur, if less frequently. This may be the result of either spelling pronunciation (which is less interesting in this context), or it may form part of a semantic-pragmatic change, where emphasizing a normally unstressed function word may give rise to both semantic and phonetic strengthening. Strengthening may be involved in degrammaticalization as well, e.g. in the development of the Dutch numeral suffix *-tig* (cognate with English *-ty*), pronounced [təx], into an independent quantifier 'dozens', pronounced [tɩx] (see section 6.9).

### 2.6.5 *Subjectification*

In general, the term 'subjectification' refers to the process whereby '[m]eanings tend to become increasingly based in the speaker's subjective belief state/attitude towards the proposition' (Traugott 1989: 35). Subjectification in grammaticalization is defined by Traugott (1995: 32) as 'the development of a grammatically identifiable expression of speaker belief or speaker attitude to what is said. It is a gradient phenomenon, whereby forms and constructions that at first express primarily concrete, lexical and objective meanings come through repeated use in local syntactic contexts to serve increasingly abstract, pragmatic, interpersonal, and speaker-based functions.'

Subjectification is attested along several (related) diachronic dimensions (Traugott 1995: 48):

Propositional function → Discourse function
Objective meaning → Subjective meaning
Non-epistemic modality → Epistemic modality
Non-syntactic subject → Syntactic subject
Syntactic subject → Speaking subject
Full, free form → Bonded form

Subjectification can be observed in both lexical and grammatical change, but in the latter case 'the interplay between morphosyntactic and pragmatic/ semantic factors leads to more complex trajectories of change than are usual in lexical change' (Traugott 1995: 32).[51] Well-known examples of subjectification in grammaticalization are the following (Traugott 1995: 31; 1997b: 199):

(38) a. Mary **is going to** visit her agent. [progressive motion verb go, purposive to]
b. Mary **is going to / gonna** visit her agent. [quasi-auxiliary]

(39) a. Mary read **while** Bill sang. [temporal connective]
b. Mary liked oysters **while** Bill hated them. [concessive connective]

(40) a. They **must** be married (some external force requires them to). [deontic modal]
b. They **must** be married (it is obvious that they are). [epistemic modal]

The (b) examples are more subjective[52] in meaning, more grammaticalized, and historically posterior to their cognates in (a) (see Traugott 1995 and 1997b for details of their development). A topic for further research, as Traugott (1995: 46) herself notes, is whether subjectification plays a role in all stages of grammaticalization. Apart from the cases exemplified in (38)–(40), subjectification has been observed in such various domains as word order change (Stein 1995), the development of modal meaning of verbs such as PROMISE and THREATEN in Dutch and English (Verhagen 1995; Traugott 1997b), the English 'have'-perfect (Carey 1995), or the grammaticalization from verb to conjunction of English *supposing* and Italian *supponendo che* (Visconti 2004).

According to Traugott (1995: 46):

> The reason for the ubiquity of subjectification presumably lies in the speaker's attempts to communicate the relevance of what is said to the communicative event, which includes hearers as well as speakers, but which ultimately depends for its occurrence on the speaker. For speakers' communicative purposes to be achieved, forms are constantly recruited from lexical domains expressing concrete, objective meanings, and are construed in terms of the perspective of the speaker, the speech event, and the discourse context.

[51] Examples provided by Traugott from the lexical domain concern the development of illocutionary speech-act verb meanings from locutionary (and often non-locutionary) meanings, e.g. *agree* (originally 'be pleasing, suitable') or *promise* (ultimately from a Latin past participle meaning 'sent forward').

[52] Note that the terms 'objective' and 'subjective' are not used in the everyday sense of 'evidence-based' and 'personal, idiosyncratic' respectively, but in the technical sense of 'pertaining to the object perceived' and 'pertaining to the perceiving individual' (Langacker 1990: 7).

A slightly different approach to subjectification is taken in Langacker (1990). Langacker's treatment of subjectification is grounded in the cognitive-semantics claim that 'an expression's meaning cannot be reduced to an objective characterization of the situation described: equally important for linguistic semantics is how the conceptualizer chooses to *construe* the situation and portray it for expressive purposes' (Langacker 1990: 5; emphasis original). For instance, Langacker accounts for the development of *be going to* into a future auxiliary as follows: 'One might suggest that it constitutes a metaphorical extension from the spatial to the temporal domain: rather than moving though space to initiate the infinitival process, the subject moves through time' (Langacker 1990: 22). But the space-to-time transfer is not the only meaning change involved: the spatial reading implies the subject's intention to accomplish the infinitival process, but this is not necessarily true of the temporal reading. Thus, in the French example in (41), or in its English translation, the subject cannot intend anything – the perspective is that of the speaker predicting the occurrence of the event. Subjectification is thus seen by Langacker (1990: 23) as a crucial factor in the development of *go* from motion verb to future auxiliary.

(41) Un tremblement de terre va détruire cette ville
'An earthquake is going to destroy that town'

According to Traugott (1995: 45) the hypothesis of unidirectional increase in subjectification is 'very robust', at least in the earlier stages of grammaticalization. In their work on regularity in semantic change Traugott and Dasher (2002: 87) furthermore assert that '[w]hat is particularly striking for our purposes in this book is that many of the counterexamples to grammaticalization that have been cited show no semantic shift..., or show regular semantic shift of the sort described in this book'. For example, the decliticization of the Japanese connective particle *ga* 'but' (see section 6.4) was accompanied by an increase in subjectification (see also Traugott 1995: 46). An increase in subjectification is also attested in the development of the Welsh preposition *yn ôl* 'after' into a verb *nôl* 'to bring', as is illustrated in example (42) (Willis 2007: 294), which reflects the first stage in the degrammaticalization of *yn ôl*. Originally, the meaning of *yn ôl* is 'after', but in example (42) it may also be interpreted as meaning 'to fetch'. This meaning change is an instance of subjectification, because the speaker infers that when the lads went after the horse and the weapons, they did so with the intention to fetch it.

(42) Yna yd aeth y gweisson **yn ol** y varch a 'e
then PART went the lads after his horse and his
arueu y Arthur
weapons for Arthur
'Then the lads went after / went to fetch his horse and his weapons for Arthur'

Examples such as (42) reveal that subjectification is not limited to grammaticalization. But is subjectification also irreversible? It seems not – its reverse, 'objectification', occurs both in degrammaticalization (e.g. in the development of Pennsylvania modal *wotte* 'would' into a full verb meaning 'to wish'; see section 4.2) and in grammaticalization, particularly secondary grammaticalization (Kranich 2008). In her study of the progressive in seventeenth and eighteenth century English, Kranich shows that while the progressive became increasingly entrenched in the English tense/aspect system (which is a kind of secondary grammaticalization; see section 1.4.1), its usage in objective constructions (example (44)) increases considerably, at the expense of its subjective usages (example (43)).[53]

(43) HARRY. Why, it is possible you may yet receive a valentine.
SOPHIA. Nay, now, but don't you go to think **that I am asking for one.**
(1792; Kranich 2008: 245)

(44) I was call'd out to see it, by the Servants, **who had been looking at it** about half a quarter of an Hour (1720; Kranich 2008: 251)

In (43), Kranich argues, the interpretative function is supported by the speaker's explicit rejection of an interpretation her interlocutor might have (ibid.: 250). Therefore, only a verb form which can be interpreted subjectively can be used in the second part – a simple tense form such as the present (*Nay, now, but don't you go to think that I ask for one*) sounds odd. In example (44), on the other hand, the description of the event is neutral rather than an interpretation by the speaker – here the focus is on duration which is made explicit by the temporal adverbial (p. 251). In other words, the function of the progressive in (44) is purely aspectual. This increasing fixation of the aspectual use of the progressive makes it less suitable for subjective constructions, because 'for an element to be available for the expression of speaker attitude, the speaker has to be free to choose whether or not to use it . . . so as soon as an element or construction has become an obligatory element of grammar, its

[53] In texts from 1600–1649, 70.8% of the progressives were used in objective constructions. This steadily increased to 80.4% (1650–1699), 86.5% (1700–1749), and 95.4% (1750–1799) (Kranich 2008: 252).

meaning cannot become enriched any more by inferences that can produce subjective meaning' (p. 253).

Similar patterns can be found in other tenses, such as the future (Kranich, in prep.). In English, future auxiliaries can be used in subjective constructions expressing obligation ((45a)) or volition ((45b)). In French, however, where the inflectional future is fully grammaticalized, corresponding constructions are ungrammatical ((46a–b)), suggesting that the French future has lost its subjective connotations.

(45) a. Shall I do it?
b. Will you marry me?

(46) a. *?Ferai-je-le?
b. *?Tu m'épouseras?

Obviously, more empirical evidence is required to establish whether secondary grammaticalization typically involves objectification, but it seems intuitively plausible that increasing obligatoriness and semantic bleaching go hand in hand with increasing objectivity.

To sum up, since neither subjectification nor objectification can be exclusively mapped onto grammaticalization or degrammaticalization, they cannot be used as a diagnostic for either type of change.

### 2.6.6 *Summary*

In the preceding sections I have discussed a number of processes which are generally held to be irreversible. As we have seen, they are indeed overwhelmingly unidirectional, but not quite, and some are 'more irreversible' than others (for instance, the reverse of univerbation is less commonly attested than the reverse of decategorialization, 'recategorialization'). Taken together, the directional preferences of semantic, phonological, and morphological processes contribute to the directional preference of grammaticalization in what is probably a cumulative manner – when they co-occur in a grammaticalization process, they usually do so in their preferred direction, that is, desemanticization co-occurs with (for example) decategorialization and phonological attrition, but not with the reverse of either of these processes. The same goes for degrammaticalization, as we will see in Chapters 4–6: here the primitive changes generally occur in the 'marked' direction, i.e. the reverses of the processes discussed above. There are some exceptions, as we will see, but the general patterns are clear. This leaves the question of *why* there are directional preferences at all, and in the next three sections I will discuss explanations for directional tendencies from different theoretical angles.

## 2.7 Explaining directional tendencies

### 2.7.1 *Usage-based approaches*

In functional, or usage-based, approaches to language change the central idea is that language changes as a result of (usually unintentional and subconscious) actions of its users.[54] At least since von der Gabelentz (1901), it has been argued that language change is to a large extent determined by the conflicting interests of the speaker and the hearer. Von der Gabelentz (1901: 256) identified these forces as the inclination towards indolence (*Bequemlichkeitstrieb*) and desire for clarity (*Deutlichkeitstrieb*) respectively. *Bequemlichkeitstrieb* is better known as '(the principle of) economy', which is attributed to 'human laziness, indolence, inertia, shirking, easygoingness, sloth, sluggishness, lack of energy or whatever other beautiful synonyms have been invented for "economy of effort" or "following the line of least resistance"' (Jespersen 1921: 263). *Deutlichkeitstrieb* evidently constrains an uninhibited trend towards ease of production, because the hearer will have to be able to process what the speaker says, or else communication will be impossible (see further Norde 2001b for a discussion of the balance of speaker and hearer strategies and their implications for language change).

On a usage-based view, grammaticalization may be defined as follows:

> Grammatikalisierung ist . . . das unbeabsichigte Resultat alltagsrhetorischer Sprecherstrategien. (Detges 1998: 23)[55]

Interestingly, a usage-based approach may account for both directional tendencies (the result of user strategies) and its exceptions:

> Grammaticalization . . . involves the interaction of linguistic structure and language use. One would not expect 100 percent regularity from strategic interaction, subject as it always is to human intervention. (Traugott and Dasher 2002: 87)

[54] The most radical usage-based approaches to change only allow for user constraints on language change. Grammatical constraints (e.g. in OT) are then said to derive from user constraints. This view is expressed e.g. by Haspelmath (1999c: 201), who argues that 'the grammatical constraints employed in optimality theory are the way they are because they arise from universal constraints on language change through a diachronic adaptive process'. This adaptive process is described as follows (p. 203): 'In language change, variants are created from which speakers may choose. Being subject to various constraints on language use, speakers tend to choose those variants that suit them best. These variants then become increasingly frequent and entrenched in speakers' minds, and at some point they may become obligatory parts of grammar.' To me, however, this approach to change seems to be too limited. I agree with Fischer (in prep.), who correctly notes that user constraints cannot form the basis of all change, since variation is constrained by structural factors in the first place.

[55] 'Grammaticalization is . . . the unintentional result of everyday rhetorical speakers' strategies.' Detges (1998:1) continues: 'Grammatik ensteht nicht deshalb, weil die Sprecher das Gefühl haben, grammatische Funktionen in ihrer Sprache bedürften dringend formaler Ausdrücksmittel, sondern

If change is a social product, the result of the interaction of language and use, how could there be no counterexamples? Humans are not machines, and do not use language mechanically... But likewise, since unidirectionality is not exceptionless, it is also not useful to adopt Lehmann's (1995 [1982]) and Haspelmath's (1999a) claims that there are no, or at least no genuine, counterexamples to grammaticalization. (Traugott 2002: 21f.)

Turning now to functional approaches to unidirectionality, I will first review two of the earliest accounts, one by Newmeyer (1998, 2001), and one by Haspelmath (1999a).

According to Newmeyer, one of the reasons for the predominance of grammaticalization is the 'least-effort effect':[56]

*Less effort* is required on the part of the speaker to produce an affix than a full form. Add the element of frequency-caused predictability to the extreme amount of redundancy in grammatical codings, and it is not difficult to see why the quick-and-easy option of affixation is frequently chosen. Other downgradings can readily be interpreted as least-effort effects as well. Functional categories require less coding material – and hence less production effort – than lexical categories. As a result, the change from the latter to the former is far more common than from the former to the latter. (Newmeyer 1998: 276)

Haspelmath (1999a) dismisses Newmeyer's argument as insufficient, and instead advances a 'theory of irreversibility' which is based on the works by Lehmann (1985 and 1995 [1982]) and, in particular, the invisible-hand framework of Keller (1994 [1990]). According to Keller's theory of change, speakers are guided by maxims, such as 'the maxim of economy' ('talk in such a way that you do not expend superfluous energy') or 'the maxim of conformity' ('talk like others talk').[57] When individuals follow the same maxims collectively, this may lead to an invisible-hand process of change. Haspelmath (1999a: 1056f.) suggests that speakers introduce an innovation in order to be noticed, guided by the 'maxim of extravagance':

What is crucial here is that the speakers' goal is not just being understood at the lowest possible cost, but rather being socially successful with their speech... The

sie ist das versteinerte Residuum bestimmter Redetechniken, welche die Sprecher zunächst mit dem Ziel erfinden, überzeugend zu sprechen.' ('Grammar does not come about because speakers have a feeling that grammatical functions in their language have urgent need of formal expression; rather it is the fossilized remains of certain speaking techniques, which speakers invent in the first place with the aim of speaking convincingly.')

[56] This effect may also be held responsible for the (overwhelmingly) unidirectional phonological changes discussed in Haspelmath (2004:19f.), e.g. the shift from /h/ to /s/, as pointed out in Luraghi (2005: 10).

[57] The names of Keller's maxims were coined by Haspelmath (1999a).

crucial point is that speakers not only want to be clear or 'expressive', sometimes they also want their utterance to be imaginative and vivid – they want to be little 'extravagant poets' in order to be noticed, at least occasionally.

Haspelmath goes on to argue that there are two reasons why speakers would not upgrade a grammatical item when they want to distinguish themselves. First, such a change would violate another maxim, 'the maxim of clarity' ('talk in such a way that you are understood'), since 'functional elements are usually less salient and less explicit than lexical elements'. Lehmann (1985: 315) similarly argues that counterdirectional changes 'would presuppose a constant desire for understatement, a general predilection for litotes'. If this were true, however, lexicalization of function words, as in (47), would *never* occur. I fail to see why the possibility of such changes would imply a *constant* desire for understatement. Understatement is a common type of expression, and it is not inconceivable that speakers would occasionally use constructions such as (47) in order to be noticed.

(47) Holly... shaved her legs and then he was a she[58]
(Lou Reed: *Walk on the Wild Side*, 1972)

Haspelmath's (1999a: 1059) second argument for the improbability of counterdirectional change runs as follows:

> [L]exical elements are freely manipulable by speakers and (more or less) accessible to consciousness, whereas functional elements are processed automatically and unconsciously. So even if a speaker had some motivation for replacing a lexical item by a functional item, s/he would not be able to do this because functional elements cannot be used outside their proper places.

Again, this claim is refuted by examples such as (47), and it seems to contradict his remark in the same paper that in such cases as *ifs and buts*, 'words are taken out of their context and employed metalinguistically'. For these reasons, I find Newmeyer's 'least effort strategy' more plausible as

[58] This usage of personal pronouns is commonly attested. For Dutch it has been suggested (Stoett 1923: 24; *WNT*) that it originates in Middle Dutch, where the noun *hie* 'male animal' and the pronoun *hi(e)* 'he' got confused, as a result of which the pronoun *si(e)* 'she' came to be used as a noun as well, denoting a female animal. In the absence of cross-linguistic parallels, this would have been a reasonable, and sufficient, explanation, but since it is so commonly attested in languages where no homonymy between the pronoun HE or SHE and a noun referring to animals existed, it is more likely that it reflects an unexceptional strategy to recruit third person personal pronouns as nouns. Compare *Är det en han eller en hon?* (Swedish); *È un lui o una lei?* (Italian); *Ist es ein Er oder eine Sie?* (German). The capitalization of *Er* and *Sie* in the German example indicates that they are conceived of as nouns, not as pronouns, though lower case *er* and *sie* are also attested, which may reflect uncertainty about their grammatical status. For Dutch, *hij* and *zij* are listed as nouns in the authoritative *Van Dale* dictionary, even with attested plural forms. They are thus a clear example of the development from grammatical element to lexical element.

an explanation for the preponderance of grammaticalization changes as compared to degrammaticalization changes.

### 2.7.2 *A psycholinguistic approach*

In a recent paper, Rosenbach and Jäger (forthcoming) adopt an entirely novel approach, which is to link findings about directional tendencies in grammaticalization studies to the psycholinguistic concept of 'priming'. Priming is defined as '"preactivation" in the sense that the previous use of a certain linguistic element will affect (usually in the sense of facilitating) the subsequent use of the same or a sufficiently similar element (the "target")'. Priming has been shown to operate on all linguistic levels (phonological, morphological, lexical, syntactic). For example, subjects are more likely to mention a violin when they have been presented with a picture of a guitar than if they had seen a picture of a table. To illustrate the connection between priming and unidirectionality, Rosenbach and Jäger cite an interesting study by Boroditsky (2000) which showed that spatial expressions may prime temporal expressions, but not vice versa. In a first experiment, the subjects got one of two types of spatial primes, an 'ego-moving prime' (e.g. *the dark can is in front of me*), or an 'object-moving prime' (e.g. *the light widget is in front of the dark widget*). They subsequently had to interpret the ambiguous temporal expression *Next Wednesday's meeting has been moved forward two days.* Boroditsky found that subjects were more likely to think that the meeting had been moved to Friday when they had been presented with the ego-moving prime (in 73.3 per cent of all cases), while they were more likely to think that the meeting had been moved to Monday when they had been presented with an object-moving prime (in 69.2 per cent of all cases). In a second set of experiments, in which the subjects were presented with temporal primes after which they had to interpret ambiguous spatial expressions, no significant correlations were found. On the basis of Boroditsky's study, Rosenbach and Jäger conclude the following:

> First, the metaphorical mapping from space to time is indeed psychologically real . . . , and second, . . . priming between space and time is asymmetric, with only spatial expressions priming temporal interpretations but not vice versa.

In the remainder of their paper Rosenbach and Jäger address the question of how asymmetric priming effects can account for long-term diachronic effects. Adopting a usage-based approach to language acquisition and change they argue, first, that grammar may continue to change in adult life (*contra* the generative view that grammar becomes fixed during childhood language acquisition; see section 2.7.3), and secondly, that priming effects may persist and even have a cumulative effect. In other words, when language users are repeatedly presented with the same prime they may develop a preference for a certain structure,[59] and the new structure may even become entrenched in the speaker's grammar. Consequently, 'what appears as diachronic trajectories of unidirectional change is ultimately decomposable into atomic steps of asymmetric priming in language use'. Although the authors concede that this still does not *explain* unidirectionality (because it is not clear why there are priming asymmetries in the first place), it does 'push the explanation considerably back to the cognitive domain'. Rosenbach and Jäger's approach has the advantage of being empirically testable with present-day speakers:

> Under the uniformitarian assumption that 'the same principles governing the world (=domain of inquiry) were the same in the past as they are now' (Lass 1997: 25) we may assume that whatever psycholinguistic mechanisms we can find to be operating today, must also have been operating in the past... Thus, investigating psycholinguistic mechanisms with present-day speakers may shed light on processes guiding language change. Under this view it is then possible to test *any* unidirectional changes that have been put forward in the literature... with respect to asymmetric priming. Very generally, the prediction is that in any reported case of change, where the development goes unidirectionally from *A* to *B*, *A* should prime *B*, but not vice versa.[60]

To my mind, Rosenbach and Jäger's novel line of research is one definitely worth exploring, because it leads to falsifiable hypotheses, where the other accounts mentioned in this section are essentially intuitive. Theirs is therefore the most promising approach to account for unidirectional preferences on all linguistic levels in the future.

### 2.7.3 *Generative approaches*

Grammaticalization studies arose out of the functionalist tradition, and it is therefore not surprising that, until quite recently, the subject was largely ignored in generative linguistics. And since grammaticalization did become noticed in generative linguistics, the two have long had 'an uneasy relationship', as van Gelderen (2004: 8) aptly summarizes. The uneasiness is undoubtedly due to theoretical premises that at first glance seem irreconcilable.

[59] This effect is reflected by the well-known fact that grammaticality judgements may become increasingly positive after repeated exposure to the same structure.

[60] Nevertheless, it is not entirely inconceivable that the uniformitarian principle ceases to work, for instance when TIME > SPACE metaphors become increasingly common (see section 2.6.1).

The principal difference between generative linguistics and functional linguistics may be characterized as follows:

> One orientation [generative linguistics] sees as a central task for linguists characterizing the formal relationships among grammatical elements independently of any characterization of the semantic and pragmatic properties of those elements. The other orientation [functional linguistics] rejects that task on the grounds that the function of conveying meaning (in its broadest sense) has so affected grammatical form that it is senseless to compartmentalize it. (Newmeyer 1998: 7)

Generativist and functionalist views on language change are likewise fundamentally different. Generative linguists traditionally conceive of language change as an abrupt phenomenon, since in their view grammars can only change when they are acquired by children, whereas functional linguists think of change as a gradual process. Another major difference between the two approaches is that functional linguists consider grammaticalization as both a synchronic and a diachronic phenomenon (with strong emphasis on the latter), whereas to generative linguists it is purely synchronic:

> Because each new learner constructs its own grammar, it is inconceivable that grammaticalization should be a diachronic process. While there is continuity in the language output, each new grammar acquired by speakers will simply assign the best-fitting status to the material encountered in the language environment. (van Kemenade 1999: 1004)[61]

It seems to me, however, that generativists and functionalists use the term 'diachrony' for different things. In the functionalist tradition, diachrony refers to a generalization over successive generations of speakers, whereas generative linguists generally view language change as a function of language acquisition, which of course is inherently synchronic. Van Kemenade (1999: 1004) makes a similar point when she writes that 'movement

[61] This position is not unique to generative linguistics, however. It also plays a central role in the writings of Janda (e.g. 2001: 267): 'Whether during youthful acquisition or adult use of language, speakers (or signers) in a given age-group never have access to the grammar of any preceding generation, and so they cannot know – either consciously or unconsciously – if the global status that earlier speakers (and signers) assigned to a particular linguistic element (= an individual unit or a multipartite construction) was lexical or grammatical, much less the precise extent to which it was either of these. As a result, there can be no cognitive restrictions which prevent a later speaker (or signer) from analyzing a given linguistic item as more lexical – or at least less grammatical – than the corresponding item was for earlier speakers (or signers), and so there can be no cross-generational "diachronic constraints" prohibiting such analyses.' On the basis of psycholinguistic research, however, Rosenbach and Jäger (forthcoming) argue *contra* Janda that speakers do follow 'natural' pathways even though they are not aware of it (see further section 2.7.2 for Rosenbach and Jäger's approach).

of a lexical head to a functional head position [which is the formalist rephrasing of grammaticalization; see below] represents the synchronic instantiation of what grammaticalization theorists regard as a diachronic process'.

Grammaticalization phenomena, in particular, are difficult to accommodate within a generativist framework of language change, because they are indicative of directional tendencies. The existence of such tendencies has long been denied in the influential work of Lightfoot (1979, 1999,[62] 2002), as is evidenced by the following passage:

> Grammaticalization, challenging as a PHENOMENON, is not an explanatory force. We have no well-founded basis for claiming that languages or grammars change in one direction but not in another, no basis for postulating algorithms mapping one kind of grammar onto another kind... Recall again that we have historical records for only a tiny fraction of language history and any inductive generalizations are perilous. (Lightfoot 2002: 126f.)

From earlier generative work such as Lighfoot's, then, one might gain the impression that the generative framework and grammaticalization phenomena were mutually exclusive and never the twain would meet, but since the mid-1990s, other generative linguists have started to acknowledge the empirical evidence for directional tendencies, which they attempted to reconcile with the generative view of language change as 'a random "walk" through the space of possible parameter settings' (Battye and Roberts 1995: 11).

Probably the best-known, and most detailed, generative approach to grammaticalization has been developed by Roberts and Roussou (1999, 2003). In their 2003 monograph, Roberts and Roussou note that the paradox that Chomskyan linguistics has to deal with is that parameter change cannot follow pathways, whereas grammaticalization research has unequivocally shown that such pathways exist. One option to deal with this paradox, Roberts and Roussou argue, is to deny that grammaticalization exists, but this goes against the empirical evidence. A second option is to reconcile 'the clear evidence for pathways of change at the descriptive level with the fact that an explanatory account of change must involve parameter change' (Roberts and Roussou 2003: 4).

Adopting the traditional generative view on language change, Roberts and Roussou (2003: 9ff.) argue that language change is the result of changes in

[62] Not surprisingly, Lightfoot's provocative views on language change have triggered fierce response from functionalists (see for instance Haspelmath 1999b).

parameter settings during language acquisition. Parameter settings are said to be triggered by 'cues' – for instance, the presence of no more than one constituent preceding the finite verb serves as the trigger for the learner that the language in question is verb-second (V2).

A change in the learner's grammar may occur when the trigger for a particular parameter value has become ambiguous. An example of a change in trigger experience is loss of inflectional morphology (van Kemenade 1999: 1004ff.). For example, when mood was still inflectionally realized in English, both main verbs and verbs which were later to become auxiliaries were moved to the functional head position Mood. But once inflectional mood was lost, the auxiliaries came to be base-generated in the functional Mood position, whereas main verbs became fixed as the head of a VP. However, such a line of reasoning is in peril of becoming circular, as Roberts and Roussou themselves (2003: 14) observe. Returning to the case of V2 just mentioned, it has been claimed that English lost this constraint because it lost the possibility of verb-movement to second position, as a result of which V2 is no longer cued. Obviously, this does not explain why this type of verb-movement was lost in the first place. I will return to this problem below.

Grammaticalization, in Roberts and Roussou's work, is defined as 'upward reanalysis', where a specific lexical item or subclass of lexical items is reanalysed as a functional head.[63] This reanalysis may be successive (corresponding to grammaticalization paths involving several stages; Roberts and Roussou 2003: 194, 202).[64] In generative terms, this means that the item is merged instead of moved, as in the (oversimplified) representations in (48) and (49) (adapted from Roberts and Roussou 2003: 16). Since merge is preferred over move, (48) (with no movement) is the unmarked option. This implies that movement as in (49) must be 'robustly triggered', or else the parameter will be set to yield the simpler structure in (48).[65]

[63] As in traditional grammar, Roberts and Roussou distinguish between lexical categories and grammatical categories, but they differ slightly in their classification of them (for instance, they regard 'some' prepositions as lexical). They furthermore argue that functional categories must be syntactically realized in some way, but that they need not be overtly expressed (Roberts and Roussou 2003: 18ff.).

[64] Also, epistemic modals are 'higher' in a syntactic tree than deontic ones (van Gelderen 2004: 157).

[65] For a slightly different generative account see van Gelderen (2004), who identifies two 'principles of economy' which, according to her, are 'motivating forces' in linguistic change, including grammaticalization. These two principles are the following (Van Gelderen 2004: 11f.): (i) HEAD PREFERENCE OR SPEC TO HEAD PRINCIPLE 'Be a head, rather than a phrase', and (ii) LATE MERGE PRINCIPLE 'Merge as late as possible'. These principles work both in the grammars of speakers and in language acquisition but, crucially, they do not always guide language change, since what is economical for the speaker may not be economical for the hearer (van Gelderen 2004: 12, following Jespersen 1921: 261ff.).

(48) 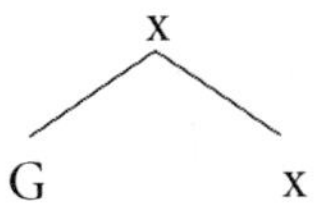

(Merge)

(49) 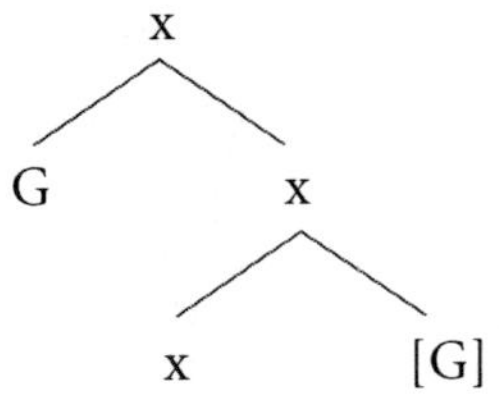

(Move)

In order to account for directional tendencies, Roberts and Roussou suggest that these are linked to the nature of the language acquirer, which is seen as 'computationally conservative', with a 'built-in preference for relatively simple representations' (Roberts and Roussou 1999: 1020). In order to refine this line of reasoning, Roberts and Roussou (2003: 210ff.) invoke the traditional notion of markedness. Presuming that a functional head is associated with a feature F, which may or may not have PF-realization, they arrive at the following hierarchy (where the diacritic '*' means that the feature must have PF-realization, and '>' means 'more marked than'):

(50) $F^{*}_{\text{Move/Merge}} > F^{*}_{\text{Move}} > F^{*}_{\text{Merge}} > F$

However, as Roberts and Roussou concede (p. 211f.), this markedness hierarchy cannot account for morphologization (e.g. their own example of the Romance future, where auxiliary HAVE becomes cliticized to the main verb) since in their model, this would be an example of $F^{*}_{\text{Merge}} > F^{*}_{\text{Merge/Move}}$. In other words, their approach may account for primary grammaticalization, but not for secondary grammaticalization (see Faarlund 2007: 75 for similar criticism). For example, in his discussion of the grammaticalization of the Swedish subordinators *om* and *ifall* (both meaning 'if, when'), Rosenkvist (2004: 216) argues that upward reanalysis is not an adequate description of the syntactic change, because here the PP was reanalysed as a CP, which is a different kind of change (see section 2.6.1 for a brief summary of the history of *om* and *ifall*). A related problem may be noted for degrammaticalization where, in line with Roberts and Roussou's approach, we would expect 'downward reanalysis', but this is not the case for secondary degrammaticalization. For instance, when the

Norwegian enclitic infinitival marker degrammaticalized into a free morpheme (see section 6.3.2), it moved from V to C, which amounts to upward reanalysis (Faarlund 2007: 76).

Not surprisingly, the generative approach has been critically reviewed by functionalists. For example, Haspelmath (1999a: 1053) notes that Roberts and Roussou's concept of upward movement merely shows how grammaticalization can be understood in their own framework, without offering an explanation for directional tendencies. According to Haspelmath, such tendencies can only be explained on a performance-based account, as opposed to Roberts and Roussou's competence-based account (see section 2.7.1 for Haspelmath's 'invisible hand' model).

As I see it, there are three fundamental problems with the generative approach to grammaticalization. First, as Fischer (2004: 728) correctly points out, one cannot explain language change on the basis of an abstraction (i.e. innate universal grammar), when there is no theory-independent evidence for how such a grammar is structured. According to Fischer, one potential source of such independent evidence is neurolinguistic research, but so far this has not yielded firm support for an innate grammar in the generativist sense. Thus, as long as universal grammar remains a theoretical construct, it cannot help explain grammar change (p. 730).

The second problem with the generative approach is that it does not deal with the question of *why* the trigger changes (Andersen 2005: 166; Traugott 2002: 20f.):[66]

> To say on the 'formal' (generative) side of the debate that all one needs in order to explain language change is: '(a) an account of how trigger experiences have shifted and (b) a theory of language acquisition that matches PLD (primary linguistic data) with grammars in a deterministic way' (Lightfoot 1999: 225) simply puts the explanation off. WHY does the trigger change?... On [the generative] view, language change is the result of innovation in the individual compared to some other, older individual... In this scenario, the individual is a processor of systems, largely passive, a logic machine, a 'language acquisition device',[67] presumably devoid of personal differences or preferences. (Traugott 2002: 20f.)

[66] According to Jan-Wouter Zwart (p.c.) this is no valid criticism of generative theorizing because generative linguistics is about competence, not performance. It is thus not the case that generative linguists deny the existence of variation in adult performance, but it is simply something that falls outside of the scope of their framework. Nevertheless, I think it is a valid point of critique of a Roberts and Roussou-style account of unidirectionality, because an explanation which rests solely on competence can only be a partial explanation at best.

[67] Indeed, Roberts and Roussou (1999: 1020) define the language learner, i.e. the child, as a 'parameter-setting device'.

This problem originates in the generativist emphasis on L1-acquisition as the only locus of change.[68] But if a trigger becomes 'obscure', this must be due to changes in adult grammar. A usage-based approach is better equipped to account for changes in adult performance. The question of whether changes in adult performance reflect changes in adult competence is trivial, because when a child is exposed to adult output, she has no way of knowing whether a given structure was acquired by the adult in childhood or in later life.

The third and final problem with the generativist view of language change as the result of abrupt parameter resettings is that it fails to account for (diachronic) gradualness and (synchronic) gradience:[69]

> For those of us who study language change, the central challenge for a restrictive theory of grammar that seeks to identify discrete parametric changes is precisely that various constructions can exist for hundreds of years without being reanalyzed or analogized into some positive parameter. Instead, they may thrive in an in-between state, like the quasi-modals [*promise* and *threaten*], sharing some properties of full raising verbs and some of full auxiliaries, without resolution of their gradient status. (Traugott 1997b: 202)

To conclude, generative approaches to unidirectionality are essentially theory-internal reformulations of observed diachronic pathways and their directional preferences. Because a generative view of language acquisition and change cannot accommodate changes that occur in actual language use, it fails to account for both variation (a *sine qua non* for change) and gradience (the observation that two or more stages of a grammaticalization chain can coexist in the grammars of several generations of speakers).[70] The forte of generative linguistics lies in its potential to formalize changes in the grammar, especially on the level of syntax, whereas usage-based approaches provide an adequate means to capture the rise of variation (or trigger change, in generativist terms). In a sense, then, the two approaches are complementary rather than orthogonal.

### 2.7.4 *Other formal explanations*

Within the functionalist tradition, linguists have not only sought explanations for directional tendencies in language usage (see section 2.7.1), but

[68] See also Croft (2000: 44ff.) for a critical discussion of child-based theories of language change.

[69] The only way of dealing with gradience from a generative point of view is to stipulate multiple grammars for individual speakers. In effect, this implies that all speakers must be multilingual, because gradience is typical of entire speech communities.

[70] The only issue upon which some formalists seem to agree with functionalists is that in the very beginning, language must have arisen out of discourse. On this view, word order was initially determined by pragmatic factors, before syntax became innate and autonomous (see Fischer in prep. for discussion and references).

they have also been concerned with formal properties of grammaticalizing items. From a formal point of view, directional preferences are essentially due to the fact that grammaticalization generally involves attrition on several linguistic levels, as correctly observed by Lehmann (2004: 181): 'One important aspect of an explanation is that grammaticalization involves loss of information. Pieces of information can go nowhere, but they cannot come from nowhere.'[71] Langacker (1977: 106f.) put it as follows:

It would not be entirely inappropriate to regard languages in their diachronic aspect as gigantic expression-compacting machines. They require as input a continuous flow of creatively produced expressions formed by lexical innovation, by lexically and grammatically regular periphrasis, and by the figurative use of lexical or periphrastic locutions. The machine does whatever it can to wear down the expressions fed into it. It fades metaphors by standardizing them and using them over and over again. It attacks expressions of all kinds by phonetic erosion. It bleaches lexical items of most of their semantic content and forces them into service as grammatical markers. It chips away at the boundaries between elements and crushes them together into smaller units. The machine has a voracious appetite. Only the assiduous efforts of speakers – who salvage what they can from its output and recycle it by using their creative energies to fashion a steady flow of new expressions to feed back in – keep the whole thing going.

For semantic change, Givón (1975: 96) presents the following account:

There are a number of reasons why such a process [of semantic enrichment] should be extremely rare. To begin with, when a verb loses much of its semantic contents and becomes a case marker, in due time it also loses much of its phonological material, becomes a bound affix and eventually becomes completely *eroded* into zero. It is thus unlikely that a more crucial portion of the information contents of the utterance – i.e., the semantic contents of a verb – will be entrusted to such a reduced morpheme. Further, while the process of change through depletion is a *predictable* change in language, its opposite – enrichment or addition – is not. (emphasis original)

And according to Croft (2000: 161f.), pragmatic inference offers a general explanation for semantic unidirectionality:

[T]he contextual property is usually entailed by the inherent property but not vice versa... For example, allative motion with a human subject usually entails intention, but not vice versa (many intended actions do not imply directed motion on the part of the intender).

[71] This is reminiscent of a Texan joke from the 1980s quoted in Hopper (1994: 31): '"What's the fastest way to become a millionaire in Houston?" The answer was: "Start out as a billionaire".' Similarly, Hopper argues, the fastest way for a phoneme to arise would be to start out as a morpheme.

One of the most straightforward observations is that grammaticalization gives rise to increasing frequency, which in turn feeds further grammaticalization (as advocated in particular by Bybee; see e.g. Bybee 2003). For frequency is not only the result of grammaticalization, but also 'a primary contributor to the process' (Bybee 2003: 602). This is evident in semantic generalization or bleaching, which goes hand in hand with an increasing number of contexts in which it can occur. This increase in frequency, then, may lead to further bleaching, since 'a stimulus loses its impact if it occurs very frequently' (p. 605). As regards phonological change, too, it is well known that frequent items tend to change more rapidly than do low frequency items (p. 615).

Also at the level of morphology it is not difficult to see why morphologization is more common than its reverse, as I have argued in an earlier paper:

> Since inflectional endings are as grammaticalized as affixes can get, they are the most specialized of grammatical items. Following Lehmann's (1985 and 1995 [1982]) parameters of grammaticalization, this implies that they have little phonological substance, are extensively desemanticized (i.e. have no concrete meaning), form part of a small, tightly integrated paradigm and are obligatory in highly specific morphosyntactic contexts. In addition, they cannot modify large syntactic units, only words or stems, and they occupy a fixed morphological position. These properties make them very unlikely candidates for lexicalization (in contrast with derivational suffixes such as *ism*). What is more, it will be obvious that inflectional suffixes have little room for change even within their own constructions... To conclude, affixal degrammaticalization is admittedly rare, but in case of favourable circumstances, such as some kind of internal *Systemstörung* (Plank 1995) and a possibility of morphosyntactic reanalysis, it is by no means impossible. (Norde 2002: 61)

Lass (1997: 295ff.) conceives of grammaticalization as movement towards a 'sink', each stage of which is irreversible in principle. This sink is a bound morpheme, and 'once this stage is reached, there is generally no way of emerging from it' (Lass 1997: 296). Lass does allow for exceptions (e.g. the s-genitive discussed in 5.3), which prove the rule in his view, but he also notes that it requires 'a rather special kick' or 'some kind of external "energy"' to get anything out of the sink (Lass 1997: 297).

In a similar vein, Fortson (2003: 657) and Willis (2007: 303) observe that the target categories of degrammaticalization – nouns and verbs – typically inflect, which implies that in order for a grammatical element to degrammaticalize into a major lexical category it has to have a form which can plausibly be reanalysed as an inflected form. Needless to say, chances of such a reanalysis are inversely proportional to the number of inflections in a given language.

The target categories of grammaticalization, by contrast, such as prepositions, pronouns, or conjunctions, are typically uninflected, which means that there are no morphological restrictions for grammaticalizing items. In addition, 'closed classes are, by definition, unproductive and generally do not contain a great number of members' (van Pottelberge 2005: 40).

For all these reasons, obsolescent inflectional categories are usually replaced by periphrastic constructions (cf. section 2.2.2) rather than by reinforcing the ailing affixes:

> Inflections, being united to the stem or root in a single phonological word, are precisely those parts of grammar which are under greatest threat from the erosive force of sound change. Periphrases, on the other hand, are clearly motivated in a syntactic sense, and may therefore serve to restore the semiotic balance. (Vincent 1987: 253)

In sum, every counterdirectional step on the cline encounters a number of different difficulties. Indeed, the very term 'cline' (see section 2.2.1) as a metaphor for grammaticalization change implies that grammaticalization proceeds easily, whereas degrammaticalization, 'up the slope' as it were, would be a Sisyphean labour. Degrammaticalization from affix to clitic is difficult because affixes are both strongly desemanticized and heavily reduced, with little room for change within the constructions in which they appear. And once an affix succeeds in doing that, and even decliticizes at a later stage, it faces a new series of hurdles. For the shift from function word to content item, too, is severely restricted because in many languages, content items such as nouns and verbs typically inflect, which means that degrammaticalization into a major lexical category requires that the gram is formally identical to an inflected form of such a category, and naturally, chances that all of this will happen are really very low.

## 2.8 Summary

In the introduction to this chapter, we saw that unidirectionality is a common theme in the writings of both grammaticalizationists and grammaticalization critics. At one extreme, unidirectionality has been claimed to be a constraint on possible changes, whereas at the other extreme, counterexamples have been over-emphasized in attempts to play down the predominance of grammaticalization changes. To my mind, the only sensible way to evaluate such conflicting views starts with a fine-grained examination of unidirectionality, or rather, directional preferences in language change. I have been arguing that irreversibility is only relevant at the type level, for counterdirectional change is not a mirror-image reversal to an earlier state of affairs, but always results in a novel gram or structure (I will return to the concept of 'novelty' in section 3.4). Another important observation is that grams can arise without a prior lexical history, as is evidenced by so-called lateral shifts and alternative sources of bound morphemes (e.g. morphological rebracketing).

Since both grammaticalization and degrammaticalization are composite changes, the directionality of each of their primitive changes must be examined in its own right (not necessarily as part of a (de)grammaticalization change). It turned out that all primitive changes have an unmarked direction, though directional tendencies are stronger in some changes than in others. Semantic and morphological changes, in particular, appear to have a strong preference for one direction (towards bleaching and bonding respectively). Taken together, the preferred directions of the primitive changes involved may account for the observation that grammaticalization is far more common than degrammaticalization.

Unidirectionality has been the focus of linguists from various theoretical persuasions, and hence explanations range from the purely language-internal (generative approaches) to the purely language-external (usage-based approaches). Although there are still some loose ends, a plausible explanation of directional preferences would run along these lines: since grammaticalization typically involves attrition on all levels, grams (particularly affixes) have little potential to gain substance on any of these levels. For instance, once the semantics of a gram have been substantially bleached, little semantic substance remains from which to infer new meanings or functions. This leaves the question of why attrition is so common in the first place, and this is most appropriately explained, I think, as a usage-based phenomenon, i.e. as a speaker strategy to save effort. In addition, psycholinguistic research has shown that directional preferences (e.g. SPACE > TIME metaphors) correspond to asymmetries in priming. Generative accounts of unidirectionality, finally, may be useful as a means of formalizing changes but offer no explanations of them.

I will conclude this chapter with some notes on unidirectionality and uniformitarianism. If unidirectionality were deterministic and concerned language change in general, we would expect that languages become more and more grammaticalized (Moreno Cabrera 1998: 224), and that all grammatical items are ultimately lexical (Lass 1997: 268n.; 2000:216). This would then violate the uniformitarian principle,[72] because such a view would

[72] This is a general principle in science, which basically says that the same physical laws apply in the entire universe, at all times. It was introduced into linguistics by the Neogrammarians, to postulate that ancient languages were not essentially different from modern ones.

presuppose that all languages must have been isolating at their earliest stages. But for this there is no evidence, quite the contrary: 'no period for which we have attested linguistic data, not even any data reconstructable by standard methods . . . shows anything other than roughly the current distribution of isolating, agglutinative, and inflectional/fusional languages' (Lass 2000: 216; see also Lightfoot 2002: 127 for a similar claim). What is more, in well-studied language families such as Indo-European, Uralic, Dravidian, Semitic, the vast majority of bound morphemes cannot be traced back to some lexical source (Lass 2000: 217). Hopper and Traugott (2003: 132), however, do not share Lass's concerns. They maintain their original claim (Hopper and Traugott 1993: 128f.) that there is no evidence that grammatical markers arise full-fledged, without prior lexical history. In their view, this has no bearing on the uniformitarian principle, because language evolution proceeded gradually, so an ultimate proto-stage cannot be established anyway. The same view is expressed in Haspelmath (2004: 25), who notes that 'since language has been around for tens of thousands of years and we know next to nothing about its origin, we really do not have to worry about the consequences of diachronic universals for prehistory'.

# 3

# Defining degrammaticalization

## 3.1 Introduction

Up until not so long ago, the title of this chapter would have been a contradiction in terms. As we have seen in Chapter 1, degrammaticalization has long been held to be non-existent or too infrequent and irregular to be of any serious concern. As a consequence, it is often not properly defined, and degrammaticalization changes were seen as unclassifiable. The following passages are typical reflections of this view:

> Whereas 'grammaticalization' refers to a process that is cross-linguistically common and regular, and can be described in a principled way…, this does not apply to the phenomena subsumed under the label degrammaticalization. Furthermore, even if one were to restrict the use of the term to one [of] its many uses, there remains the following problem: The term suggests directionality, e.g. from more grammatical to less grammatical forms. However, as we saw above, none of the processes underlying degrammaticalization, be it lexicalization, euphemism, exaptation, or adaptation, clearly exhibits any directionality. Furthermore…these processes do not seem to share any common denominator. Thus, it would seem that this term is not of much help for describing or understanding grammatical change, except for referring to the epiphenomenal effect some of the processes have in specific situations. (Heine 2003a: 175)
>
> If one is interested in generalizations rather than arbitrary facts, one must put aside the exceptions, because unless they can be subsumed under some further generalization, they cannot be explained. (Haspelmath 2004: 23)

It seems to me, however, that ignoring exceptions would make grammaticalization studies (or indeed historical linguistics in general) potentially defective, because an untimely dismissal of unwelcome evidence may lead to false generalizations, which in turn may form the basis of erroneous reconstructions (see section 1.6.4).[1] For instance, in the case of the rise of the English s-genitive

[1] Fischer (2000: 153) makes a similar point: 'I also think that grammaticalisation processes themselves can only be discovered with hindsight, which means that if we have a preconceived notion of what grammaticalisation is, we will indeed discover mainly those processes that have run a full or "fullish" course, and we will not realise that there may be many cases where the path of grammaticalisation proceeded differently. So it may only seem that grammaticalisation usually follows the same channel.'

(see 5.3.3) one might be tempted to accept Janda's (1980) theory that it arose as a reanalysis of the suffix *-es* as the possessive pronoun *his*. This is indeed what Lehmann (1995 [1982]: 19) did, simply because in his view the alternative, the 'upgrading' from affix to clitic, is ruled out by a principle of unidirectionality. If one regards the unidirectionality hypothesis as a universal constraint on possible language change (see section 2.1), one is in danger of taking no notice of developments in the opposite direction. Even if such developments are rare, they are valuable, as Fischer and Rosenbach (2000: 21) point out:

> [T]he role of counter-examples is to modify the hypothesis in such a way that it can also account for these hitherto unpredicted cases... In the Popperian sense of scientific research we should always look for counterexamples and not for cases which conform to our hypotheses.

Another way of dealing with unwelcome counterexamples to unidirectionality has been to say that they are not instances of degrammaticalization, but 'really something else'. I find it hard to see what is gained by such a line of reasoning, and fully agree with Newmeyer when he writes:

> Occasionally, one reads about certain upgradings not really counting as counterexamples to unidirectionality because they are not genuine cases of 'grammaticalization reversing itself'. Rather, they are said to manifest some other process, such as, say 'lexicalization'. My feeling is that attributing upgradings to some process distinct from the inverse of grammaticalization is tantamount to covertly building unidirectionality into the definition of grammaticalization. Certainly it would have the effect of ruling out the great majority of potential counterexamples to unidirectionality. (Newmeyer 1998: 363)

The main aim of this chapter, then, will be to examine whether it is possible to define and classify degrammaticalization. In order to do so, I will first provide a *Forschungsgeschichte* of degrammaticalization terminology, considering both the alternative terms 'regrammaticalization' and 'antigrammaticalization' (section 3.2), and other changes with which degrammaticalization has frequently been mixed up (3.3). In the subsequent section, I will discuss the primary defining characteristics of degrammaticalization: counterdirectionality, novelty, lack of cross-linguistic replication, and the absence of degrammaticalization chains. Section 3.5 is concerned with a model to classify degrammaticalization changes, based on Lehmann's 'parameters of grammaticalization' and Andersen's 'levels of observation'.

## 3.2 Regrammaticalization and antigrammaticalization

Two terms are sometimes used as synonyms, or rather hyponyms, of degrammaticalization. The first, 'regrammaticalization', was introduced by Greenberg

(1991: 301) for a shift in function of heavily grammaticalized grams. Greenberg was thus one of the first to demonstrate that the ultimate stage in grammaticalization need not be loss. Among the great many examples discussed by Greenberg is Chibchan-Paezan[2] **-kwa* (Greenberg 1991: 309f.). Comparative evidence suggests that this was originally a noun denoting a specific round object (it still is in e.g. Terraba *gwa* 'egg' or Cuna *kwa-kwa* 'nut'). In many Chibchan languages, this noun grammaticalized into a suffix which functions as a classifier for round objects, e.g. Chibchan proper *up-kwa* 'eye' or *pihi-gwa* 'hole', from where it spread to other nouns, e.g. *kip-kwa* 'place'. In some languages, it subsequently 'regrammaticalized' into other functions. In Cuna, for example, it serves to form singulatives from collectives, e.g. *win-kwa* 'a single bead' (from *wini* 'beads'), whereas in Millcayak it functions as a nominalizer, e.g. *cherigwe* 'gift' (from *cheri* 'to give').

Although regrammaticalization changes are sometimes cited as potential counterexamples to grammaticalization (e.g. in Heine, Claudi, and Hünnemeyer 1991: 4; Hopper and Traugott 2003: 135), they differ from degrammaticalization in that the grams do not become 'less grammatical'. Instead, they substitute one grammatical function for another, and for this reason they are more appropriately regarded as instances of lateral shift (see section 2.4).

The second term, 'antigrammaticalization', has been proposed by Haspelmath (2004) to replace the term degrammaticalization. Haspelmath has coined this new term to separate true exceptions to unidirectionality from other changes that have been labeled degrammaticalization (see section 3.3). The term is intended to cover 'any type of change that goes against the general direction of grammaticalization (i.e. discourse > syntax > morphology).' (Haspelmath 2004: 28). His definition of antigrammaticalization runs as follows:

> By [antigrammaticalization] I mean a change that leads from the endpoint to the starting point of a potential grammaticalization and also shows the same intermediate stages. For instance, a change from a case suffix to a free postposition with the intermediate stage of a postpositional clitic would be an antigrammaticalization. This implies that the change occurs in a construction which can be seen as preserving its identity before and after the change, as in grammaticalization, where we also have a gradual change of the properties of a construction, but we do not get a new construction. (Haspelmath 2004: 27f.)

According to Haspelmath, the following changes qualify as antigrammaticalization (p. 29):[3]

[2] Chibchan-Paezan is a subbranch of Chibchan, a family of Native American languages spoken in (among others) Colombia and Central America.

[3] See Chapters 5 and 6 for discussion of these cases.

(1) a. English and Mainland Scandinavian genitive suffix *-s* > clitic =*s*
b. Irish first person plural suffix *-muid* > independent pronoun *muid*
c. Japanese adverbial subordinator *-ga* 'although' > free linker *ga* 'but'
d. Saami abessive suffix **-ptaken* > clitic =*taga* > free postposition *taga*
e. Estonian question marker *-s* > =*es* > free particle *es*
f. English infinitive prefix *to-* > proclitic *to*
g. Modern Greek prefix *ksana-* 'again' > free adverb *ksana* 'again'
h. Latin rigid prefix *re-* 'again' > Italian flexible prefix *ri-* (e.g. *ridevo fare* 'I must do again')

What is striking about Haspelmath's shortlist is not merely that so few items seem to have made it to it, but in particular that, with the exception of (d), none of these cases meet Haspelmath's own definition of antigrammaticalization. For all changes except (d) involve only a single counterdirectional shift, not a series of gradual transitions with the same intermediate stages as observed in grammaticalization chains.

Judging from the examples rather than from the definition, Haspelmath's 'antigrammaticalization' covers secondary degrammaticalization only,[4] so it is not fully synonymous with 'degrammaticalization' as provisionally defined in section 1.3.2. Therefore, I will not use the term in the remainder of this book. Up until now, the term 'antigrammaticalization' has not been adopted into mainstream grammaticalization studies, and to my mind we may just as well stick to the term 'degrammaticalization', provided it is defined properly, a task to which I will turn in sections 3.4 and 3.5.

## 3.3 Terminological proliferation and confusion

The term 'degrammaticalization' has been used to refer to a strikingly heterogeneous group of changes. Unfortunately, this adds to the confusion commonly associated with the term and its rejection by some. One of the most exhaustive treatments of this terminological pandemonium is Heine (2003a), who lists the following 'definitions' of degrammaticalization:

(2) Uses of the term degrammaticalization (where L = lexical form, $G_1$ = grammatical form, $G_2$ = more grammatical form, $G_0$ = grammatical form which has no more grammatical meaning, and '>' = 'develops diachronically into'; Heine 2003a: 165)

[4] More precisely, seven of Haspelmath's examples concern debonding (see Chapter 6) with the exception of the s-genitive, which is considered a case of deinflectionalization in the present work (see Chapter 5).

| | | | | | |
|---|---|---|---|---|---|
| a. | | | $G_2$ | $>$ $G_0$ | Loss of grammatical meaning |
| b. | L | $<$ | $G_1$ | $<$ $G_2$ | Mirror image reversal |
| c. | L | $<$ | $G_1$, $G_2$ | | Lexicalization |
| d. | L | $<$ | $G_1$ | | Euphemism |
| e. | | | $G_1$ | $<$ $G_0$ ($G_2$) | Exaptation |
| f. | | | $G_1$ | $<$ $G_2$ | Adaptation |
| g. | | | $G_1$ | $<$ $G_2$ | Replacement |
| h. | (L) | $<$ | ($G_1$) | $<$ ($G_2$) | Upgrading |

Basically, it seems that three different phenomena have been mixed up in (2). In fact, only (a–c) have, as far as I can tell, been used as equivalents of degrammaticalization. The terms (c–g) are processes that *may* be involved in counterdirectional changes (but none of them are inherently counterdirectional) and (h) is simply a superordinate term for all counterdirectional changes (cf. Plank 2003 [2000]: 177). In the following sections, I will discuss the phenomena in (2) and argue why they should be distinguished from degrammaticalization proper.

### 3.3.1 *Loss of grammatical meaning*

Especially in earlier works, degrammaticalization is defined as the loss of grammatical meaning or function, resulting in 'empty morphs' (e.g. Heine, Claudi, and Hünnemeyer 1991: 26; Ramat 1992: 551ff.; Allen 1995: 5; Koch 1996: 241). Examples of such 'ghosts of old morphology' (Lass 1997: 307) are former derivational suffixes that are no longer recognizable as such and have fused with the stem, such as the Proto-Germanic suffix *-m* to form nouns from verbs, as in (Dutch / German / Swedish) *bloem* / *Blume* / *blomma* 'flower', *helm* / *Helm* / *hjälm* 'helmet', or *storm* / *Sturm* / *storm* 'storm'; cf. the (Modern) Dutch verbs *bloeien* 'to bloom', *helen* (originally) 'to cover' and *storen* 'to disturb'.

Another example of functional loss which has been termed 'degrammaticalization' concerns the suffix *-sc* in the Romance languages (Ramat 1992: 551ff.; Allen 1995). In Latin, some *sc*-verbs lent themselves to an inchoative interpretation (e.g. *crēscere* 'to come into existence', *nōscere* 'to get to know') and as a consequence, *-sc* became a productive suffix to derive inchoative verbs from nouns (*iuvenis* 'young man' > *iuvenēscere* 'to grow up'), or verbs (*calēre* 'to be warm' > *calēscere* 'to become warm'). All these verbs are intransitive, but in Late Latin some of them became transitive, such as *innōtēscere* 'to become known' > 'to make known' (Allen 1995: 4). This development continued in the Romance languages, for example in French where such verbs may be intransitive (*verdissent* '(they) become green'),[5] transitive (*blanchissent* '(they) whitewash') or both (*finissent* '(they) finish ([NP])'). Accordingly, the inchoative meaning became increasingly backgrounded, such that Ramat (1992: 552) argues for Italian *finisco* 'I finish' that *-isc-* has become part of the 1SG person ending (cf. e.g. 1PL *finiamo* 'we finish'). Thus, a derivational suffix marking inchoative became part of the (inflectional) conjugational system in Italian, marking the singular and the 3PL persons in the present indicative.

None of the examples given above will be regarded as degrammaticalization in this book. For as Heine (2003a: 165) correctly points out, loss of grammatical meaning is indicative of advanced grammaticalization, not degrammaticalization.

### 3.3.2 *Mirror image reversal*

A severe problem with the term *de*grammaticalization is that it seems to suggest that it is 'grammaticalization reversed'. When thus interpreted, one may expect degrammaticalization to be a process which can be described in terms of degrammaticalization chains, with grams stepwise moving 'up the cline', and with changes in content following changes in form:

> A good case of degrammaticalization would consequently be one in which, for instance, an infix first becomes a peripheral affix, this then becomes a free form, gaining more concrete semantic features and a few more phonological segments. All the while, the paradigm of forms with a similar distribution fills up by other items taking the same course, expanding into a larger class of more heterogeneous elements. In the further course of events, the degrammaticalized item joins the lexical (rather than grammatical) subclass of its category, passing, for instance, from an adposition to a relational noun, typically sprouting a case suffix that had not been there. The reverse of such a process is an everyday grammaticalization phenomenon. (Lehmann 2004: 170)

Such degrammaticalizations are yet to be discovered, but it seems most implausible that they will, for reasons I have discussed in section 2.7.4. In a thought-provoking contribution to a discussion on unidirectionality at *Linguist-list* in 1996, Östen Dahl puts it this way:

> I think grammaticalization is unidirectional in about the same sense as biological processes such as growth, maturation, and ageing are. As we grow up, we become taller; in old age, we may shrink a little. However, we would not expect a child to start becoming shorter and shorter and finally return to its mother's womb. Similarly,

[5] Third person plural forms are used because these, unlike the infinitive, still contain a vestige of the inchoative suffix (*-iss-*).

eyesight generally deteriorates with age, but myopic persons may actually become less so due to their eye lenses getting more rigid and compensating the myopia. In other words, the biological processes that take place during our lives sometimes give rise to contradictory results but there can be no doubt that they are basically irreversible. In the same way, we would not expect, say, that the French future tense endings would start separating from the verb, become auxiliaries and then end up as full verbs meaning 'to keep' (the presumed etymology of Latin *habere*, the source of the French future).

In other words, degrammaticalization is not the mirror image of grammaticalization in the sense that it cannot be the complete reverse of a grammaticalization chain, neither on the token nor on the type level.

### 3.3.3 *Lexicalization of function words and affixes*

The reason why lexicalization is so frequently seen as the 'opposite' of grammaticalization is rooted in the cline of grammaticality, in which grammar and lexicon are the two extreme poles which, as Douglas Lightfoot (2005: 586) aptly notes, suggests that the two are in opposition: 'The reasoning seems logical: if a single continuum exists which has "the lexical" at one end and "the grammatical" at the other, one could readily interpret movement along the cline toward "the grammatical" as grammaticalization, and toward "the lexical" as lexicalization.'[6]

As I have explained in section 1.3.3, I use a broad definition of lexicalization in this work, encompassing most changes that result in new lexemes, with the exception of regular word formation. On this view, lexicalization is essentially non-directional. Any linguistic material may serve as its input – phrases such as *forget-me-not*, *has-been*; acronyms such as *sms* (*short message service*), which can be used both as a verb (*to sms*, *she smses*, etc.) and as a noun (*an sms*, *smses*); and parts of words, sometimes irrespective of morpheme boundaries, as in the well-known *burger* from *hamburger* (originally a German derivation: *Hamburg-er* 'a Hamburg delicacy').

The only cases of lexicalization that need concern us here are those in which lexicalization has been interpreted as a synonym or subset of degrammaticalization (e.g. Anttila 1989: 151; Ramat 1992, 2001; Hopper and Traugott 1993: 127; Newmeyer 1998: 269f.; Brinton and Traugott 2005: 60; see van der Auwera 2002 for discussion). These are changes where a grammatical morpheme (e.g. an affix or a preposition) comes to be employed as a lexical item (primarily as a noun or verb). This is a common cross-linguistic

[6] See also Lehmann (2002), Himmelmann (2004), and Lindström (2004) for extensive arguments why lexicalization is not the opposite of grammaticalization.

strategy, rightly characterized as 'the recruitment of linguistic material to enrich the lexicon' (Hopper and Traugott 2003: 134). In fact, lexicalization is so common that Ramat (1992: 557) even suggests that Givón's well-known slogan 'Today's morphology is yesterday's syntax' might well be completed with 'and today's grammar may become tomorrow's lexicon'.

The best-known example of the lexicalization of an affix is *-ism* which can be used as a count noun in many languages, as a hypernym for 'ideology' (English *isms*, Dutch *ismen*, Swedish *ismer*, French *ismes*, etc.). This kind of change is clearly different from degrammaticalization for two reasons: (i) the suffix is taken out of its context to serve as a noun, whereas degrammaticalization is a context-internal change, and (ii) it is not the reverse of a grammaticalization change, because there is no evidence of nouns becoming a suffix 'in one bang'.

English examples of the lexicalization of function words include the shift from adverb to noun (*ups and downs*); adverb to verb (*up the price*) and conjunction to noun (*ifs and buts*). Other examples are lexicalizations of pronouns: from pronoun to verb (French *tutoyer* (< *tu*, *toi*), Swedish *dua* (< *du*), German *duzen* (< *du*), Dutch *jijen en jouen* (< *jij*, *jou*) 'to use the informal pronoun of address'); and from pronoun to noun (Dutch *Is het een hij of een zij?* / English *Is it a he or a she?*). It has been noted (Norde 2001a: 235n., Brinton and Traugott 2005: 38) that such conversions are more common in languages with little inflection, that is, where word-class membership is not formally marked, for example by means of specific derivation or word-class-specific inflections. Brinton and Traugott (ibid.) also claim that there is a distinction between zero conversions such as *to off* and derivational conversions such as German *duzen* 'to use the informal form of address', which is derived from the 2SG personal pronoun *du* by means of adding an infinitival suffix.[7] Whether English and German are truly distinct in this respect remains a matter of debate, however. The principal difference between these two languages is that the infinitive is formally marked in German, but not in English. This raises the question of whether it is the infinitive which is the result of derivation/conversion and forms the basis for inflection. One might also say that English has derivational conversion in a sentence such as *he offed himself* in the sense that the verbal form *offed* is derived by means of a tense inflection from the adverb *off*. Willis (2007: 275) makes a similar case to treat *to down* as a case of zero derivation, which is not essentially different from derivation such as German *duzen* with an overt derivational suffix. Beard

[7] Actually, *duzen* is more complex than that, because the infinitival suffix *-en* is attached to a stem *duz-*, with an epenthetic consonant. A better example would have been Swedish *du-a* you.2SG-INF 'to use the informal form of address'.

(1998: 62), too, argues against a distinction between conversion and derivation for two reasons. First, exactly the same semantic relations can be expressed by either conversion (*to wet, to empty*) or derivation (*to shorten, to normalize*). Secondly, conversion and derivation are in complementary distribution, in that stems which 'convert' are precluded from affixation (**to wetten*, **to emptify*), whereas those that can be affixed are precluded from conversion (**to short*, **to normal*). Beard therefore proposes to regard forms without derivational affixes as 'null-marked variants of the same derivation which is otherwise marked by a variety of affixes' (ibid).

The primary reason why conversions will not be considered degrammaticalization is that the function words are taken out of context. As Himmelmann (2004: 30) correctly observes, there is no fundamental difference between conversions between major word classes, for instance the shift from the noun *average* to a verb or adjective, and the conversion from function word to lexical item, for instance the use of the subordinator *if* as a noun.

To conclude, lexicalization of affixes or function words is a change which is fundamentally different from degrammaticalization as here defined. Nevertheless, it is important to bear in mind that some developments into lexical items *can* be characterized as degrammaticalizations. In cases where a lexical form emerges from a more grammatical form such as an adverb or modal auxiliary within the boundaries of its own construction it may be regarded as a degrammaticalization change (see the cases discussed in Chapter 4).

### 3.3.4 *Euphemism*

Euphemism is a common force behind the lexicalization of function words, as acknowledged by Heine:

> According to one of the main premises underlying this work, established in a number of previous works, grammaticalization is a unidirectional process... This is a strong claim, and a number of exceptions to the principle have been pointed out... The exact status of such exceptions remains to be investigated; for the time being, I will assume that certain specific forces can be held responsible for exceptions. Such forces will have to do, in particular, with the pragmatics of linguistic communication... and relate to psychological and sociological factors such as taboo strategies and euphemism, politeness, humbleness, paternalism, and the like. (Heine 1997: 152f.)[8]

For example, body parts (particularly private parts) may be euphemistically denoted by locative expressions (cf. French *derrière* / English *behind*).

[8] Note that this observation of Heine's appears incompatible with his claim (in this particular work and elsewhere), that the unidirectionality hypothesis predicts that if a given language uses the same or a similar word for both a body part and a spatial concept (e.g. an adverb), the latter must be derived from the former.

Subsequently, these expressions may even be conventionalized as the only word for that particular item. Similarly, the German modal auxiliary *müssen* 'to have to' (Janda 2001: 313) and its Dutch equivalent *moeten* can be used as a lexical verb meaning 'to relieve oneself', as in Dutch *ik moet* 'I need to go to the bathroom'.

Euphemism is not synonymous with degrammaticalization, but in a few cases it is relevant as a prompting factor. The clearest example is the development of the Pennsylvania German auxiliary *wotte* into a full lexical verb meaning 'to wish' (see section 4.2).

### 3.3.5 *Adaptation and exaptation*

Adaptation and exaptation are discussed in one section, since it is not quite clear to me that the two are really different. The term 'adaptation' basically refers to the fact that in all category changes (whether grammaticalization or degrammaticalization) linguistic items are adapted to the morphosyntactic layout of their new grammatical category. This is a rather trivial observation, which holds true for many kinds of morphosyntactic change and has no bearing on directionality claims. Hence it is not a synonym of degrammaticalization (and, apart from Heine 2003a, I know of no authors who have used the term in this sense). 'Exaptation' can be seen as a specific kind of adaptation,[9] and this is a type of change that has often been associated with degrammaticalization, even though exaptation is not necessarily counterdirectional.

Exaptation is a term borrowed by Roger Lass from evolutionary biology (see Lass 1990; 1997: 316ff.).[10] The term was coined by Gould and Vrba (1982) to refer to the co-optation, during evolution, of structures that originally served some other purpose. Well-known examples are the exaptation of feathers (originally a thermoregulatory device) for flight, or the exaptation of respiratory and digestive structures for sound production. In linguistics, exaptation may be defined as 'the use of relatively marginal grammatical material as more productive morphology with a different function' (Traugott 2004). According to Lass, exaptation is an 'opportunistic' change, which requires that a grammatical distinction is lost prior to the loss of the morphological material that used to code it. This results in 'junk morphology', which, in Lass's view, is crucial in language change:

[9] See also Willis (forthcoming) for discussion of the definitional overlap between exaptation and adaptation.

[10] Lass's concept is similar to Greenberg's (1991) 'regrammaticalization', discussed in section 3.2, Brinton and Stein's (1995) 'functional renewal' and Croft's (2000) 'hypoanalysis'.

[O]ne might say that 'junk makes the world go round'. Languages are constantly losing (relatively) 'deep' contrasts, but retaining the 'surface' material that used to underwrite them, and then (if they don't dump it), reusing it for new purposes, often at quite different structural levels. In fact junk is crucial, because if languages were 'perfect' systems they'd have no room for play, and hence no freedom to change. (Lass 1997: 317)

Basically, then, the junk morpheme has three options:

(i) it can be dumped entirely;
(ii) it can be kept as marginal garbage or nonfunctional / nonexpressive residue (suppletion, 'irregularity');
(iii) it can be kept, but instead of being relegated as in (ii), it can be used for something else, perhaps just as systematic (Lass 1990: 82).

Option (i) is probably most commonly attested, typical examples in the history of English being the loss of case marking on nouns and the loss of mood marking on verbs. Option (ii) is the maintenance of inflections in petrified expressions and suppletive forms, such as the plural *-en* in *oxen* or subjunctive *I were*. Option (iii) is linguistic exaptation.[11]

One of Lass's (1990: 88ff.) own examples concerns the exaptation of adjectival suffix *-e* in Afrikaans. In the rudimentary system that was seventeenth-century Dutch adjectival inflection, the contrast between common and neuter gender, the contrast between 'strong' (indefinite) and 'weak' (definite) inflection, and the contrast between singular and plural had all been retained, using no more than two suffixes: *-ø* and *-e*.[12] In Early Afrikaans, this system collapsed completely, with gender being the first to be given up. As a result, both forms of the adjective were used in similar contexts, in completely random distribution. This difference between the original stage (gender retained) and the genderless stage is illustrated in (3a) and (3b) respectively.

[11] Most examples of exaptation adduced in the literature concern bound morphemes, but Fanego (2004) has extended the term to include the Early Modern English gerund constructions such as *he may probably miss* **the seeing** *some curious productions of nature which will be observed by the slower and more accurate reader* (1742) in which a verbal gerund is preceded by *the*, which according to Fanego functions as a complementizer. Since this change (from definite article to complementizer) involves none of the primitive changes typical for grammaticalization, Fanego suggests that it is a case of exaptation.

[12] Naturally, with only two suffixes, the contrasts could not be preserved in all paradigms. In Modern Dutch (which has basically the same system), there is for instance no 'weak'/'strong' contrast with common nouns since both adjectives end in *-e*: *een grote kamer* 'a big room' (strong) / *de grote kamer* 'the big room' (weak). In fact, this contrast is only found in singular neuter nouns: *een groot-ø huis* 'a big house' (strong) / *het grote huis* 'the big house' (weak).

| | | | | | | | | | |
|---|---|---|---|---|---|---|---|---|---|
| (3) | a. | een | kleyne | harpoen | / | een | kleyn | stuk | |
| | | a | small-COMM | harpoon | / | a | small-NEUT | piece | |
| | b. | een | kleyn ~ kleyne | harpoen | / | een | kleyn ~ kleyne | stuk | |
| | | a | small | harpoon | / | a | small | piece | |

According to Lass (1990: 91), adjectival *-e* had now become a 'junk morpheme', which makes it a good candidate for exaptation, and this is indeed what happened. The suffix *-e* came to mark a particular class of adjectives, which are either morphologically complex (e.g. affixed adjectives such as *ge-heim* 'secret' or *stad-ig* 'slow') or morphophonemically complex (adjectives with stem allomorphy, e.g. *sag/sagt* 'soft'). This, Lass argues, is a system unique to Germanic, because it is not the morphosyntactic context which determines the inflection of the adjective, but the very form of the adjective itself.

In Vincent (1995), Lass was criticized for his use of the term 'junk', because according to Vincent:

> [L]anguages are sign systems and no part of a sign system is without function, even if we as analysts have not yet worked out what the function in question is . . . one can never be sure that there is not a generalization still lurking out there waiting to be captured which will encompass just the piece of linguistic form that has heretofore been written off as junk. (Vincent 1995: 435)

Vincent is right to some extent, in the sense that it is evident that, once a morphological rule has ceased to be productive and the 'junk' morpheme has become an indistinguishable part of the word (as in the case of formerly morphemic *-m* in Dutch *bloem* 'flower'; see section 3.3.1), exaptation is not possible. Therefore, it would be more appropriate to use the term 'obsolescent morphology' (Willis, forthcoming) instead of 'junk' for morphemes that are in the process of losing their function. In his 1997 work, Lass seems to acknowledge this when he extends his definition of exaptation to 'non-junk'. In the parallels from the organic world that he quotes, the exaptata did not lose their original function either. Feathers, for instance, were co-opted for flight, yet they continue to be a thermoregulatory device for reptiles in high latitudes (which was their original purpose).

A final point that needs to be stressed is that in exaptation, a gram acquires a new function. Lass (1990: 82) considers this notion of linguistic novelty as basic to the definition of exaptation. Thus, the generalization of *-s* as the plural marker of (virtually) all English nouns is not a case of exaptation, because here *-s* is simply continuing a function it already possessed.

So how does exaptation relate to degrammaticalization?[13] It is certainly not synonymous with it – although there are cases of degrammaticalization where exaptation is involved (e.g. in deinflectionalization, see Chapter 5), there are far more cases where exaptation is not an adequate characterization of the change in question. For example, the infinitival marker *to* was by no means marginal when it degrammaticalized from prefix to proclitic (section 6.3.1), nor did it acquire a new function. Conversely, not all cases of exaptation are degrammaticalizations – they may also involve lateral shift (as in Lass's example of adjective inflections above).[14] But exaptation *is* relevant to the unidirectionality of grammatical change, as noted in Traugott (2004):

> Exaptation in language change can be thought of as the phenomenon of the emergence of a new grammatical function at what could otherwise be expected to be the end of a cline of grammaticalization. Since this phenomenon is attested, it does serve as a counterexample to the hypothesis of unidirectionality.

Potential cases of exaptation may be difficult to identify, however, because exapted affixes are synchronically indistinguishable from other affixes. Exaptation changes can only be detected in languages with (long) written histories, such as Indo-European or Japanese (Narrog 2007: 19).

To conclude, degrammaticalization may involve exaptation, but not necessarily so, and not all cases of exaptation can be classified as degrammaticalization. The two terms should therefore not be treated as synonyms.

### 3.3.6 *Replacement*

In some cases that have been presented as degrammaticalization, a highly grammaticalized item (typically an inflectional affix) is replaced by a (near-) homophonous, less grammatical item. Although such changes are counterexamples to unidirectionality in that they represent a pathway which deviates from the cline of grammaticality, I do not regard them as instances of degrammaticalization, because the affixes do not degrammaticalize 'on their own'. Instead, they are confused with a similar, less grammatical item,

[13] See also Traugott (2004) for a careful discussion of the relation between exaptation and grammaticalization.

[14] In two earlier papers (Norde 2001a: 245; 2002: 53) I have written that, according to Lass (1997: 318) exaptation may lead to grammaticalization, but Lass actually did not claim that. Instead he wrote that exaptation may lead to 'grammaticization', which I interpreted as the Bybeean synonym for grammaticalization, but which Lass (1997: 256n) defines as 'having become grammatically obligatory', to be explicitly distinguished from grammaticalization, which he defines as 'routinized, bleached, downgraded from lexical to grammatical status'. The difference seems marginal to me, however (according to Lehmann obligatorification is characteristic of grammaticalization, see section 3.5.1). In any event, this has no consequences for my observation that exaptation is not necessarily counterdirectional.

which eventually comes to occupy the morphosyntactic position of the erstwhile affix.

One of the best-known examples is the New Mexican Spanish 1PL verbal ending *-mos*, which has been reanalysed as the (already existing) 1PL enclitic pronoun *=nos* (Janda 1995; 2001: 270f., 287f.).[15] However, this is not a case of a suffix degrammaticalizing into a clitic,[16] but of substitution, as also noted by, among others, Klausenburger (2002: 39f.), and Heine (2003a: 170f.). Another example, which was also made famous by Janda, is the hypothesis that Old English MASC.SG.GEN *-es* was reanalysed as (i.e. replaced by) *his*, which eventually resulted in the s-genitive. If this is indeed what happened (see section 5.3.3 for an argument against this hypothesis), the Modern English s-genitive would not be an example of degrammaticalization, since it would not be the direct continuation of the inflectional genitive suffix.

A third example is the reanalysis, in some varieties of Slavonic, of the second person plural conditional auxiliary *byste* (where *-ste* denotes 2PL) as a conditional particle *by* + the (existing) perfect auxiliary *este*, yielding a new conditional form (e.g. Old Russian *by este*; Willis, forthcoming). In this case, too, the rise of a phonologically strengthened independent auxiliary was made possible because of an accidental phonological likeness.

In the three examples mentioned thus far, the suffix and the pronoun by which it was (claimed to be) replaced were both semantically and phonologically similar, but this need not be the case. An interesting example where there is no semantic correspondence is discussed in van der Horst and van de Velde (2007). This example concerns the construction *so good a bargain* and its Dutch equivalent (which disappeared in the nineteenth century). According to traditional analyses (of whatever theoretical persuasion), the adjectival phrase *so good* has been fronted, but van der Horst and van de Velde provide an extensive line of reasoning against this view. Instead, they argue that the indefinite article in this construction derives from an inflectional ending on the adjective in both English and Dutch, as exemplified in (4a–d):

(4) a. And tolde whi þat tempest **so longe tyme** dured
(English, 14th century)

[15] This change has also occurred in other regional varieties of Spanish, in both Spain and the Americas (Janda 1995: 122). Note, however, that the analysis of *nos* as a clitic is not uncontroversial (Newmeyer 1998: 268n.).

[16] Janda himself (1995: 119) treats this change as equivalent to e.g. the deaffixation of the Irish 1PL verbal ending *-muid* into an independent pronoun (see section 6.6), but to me these changes are fundamentally different, because in the Irish case, there is no formal change and moreover, there was not even a phonologically similar pronoun with which the suffix could have become confused.

b. The only place where they could remain, for **so long a time** (English, 18th century)

c. Ic hebbe **soo** **grooten** **lost** (Dutch, 15th century)
I have so big-MASC.SG.ACC desire
'I have such a strong desire'

d. dat zij **zo** **groot** **een** **lust** had (Dutch, 18th century)
that she so big a desire had
'that she had such a strong desire'

In these examples, replacement of a suffix by a function word appears to be purely formally motivated.

In sum, although these changes are relevant to the unidirectionality debate, they are not consistent with the definition of degrammaticalization in the present work because they involve two different morphemes. Therefore, I consider replacement as a separate kind of change.

## 3.4 A generic definition

If all the changes discussed in the previous sections do *not* fall under the definition of degrammaticalization, then what *does*? Even if we exclude the lexicalization of grams and cases of replacement, we are left with a very heterogeneous group of changes, which are usually endemic to a single language or language family. As I will argue later on in this chapter, there are three basic types of degrammaticalization, each with its own definition and distinctive primitive changes, but it will also be seen that there are a few basic characteristics that all types of degrammaticalization have in common. As a superordinate definition for all types of degrammaticalization, I propose the following:

(5) Degrammaticalization is a composite change whereby a gram in a specific context gains in autonomy or substance on more than one linguistic level (semantics, morphology, syntax, or phonology).

This is a generic definition that covers all three types of degrammaticalization that will be identified later on in this work. In addition, I will briefly discuss four basic characteristics that all types of degrammaticalization have in common:

(i) counterdirectionality
(ii) novelty

(iii) infrequency
(iv) discontinuity

(i) *Counterdirectionality.* The most obvious criterion to select a potential case of degrammaticalization, which is also implicit in the definition in (5), is the direction of the change. In section 1.3.2, degrammaticalization was provisionally defined as a single shift from right to left on Hopper and Traugott's (2003: 7) cline of grammaticality:[17]

(6) content item > grammatical word > clitic > inflectional affix (> ø)

Such a cline-based definition primarily refers to decreasing bondedness (in the broadest sense), and as we will see later on, this is indeed what all degrammaticalization types have in common.

(ii) *Novelty.* A crucial prerequisite for a case to qualify as degrammaticalization is that it must result in a novel gram, as I will now illustrate by a brief discussion of the development of English *dare.* In Beths (1999), the history of *dare* is classified as a case of degrammaticalization, a view which is contested in Traugott (2001). According to Beths, historical evidence suggests that the predecessor of *dare* (**durran*) was a main verb in Old English which soon came to acquire modal properties and continued to do so until the Early Modern English period. These properties included lack of an infinitive form, increasingly deontic meaning, and no *do*-support. From the fifteenth century onwards, however, main verb uses of *dare* started to appear (as evidenced by, among other things, *to*-infinitives, an NP direct object, and *do*-support). In present-day English, Beths claims, *dare* is exclusively used as a main verb.

Arguing against Beths, Traugott (2001) cites data from Krug (2000), which show that *dare* did not cease to be a modal verb at all. But even if modal *dare* had become obsolete, Traugott argues, this is not a case of degrammaticalization because main verb uses and modal verb uses had always coexisted, which means that there is no evidence that (new) main verb uses arose out of previous modal ones. She concludes 'that main verb and emerging auxiliary uses have coexisted for over a thousand years, with one type predominating over the other at different periods and in different styles'. This kind of change, where more grammaticalized usages become marginalized (or even obsolete), with less grammatical usages increasing in frequency, has been termed 'retraction' by Haspelmath (2004: 33ff.).

[17] An alternative to counterdirectional movement on the cline of grammaticality is movement from one cline to another, as has been proposed by Rosenbach (2004) for the rise of the English s-genitive (see section 5.3.4 for discussion of this view).

I agree with Traugott and Haspelmath that these are not cases of degrammaticalization. In degrammaticalization, 'less' grammaticalized functions must be shown to derive from 'more' grammaticalized functions. If they continue, or develop out of, a less grammatical function that had always been around, however marginalized, the change will not qualify as a case of degrammaticalization.

(iii) *Infrequency.* A striking difference between grammaticalization and degrammaticalization, observed by grammaticalizationists and their critics alike, is that the number of degrammaticalization case studies is outnumbered by far by the number of grammaticalization case studies. Estimates of the grammaticalization/degrammaticalization ratio range from '10:1' (Newmeyer 1998: 275–6) to '100:1' (Haspelmath 1999: 1046). These differences are partly due to the definition of degrammaticalization – if one adopts a very restrictive definition of degrammaticalization (Haspelmath), the number of occurrences is evidently much smaller than when one adopts a large definition including lexicalization of bound morphemes and function words (Newmeyer, but also Ramat 1992, 2001). But they may also be due to theoretical bias. A linguist who is convinced that grammatical change is strictly unidirectional will be less likely to find, or accept, potential counterexamples (Luraghi 2005: 15). The importance of this methodological point is also stressed by Lass:

> Say in the course of your work you have found 542 changes that confirm a direction, and none that don't. Question is, 542 out of *what*? Does a UD-believer's inability to find the counterexamples, and/or the observed frequency of the confirming instances, reflect a 'real' property of the domain or merely the accidental tendentiousness of a chosen database? Note that not finding things is an *argumentum ex silentio*, which is not at the top of anybody's hierarchy of epistemic goodness. (Lass 2000: 214)

Joseph (2005: 4) similarly argues: 'the issue of statistical preponderance of grammaticalization as opposed to "counter-/de-/anti-grammaticalization", often claimed as a reason for being able to ignore any examples of counter-directional developments, is a nonissue in the absence of any meaningful way of counting tokens of the latter'.

Authors like Luraghi, Lass, and Joseph are of course right that it is impossible to establish an exact grammaticalization/degrammaticalization ratio, but the study of grammaticalization phenomena is not the exclusive territory of 'UD-believers', and in spite of all the efforts by avid 'unbelievers' to collect as much counterevidence as possible, the number of degrammaticalization changes remains relatively small.

(iv) *Discontinuity.* As we have seen in Chapter 2 and section 3.3.2, some authors dismiss degrammaticalization as a valid type of change on the basis of a distorted definition of degrammaticalization as a mirror-image reversal of grammaticalization, even though no one, to the best of my knowledge, has ever claimed the existence of such a full reversal. Such developments verge on the impossible, as I have argued on several occasions in this book. What sets apart degrammaticalization from grammaticalization is that in most cases, degrammaticalization entails a *single* shift from right to left on the cline of grammaticality. There may be some subsequent change (as in the case of Saami *haga*, which developed from suffix to postposition to preposition; see section 6.7), but in general we may say that there is no 'domino effect'.

This is mainly an observation, not something which is inherent in the definition of degrammaticalization. The reason why there are no degrammaticalization chains is that circumstances under which a degrammaticalization can take place are very rare, and it is quite unlikely that such circumstances would arise twice in the history of a given morpheme (see section 2.7.4).

## 3.5 Classifying degrammaticalization

The remainder of this chapter will be concerned with the question of how we can identify a degrammaticalized form. If increasing grammaticality involves desemanticization, context generalization, decategorialization, and phonological reduction, decreasing grammaticality might be expected to go hand in hand with the opposite primitive changes, that is, resemanticization, context contraction, recategorialization, and phonological strengthening. Willis (2007: 272) makes a similar point:

> [I]n order to be theoretically interesting, degrammaticalization must be parallel to and linked to grammaticalization. That is, the nature of the mechanisms involved must, in some sense, be the same in both cases, but they must lead to opposite results. (Willis 2007: 272)

If degrammaticalization indeed involves the opposite primitive changes from those commonly attested in grammaticalization, the first thing we need is a descriptive framework for grammaticalization changes. For this reason I will start with a section on the classification of grammaticalization (without however offering an exhaustive typology), using two taxonomic tools: Lehmann's (1995[1982]) six 'parameters of grammaticalization' and Andersen's (2005, 2006, 2008) four 'levels of observation'. Once it has been shown how these tools can be applied to grammaticalization chains, I will demonstrate how they can be used to generate a degrammaticalization typology.

### 3.5.1 *Lehmann's parameters*

Before turning to Lehmann's parameters of grammaticalization, let us first briefly reconsider Kuryłowicz's 'classical' definition of grammaticalization in (7), and the terms 'primary' and 'secondary' grammaticalization that can be derived from it.

(7) Grammaticalization consists in the increase of the range of a morpheme advancing from a lexical to a grammatical or from a grammatical to a more grammatical status. (Kuryłowicz 1975 [1965]: 52)

With this bipartite division as a point of departure, it may be interesting to examine how these two types relate to Lehmann's (1995[1982]) parameters of grammaticalization. Lehmann's model has been criticized for being a taxonomic system rather than a descriptive model with explanatory force (e.g. in Detges and Waltereit 2002: 172), or for being formalistic rather than founded on empirical evidence (von Mengden 2008). But nowhere does Lehmann claim that his parameters were intended to explain grammaticalization phenomena, and I think it is safe to say that, as a taxonomy, Lehmann's system has proven quite successful, though some parameters appear more useful than others (see below). And as I aim to demonstrate later on, it is also useful for classifying different types of degrammaticalization.

Lehmann (1995 [1982]: 121ff.) distinguishes three aspects that determine the autonomy of a linguistic sign: *weight*, *cohesion*, and *variability*, which can be analysed from a paradigmatic and syntagmatic point of view. This results in six parameters, or criteria, that can be used to determine which of two linguistic items is *more grammatical* than the other (see Table 3.1). Each parameter is associated with a number of primitive changes, the most important of which are listed below:

TABLE 3.1. Lehmann's parameters (Lehmann 1995 [1982]: 123)

| | Weight | Cohesion | Variability |
|---|---|---|---|
| **Paradigmatic** | integrity | paradigmaticity | paradigmatic variability |
| **Syntagmatic** | structural scope | bondedness | syntagmatic variability |

(1) **Integrity:** *desemanticization* (loss of semantic substance); *phonological attrition* (loss of phonological substance); *decategorialization* (loss of morphosyntactic properties)[18]

[18] This term is not from Lehmann, but introduced by Hopper (1991) to refer to the transition from open class to closed class and its accompanying changes (see also Hopper and Traugott 2003: 110ff.). I have chosen this term because it is so well established (see also section 2.6.2). Lehmann himself (p. 132) uses the term 'morphological degeneration', which he sees as inherently linked to both phonological and semantic attrition.

(2) **Paradigmaticity:** *paradigmaticization* (1: from major to minor word class; 2: integration into a paradigm)
(3) **Paradigmatic variability:** *obligatorification* (becoming obligatory in specific morphosyntactic contexts)
(4) **Structural scope:** *condensation* (reduction of syntactic scope)
(5) **Bondedness:** *univerbation* (boundary loss); *coalescence* (increase in morphophonological integration)
(6) **Syntagmatic variability:** *fixation* (decrease in syntactic freedom)

The interaction between Lehmann's parameters is very complex and cannot be treated in much detail (see Lehmann 1995 [1982]: 160ff. for extensive discussion). However, a few things need to be mentioned. First, there is a crucial difference between the parameters associated with syntagmatic and paradigmatic variability, as von Mengden (2008) correctly observes: where the aspects of 'weight' and 'cohesion' are about individual expressions, the aspect of 'variability' is about categories. This implies that changes on the level of paradigmatic or syntagmatic variability naturally follow from changes in category membership. For example, when a noun grammaticalizes into a preposition, its syntactic freedom (i.e. the number of positions in which it may appear) is inherently reduced because prepositions are generally more fixed than are nouns. On the other two levels however, changes are connected to the individual properties of the original lexeme. For example, spatial expressions typically derive from body-part items (e.g. 'head' for 'up', 'face' for 'front', or 'back' for 'back, behind'), or environmental landmarks (e.g. 'sky' for 'up', 'earth' for 'down') (Heine 1997: 35ff.). The meanings of such spatial expressions are not related to category membership (e.g. adverb or adposition) but to the meaning of the source lexeme.

Secondly, not all primitive changes need to be attested in a given grammaticalization change. This holds true, in particular, for phonological attrition. Especially during the first stage, from lexical item to function word, there need not be any change, as in prepositions such as *considering* or *notwithstanding*. Serious reduction is often not attested until the later stages, when the grammaticalizing gram becomes bound and fuses with its host (in the case of clitics) or stem (in the case of inflections).

Thirdly, some parameters work 'continuously', whereas others have very different effects at different stages in grammaticalization chains. An example of a continuous parameter is integrity. Desemanticization, for example, is a continuous process which goes hand in hand with increasing grammaticalization. An example of a parameter with quite different effects in primary and secondary grammaticalization is paradigmaticization. In primary grammaticalization, this implies a shift from an open category (e.g. nouns or verbs), with thousands of members, to a closed category (e.g. prepositions or subordinators, which is much smaller in size (Lehmann 1995 [1982]: 133).[19] For instance, when the participle *considering* grammaticalized into a preposition it joined the 'paradigm' of prepositions. In secondary grammaticalization on the other hand, paradigmaticization implies that grams (eventually) become part of inflectional paradigms.

Fourthly, some parameters appear to be relevant to only one type of grammaticalization (primary or secondary). The parameter of bondedness only applies in secondary grammaticalization, because it is first here that a gram becomes bound (in primary grammaticalization, the gram remains a free morpheme). Conversely, the parameter of syntagmatic variability only applies in primary grammaticalization, because bound morphemes are inherently fixed in a certain position. In other words, bondedness and syntagmatic variability can be seen as essentially one and the same parameter, with different effects in different types of grammaticalization.

Finally, the parameter of scope has been the subject of much debate. I will therefore treat it in some more detail in section 3.5.2.

The relation between Lehmann's parameters and primary and secondary grammaticalization is summarized in Table 3.2.[20]

### 3.5.2 *Some notes on the parameter of structural scope*

Scope change in grammaticalization is a controversial issue. According to Lehmann (1995[1982]: 143), '[t]he structural scope of a sign decreases with increasing grammaticalization'. For example, when an adposition grammaticalizes into a case affix the scope is reduced from (inflected) full NP to bare noun. Similarly, when a main verb grammaticalizes into an auxiliary the scope is reduced from the clause level to the VP level (Lehmann 1995[1982]: 144).

Traugott (1997a) and Tabor and Traugott (1998), however, have claimed that in terms of c-command, scope is not reduced but expanded in grammaticalization. Visconti (2004: 177) likewise notes that the grammaticalization of English *supposing* involves scope expansion. Another case of grammaticalization involving scope expansion is the well-known development of deontic modals into epistemic ones, as illustrated in (8). In (8a), syntactic scope of *must* is restricted

[19] Naturally, the term 'closed class' does not mean that no new members can be added, because if that were the case, there would no grammaticalization. It does mean that the number of members is and remains limited, as opposed to open classes, where new members are being added continuously, and in great numbers.

[20] Some of the examples in Table 3.2 are from Lehmann, others have been added by me.

TABLE 3.2. Lehmann's parameters in primary and secondary grammaticalization

| Parameter | Primary grammaticalization | Secondary grammaticalization |
|---|---|---|
| **Integrity** | *desemanticization*: from lexical content to grammatical content<br>e.g. English *to be going to:* lexical verb ('to walk') > future auxiliary | *desemanticization:* increasing conceptual abstraction<br>e.g. Old Norse enclitic =*sk* (REFLEXIVE) > Norwegian inflectional -*s*(*t*) (PASSIVE) |
| | *phonological attrition*<br>e.g. Latin noun *homo* 'man' > French 3SG indefinite pronoun *on* 'one' | *phonological attrition*<br>e.g. Latin periphrastic future 1SG *cantare habeo* > French synthetic future 1SG *chanterai* |
| | *decategorialization*: loss of inflection and other morphosyntactic properties<br>e.g. ModE conjunction *while* cannot inflect, take articles or quantifiers (unlike its predecessor, the OE noun *hwíl* 'length of time') | *decategorialization*: not relevant in secondary grammaticalization |
| **Paradigmaticity** | *paradigmaticization:* from open class to closed class<br>e.g. English *to be going to:* from lexical verb (open class) to auxiliary (closed class with limited number of members) | *paradigmaticization:* integration into an inflectional paradigm<br>e.g. French inflectional future paradigm (1SG *chanterai*, 2SG *chanteras*, 3SG *chantera*, etc.) |
| **Paradigmatic variability** | *obligatorification:* from optional to obligatory element in syntactic constructions<br>e.g. Latin demonstrative *ille* (optional modifier of nouns) > French definite article *le* (obligatory in definite contexts) | *obligatorification:* obligatory inflectional expression of grammatical categories<br>e.g. CASE and NUMBER in Latin |

(*Continued*)

TABLE 3.2. (Continued)

| Parameter | Primary grammaticalization | Secondary grammaticalization |
|---|---|---|
| **Structural scope** | *condensation:* scope diminution from clause level to phrase level e.g. the development from possessive HAVE (cf. English [*I* [*have* [*the letter written*]]]to perfective HAVE (cf. English [I [have written] [the letter]]] | *condensation:* scope diminution from phrase level to word level e.g. Latin [*humili et dulci*] *mente* 'with a humble and gentle mind' > French *humblement et doucement* 'humbly and gently' |
| **Bondedness** | not relevant in primary grammaticalization | *univerbation only:* boundary loss without reduction; gram becomes bound e.g. Latin *tota mente* 'with one's entire mind' > Italian *totamente* 'entirely'<br><br>*univerbation and coalescence:*[a] boundary loss and reduction; gram becomes bound e.g. Proto-Scandinavian *hali hino* (stone-ACC this-ACC) 'this stone' > Old Norse *hallinn* (stone-DEF.ACC) 'the stone'[b] |
| **Syntagmatic variability** | *fixation* e.g. Latin possessive HAVE: *epistulam scriptam habeo* 'I have a letter written', which could appear in any order (*habeo epistulam scriptam, scriptam habeo epistulam,* etc.) > Italian auxiliary HAVE, with fixed order, *ho scritto una lettera* 'I have written a letter' | not relevant in secondary grammaticalization |

[a] Following Brinton and Traugott (2005: 27f.), I will distinguish between univerbation or fusion (boundary loss) and (subsequent) coalescence (loss of phonological segments).
[b] The Proto-Scandinavian example is from the inscription on the Strøm whetstone (Norway, *c.* 600).

to the VP, but in (8b), *must* takes scope over the entire proposition (it can be paraphrased as *it is necessarily the case that he is home by now*).

(8) a. I **must** do this first (deontic)
b. He **must** be home by now (epistemic)

At a superficial glance, then, the shift from deontic to epistemic modality is problematic in terms of scope change. But according to Fischer (2008: 363ff.), it is problematic only when it is reduced to a mere comparison of the initial and the final stage, without considering the actual changes involved. For upon closer scrutiny it turns out that the modals went through an intermediate stage of clause combining. In Old English, epistemic modals only occur in subjectless constructions, such as (9a) (rare), impersonal verb constructions such as (9b), and a construction in which the modal is combined with an intransitive infinitive, followed by a *þæt*-clause, as in (9c).

(9) a. Eaðe **mæg** þæt me Drihten þurh his
Easily can that me Lord through his
geearnung miltsigan wille
merit show-mercy will
'It may be that the Lord will show me mercy because of his merit'
(Bede 3 11.192.5)

b. þonne **mæg** hine scamigan þære brædinge his hlisan
then can him shame of-the spreading of-his fame
'then he may be ashamed of the extent of his fame' (Bo 19.46.5)

c. Đeah þe hit swa beon **mihte** þæt he þas blisse
Though it so be could that he those favours
begitan mihte
beget could
'Though it could be the case that he would receive those favours'
(Æls (Ash Wed) 106)

Fischer points out that the construction in (9c) is of particular interest, because it exemplifies a bi-clausal construction which is not attested for deontic modals. She furthermore argues that it was this construction from which epistemic constructions involving agentive verbs evolved. If this scenario is correct, the English epistemic modals did decrease their scope from Old to Middle English. In Old English, they appeared in a matrix clause and took scope over the subordinate clause, whereas in Middle English, they were 'raised' to the same clause as their infinitival object. Fischer (2008: 368) concludes that the modals became epistemic 'only via a more elaborate construction type'. This is corroborated by British English corpus data which show that epistemic modals are (still) usually followed by the infinitive *be* or *have*, and only rarely by an agentive verb. Indeed, constructions such as *he must be lying* or *he must have lied* are easily interpreted as epistemic, whereas *he must lie* is more likely to be interpreted as deontic (e.g. when said about a spy who must lie for his country). A final piece of evidence is the occurrence of epistemic adverbs such as *maybe* (with cognates in many other languages), which likewise suggests that infinitival *be* played a crucial part in the rise of the epistemic construction. However, though Fischer makes a convincing case for scope reduction in the epistemic modals from Old to Middle English, the constructions in (9) can still be said to involve scope expansion when compared to the (older) construction involving deontic modals, because the latter cannot be followed by a *that*-clause.

In sum, it seems as if the jury is still out on the subject of scope change in grammaticalization. Nevertheless, it will be interesting to see what happens to syntactic scope in the degrammaticalization changes.

### 3.5.3 *Parameters of degrammaticalization*

As I have done in the previous section, I will start the classification of degrammaticalization changes with the observation that there is primary degrammaticalization, whereby a function word becomes a full lexical item, and secondary degrammaticalization, whereby a bound morpheme (inflectional, derivational, or enclitic) becomes 'less grammatical'. It will be seen later on in this section that there are two subtypes of secondary degrammaticalization, one in which affixes become 'less bound', and one in which bound morphemes become free morphemes. But first I will consider Lehmann's parameters and their connection to primary and secondary degrammaticalization.

Since degrammaticalization is a composite change in the opposite direction from grammaticalization, we may expect Lehmann's parameters to work in the reverse way as well. Hence I will assume the following 'parameters of degrammaticalization' and its associated primitive changes (concrete examples of these primitive changes will be given in Chapters 4–6.):[21]

(1) **Integrity:** As far as integrity is concerned, a degrammaticalized item can be expected to *gain* semantic and phonological substance, which will be termed *resemanticization* and *phonological strengthening*

[21] Note that these terms are not Lehmann's, but antonyms coined by me. Lehmann would probably not use his parameters in this sense, since he remains critical of degrammaticalization (Lehmann 2004), but to me it only shows the strength of his framework that it works 'both ways'.

respectively. It is also likely to involve *recategorialization*, the acquisition of morphosyntactic features of members of major word classes (only to be found in primary degrammaticalization).

(2) **Paradigmaticity:** The reverse primitive change associated with this parameter is *deparadigmaticization*, which is expected to have different effects in primary degrammaticalization, where it signifies movement from a closed word class to an open word class, and in secondary degrammaticalization, where it refers to 'discharge' from an inflectional paradigm.

(3) **Paradigmatic variability:** Degrammaticalization can also be expected to go hand in hand with increasing paradigmatic variability, or becoming optional in specific morphosyntactic contexts (*deobligatorification*).

(4) **Structural scope:** Where scope has proved a problematic parameter in grammaticalization, it appears to be no less so in degrammaticalization. For the time being however, degrammaticalization will be expected to involve *scope expansion.*

(5) **Bondedness:** A decrease in bondedness (*severance*) is typically found in secondary degrammaticalization. As we will see in Chapters 5 and 6, severance comes in several forms. In the second type of degrammaticalization (deinflectionalization, see below), inflectional affixes may become either enclitic or derivational. In the third type of degrammaticalization (debonding), bound morphemes become free morphemes, accompanied by a change in meaning or function (if the debonding gram is derivational), or without such change (in most cases of debonding inflectional affixes or clitics).

(6) **Syntagmatic variability:** As regards this parameter, the expected primitive change is *flexibilization*, i.e. an increase in syntactic freedom. Unlike in grammaticalization, this parameter is relevant in both primary and secondary degrammaticalization. I will return to this issue below.

As was the case with the grammaticalization parameters, these degrammaticalization parameters do not apply to all instances of degrammaticalization. The parameter of integrity has different effects in different types of degrammaticalization – when a grammatical word becomes a content item, it naturally gains full lexical content, but in other cases there is not so much an increase in semantic substance as in grammatical function (other functions are being added).

The parameter of bondedness is restricted to secondary degrammaticalization, just as it was restricted to secondary grammaticalization. However, the parameter of syntagmatic variability, which is only relevant to primary grammaticalization, can be involved in both primary and secondary degrammaticalization. In secondary grammaticalization, a gram becomes bound and hence inherently fixed, so that the parameter of syntagmatic variability is no longer relevant. But in secondary degrammaticalization, a bound morpheme may become a free morpheme (notably in cases of debonding), and as a free morpheme it need not be fixed in a specific syntactic slot. There is thus an asymmetry between grammaticalization and degrammaticalization with respect to this parameter.

### 3.5.4 *Andersen's levels of observation*

A second way to classify different types of grammaticalization or different stages in a grammaticalization chain is proposed in Andersen (2005, 2006, 2008) who identifies four 'levels of observation' in grammaticalization:

> A Grammaticalization . . . is typically a complex of interrelated changes in (i) content (or function), (ii) content syntax, (iii) morphosyntax (expression syntax), and (iv) expression. (Andersen 2006: 232)

Since there is no terminology to capture these changes, Andersen (2006: 232) proposes the following:

(1) **Changes in content.**
  (1.1) *Grammation:* a change by which an expression through reanalysis is ascribed grammatical content (change from any other, including zero, content to grammatical content).
  (1.2) *Regrammation:* a change by which a grammatical expression through reanalysis is ascribed different grammatical content (change within and among grammatical paradigms).
  (1.3) *Degrammation:* a change by which an expression through reanalysis loses grammatical content (change from grammatical content to other, including zero, content).
(2) **Changes in content syntax.**
  (2.1) *Upgrading:* a change from dependent to head or an enlargement of scope.
  (2.2) *Downgrading:* a change from head to dependent or a scope diminution.
(3) **Changes in morphosyntax.**
  (3.1) *Bond weakening* (*emancipation*) (affix > clitic, clitic > word, compound word > phrase).
  (3.2) *Bond strengthening* (*integration*) (phrase > word, word > clitic, clitic > affix).

(4) **Changes in expression.**
 (4.1) *Reduction.*
 (4.2) *Elaboration.*

Applying Andersen's model to all types of grammaticalization is way beyond the scope of this paper (for this the reader is referred to the papers of Andersen himself), but I will use it to classify degrammaticalization in the next section.

### 3.5.5 *Three types of degrammaticalization*

In section 3.5.3, I discussed the primitive changes that can be expected to operate in degrammaticalization, and now I will consider the relevance of Andersen's levels of observation to types of degrammaticalization. A systematic comparison of all attested degrammaticalization changes (Chapters 4–6) reveals that degrammaticalization can be observed on three of Andersen's levels, yielding three clearly distinguishable types of degrammaticalization:

(1) **Content level:** shift from grammatical content to lexical content (resemanticization). Degrammaticalization at the content level is primary degrammaticalization and will be termed 'degrammation'.
(2) **Content-syntactic level:** shift from 'more grammatical' to 'less grammatical', or movement out of a paradigm accompanied by a change in grammatical content. Degrammaticalization at the content-syntactic level is the first subtype of secondary degrammaticalization and will be termed 'deinflectionalization'.
(3) **Morphosyntactic level**: shift from bound morpheme (affix, clitic) to free morpheme. This is the second subtype of secondary degrammaticalization and will be termed 'debonding'.

To prevent terminological confusion, I have chosen to use terms that have not been used to refer to other kinds of change. The term 'degrammation' was coined by Henning Andersen, as we have seen, to refer to loss of grammatical content. Andersen uses the term in a slightly wider sense in that he includes loss of grammatical content resulting in empty morphs, such as *to* (originally a prefix) in *tomorrow.* I use it in the narrow sense, that is, the loss of grammatical content in exchange for lexical content. 'Deinflectionalization' was chosen because that term appears not to have been used in other contexts. 'Debonding', finally, is preferred to the term 'demorphologization', because that term has been used in a number of different senses already. For instance, in Joseph and Janda (1988) it refers to the relocation of morphological phenomena to either phonology or syntax, whereas in Hopper (1994) it is a synonym for 'phonogenesis', the degradation from morpheme to phoneme(s), or empty morphs. The term 'debonding' is used in chemistry and related sciences for the severance of inter- and intra-molecular ties.

## 3.6 Summary

As it is one of the main aims of this work to describe and classify degrammaticalization, an unambiguous definition is badly needed. For such is the definitional inconsistency in current theorizing, that sometimes authors are talking about entirely different phenomena when they speak of 'degrammaticalization'. In section 3.3, we saw that quite a few changes have been associated with degrammaticalization, either as primitive changes or mechanisms involved in degrammaticalization, or as straightforward synonyms.

I have chosen to retain the term 'degrammaticalization' as a hypernym, partly because it is so well-established, partly because the alternatives (re- and antigrammaticalization) do not quite refer to the same thing. 'Regrammaticalization' is rather a synonym of 'lateral shift' (see section 2.4) than of degrammaticalization. And the definition of 'antigrammaticalization' is much narrower than the one proposed here. On the other hand, the definition used in the present work is more restrictive than many others, excluding, among other things, the lexicalization of affixes and function words, and cases of replacement.

In order to classify all potential cases of degrammaticalization, one evidently needs a set of well-defined criteria. The best-known, and most detailed, model is Lehmann's 'parameters of grammaticalization'. Lehmann's parameters are frequently applied in both grammaticalization and degrammaticalization studies, but often in an *à la carte* fashion, whereby only those parameters are selected that serve the argument. This is understandable to some extent, since not all parameters apply in all types of either grammaticalization or degrammaticalization. This will become evident in the next three chapters, where each individual case will be analysed in terms of Lehmann's parameters, and I will return to the theoretical implications of this in Chapter 7.

A final important observation in this chapter is that change (including (de)grammaticalization) may occur at different linguistic levels (Andersen 2005, 2006, 2008). Although this became apparent first after a systematic comparison of the case studies discussed in Chapters 4–6, Andersen's levels are briefly mentioned at the end of this chapter, to account for the classification of degrammaticalization in three different types. For further discussion of this classification, too, the reader is referred to Chapter 7.

# 4

# Degrammation

## 4.1 Introduction

In this chapter, I will discuss a few cases of 'degrammation', the type of degrammaticalization which is least frequently attested. It will be defined as follows:

(1) Degrammation is a composite change whereby a function word in a specific linguistic context is reanalysed as a member of a major word class, acquiring the morphosyntactic properties which are typical of that word class, and gaining in semantic substance.

Degrammation typically occurs in ambiguous contexts, which facilitate the reanalysis of the function word as a member of a major word class, and it gains in semantic substance by means of pragmatic inferencing.[1] It is therefore different from lexicalization changes such as *to **up** the volume*, because in the latter case the function word is torn out of context, and neither reanalysis nor pragmatic inferencing is involved. The reason why degrammation is so rare is, as I have argued in section 2.7.4, that members of major word classes, such as nouns and verbs, are often inflected. As a consequence, for a function word to be reanalysed as an inflected noun or verb, it must have a form which happens to be identical (or at least similar) to an inflected noun or verb, *and* this form must be the appropriate one in the context in which the reanalysis takes place. This is obviously a needle in the haystack phenomenon, becoming progressively more difficult the more inflections a language possesses.

[1] Willis (2007) uses the term 'syntactic lexicalization' for this kind of change. I have avoided this term because of the potential confusion with other types of lexicalization. Note also that Willis's use of the term differs from that found in Bauer (1983: 59ff.), where it refers to syntactic reflections in word formation, for instance the order of elements in compounds such as *scarecrow* or *telltale*, which corresponds to the syntactic ordering of the verb and the direct object.

## 4.2 From modal auxiliary to lexical verb

One of the most-cited cases of degrammaticalization concerns a shift from modal verb to lexical verb. Examples that have been suggested are English *dare* and *need* (Beths 1999; Taeymans 2004), Swedish *må* 'may' > 'feel' (van der Auwera and Plungian 1998), and Danish *turde* 'dare' (Andersen 2008). In none of these cases, however, is the evidence conclusive.

With the exception of Swedish *må*, none of the above-mentioned verbs changes semantically. Therefore, some authors (e.g. Taeymans 2004) have chosen to use the term 'semi-modal' to refer to the (formally) less grammaticalized variant. The changes that can be observed are purely formal: showing regular verb morphology (see example (2)), having non-finite forms (example (3)), as well as the possibility of selecting *to*-infinitives (also in example (2)), and (in the case of English) auxiliary DO-support (see example (4); Taeymans 2004: 100ff.).

(2) a. Somebody **needs** to be a contact for getting all the information to by a given date.
  b. No one **dared** to say anything.

(3) a. Why do I **need** to practice that...?
  b. He shivered, not **daring** to move in case they noticed and dragged him out.

(4) a. You do not **need** to be very rich.
  b. Don't you **dare** come over smoking!

In my brief discussion of *dare* in section 3.4, we have already seen that the history of *dare* is most appropriately analysed as a case of retraction – although main verb usage is becoming increasingly common at the expense of modal verb usage, *dare* had in fact never become entirely obsolete as a main verb. As a consequence, we cannot conclude that the main verb usage developed out of the modal usage, and hence this is not a case of degrammaticalization. In her corpus-based study of *dare* and *need* in spoken and written British present-day English, Taeymans arrives at a similar conclusion. As to *dare*, Taeymans's frequency analysis suggests that the use of *dare* as a modal verb is increasing, but she also notes that modal *dare* has become very rare in American English, which is generally considered less conservative than British English. Taeymans (2004: 111) therefore concludes that *dare* 'is not evidently moving in a clearly identifiable direction'. In the case of *need* (Taeymans 2004: 108), the formal development is counterdirectional, because *need* has acquired morphosyntactic characteristics of a main verb. On the semantic side, however, semi-modal *need* has shifted from 'internal' to 'external' necessity, which is a kind of change typically associated with grammaticalization. It is therefore not an example of degrammation as defined in (1).

A comparable case is Danish *turde* 'dare' (Andersen 2008), which can occur both with an *at*-infinitive and a 'bare' infinitive:

(5) a.

| | | | | | |
|---|---|---|---|---|---|
| Jeg | **tør** | ikke | **at** | spørge | ham |
| I | dare | not | to | ask | him |

b.

| | | | | |
|---|---|---|---|---|
| Jeg | **tør** | ikke | spørge | ham |
| I | dare | not | ask | him |

Here the evidence does seem to suggest that the occurrence of infinitival markers is a fairly recent development. It was probably first noted by Hansen in 1977 (Davidsen-Nielsen 1990: 37), but the *at*-infinitive is still not generally accepted in reference grammars (cf. e.g. Zola Christensen and Christensen 2005: 116; Jacobsen and Jørgensen 2005: 89). But apart from the use of the infinitival marker, nothing has changed – there is no change in either meaning or inflection.

A change which has been claimed to involve both formal and semantic change is Swedish *må* (van der Auwera and Plungian 1998; van der Auwera 2002; Andersson 2007). This verb can indeed be used in two different senses, exemplified in (6) and (7). Modal *må* 'may' is not inflected in the present tense ((6a)), and has an irregular past tense *måtte* ((6b)), which is rather formal/archaic and can be used, among other things, as an epistemic modal. Because of the semantic discrepancy between the present and the past tense, *måtte* is sometimes classified as a separate modal verb (Teleman, Hellberg, and Andersson 1999a: 573). As a main verb meaning 'feel', exemplified in (7), *må* has regular verb inflection.

(6) a.

| | | | | | | |
|---|---|---|---|---|---|---|
| Hon | **må** | inte | vara | världens | bästa | sångerska |
| She | may | not | be | the world's | best | singer |

'She may not be the best singer in the world'

b.

| | | | | |
|---|---|---|---|---|
| Hon | **måtte** | vara | lyckligt | gift |
| She | must | be | happily | married |

(7) a.

| | | | |
|---|---|---|---|
| Jag | **mår** | bra | idag |
| I | feel | well | today |

b.

| | | | | |
|---|---|---|---|---|
| Jag | **mådde** | inte | bra | igår |
| I | felt | not | well | yesterday |

'Yesterday, I did not feel well'

Van der Auwera and Plungian (1998: 105), and van der Auwera (2002: 24) suggest a split in the history of *må*, when the original auxiliary meaning was continued and a new verb with regular inflection was developed. But in his detailed diachronic study of Swedish *må*, Andersson (2007) has shown that the sense of 'feel' dates back to the oldest Swedish texts available, and that both modal *må* and lexical *må* can be traced back to an earlier lexical verb *magha* 'to be strong, powerful' (Andersson 2007: 65). Two examples of *magha* as a lexical verb are given below:

(8) a. Jak hugdhe thik wara vældogastan hærra
I imagined you to.be most.powerful-ACC man-ACC
nu findar iak at christus **ma** mer æn thu
now find I that Christ can more than you
'I thought you were the most powerful man. Now I think that Christ has more powers than you'

b. ... sende faustianius budh til athenas At wita
... sent Faustianius messenger to Athens to learn
wm sina hustru Ok syni huru the **mattu**
about his-ACC wife-ACC and sons-ACC how they felt
'Faustianius sent a messenger to Athens to find out how his wife and sons were doing'[2]

In the above examples, the Old Swedish main verb *ma* has the same (irregular) inflection as modal *ma*, with lack of *-r* in the third person of the present indicative, and a preterite stem *matt-*. Interestingly, the formal split-off of *må* occurs much later – present tense *mår* is not attested before the second half of the sixteenth century, and preterite *mådde* not before the beginning of the seventeenth century (Andersson 2007: 191). Lexical *må* joined a new conjugation of monosyllabic verbs ending in a vowel. The change may thus very well be motivated by analogy (after such verbs as *nå* 'to reach' or *spå* 'prophesize'), and Andersson (ibid.) correctly concludes that the divergence of lexical *må* and modal *må* as a result of morphological change alone is insufficient to qualify as a case of degrammaticalization.

A genuine example of degrammation of a modal verb is the development of the full verb *wotte* 'to wish' from the preterite subjunctive of modal *welle* 'to want to' in a variety of Pennsylvania German spoken in Waterloo County, Canada (Burridge 1995, 1998).

[2] Both examples are from the *Codex Bildstenianus* manuscript (*c.* 1350) of the Old Swedish book of legends, which were first written down towards the end of the thirteenth century.

Pennsylvania German has seven modal verbs: *misse* 'to have to, must', *selle* 'to be supposed to, to be to', *kenne* 'to be able to, can', *welle*, 'to want to', *daerfe* 'to be allowed to', *maage* 'to like to, may' (now rare), and *brauche* 'to need to'. As a result of the decreasing productivity of the subjunctive mood in Pennsylvania German,[3] the original preterite subjunctive forms of these verbs have established themselves as separate modal verbs, 'in ways that are reminiscent of the developing independence of the originally preterite forms *would*, *could*, *should*, and *might* in English' (Burridge 1998: 25). This lexical split between the present indicative and the preterite subjunctive was facilitated by three factors that determine the likelihood of such a dissociation (Bybee 1985b: 88ff.): semantic distance, phonological distance, and frequency. The semantic relationship between the present indicative and the preterite subjunctive has become increasingly opaque, especially since the modals were among the handful of verbs retaining synthetic forms. Phonologically, they became more divergent than they already were (being irregular verbs), for example when *sollt-/söllt-* and *wollt/wöllt-* became *sett-* and *wett-*. And the high discourse frequency of the preterite subjunctive forms may have promoted their increasing autonomy. The lexical split is exemplified by constructions such as (9a–b) (quite commonly used by younger speakers), where instead of the expected infinitive (as in (9c)), preterite subjunctive forms are found.

(9) a. Er hett nach[4] Mt Forest geh **sette**
He had to Mt Forest go should
'He ought to have gone to Mt Forest (but he didn't)'

b. Er hot nach Mt Forest geh **sette**
He has to Mt Forest go should
'He ought to have gone to Mt Forest (but he didn't)'

c. Er hett nach Mt Forest geh **solle**
He had to Mt Forest go should
'He ought to have gone to Mt Forest (but he didn't)'

[3] In present-day Pennsylvania German the subjunctive is primarily expressed by the subjunctive forms of the modal *due* 'to do' + infinitive, but some synthetic forms have been retained, varying from dialect to dialect. Indeed there are varieties (Amish and Mennonite) where both the finite verb and the modal infinitive are marked for the subjunctive, as in *ich hett gehe missde* 'I would have had to go', where *-d-* in *missde* marks the subjunctive (which is quite uncommon for infinitives; Mark Louden, p.c.).

[4] According to Mark Louden (p.c.) the correct form of this preposition is actually *noch*.

This strongly suggests that these verbs are in the process of becoming separate modal verbs. But Waterloo County Pennsylvania German witnessed a second split: the preterite subjunctive form *wotte* (retaining the earlier rounded vowel) is now distinct from both *welle* 'to want to' and *wette* 'would'. At present, *wotte* is rapidly establishing itself as an autonomous verb with full lexical meaning 'to wish, desire', thus becoming synonymous with the verb *winsche* 'to wish'.[5] In its shift from a modal verb to a lexical verb, *wotte* gained a number of morphosyntactic properties, exemplified in (10) (Burridge 1998: 28f.). Thus, it can no longer take infinitival complements ((10a)), it can be nominalized, as in (10b), it has acquired verbal inflections such as the imperative in (10c), or a participle as in (10d), and it can itself be the complement of a modal auxiliary, as in (10e), or auxiliary DO as in (10f).

(10) a. *Ich **wott** kumme
I want come
'I want to come'

b. Er ist juscht am **wotte**, er kennt noch eens
He is just at.the wishing, he could again one
vun die Ebbel hawwe
of the apples have
'He is just wishing he could have one more of the apples'

c. **Wott** net fer sell
Wish not for that
'Don't wish for that'

d. Er hat **gewott** er kennt noch eens vun die
He has wished he could again one of the
Ebbel hawwe
apples have
'He wished he could have one more of the apples'

e. Ich muss **wotte** er brauch net lang Schmaetze hawwe
I must wish he need not long pain have
'I do wish, he didn't need to be in pain for long'

f. Er dut als **wotte**, er kennt noch eens vun
He does always wish, he could again one of
die Ebbel hawwe
the apples have
'He is always wishing he could have one more of the apples'

[5] The verb *winsche* has not disappeared entirely – it survives in a subjunctive form, and both *Ich* ***wott****, er kennt mitkumme* and *Ich* ***winscht****, er kennt mitkumme* (both meaning 'I wish he could come with us') are possible in present-day Pennsylvania German (Mark Louden, p.c.).

It is not uncommon per se for the past subjunctive of certain modal verbs to be used in modest expressions of volition, as in the German example below, involving the modal *mögen* 'may':

| | | | | | | |
|---|---|---|---|---|---|---|
| (11) | Ich | **möchte,** | dass | er | mal | aufhört |
| | I | may-PAST.SUBJ | that | he | once | stops |
| | 'I wished he would just stop doing that' | | | | | |

What is special about Pennsylvania German *wotte* is, however, that this subjunctive modal went on to develop into a lexical verb, something which Standard German *möchte* did not do. According to Burridge, the explanation for this remarkable development has to be sought in extralinguistic factors. She points out that Pennsylvania German speakers, in particular the Old Order Mennonites which formed the focus of Burridge's studies, are a deeply religious people, whose self-will and self-love is entirely subordinated to the will of God:

> Speakers are quite clearly uncomfortable with blunt expressions of desire or will. It is hardly surprising then that the usual German verb of 'wishing' and 'desiring' *winsche* has all but disappeared from this language. The use of the past subjunctive has always had a range of different tentative or remote applications in Germanic. Its element of

TABLE 4.1. Parameter analysis of Pennsylvania German *wotte*

| Parameter | Primitive change(s) |
|---|---|
| **Integrity** | *resemanticization:* ☑; there has been a shift from grammatical (modal) meaning ('would') to full lexical meaning ('to wish').<br>*phonological 'strengthening':* ☐; there is no change in the verb stem at the phonological level.<br>*recategorialization:* ☑; lexical *wotte* has acquired regular verb morphology. |
| **Paradigmaticity** | *deparadigmaticization:* ☑; *wotte* has shifted from a minor word class (modal verbs) to a major word class (lexical verbs). |
| **Paradigmatic variability** | *deobligatorification:* ☑; the selection of *wotte* as a full verb meaning 'to wish' depends on the lexical context, not on the syntactic construction (as was the case with modal preterite subjunctive *wotte*, which was obligatory in modal constructions). |
| **Structural scope** | *scope expansion:* ☑; modal verbs only take scope over a VP, but lexical *wotte* may take clausal complements, as in some of the examples above. |
| **Bondedness** | not relevant in primary degrammaticalization. |
| **Syntagmatic variability** | *flexibilization:* ☑; as a full verb, *wotte* can appear in more construction types (both finite and infinite). |

unreality means it can offer a more indirect, a more cautious, a more modest, a more polite, even a more objective mode of expression than the more pedestrian indicative. (Burridge 1998: 32)

A second example which might be a case of degrammation is Chinese *děi/dé* (Ziegeler 2004). In Old Chinese (500 BC – AD 200), this was a lexical verb meaning 'to obtain', as in (12):

| | | | |
|---|---|---|---|
| (12) | ér | **dé** | tiānxià |
| | and | obtain | world |

'and have the kingdom'

The object of the verb could be either physical or abstract. In addition, *dé* could be used as a preverbal modal of permission in negative or rhetorical contexts (example (13), which can be seen as an extension from 'to obtain an object (NP)' to 'to obtain an act (V)' (Ziegeler 2004: 122). The permissive usage, in turn, gave rise to a deontic usage of *dé* (ibid.: 123f.), and in Modern Chinese, deontic obligation is still the main modal meaning of *děi* (example (14)).

| | | | | | | |
|---|---|---|---|---|---|---|
| (13) | zǐkuài | bu | **dé** | yǔ | rén | yàn |
| | Zi Kuai | NEG | permit | give | other | Yan |

'Zi Kuai is not permitted to give other(s) the state of Yan!'

| | | | | |
|---|---|---|---|---|
| (14) | hái | **děi** | chī | ròu |
| | still | should | eat | meat |

'(One) still has to eat meat'

Thus far, the development of *dé/děi* appears to be a regular case of grammaticalization. In present-day Chinese, however, *děi* developed a new, lexical meaning 'need, take, require'. It can be used in two contexts: preceding a numeral classifier (example (15a)), or preceding a noun clause (example (15b)) (Ziegeler 2004: 124):

| | | | | | | | | |
|---|---|---|---|---|---|---|---|---|
| (15) | a. | zhè | ge | gōngzuò | **děi** | sān | ge | rén |
| | | this | CL | work | needs | three | CL | people |

'this work needs three people'

| | | | | | | | | |
|---|---|---|---|---|---|---|---|---|
| b. | bié | rén | qù | bù | xíng | **děi** | nǐ | qīnzì | qù |
| | other | people | go | not | ok | need | you | in-person | go |

'It's not ok for other people to go, it requires that you go in person'

That the new lexical verb developed from the modal and not from the original lexical verb meaning 'to obtain' is evidenced by its phonological form: the modal and the verb meaning 'need' are both *děi*, whereas the original verb 'to obtain' has retained the form *dé* (ibid.: 125).

TABLE 4.2. Parameter analysis of Chinese *dĕi*

| Parameter | Primitive change(s) |
|---|---|
| **Integrity** | *resemanticization:* ☑; there has been a shift from grammatical (modal) meaning ('should') to full lexical meaning ('to need').<br>*phonological 'strengthening':* ☐; there is no change at the phonological level.<br>*recategorialization:* ☐; this is probably not relevant for an isolating language such as Chinese. |
| **Paradigmaticity** | *deparadigmaticization:* ☑; *dĕi* has shifted from a minor word class (modal verbs) to a major word class (lexical verbs). |
| **Paradigmatic variability** | *deobligatorification:* ☑; the selection of *dĕi* as a full verb meaning 'to wish' depends on the lexical context.[a] |
| **Structural scope** | *scope expansion:* ☑; modal verbs only take scope over a VP, but *dĕi* may take clausal complements, as in example (15b). |
| **Bondedness** | not relevant in primary degrammaticalization. |
| **Syntagmatic variability** | *flexibilization:* ☐; on the basis of the available evidence, it is not possible to say whether *dĕi* gained in syntactic freedom. |

[a] Ziegeler (2004: 124) remarks, however, that the construction with *dĕi* meaning 'need' is not generally accepted by native speakers – some regard it as highly idiomatic, others as dialectal.

## 4.3 Bulgarian *nešto*: from indefinite pronoun to noun 'thing'

This example (Willis 2007: 278ff.) represents the reverse development from a cross-linguistically common shift from generic nouns such as 'person' or 'thing' to indefinite pronouns such as 'something' or 'someone' (Haspelmath 1997a; Heine and Kuteva 2002: 208f., 232f., 295f.; see also section 2.6.3). Bulgarian *nešto* 'thing' (cf. Old Church Slavonic *něčĭto*) was used as an indefinite pronoun meaning 'something' (see (16a)). Although *něčĭto* may be semantically ambiguous, its morphosyntactic behaviour is clearly that of a pronoun. For example, modification is largely limited to adjectives in the short (indefinite) form, as in (16b).[6] Modern Bulgarian *nešto*, on the other

[6] There was no fixed order between adjectives and nouns or pronouns in Old Church Slavonic, so the position of the adjective in (16b) is not indicative of the word-class status of *něč'to*. One might thus interpret *něč'to* as a noun here, but since it is always accompanied by the short (indefinite) form of the adjective, this would mean that *něč'to* is a noun which only appears in indefinite contexts, which would be very odd. Hence, it is most appropriately analysed as a pronoun (David Willis, p.c.).

hand, functions both as a pronoun and as a neuter noun. As a noun, it has regular neuter inflection (plural *nešta*, definite form *neštoto*, with enclitic definite article) and may be modified by adjectives, as in (16c). As a pronoun, it is morphosyntactically much more restricted, as was Old Church Slavonic *něčĭto*. The differences between its use as a noun and as a pronoun are illustrated in (16c–d) (Willis 2007: 279f.; 282)).

(16) a. Simone imamŭ ti ***něčŭto*** rešti
Simon have-PRES.1SG you-DAT something say-INF
'Simon, I have something to say to you'

b. **něč'to** ino zŭlo **něč'to**
something else-NEUT evil-NEUT something
'something else' 'something evil'

c. vsjako novo **nešto** e dobre zabraveno staro
every new thing is well forgotten old
'every new thing is a well-forgotten old one'

d. Predi dve godini xorata glasuvaxa
before two years people-the voted-3PL
sigurno za promjanata, iskajki **nešto** po-dobro
decisively for change-the, seek-GER something better
'Two years ago people voted decisively for change, wanting something better'

Although the transition from pronoun to noun appears to be rare cross-linguistically, in this particular case it is not difficult to conceive how this change could have occurred both from a semantic and a morphosyntactic point of view, as Willis convincingly demonstrates. In some contexts, 'something' can easily be interpreted as an unspecified, unknown 'thing'.[7] This change was facilitated by the relatively free word order in Old Church Slavonic, in which a pronoun modified by an adjective could easily have been interpreted as a full noun phrase, as well as by the coincidental circumstance that *nešto* could be the nominative singular form of a neuter noun. Finally, thanks to the erosion of the Bulgarian case system, irregular (pronominal) case forms that might have inhibited the reanalysis of *nešto* as a noun disappeared.

[7] A parallel shift is attested in Modern Dutch, where one can say things like *een geschikter iemand* 'a more suitable someone (person)', or *een heel ander iets* 'a very different something (thing)'. Although *iemand* and *iets* still have a long way to go to noun-hood (they cannot be pluralized or take a definite article), the semantic shift is similar.

TABLE 4.3. Parameter analysis of Bulgarian *nešto*

| Parameter | Primitive change(s) |
|---|---|
| **Integrity** | *resemanticization:* ☑; there has been a shift from pronoun with abstract meaning ('something') to noun with concrete meaning ('thing'). *phonological 'strengthening':* ☐; there is no change at the phonological level. *recategorialization:* ☑; *nešto* acquired noun morphology. |
| **Paradigmaticity** | *deparadigmaticization:* ☑; there has been a shift from pronoun (closed class item) to noun (open class item). |
| **Paradigmatic variability** | *deobligatorification:* ☑; the selection of *nešto* as a noun is only dependent on the lexical context. |
| **Structural scope** | *scope expansion:* ☐; both pronouns and nouns can be the head of an NP, but generally nouns can take more kinds of complements; it is not clear however whether this qualifies as scope expansion. |
| **Bondedness** | not relevant in primary degrammaticalization. |
| **Syntagmatic variability** | *flexibilization:* ☑; generally, nouns can appear in more construction types (definite and indefinite; modified by quantifiers (*mnogo nešta* 'many things') or numerals (*pet nešta* 'five things')). |

## 4.4 Welsh *eiddo*: from possessive pronoun to noun 'property'

As in the example discussed in the previous section, the case of Welsh *eiddo* (Willis 2007: 283ff.) involves the emergence of a generic noun from a pronominal form. In Modern Welsh, *eiddo* functions both as a noun meaning 'property' and as a MASC.3SG possessive pronoun 'his'. The Middle and Modern Welsh possessive pronominal paradigm is given in Table 4.4. These pronouns, which are rather formal, are preceded by a definite article and are optionally followed by a reinforcing pronoun when they are used independently as absolute possessive pronouns, as in example (17) (Willis 2007: 284):

| | | | | | | | | | |
|---|---|---|---|---|---|---|---|---|---|
| (17) | 'Rwy | 'n | hoffi | ... ei | gwmni | a | 'i | wlad | yn |
| | am | PROG | like.INF | ... his | company | and | his | country | PRD |

well na 'r ***eiddot*** ti
better than the yours you
'I like . . . his company and his country better than yours'

Table 4.4. Paradigm of the possessive pronoun in Welsh (Willis 2007: 284)

| | Middle Welsh | | Modern Welsh | |
|---|---|---|---|---|
| | Singular | Plural | Singular | Plural |
| 1st person | *meu* | *einym* | *eiddof* | *eiddom* |
| 2nd person | *teu* | *einwch* | *eiddot* | *eiddoch* |
| 3rd person | *eidaw* (masc.)<br>*eidi* (fem.) | *eidu(nt)* | *eiddo* (masc.)<br>*eiddi* (fem.) | *eiddynt* |

As a noun, *eiddo* may be modified by adjectives, demonstratives, and quantifiers,[8] which clearly separates *eiddo* from other members in the possessive pronominal paradigm, such as FEM.3SG *eiddi*:

(18) a. eiddo lledrad
EIDDO stolen
'stolen property'
b. *eiddi ledrad
EIDDI stolen
'stolen things of hers'

(19) a. yr eiddo hwn
the EIDDO this-MASC
'this property'
b. *yr eiddi hwn
the EIDDI this-MASC
'these things of hers'

Etymologically, *eiddo* derives from a Common Celtic possessive, so this, too, is clearly a case of a grammatical element becoming lexical. The development from pronoun to noun proceeded gradually, in a series of semantic and syntactic changes in ambiguous contexts.

(i) In Middle Welsh constructions such as (20a), the pronoun was inflectionally similar to a preposition (which in Welsh are inflected), and could thus be interpreted to mean 'of him' rather than 'his'. This interpretation was further facilitated by the accidental formal similarity of *eidaw* to the 3SG. MASC form of prepositions, such as *hebdaw* 'without (him)'. And when *eidaw* was used independently (i.e. when it did not modify a noun), it must be preceded by an article, as in (20b) (Willis 2007: 285).

[8] However, since *eiddo* is a mass noun, it cannot be pluralized (David Willis, p.c.).

(20) a. ef... a gymyrth y dyrnas yn **eidaw**
he... PRT took the kingdom PRD his
ef ehvn
3MASC.SG himself
'he... took the kingdom as his own'

b. emelltith Duw a 'r **eidaw** ynteu
curse God and the his 3MASC.SG
'the curse of God and his own'

(ii) The inflected prepositions could occur with a null object, since their inflection indicated person and number of the object. Because of the similarities between inflected prepositions and possessive pronouns, the latter, too, could be used independently, that is, without a reinforcing pronoun following it.

(iii) In cases where there is no overt possessor and *eiddo* is preceded by an article, an ambiguous context arises, in which *eiddo* can be interpreted either as 'the (X which is) his', in which case it is a pronoun, or as a noun meaning 'property', by means of a plausible semantic shift. Another ambiguous context is one in which EIDDO is followed by a possessor phrase, as in (21). Here EIDDO does not occur in absolute position (and is hence not preceded by an article), but with possessive noun phrases the definite article is precluded anyway, so that EIDDO here, too, may be reinterpreted as a head noun, with the possessor phrase as its modifier (Willis 2007: 288).

(21) nyt **eydav** vn tewyssav[c] e vudvgolyaeth
NEG EIDDO one prince the victory
'the victory is not a single prince's (property)'

That EIDDO indeed had been reinterpreted as a noun becomes evident in texts from the fourteenth century onwards where it is preceded by a proclitic possessive, as in (22). In this example, it is also clear that 'property' is the only sensible interpretation:

(22) Pan vo marw righill yn trugared
when be-PRES.SUBJ.3SG dead sergeant in mercy
yr arglwyd y byd y **eidaw**
the lord PRT be-FUT.3SG his property
'Whenever a sergeant dies, his property is at the mercy of the lord'

The case of EIDDO is an interesting one, because it involves a series of both semantic-pragmatic and syntactic reanalyses, which makes it quite similar to

TABLE 4.5. Parameter analysis of Welsh *eiddo*

| Parameter | Primitive change(s) |
|---|---|
| **Integrity** | *resemanticization:* ☑; *eiddo* acquires lexical content ('property').<br>*phonological 'strengthening':* ☐; there has been no change at the phonological level.<br>*recategorialization:* ☑; as a noun, *eiddo* can, among other things, be preceded by adjectives or possessives. |
| **Paradigmaticity** | *deparadigmaticization:* ☑; there has been a shift from pronoun (closed class item) to noun (open class item). |
| **Paradigmatic variability** | *deobligatorification:* ☑; the selection of *eiddo* as a noun is only dependent on the lexical context. |
| **Structural scope** | *scope expansion:* ☐; generally, nouns can take more types of complements than do pronouns (e.g. possessives, articles, or PPs), but it is not quite clear whether this is scope change in the Lehmannian sense. Also, the noun *eiddo* cannot take PP complements (David Willis, p.c.) so there is no conclusive evidence for scope change in this case. I will therefore disregard this parameter here. |
| **Bondedness** | not relevant in primary degrammaticalization. |
| **Syntagmatic variability** | *flexibilization:* ☑; As a pronoun, *eidaw* had to be preceded by a predicate marker *yn* or a definite article *yr*, but modern *eiddo* can function as an NP in its own right (David Willis, p.c.). |

grammaticalization, with the crucial difference being the direction of the change.

## 4.5 Middle Welsh *yn ol*: from preposition to Modern Welsh full verb *nôl* 'to fetch'

The third and final type of degrammation discussed in Willis (2007) is the development of the Welsh preposition *yn ôl* 'after' into a verb *nôl* 'to bring'. Middle Welsh *yn ol* 'after' (both spatial and temporal)[9] is itself a grammaticalized compound preposition which derives from the preposition *yn* 'in' + a noun

[9] The temporal meaning 'after' developed further into the meaning 'according to', and the Modern Welsh preposition *yn ôl* has lost the spatial and temporal meanings entirely.

*ol* 'track(s), path, trail' (Willis 2007: 292).[10] The spatial use is illustrated in example (23a), where there is still a hint of the original meaning of 'in (its) tracks' (ibid.: 292). The temporal usage gave rise to an additional meaning 'according to'; example (23b) is ambiguous between these two interpretations (ibid.: 293).

(23) a.

| | | | | | | | | |
|---|---|---|---|---|---|---|---|---|
| a | 'r | baed | yn | kyrchu | yr | gaer | yn | uuan, |
| and | the | boar | PROG | head.for | to.the | fortress | PRD | swift |

| | | | | | |
|---|---|---|---|---|---|
| a | 'r | cwn | **yn** | y | **ol** |
| and | the | dogs | in | his | track |

'and the boar was heading for the fortress swiftly, with the dogs behind/after it'

b.

| | | | | | |
|---|---|---|---|---|---|
| A | gwedy | hynny | Lawnslot | a | dyngawd |
| And | after | that | Lawnslot | PRT | swear.PAST.3SG |

| | | | | | | |
|---|---|---|---|---|---|---|
| a | Gwalchmei | a | Pheredur | a | Bwrt | a |
| and | Gwalchmai | and | Peredur | and | Bwrt | and |

| | | | | | | | |
|---|---|---|---|---|---|---|---|
| Lionel | a | chwbyl | o'r | milwyr | ereill | pob | un |
| Lionel | and | all | of.the | warriors | other | every | one |

| | | |
|---|---|---|
| **yn ol** | y | gilyd |
| after | each | other |

'And after that, Lawnslot swore an oath, and Gwalchmai and Peredur and Bwrt and Lionel and all the other warriors, each one after the others / each one in the same way as the others'

In late Middle Welsh however, *yn ol* began to appear in ambiguous contexts where it could be interpreted either as a preposition meaning 'after', or as a verb meaning 'to fetch', as in (24a). Subsequently a split occurs ('divergence' in Hopper and Traugott's (2003: 118) terminology) – *yn ol* continues as a preposition whereas the verb is reduced to *nôl*. The first examples of *nôl* occur in the sixteenth century, and from the seventeenth century onwards unambiguously verbal forms are attested, as in (24b) (Willis 2007: 294, 297).

(24) a.

| | | | | | | | | |
|---|---|---|---|---|---|---|---|---|
| Yna | yd | aeth | y | gweisson | ***yn ol*** | y | varch | a |
| then | PART | went | the | lads | after | his | horse | and |

| | | | |
|---|---|---|---|
| 'e | arueu | y | Arthur |
| his | weapons | for | Arthur |

'Then the lads went after / went to fetch his horse and his weapons for Arthur'

[10] The grammaticalization path FOOTPRINT > BEHIND is also known from African languages (Heine and Kuteva 2002: 141).

b. **Nolwch** y Brenin i 'w examnio
fetch-2PL.IMP the King to 3MASC.SG examine-INF
'Fetch the king to be cross-examined'

The semantic change from 'go after' to 'go and fetch' seems to involve the same kind of pragmatic inferencing as do standard examples of grammaticalization. For if someone is going after something, it is reasonable to assume that s/he has the intention of bringing it back. What we witness here, then, is a metonymic shift which is commonly attested in (incipient) grammaticalization. According to Willis (2007: 299), this leads to the surprising conclusion that pragmatic inferencing is a bidirectional process (Willis 2007: 299). Apart

TABLE 4.6. Parameter analysis of Welsh *nôl*

| Parameter | Primitive change(s) |
| --- | --- |
| **Integrity** | *resemanticization:* ☑; there has been a shift from a more abstract spatial meaning ('after') to full lexical meaning ('to fetch').<br>*phonological 'strengthening':* ☒; on the contrary, *yn ol* is reduced to *nôl.*<br>*recategorialization:* ☑; *nôl* has acquired full verbal morphology. |
| **Paradigmaticity** | *deparadigmaticization:* ☑; there has been a shift from closed class item (preposition) to open class item (verb). |
| **Paradigmatic variability** | *deobligatorification:* ☑; the selection of *nôl* as a verb is only dependent on the lexical context. |
| **Structural scope** | *scope expansion:* ☐; again, the change is inconclusive with respect to scope – the preposition *yn ol* only takes scope over its prepositional object, which can be a full NP, whereas the transitive verb *nôl* takes scope over the entire clause, which can likewise be a full NP. |
| **Bondedness** | not relevant in primary degrammaticalization. |
| **Syntagmatic variability** | *flexibilization:* ☑; the verb *nôl* enjoys more syntactic freedom than the preposition *yn ol,* because the preposition obligatorily precedes its (prepositional) object whereas a verb can often both precede and follow its (direct) object. In Welsh, the unmarked order is VSO, but the object can be fronted for emphasis, yielding OVS (David Willis, p.c.). |

from pragmatic inferencing, the history of *nôl* shares another characteristic with grammaticalization: phonological reduction or attrition. This reduction is the result of reanalysis of morpheme boundaries – the phrase *yn ol y varch* in (24a) could be reinterpreted as *y nol y varch* 'to fetch his horse'. And finally, this change involves divergence, in that the 'more grammaticalized' preposition *yn ol* is still used as a preposition (in unambiguous contexts) whereas the 'less grammaticalized' verb developed into *nôl* (Willis 2007: 296).

# 5

# Deinflectionalization

## 5.1 Introduction

Deinflectionalization is the first type of secondary degrammaticalization. Like degrammation, it involves changes in both form and function, but unlike in degrammation, the gram remains bound:

(1) Deinflectionalization is a composite change whereby an inflectional affix in a specific linguistic context gains a new function, while shifting to a less bound morpheme type.

Potentially valid examples of deinflectionalization will be changes where an inflectional affix becomes either enclitic or derivational. It is a subtle kind of degrammaticalization, because it involves a shift from one type of bound morpheme to another. This immediately raises two fundamental questions: (i) how can we establish (changes in) morphological status, and (ii) how can we establish which bound morphemes are 'less grammatical' than others? I will therefore start this chapter with a section on morphological demarcations, including differences in grammaticality.

## 5.2 Classifying bound morphemes

Delineating the boundaries between different kinds of bound morphemes is a major issue in current morphological theory. A number of tests have been proposed to distinguish inflection from derivation, inflection from cliticization, and derivation from compounding, and although these tests have proven useful for the classification and demarcation of different kinds of morphemes, none of them is exceptionless. In the next two sections, I will provide a brief discussion of the inflection–derivation interface, and of the inflection–cliticization interface, which will serve as the theoretical grid for the analysis of the deinflectionalization changes discussed in the last sections of this chapter.

### 5.2.1 *Inflectional versus derivational affixes*

Most linguists appear to have an intuitive understanding of the differences between inflectional and derivational morphology, but it is obvious that there is no strict boundary between the two. Various criteria to distinguish inflection from derivation have been proposed in the literature (see e.g. Bybee 1985b: 81ff.; Anderson 1992: 77ff.; Haspelmath 1996; Beard 1998: 44ff.; Stump 1998: 14ff.), the most common of which are (i) obligatoriness, (ii) the ability to change word class, and (iii) cumulative exponence. I will provide a brief discussion of these three criteria, and it will be seen that none of them is entirely without exceptions.

(i) *Obligatoriness.* Inflections are obligatory in a given morphosyntactic context, but derivational affixes are not. As Anderson (1992: 101) put it: 'inflectional morphology is the area in which principles of syntactic structure and of word formation interact with one another'. In other words, unlike derivation, inflection is syntactically relevant, and hence more grammatical. For instance, derived words can generally be substituted by monomorphemic words. Thus, the (derivational) suffix *-ling* is not obligatory, as example (2b) shows, but the (inflectional) verbal suffix *-ing* cannot be left out in progressive constructions, as in (2c) (Bybee 1985b: 81):

(2) a. the duckling was swimming
b. the duck was swimming
c. *the duckling was swim

An interesting exception to this criterion are Dutch derivations for female inhabitatives, described in van Marle (1996: 70f.). In contrast to other female derivations (cf. (3a)), inhabitative female suffixes are compulsory, as is shown in example (3b):

(3) a. Zij is een goede verteller / vertelster
She is a good story-teller (NEUTRAL / FEMALE)[1]
b. Marie is een echte *Amsterdammer / Amsterdamse
Marie is a real *[neutral inhabitant] / [female inhabitant] of Amsterdam

However, such exceptions appear to be very rare, which makes obligatoriness a potentially useful criterion. And as obligatorification is considered as a primitive change typically involved in grammaticalization (see section 3.5.1), the obligatoriness of inflections suggests that these are 'more grammatical'.

[1] In these examples, NEUTRAL means that the noun is not specified for gender, and can hence be used when the sex of the person is unknown.

(ii) *Change in word class.* Derivational affixes can (but need not) change word class. Thus the adjective *beautiful* is derived from the noun *beauty,* and the noun *greatness* is derived from the adjective *great.* To this criterion there appear to be far more exceptions than to the criterion of obligatoriness, for there are many known cases of word-class-changing inflection. For instance, both the Swedish inflectional suffix *-t* (originally the neuter suffix of adjectives) and the English suffix *-ly* (which is 'moving towards inflectional status' (Brinton and Traugott 2005: 136)) can be used to form adverbs from adjectives.[2] A particularly interesting example is provided by Haspelmath (1996: 44), who argues that the German inflectional present participial ending *-ende* changes word class, as in the following example:

| | | | | | | |
|---|---|---|---|---|---|---|
| (4) | der | im | Wald | laut | sing**ende** | Wanderer |
| | the | in.the-DAT | forest | loud | sing-PTCP | hiker |
| | 'the hiker (who is) singing loudly in the forest' | | | | | |

The suffix *-ende* is a verbal inflection, but in example (4) the participle has properties of both verbs and adjectives. It is verbal in that it is modified by both a locative phrase (*im Wald*) and a manner adverb (*laut*), but it is adjectival in that it occurs in prenominal position as a modifier of a noun. In sum, the ability–to-change-word-class criterion does not appear strict enough to distinguish derivations from inflections.

(iii) *Cumulative exponence.* According to Anderson (1992: 76) 'portmanteaux are much rarer in derivation (if indeed such elements exist at all)'. In other words, a cumulative (portmanteau) morpheme which denotes more than one category (e.g. gender and number) is most likely to be inflectional. For example, the Latin inflectional ending *-us* in *servus* 'slave' denotes gender (MASC), number (SG), and case (NOM).

However, Ricca (2005: 200) has shown that derivational suffixes may be cumulative as well, with feminine agentive suffixes as a case in point, e.g. Italian *gioca**trice*** 'female player' or French *vend**euse*** 'female seller'. Unlike their masculine non-cumulative counterparts (as in *gioca**tore*** and *vend**eur***) respectively), the feminine suffixes denote both gender and agentivity, and are therefore cumulative derivational suffixes.

In sum, of the three criteria to distinguish inflection from derivation obligatoriness will probably prove the most useful one, but it is evident

[2] That the Swedish forms in *-t* are not merely neuter forms of the adjective is evidenced by the fact that there are adverbs in *-t* without an adjectival counterpart, e.g. *enbart* 'only' (there is no adjective **enbar*).

that there are no clear-cut boundaries between inflection and derivation. The same stance is taken by Booij (2002), who argues against the 'split morphology hypothesis' (advocated in e.g. Anderson 1992), which says that inflection and derivation belong to different modules of the grammar. In his own classification, Booij (2002: 19f.) makes a distinction between inherent inflection ('that kind of inflection that adds morpho-syntactic properties with an independent semantic value to the stem of the word'), and contextual inflection ('that kind of inflection that is required by syntactic context, but does not add information'). An example of contextual inflection is the marking of number and person on tensed verbs: these categories have to be expressed because the verb has to agree in number and person with the subject. An example of inherent inflection is number on nouns, because this category is not exclusively dictated by syntax.

Inherent inflection is closer to derivation than contextual inflection (Booij 2002: 20ff, 29, 42). Like derivation, inherent inflection:

(1) adds information to the base, which is particularly apparent in minimal pairs such as Dutch *portiers* 'door-keepers' / *portieren* 'car doors'.
(2) may have gaps in the paradigm, usually for semantic reasons, e.g. the absence of plural forms of mass nouns such as Dutch *aandacht* 'attention', *hooi* 'hay', or *Nederlands* 'the Dutch language', or suppletion with adjectives, e.g. *goed* 'good' / *beter* 'better' / *best* 'best'.
(3) may have a non-existing word as its base, as in pluralia tantum: Dutch *hersenen* 'brains' (**hersen*), *notulen* 'minutes of a meeting' (**notuul*).
(4) may acquire idiosyncratic meanings, e.g. participles such as Dutch *gesloten* 'closed, tight-lipped' (< *sluiten* 'to close'), or *geslepen* 'sharpened, sly' (< *slijpen* 'to sharpen').
(5) may be borrowed from another language, e.g. Dutch *musea, rectores.*

Thus far, I have only discussed synchronic properties of derivation and inflection, but diachronically too, derivation and inflection behave differently. These differences are summarized in Table 5.1.

When comparing derivation and inflection, both synchronically and diachronically, it makes sense to conclude that derivation is generally 'less grammatical' than inflection – it is not obligatory, and does not convey grammatical meaning. In addition, derivational affixes may take scope over an entire phrase, whereas inflectional affixes do not. In Dutch, for example, adding a derivational suffix to an entire phrase is a common process of word-formation:

TABLE 5.1. Diachronic characteristics of derivation and inflection

| Derivational affixes | Inflectional affixes |
|---|---|
| may fossilize<br>PGmc *-*ni*- (to derive abstract N from V): MoSw ***början*** 'beginning' (cf. *börja* 'to begin'), ***syn*** 'view' (cf. *se* 'to see')<br>PGmc *-*iþō* (to derive abstract N from Adj): MoSw *längd*, Dutch *lengte*, English *length* | may fossilize<br>MoDu *schoen* 'shoe' (< plural of older *schoe* 'shoe')<br>French *fils* 'son' (< Lat. MASC.SG.NOM *filius*) |
| do not usually become zero (fossilize instead) | may become zero (frequently)<br>most of OE verbal and nominal morphology |
| may lexicalize<br>*isms* and *ologies* | do not lexicalize |
| may become inflectional<br>ModE adverbial -*ly* | may become derivational (cf. sections 5.4–5.6) |

(5)[3] a. 'kleed je favoriete barbie aan'-**achtige** spelletjes
[dress your favourite barbie]-like games
'games of the type "dress your favourite barbie"'

b. geld-over-de-balk-gooi**erij**
[money-over-the-beam-throw]-ing
'(the act of) throwing one's money about'

Indeed, both Kuryłowicz (1975: 52) and Heine, Claudi, and Hünnemeyer (1991: 213) regard the shift from a derivational affix to an inflectional one as grammaticalization, which implies that inflectional affixes are 'more grammatical'. The reverse, from inflection to derivation, would hence be an example of degrammaticalization. According to Haspelmath (2004: 32), however, an inflectional affix becoming derivational does not count as an instance of degrammaticalization, because '[i]nflectional patterns do not show stronger internal dependencies than derivational patterns'. This is a questionable position, however. On the basis of the criteria to distinguish inflection from derivation listed above, inflection can be interpreted as showing exactly these stronger internal dependencies, or a higher degree of

[3] The examples in (5) were found on http://tweakers.net/nieuws/52752/online-gaming-minder-populair-dan-gedacht.html, and http://luxereizen.blog.nl/algemeen/2007/11/16/first-class-mas-dat-is-pas-klasse-vliegen respectively.

grammaticality. Another argument against Haspelmath's claim is provided by Luraghi (2005: 10), who shows that derivational affixes may be less specific in stem selection than inflectional ones. Italian (derivational) *-ante*, for example, can be attached to both verbal stems and nominal stems, as exemplified in (6):

(6) a. insegnare insegn**ante**
'to teach' 'teacher'

b. edicola edicol**ante**
'newspaper booth' 'newspaper seller'

Luraghi goes on to argue that, following Lehmann's (2004) definition that '[g]rammaticalization of a linguistic sign is a process in which it loses in autonomy by becoming more subject to constraints of the linguistic system', the change from derivational to inflectional must be considerd degrammaticalization, 'since derivational affixes are less subject to constraints of the linguistic system than inflectional affixes'.

Summing up the discussion thus far, inflections can generally be said to be more grammatical than derivational affixes. In sections 5.4–5.6, I will examine whether a shift from inflection to derivation amounts to degrammaticalization in terms of Lehmann's parameters as well.

### 5.2.2 *Inflectional affixes versus clitics*

Demarcating inflectional affixes from clitics is no less complicated than demarcating inflectional affixes from derivational ones. Most linguists agree that clitics and affixes form a continuum, and indeed they form two contiguous points on the cline of grammaticality (see (8) below).

Clitics alone are a subject of monographic proportions, such as Anderson (2005), to mention but one, and I will therefore confine myself to some general properties that separate them from affixes. Stressing once more that the differences are gradient rather than absolute, I will show how a well-defined set of criteria (such as Zwicky and Pullum 1983, which I will discuss shortly) suffices to show if indeed an affix has degrammaticalized into a clitic, as in the case of the s-genitive (section 5.3).

Traditionally, clitics have been split into two major types: 'simple clitics' and 'special clitics'. Simple clitics are reduced forms of full words, which are prosodically dependent on a 'host', and which appear in the same syntactic position as the full form. An example is English *'re* as in *they're fine*, which corresponds to the full form *are*, and appears in the same position as the full form. Special clitics, on the other hand, often lack a stressed counterpart and/or display special syntax.[4] A prototypical special clitic is the enclitic conjunction *-que* in Latin, which does not appear between conjoined phrases, as does the independent conjunction *et* (*senatus et populus Romanus* 'the senate and the people of Rome'), but on the first word of the last element in a sequence of conjoined phrases: *senatus populusque Romanus* (Anderson 1992: 199ff.).

There are many alternative classifications of clitics (e.g. Halpern 1995 or Börjars 2003), but for the present purpose the most workable model is one in which prototypical affixes and prototypical ('simple') clitics are viewed as the two extremes on a continuum (for a similar view see Allen 1997: 122). The points that are in between are difficult to establish (and probably language-specific).

In Zwicky and Pullum's seminal paper from 1983, the authors identify six criteria for distinguishing affixes from clitics, given in (7).

(7) Zwicky and Pullum's criteria
   a. Clitics can exhibit a low degree of selection with respect to their hosts, while affixes exhibit a high degree of selection with respect to their stems.
   b. Arbitrary gaps in the set of combinations are more characteristic of affixed words than of clitic groups.
   c. Morphophonological idiosyncrasies are more characteristic of affixed words than of clitic groups.
   d. Semantic idiosyncrasies are more characteristic of affixed words than of clitic groups.
   e. Syntactic rules can affect affixed words, but cannot affect clitic groups.
   f. Clitics can attach to material already containing clitics, but affixes cannot.

The careful way in which the criteria are formulated reflects the fact that there is no absolute line of division between affixes and clitics. Nevertheless, these criteria are sufficiently explicit to make a very workable set of tests, with one important proviso. Four of the criteria have primarily something to say about affixes, and only two (the first and the sixth criterion) can be used to positively identify a clitic. In other words, four of the criteria can only be used to show that a given morpheme is *probably not an affix*.[5] Nevertheless, in section 5.3.2 it will be seen that Zwicky and Pullum's criteria prove useful as

[4] An example of special clitics which correspond to a full form but display special syntax nevertheless are the Romance pronominal clitics (Anderson 1992: 202).

[5] I owe this observation to Lars Heltoft.

*relative* criteria to assess whether a given morpheme has moved towards the affix end or towards the clitic end of the affix–clitic continuum.

### 5.2.3 *Continua*

Diachronically, the bound suffixes are assumed to derive from different sources. Clitics and inflectional affixes are cluster points on the cline of grammaticality (repeated here as (8)), while derivational affixes usually arise out of compounds, via the cline of lexicality (repeated here as (9)):

(8) content item > grammatical word > clitic > inflectional affix

| | | | | |
|---|---|---|---|---|
| (9) part of phrase | > | part of compound | > | derivational affix |
| a basket **full** (of eggs) | > | a cup**ful** (of water) | > | hope**ful** |

If these clines were universal, clitics could become inflectional affixes (grammaticalization), or vice versa (degrammaticalization), but clitics and inflectional affixes could not become derivational or vice versa. Yet there is ample evidence that derivational affixes can become inflectional (see section 5.2.1 for examples), and that inflectional affixes can become derivational (see sections 5.4–5.6). Therefore, there appears to exist a cline involving both inflection and derivation as well. Such clines have indeed been proposed, e.g. (10) (Dalton-Puffer 1996: 175), and (11) (Booij 2002: 19f.; cf. section 5.2.1).

(10) lexical > lexical-derivational > quasi-syntactic > inflectional[6]

(11) lexical > derivational > inherent inflectional > contextual inflectional

Clitics and derivational affixes may also form part of the same cline, as argued by Hopper and Traugott:

> While there is not always evidence of a clitic pre-stage in the grammaticalization of affixes out of autonomous lexical words, the fixing or 'freezing' and loss of lexical autonomy involved in the process *presupposes a clitic stage.* In the example of French *-ment*, Spanish *-mente*..., and in other examples of derivational affixes such as English *-hood*, *-ly* etc. out of full nouns, it may be assumed that at one stage the eventual affix was attracted to what came to be its future stem and came to form an accentual unit with it. *Clitics obviously have a central role in establishing the sorts of structures that undergo morphologization.* It is the frequent syntactic collocation of a

[6] In her discussion of English *-ly*, Dalton-Puffer (1996: 175) uses the term 'lexical-derivational' for adjectival *-ly*, because its productivity is limited and it may have idiosyncratic meanings, and 'quasi-syntactic' for adverbial *-ly*, because it is very productive and general in meaning. In a similar vein, Hopper and Traugott (2003: 5) distinguish between derivational forms that add a meaning component without changing the categorial status of the word they attach to, e.g. *un-* as in *unhappy* or *-ling* as in *duckling*, and derivational forms that do affect the grammatical category, such as *-ly* (Adj > Adv) or *-er* (V > N). These are termed 'lexical derivational morphemes' and 'grammatical derivational morphemes' respectively.

particular word class, such as a noun, with a particular type of clitic, such as an adposition, that most typically leads to morphologization (e.g. as a noun with a case affix). (Hopper and Traugott 2003: 142; emphasis mine)

It is rather unfortunate that Hopper and Traugott use derivational *-mente* and *-ly* as cases for which a clitic stage is presupposed, because in these examples it is quite clear that they derive from compounds (in the case of *-ly*, from OE compounds with *līċ* 'body'; for *-mente* see section 1.6.5). But there do seem to exist examples of changes involving both cliticization and derivation.

For the Scandinavian *-s(t)* passive it has even been claimed that it involved an enclitic, a derivational, and an inflectional stage. The first stages are undisputed (the passive suffix originates in a Proto-Scandinavian reflexive pronoun **sik* (ACC) or **sēr* (DAT) which was cliticized to the verb), but what happened next is not quite clear. According to the general cline suggested in Harris and Campbell (1995: 337), the inflectional stage would have preceded the derivational stage, as in (12). But for the specific case of the *-s(t)* passive, Faarlund (2005: 63) proposes the cline in (13), while Enger (2002: 93, 97) proposes the cline in (14):

(12) clitic > inflectional affix > derivational affix

(13) simple clitic > special clitic > inflectional affix > derivational affix

(14) clitic > derivational affix > inflectional affix (inherent) > inflectional affix (contextual)

A discussion of these clines and their implications goes beyond the scope of this work, but all authors assume that the Scandinavian passive has been both inflectional and derivational at some point. The gradient transition between the derivational and the inflectional stage is also reflected by the fact that some Old Norse verbs in *-st* are inflectional, whereas others are more derivational (Enger 2002, 2003). What this case teaches us is that it is not always possible to assess some gram's morphological status with absolute certainty. Therefore, each individual case needs to be scrutinized, and sometimes all we can see are delicate shifts in a given direction (as I will argue for the Swedish s-genitive, section 5.3.2). Faarlund (2005: 53) likewise argues that 'it may be more interesting to see how individual items and elements acquire, retain or lose features, than trying to determine their strict category membership at any given point in history'.

## 5.3 The s-genitive (English and Mainland Scandinavian)

### 5.3.1 *Introduction*

One of the most-quoted examples of degrammaticalization is the development of genitive *-s* from inflectional affix to phrase-final (enclitic) determiner. This so-called s-genitive is found in English, Danish, Swedish,[7] and Bokmål Norwegian.[8] The primary distinction between the morphological genitive and the s-genitive is that the former operates on the word level, whereas the latter operates on the phrase level.[9] This is illustrated by the following contrastive pair of sentences from Old and Modern Swedish:

(15) a. ens riks mans hws (Bild 642)
a-MASC.SG.GEN rich-MASC.SG.GEN man-MASC.SG.GEN house

b. en rik mans hus
[a rich man]'s house
'a rich man's house'

In the OSw[10] noun phrase, *ens riks mans*, *-s* is attached to each element separately, whereas in the MoSw counterpart *en rik mans* it is attached to the noun phrase as a whole. A similar contrast is found between Old and Modern English:

(16) a. þæs deofles bearn — Old English[11]
b. the devil's children — ModE

Even more striking examples are the so-called group-genitives, in which *-s* is separated from the head noun by a postmodifying prepositional phrase or relative clause, as in the Swedish examples in (17) and the English examples in (18).[12]

[7] The s-genitive is not found in all varieties of Mainland Scandinavian – it is largely confined to the central part of the continent (including the standard languages, with the exception of *Nynorsk* Norwegian; cf. note 8). For a survey of other possessive constructions attested in the area see Norde (1997: 49ff.), or Dahl (2007: 149ff.).

[8] Norway has two official languages, which were developed in the nineteenth century: *Bokmål* ('Book Language') based on upper-class speech heavily influenced by Danish, and *Nynorsk* ('New Norwegian'), based on a comparative study of Norwegian dialects.

[9] Note that the discussion in this section is confined to attributive possessives where the genitive phrase functions as a determiner, because this is the only construction in which the genitive developed into a clitic (as evidenced by the occurrence of group genitives). This excludes a number of other constructions, among them qualifying genitives (*a children's book*), predicative genitives (*my garden is smaller than Fred's*), or locative genitives (*at the dentist's*).

[10] The main periods of the Swedish language are: Runic Swedish (RSw) 800–1225; Old Swedish (OSw) 1225–1375; Middle Swedish (MiSw) 1375–1526; Early Modern Swedish (EMoSw)1526–1732; Modern Swedish (MoSw)1732–present.

[11] The example is from the eleventh-century Old English translation of Adso of Montièr-en-Der's treatise on the Antichrist (http://webpages.ursinus.edu/jlionarons/wulfstan/frameset2.html). It was suggested to me by Olga Fischer.

[12] All examples were found on the web during Google searches on 3 May 2008.

(17) a. killen mittemot migs ansikte
[guy-DEF opposite me]=GEN face
'the guy opposite me's face'

b. en av dom jag har vuxit upp meds
[one of them I have grown up with]=GEN
lillasyster
little.sister
'one of the people I grew up with's little sister'

(18) a. some R'n'B crap out of the guy opposite me's headphones
b. The blonde I had been dancing with's name was Bernice

The grammatical status of the English and Mainland Scandinavian s-genitives has been the subject of much discussion recently. In Norde (2006a), I have argued that the Swedish s-genitive is a special clitic and hence a genuine example of degrammaticalization, and Anderson (2008) arrives at the same conclusion for English. Another important characteristic of the contemporary s-genitives is that they function as determiners (see e.g. Delsing 1991; Perridon 1994 or Platzack 1998: 188ff. for Swedish; Herslund 2001 for Danish; Abney 1987 and Rosenbach 2004 for English).

### 5.3.2 *The s-genitive in Swedish*

In the following, I will summarize the argument in Norde (2006a). I wish to stress that the Swedish and English s-genitives, though superficially similar, are crucially different in some respects (most importantly as regards the genitive plural). For details about the historical development of the English s-genitive the reader is referred to the works of Jespersen (1894, 1918) and Allen (1997, 2003).

In the history of the Swedish genitive, three stages can be discerned. The transition between these three stages was subtle and gradual, and historical textual evidence suggests that two diachronically contiguous constructions may have formed part of the grammar of one and the same speaker.

(i) Initially, Swedish *-s* was a word marker, which implied that all elements in a noun phrase were inflected. This is the common Indo-European type of case-marking known as concordial case:

(19) af mangs riks manz
of many-MASC.SG.GEN rich-MASC.SG.GEN man-MASC.SG.GEN
vlyko (Bur 153)
bad.luck-OBL
'of the bad luck of many a rich man'

The genitive at this stage will be called 'word-marking genitive' (or simply '*-s*'), and will be glossed as '-GEN'.

(ii) When in the Old and Middle Swedish periods this system of concordial case-marking gradually disappeared, *-s* was the only case suffix that developed into a phrase marker[13] regardless of the internal structure of the noun phrase, as in (20a–b):

(20) a. mangen riddaris blod (Did 10)
many-ø knight~GEN blood
'the blood of many a knight'

b. ... kom iak heem til fadhir[14] mins
... came I home to father-ø my~GEN
hws (Bir 26)
house
'I came home to my father's house'

Genitives from this stage are termed 'phrase-marking genitives' (or simply '*~s*'), and glossed as '~ GEN'. At this stage, *~s* also started to expand to other declensions (e.g. female nouns) and the plural (see Norde 1997: 116ff. for details).

At a superficial glance, it might seem that the only thing that changed at this stage was that concordial marking has been replaced by single case marking, with *~s* mostly being attached to nouns, since by this time, word order within the NP had become fairly rigid Modifier-Noun. That the genitive was not merely a head marker is however evidenced by examples in which *~s* is attached to all kinds of inflected forms, e.g. to FEM.SG.OBL *domkirky-o ~s* 'cathedral', to PL.GEN.DEF *ox-a-nna~s* 'the oxen' or to FEM.PL. NOM/ACC *menniski-or~s*. These examples show that *~s* had developed into an edge-located morpheme that could be attached to inflectional suffixes of various kinds.[15] The examples furthermore show that *~s* is not attached to

[13] The term 'phrase marker' is based on Blake's classification of case-marking languages. According to Blake (1994: 100f.; 2001: 99f.) there are two common distributions for case affixes (besides some minor types): one in which the case suffix is attached to every single element in a noun phrase and one in which the case marker appears on the final word in a noun phrase, which is in most cases the head but can also be some other element, depending on the basic word order in the noun phrase. Blake regards both types as affixal.

[14] Perhaps unnecessarily, I wish to point out that the form *fadhir* is an uninflected form (lacking *s*), not an oblique form, in which case there would be concordial case after all. Although r-stems such as *fadhir* originally did not possess a genitive in *-s*, but an oblique form ending in *-ur*, genitives in *-s* are attested since Runic Swedish times (Norde 1997: 118ff.). The text from which this example has been taken is from the 1380s and generally has genitives of r-stems ending in *-s*, even with feminine r-stems (e.g. *modhirs* 'mother's').

[15] This phenomenon has an interesting parallel in the contemporary Swedish dialect of Älvdalen, where the dative has been preserved and the genitive is attached to inflected dative forms, as in *skaulmiesterames lägeniet* 'schoolteacher-DAT.DEF-S' apartment (Levander 1909, Ringmar 2006).

stems, as was word-marking *-s.*[16] Another argument against the analysis of *∼s* as a mere head marker is that examples of single marking are not attested in lexical genitive constructions where the genitive is governed by a preposition or a verb. Examples such as **til min fadhurs* 'to my father' are not found. To conclude, the development had not been one from concordial marker to 'once-only' marker (for in that case we would expect *∼s* to appear in non-attributive contexts as well), but to phrase marker in a specific type of construction.

On the other hand, *∼s* also needs to be distinguished from the s-genitive, because group genitives do not yet occur.

(iii) 'True' group genitives, of the type exemplified in (17), appear at a later stage, probably not before the second half of the fifteenth century (Delsing 1991: 28). Texts from the Early Modern Swedish period still show considerable variation as regards genitive constructions involving complex NPs. Example (21a) is a group genitive construction taken from a text from *c.* 1640, but the same text contains constructions such as *konungens i Pålandz skipp* (296) 'the king of Poland's ships', with the genitive marked twice, and *konungens i Poland skipp* (312) 'the king of Poland's ships' with the genitive only marked on the core NP,[17] not on the postmodifying PP as in (21a). In earlier texts, from the fifteenth century, the original construction with NPs with a postmodifying PP, in which the PP follows the possessee, is also still commonly attested. An example of the latter construction is given in (21b). In spite of all this variation, the s-genitive appears to become increasingly common, and since this morpheme is best analysed as a clitic, as I intend to show below, I will use the notation '*=s*' for it (and gloss it as '=GEN').

(21) a. konungen i Sveriges felltherre (Gyll 339)
[king-DEF in Sweden]=GEN general
'the king of Sweden's general'

b. konung Valdemars dotter aff Danmark (Petri 60)
[king Valdemar]∼s daughter of Denmark
'King Valdemar of Denmark's daughter'

[16] For a similar argument about the introduction of *∼s* to the n-declensions or 'weak' stems (distinguishing only between nominative and oblique in the singular) see Trosterud (2001: 180). I do not however share Trosterud's conclusion that this expansion implies that *∼s* has become enclitic at this stage. According to the analysis presented here, *∼s* was still affixal.

[17] This construction type appears to have been more common in earlier stages of Swedish than what is assumed in Norde (2006a: 227).

To sum up the findings thus far, the s-genitive does not appear to have changed from word-marking inflection to clitic in a single step, but went through an intermediate stage of phrase-marking inflection.

Under a DP analysis, the changes can be represented in the following way. In Modern Swedish, =*s* is generated in D(eterminer) position (Delsing 1991: 24ff. and 1993: 172 ff.), separated from the possessor:[18]

(22) *min fars hus* 'my father's house'
$[_{DP}[_{SPEC}\text{ min far}_i]\ [_{D'}[_{D}\text{s}]\ [_{NP}[_{POSS}\ \text{t}_i]\ [_{N'}\text{ hus}]]]]$
(adapted from Delsing 1991: 27)

If this representation is correct, the s-genitive cannot possibly be an affix.

In Old Swedish, on the other hand, when -*s* was still a word-marking affix, it could obviously not be separated from (all individual elements in) the possessor NP, so for this stage Delsing proposes (23), in which the entire genitive phrase in found in SPEC:

(23) *mins faþurs hus* 'my father's house'
$[_{DP}[_{SPEC}\text{ mins faþurs}_i]\ [_{D'}\text{ D }[_{NP}[_{POSS}\ \text{t}_i]\ [_{N'}\text{ hus}]]]]$
(adapted from Delsing 1991: 27)

Delsing does not offer an analysis of the subsequent stage, in which ~*s* functions as an inflectional phrase marker, but for this stage I will assume that the genitive phrase is still found in SPEC in its entirety:

(24) *min fadhurs hus* 'my father's house'
$[_{DP}[_{SPEC}\text{ min fadhurs}_i]\ [_{D'}\text{ D }[_{NP}[_{POSS}\ \text{t}_i]\ [_{N'}\text{ hus}]]]]$

Now, what seems crucial in the development of the s-genitive is that learners at some point reanalysed (24) as (22),[19] that is, phrase-marking ~*s* was reanalysed as a separate element in D. The phrase-marking stage is essential for this reanalysis, because the 'surface' structures (disregarding the phonological change from *faþur* to *far*) of (22) and (23) are not the same (and hence there cannot have been a 'direct' reanalysis from (23) to (22)).

Once the reanalysis had been accomplished, it became possible to add =*s* to larger NPs and virtually every word class, yielding group genitives. In sum, the rise of the Swedish s-genitive was motivated by the loss of concordial case (and deflexion in general) and supported by the emergence of a fixed prepositive

[18] Delsing (1993) assumes a more complex structure, involving an additional level PossP, where =*s* is raised to D: $[_{DP}[_{XP}\text{ Per}_j]\ [_{D'}[_{D}\text{ s}_i]\ [_{PossP}[_{SPEC}\ \text{t}_j]\ [_{Poss'}[_{Poss}\ \text{t}_i]\ [_{NP}[_{SPEC}\ \text{t}_j]\ [_{N'}[_{N}\text{ hus}]\ [_{XP}\ \text{t}_j]]]]]]]$ *Pers hus* This difference is however not crucial to the argument presented here.

[19] See Seppänen (1997: 201) and references there for a similar argument for English.

position for determiners.[20] This would imply that in varieties where the s-genitive did not become a determiner, group genitives are not found either. Interestingly, this seems to be the case. For example, in dialects of Swedish in which the genitive is not a determiner, such as the Lappträsk dialect spoken in Finland (Vangsnes 1998), group genitives do not appear to be possible.

In the following, I will describe how the three stages in the history of the Swedish genitive identified above relate to Zwicky and Pullum's criteria. Especially for the older stages, it is not always possible to state in absolute terms whether < s> is an affix or a clitic. In relative terms, however, it can be argued that < s> becomes progressively more clitic-like (see Norde 2006a: 214ff. for a more detailed discussion).

> Criterion 1. *Clitics can exhibit a low degree of selection with respect to their hosts, while affixes exhibit a high degree of selection with respect to their stems.*

The OSw word-marking genitive was confined to specific nominal stems, to wit (some) masculine and neuter nouns and adjectives in the singular, as well as some pronouns (Norde 1997: 93ff.). This clearly makes *-s* an affix according to criterion 1.

Phrase-marking ∼*s* is still quite selective about the word it attaches to, because it is never added to a non-(pro)nominal element. On the other hand, it spreads rapidly to other declensions and the plural, which makes it less specific than word-marking *-s*. The genitive at Stage (ii) is hence most appropriately analysed as an affix still, but it has clearly become more generalized, which makes it less affix-like than *-s*.

MoSw =*s*, finally, is clearly a clitic according to criterion 1, since it may be added to most parts of speech,[21] as illustrated in (25): in (a), =*s* is attached to a noun, in (b) to an adjective, in (c) to a demonstrative pronoun, in (d) to a (postpositive) possessive pronoun, in (e) to the object form of a personal pronoun, in (f) to a numeral, in (g) to an adverb, in (h) to a (stranded)

[20] Note that the order of events as attested in the history of Swedish differs slightly from the relative chronology that has been suggested for the English s-genitive (see. e.g. Jespersen 1894, Carstairs 1987, and Plank 1992 and 1995), but this discussion need not concern us here (see Norde 1997: 225ff.; 2001a: 254). For a discussion on the relative chronology of the changes in Swedish see Delsing (1999, 2001) and Norde (2001b).

[21] Notable exceptions are the subject forms of personal pronouns (**jags* '*I's', **dus* '*you's', etc.), possibly because these forms are 'blocked' by existing possessive pronouns (*min* 'my', *din* 'your' etc.), and plural nouns in *-s*, which are mostly of English origin. But since s-plurals are problematic to Swedish morphophonemics anyhow (Teleman, Hellberg, and Andersson 1999a: 112), as a result of which there is a tendency to incorporate English nouns in native Swedish declensions with plurals other than *-s*, this is not a very significant exception either.

preposition, in (i) to a verbal particle, and in (j) to an inflected verb form (Norde 2006a: 215f.):

(25) a. de fattiga människornas ögon
[the poor people-DEF]=GEN eyes
'the poor people's eyes'

b. de fattigas ögon
[the poor-PL]=GEN eyes
'the eyes of the poor'

c. alla dessas musik
[all those]=GEN music
'the music of all those people'

d. far mins plånbok[22]
[father my]=GEN wallet
'my father's wallet'

e. en kompis till migs farsa
[a pal to me]=GEN daddy
'a pal of mine's daddy'

f. barn nummer tvås ankomst
[child number two]=GEN arrival
'the arrival of child number two'

g. grannen ovanpås hund
[neighbour-DEF upstairs]=GEN dog
'the dog of the neighbour upstairs'

h. personen du pratar meds mobil
[person-DEF you talk with]=GEN mobile.phone
'the mobile phone of the person you're talking to'

i. en artist som jag inte tycker oms platta
[an artist that I not care about]=GEN record
'the record of an artist I do not like'

j. den man älskars lycka
[the.one one loves]=GEN happiness
'the happiness of one's loved one'

[22] This construction is generally considered dialectal or archaic. According to Teleman, Hellberg, and Andersson (1999a: 263), the possessive pronoun is enclitic here.

Criterion 2. *Arbitrary gaps in the set of combinations are more characteristic of affixed words than of clitic groups.*

Inflectional paradigms sometimes idiosyncratically lack one or several members, which may either be filled by suppletive forms, e.g. in the comparison of some adjectives (*good – better – best*), or simply remain a gap (e.g. the Swedish verb *stinga* 'to prick' lacks past tense and imperative forms). In none of the three stages in the development of the genitive are such arbitrary gaps found, but that does not make the (s-)genitive a clitic, since the criterion does not say that the absence of gaps implies that a morpheme is enclitic. Hence, this criterion cannot be used to identify the morphological status of the genitive at any of its three stages.

Criterion 3. *Morphophonological idiosyncrasies are more characteristic of affixed words than of clitic groups.*

It is not uncommon for an inflectional affix to affect its root phonologically, for instance by changing vowel quality or quantity. The OSw inflectional genitive also had a phonological impact on the root to which it was suffixed: when the root ended in a voiced consonant, the consonant was devoiced, and when the root vowel was long, it was shortened. Evidence for devoicing of [g] and [d] is found in such OSw spellings as <x>([ks]) and <z>([ts]) respectively, e.g. *dax* (NOM *dagher* 'day'), or *lanz* (NOM *land* 'land'). Etymological orthographies such as *skogs* also occur, but less frequently (Norde 1997: 94). Vowel shortening is not reflected in OSw orthography, but is evidenced by vestiges of the inflectional genitive in Modern Swedish, namely compounds and petrified prepositional constructions, such as *skogsbruk* [skuks-] 'forestry' and *till skogs* [skuks] 'to the forest'. For the phrase-marking stage, it is difficult to establish whether consonants were still devoiced, because both voiceless and voiced consonants appear in writing, though the latter appear to be on the increase. The Modern Swedish s-genitive, however, has neither of these phonological effects. When native speakers are presented with examples such as (26),[23] the word *skogs* is pronounced [sku:gs]. The loss of consonant devoicing and vowel shortening clearly marks a transition from the affix to the clitic end of the continuum.

| | | | |
|---|---|---|---|
| (26) | en | skogs | fågelrikedom |
| | [a | forest]=s | bird.species.abundance |
| | 'bird species abundance in a forest' | | |

[23] Naturally, the examples were presented in context, and the informants were not told what the task was about. The example is from www.skogsfaglar.info/praktiska_rad-bedomning.html (excerpted 10 April 2008). Thanks to Therese Leinonen for suggesting it to me.

Criterion 4. *Semantic idiosyncrasies are more characteristic of affixed words than of clitic groups.*

This is not a very helpful criterion as far as the three stages in the development of the s-genitive are concerned, because idiosyncratic meanings have always been rare. One exception is Swedish *dags* (originally the genitive form of *dagher* 'day') in expressions such as *det är dags* 'it is time' or *hur dags?* 'at what time?', but it is not quite clear how far forms with non-compositional semantics date back. It is thus not possible to say when such semantic idiosyncrasies ceased to arise. In any event, no such 'quirky' semantics are found with the MoSw s-genitive, but then again this is not conclusive evidence that it is a clitic, but merely that it has lost a property that is more common in affixes.

Criterion 5. *Syntactic rules can affect affixed words, but cannot affect clitic groups.*

Put differently, this criterion says that affixes are inseparable from their roots, and hence obligatorily follow them in syntactic operations. When word-marking *-s* was still attached to every single element in an NP (as in (15a)), it could obviously never be separated from its stem, so it is clearly an affix according to this criterion. With phrase-marking *∼s*, the attachment has become slightly weaker, because *∼s* is always attached to the final element in the NP. Thus, when Adjective – Noun order in an NP such as *min fadhurs* is reversed, we do not get **fadhurs min* but *fadhur mins.* On the other hand, *∼s* was not as flexible as MoSw =*s*, because it cannot be used to form group genitive constructions. The MoSw s-genitive is clearly different, because =*s* does not move along with its host. For instance, when the order of two co-ordinated NPs is reversed, =*s* is still found on the second NP, which strongly suggests that =*s* is a clitic: [24]

(27) a. Björn och Bennys nya musikal[25]
[Björn and Benny]=*s* new musical
'Björn and Benny's new musical'

b. *Bennys och Björn nya musikal / Benny och Björns nya musikal
Benny=*s* and Björn new musical / [Benny and Björn]=*s* new musical
'Benny and Björn's new musical'

[24] In formal written Swedish, group genitives are avoided, yielding such constructions as *institutionens för slaviska språk prefekt* 'the head of the department of Slavonic languages' (Börjars 2003: 149), but such constructions are generally considered 'unnatural' (Dahl 2003: 47; Hultman 2003: 212).

[25] The examples in (27a–b) are from *Språkriktighetsboken* (SRB; a prescriptive work on Swedish grammar), p. 54.

Criterion 6. *Clitics can attach to material already containing clitics, but affixes cannot.*

Constructions in which word-marking *-s* is attached to a clitic are not attested at all, which makes *-s* clearly affixal. Phrase-marking ~*s* behaves less like an affix for two reasons. First, phrase marking *-s* is attached to inflected nouns (as in *domkirkyos* [cathedral-FEM.SG.OBL~*s*] 'cathedral's' or *ox-a-nna-s* [OX-MASC.PL.GEN-the-MASC.PL.GEN~*s*] 'oxen's' (Norde 2002: 57). Thus, although examples such as *domkirkyos* are not examples of ~*s* attached to material containing *clitics*, the implications are similar. It is no longer possible to regard phrase-marking ~*s* as an affix on the same level as the (older) inflectional case suffixes. Secondly, ~*s* can be attached to a postnominal possessive pronoun (as in *fadhir mins hws* 'my father's house'), which according to some analyses is enclitic (e.g. Wessén 1965: 115). If this is indeed the case, ~*s* must be considered enclitic, because affixes cannot be attached to clitics. The MoSw s-genitive, finally, is clearly a clitic, because it occurs in such constructions as (25d) and (28).

(28) Han som såg'na-s cykel
[He who saw=her]=*s* bike
'The bike of the one who saw her'

Having thus examined the three stages in the history of the Swedish genitive with respect to Zwicky and Pullum's criteria, I will now summarize my findings in Table 5.2. In this table I have indicated what can be inferred from each criterion about the morphological status of -*s*, ~*s*, and =*s*. From the criteria which can only be used to positively identify affixes (3, 4, and 5) it can only be inferred whether the genitive at some stage is either 'affixal' or 'not affixal'. Criteria which identify both affixes and clitics (1 and 6) can be used to establish both affixhood and clitichood. Criterion 2 could not be used

TABLE 5.2. (Changes in) the morphological status of -*s*, ~*s*, and =*s* (Norde 2006a: 223)

| | -*s* | direction | ~*s* | direction | =*s* |
|---|---|---|---|---|---|
| **Criterion 1** | affixal | → | affixal | → | enclitic |
| **Criterion 2** | – | – | – | – | – |
| **Criterion 3** | affixal | – | (affixal) | → | not affixal |
| **Criterion 4** | affixal | – | (affixal) | → | not affixal |
| **Criterion 5** | affixal | → | affixal | → | not affixal |
| **Criterion 6** | affixal | → | enclitic | → | enclitic |

TABLE 5.3. Parameter analysis of the Swedish s-genitive

| Parameter | Primitive change(s) |
|---|---|
| **Integrity** | *resemanticization:* ☑; the MoSw s-genitive not only marks possession (in the widest sense) but gained a new function: that of determiner (Delsing 1991; Norde 1997, 2001a2002, 2006a), which can be considered a case of functional enrichment.<br>*phonological 'strengthening':* ☐; there is no change at the phonological level.<br>*recategorialization:* not relevant in deinflectionalization. |
| **Paradigmaticity** | *deparadigmaticization:* ☑; the OSw suffixal genitive formed part of an intricate system of noun declensions with different inflectional patterns, the MoSw s-genitive does not. |
| **Paradigmatic variability** | *deobligatorification:* ☑; when OSw case marking was still productive, it was obligatory, and hence inflectional *-s* was obligatory when nouns of certain declensions appeared in constructions requiring the genitive case. The MoSw s-genitive, on the other hand, is not obligatory, because a noun is not ungrammatical when it is not 'marked' by a clitic. |
| **Structural scope** | *scope expansion:* ☑; scope of inflectional *-s* was confined to the word level, because in full NPs, it had to be attached to both the noun and its (adjectival) modifiers. But when inflectional *-s* developed into an enclitic s-genitive scope was expanded to the NP-level (including its postmodifiers), as the examples in (25) show. |
| **Bondedness** | *severance:* ☑; the s-genitive remains bound, but with a weaker degree of attachment (host–clitic boundary), which is evidenced by the loss of word-internal sandhi (vowel shortening and consonant devoicing) and the possibility of attachment to phrases. |
| **Syntagmatic variability** | not relevant in deinflectionalization. |

to distinguish between the three stages but will be added here for the sake of completeness. An arrow < →> indicates that a change towards less affixal / more enclitic can be identified. When it has been unclear whether something has changed between Stage 1 and Stage 2, this is indicated by a dash < – >. At first glance, it may seem strange to see an arrow in the row between *-s* and *~s* when both are considered affixal. These arrows, however, indicate that ~*s*, though still affixal, has shifted away from the affixal end of the continuum, for example because it has become less specific about the element it attaches to (cf. criterion 1).

To summarize thus far, it is evident that word-marking -*s* is affixal. Phrase-marking ~*s* has become less prototypically affixal according to criteria 1 and 5, but it is certainly not enclitic. The s-genitive (=*s*) is even less affixal according to three criteria (3, 4, and 5), and positively enclitic according to two (1 and 6). Zwicky and Pullum's criteria have thus proven useful to reveal that there have been gradual changes in morphological status between the subsequent stages.

Crucially, these changes can be shown to be directional towards the enclitic end of the affix–clitic continuum. In some cases there has been no change or perhaps a change too subtle to perceive, but the overall direction of the changes is clear, and there is no evidence of movement towards the affixal end of the continuum. To me, the evidence in Table 5.2 suffices to analyse the MoSw s-genitive as a (special) clitic. The direction of the change clearly makes this a case of degrammaticalization.

### 5.3.3 *The s-genitive in English*

The major difference between the Swedish and the English s-genitive is that the latter is less easily analysed as a clitic according to Zwicky and Pullum's first criterion. On the one hand, the English s-genitive can, just like its Swedish equivalent, be attached to most parts of speech, as the examples in (29) demonstrate (Anderson 2005: 90): in (29c) the s-genitive is attached to a finite verb, in (29d) to a preposition and in (29e) to the object form of a pronoun (for more examples see Plank 1992: 27f.).

(29) a. Fred's taste in wallpaper is appalling.
b. The man in the hall's taste in wallpaper is appalling.
c. Every man I know's taste in wallpaper is appalling.
d. That brother-in-law of mine that I was telling you about's taste in wallpaper is appalling.
e. Even that attractive young man who is trying to flirt with you's taste in wallpaper is appalling.

On the other hand, the English s-genitive has one crucial exception – plurals in -*s* (see e.g. Kruisinga 1932: 39; Carstairs 1987; Zwicky 1987 and 1988; Halpern 1995: 99ff.; Anderson 2005: 89ff.). This is illustrated by the examples in (30), as well as those in (31), which show that the suppression of the s-genitive is not phonologically conditioned – nouns or irregular plurals ending in a sibilant do allow s-genitives (Halpern 1995: 102f.):

(30) a. the girls' parents [grlz] *[grlzəz]
b. the card players' hats [plejrz] *[plejrzəz]
c. the bees' hives [biz] *[bizəz]

(31) a. the fuzz's sirens [fəzəz] *[fəz]
b. the cheese's aroma [čizəz] *[čiz]
c. the mice's tails [məˈsəz] *[məˈs]

According to some scholars (e.g. Carstairs 1987; Zwicky 1987 and 1988), the absence of a genitive plural in English has serious implications for the establishment of the grammatical status of the s-genitive. Zwicky (1987: 139) is most radical in his conclusion, namely that the English s-genitive is an (edge-located) inflectional affix; Carstairs (1987: 160) suggests that only the genitive plural involves inflection, not clisis. I will briefly discuss both possibilities.

According to Zwicky (1988: 400), the incompatibility of =*s* with plural nouns and group genitives are two separate issues. In *kids'* (example (32a)), the genitive is suppressed because it follows the plural suffix -*s*, and according to Zwicky the s-genitive is never realized after 'Z-suffixes'.[26] Compare the irregular plural *children* in (32d), where the addition of 's is not precluded:

(32) a. Anyone who likes kids' life is easy.
b. *Anyone who likes kids's life is easy.
c. *Anyone who likes children life is easy.
d. Anyone who likes children's life is easy.

In group genitives, on the other hand, plural nouns can never occur, regardless of their form:

(33) a. My father-in-law's head is as bald as an egg.
a′. *Our fathers-in-law's heads are all bald as eggs.
b. A passer-by's arm was hurt in the accident.
b′. *Two passers-by's arms were hurt in the accident.
c. The queen of England's reign is usually long.
c′. *The queens of England's reigns are usually long.
d. Any child from Chicago's hair is straight and brown.
d′. *Many children from Chicago's hair is straight and brown.

On the basis of these examples, Zwicky (1988: 402) concludes that 'An NP is ungrammatical if its last, CASE:GEN, word is distinct from its head, NUM:PL word.'

[26] 'Z' refers to suffixes that are phonetically realized as [s], [z], or [ɨz], such as the plural or the 3.SG.PRES verbal ending.

Zwicky's conclusion is however challenged by Picard (1990), who points out that many of the starred sentences given by Zwicky to support his rule are in fact considered to be grammatical by a significant number of native speakers of English. Picard presented forty-four native speakers (mostly from Canada) with the following sentences:

(34) a. Anyone who drives trucks' life is pretty monotonous.
b. It's funny how our fathers-in-law's heads are all bald as eggs.
c. There was an explosion, and the passers-by's legs were injured.
d. Maybe you never noticed, but all the queens of England's reigns were rather long ones.

Picard found that only three out of forty-four subjects judged (34a) (corresponding to Zwicky's (32a)) to be grammatical. Conversely, the types exemplified in (34b–d), which had been marked with an asterisk by Zwicky, were deemed acceptable by twenty-five, twenty-four, and twenty-one subjects respectively.

Unfortunately, Picard did not examine the acceptability of (33d′), but Carstairs (1987: 160) does not appear to regard this type as ungrammatical, for he gives some examples of group genitives with irregular plural heads such as *the children over there's uniforms* and *the women of that parish's reaction to the problem.*

As noted above, Carstairs (1987) regards the *s* in the singular and in the plural as two different morphemes: with singular and irregular plural nouns, =*s* is a clitic, but in regular plurals, -*s* is a cumulative inflectional ending, denoting the features PLURAL and GENITIVE simultaneously. Carstairs's proposal has the advantage of accounting for the ungrammaticality of group genitives with plural heads in -*s*: 'The fact that the head of the possessor noun phrase has a Plural in -s imposes a requirement that possession should be expressed inflexionally, through the genitive Plural affix -s'; but the fact that the head of the possessor noun phrase is not phrase-final leads us to expect the phrase-final clitic -'s as a possessive marker too.' Therefore, sentences such as (33a′), (33b′), and (33c′) 'seem odd because they contain double marking of possession, both on the head of the noun phrase and at the end of it' (Carstairs 1987: 161).

In order to account for the irregularities in English, other authors have proposed that the 'possessive feature' has 'percolated down' to the rightmost element in a possessive NP, where it triggers the insertion of an inflected lexical item (see Halpern 1995: 104ff. and references there). Although such an analysis would explain the suppression of the s-genitive in NPs with a 'Z' on its final element, it has some serious disadvantages. First, it would imply that every item in the lexicon would have an 'inflected possessive' form (in -ø for items ending in 'Z', in 's for all others), including word classes that are generally not inflected in English, such as prepositions (*a woman I work with's apartment building*) or even inflected forms (*the guy you were kissing's laptop*). This is intuitively unappealing, for it would require a radical redefinition of the lexicon and grammatical properties of word classes.

According to criterion 1, then, the English s-genitive can only be regarded as enclitic in the singular. Note also that since the absence of plural s-genitives is regular, this is not an example of an 'arbitrary gap' according to criterion 2. In the singular, no such gaps appear to occur either, so the English s-genitive is not affixal according to this criterion. As regards criterion 3 (morphophonological idiosyncrasies), it is worth noting that there is a difference in pronunciation between English *wives* and *wife's* (Kreidler 1989: 263ff.), but that in Old English both were pronounced with /v/ (Jespersen 1894: 165f.; Plank 1985: 212ff.). This suggests that English lost a devoicing rule with the genitive, which makes the Modern English genitive less affixal than the Old English one. Semantic idiosyncrasies (criterion 4) are as rare in English as they are in Swedish, and they are not found in s-genitives, which suggests that the s-genitive is more enclitic according to this criterion. According to criterion 5, the English s-genitive is non-affixal, as becomes evident from the English translations in example (27). Finally, the English s-genitive is enclitic according to criterion 6, because it can be attached to material already containing clitics, e.g. *y'all* (with proclitic *y* < *you*), as in example (35) (non-standard American English):[27]

(35) Y'all's nasty attitudes are just ugly.

In terms of Lehmann's parameters, the English s-genitive can be analysed in a way similar to the way the Swedish s-genitive has been analysed (see Table 5.3), as far as the singular and irregular plurals are concerned.

### 5.3.4 *Alternative analyses*

For English it has been suggested that *-s* did not degrammaticalize 'on its own', but is instead a reduced form of the pronoun *his*, and hence a case of grammaticalization. This scenario was first suggested in Jespersen 1894, and made famous by Richard Janda in his 1980 paper. According to Jespersen (1894: 319), such constructions as *for Jesus Christ his sake* originate in anacoluthon-like sentences or in indirect object constructions such as *þet tu wult... reauen God his strencðe.* Subsequently, as *his* had lost initial

[27] The example in (35) is from http://www.prometheus6.org/node/16285.

*h* in unstressed positions, the *his*-construction was confused with the old morphological genitive. In Jespersen's view, the s-genitive and the *his*-construction had developed independently, but the homophony of inflectional -(*e*)*s* and the unstressed variant of the possessive pronoun *his* / *ys* provided just the catalyst the old inflection needed in its development from word marker to phrase marker.

In a later paper (Janda 2001) Janda expresses the slightly different view that *his/ys* was homophonous, but not identical, with the possessive pronoun *his*. Janda's hypothesis has been challenged by Carstairs (1987), Allen (1997, 2003), and myself (Norde 1997, 2001a). Both Carstairs (1987: 156) and Allen (1997: 111) consider separated *his/ys* as a mere orthographic variant of -(*e*)*s*, since constructions with feminine or plural pronouns (*Juno hir bedde*; *Canterbury and Chillingworth their books*) do not appear until the late sixteenth century. Allen (p. 116) furthermore observes that the *his*-construction and -(*e*)*s* had exactly the same distribution. Another convincing argument put forward by Allen is that in texts where initial <h> was not omitted, *his* and *ys* are usually distinct. Hence it does not seem likely that separate *ys* was perceived as an unstressed variant of the possessive pronoun *his*.

As regards the rise of the s-genitive in some Scandinavian languages, Janda asserts that in these cases, too, genitive -*s* could have been associated with possessive pronouns (reflexive *sin*, comparable to Lat. *suus*, and non-reflexive *hans*, comparable to Lat. *eius*), but in view of the diachronic Swedish data outlined in section 5.3.2, it is more likely that -*s* developed independently into a phrase marker, without mediation from possessive pronouns. In the first place, unlike in English, Scandinavian -*s* had not become homophonous with any pronoun and secondly, there is no evidence that such constructions as *for Jesus Christ his sake* were ever relevant in Swedish. There are a few unclear examples, usually anacoluthon-like constructions, and these date from a relatively late period, i.e. (long) after the first examples of -*s* as a phrase marker are attested. Moreover, the possibility of Low German influence cannot be excluded in these cases (see Norde 1997: 61ff. and 89ff.). In conclusion, the claim that the s-genitive is a reduced possessive pronoun can be safely dismissed, both for English and Swedish.

A slightly different approach from the one adopted here is proposed in Rosenbach (2004). Instead of moving back along the cline of grammaticality, Rosenbach argues, the s-genitive became part of a 'cline of definiteness' (because it developed into a determiner). Following the type/token distinction, Rosenbach defines unidirectionality as a property of types (i.e. clines), and since a token can form part of several clines, she concludes that unidirectionality on the type level is preserved. Rosenbach's view is not necessarily incompatible with the view presented here, because degrammaticalization as a counterdirectional change along the cline of grammaticality primarily concerns its degree of bondedness (from affix to clitic), whereas Rosenbach's 'cline-swapping' pertains to the semantic-functional properties of the s-genitive.

More serious challenges to the claim that the s-genitive is a case of degrammaticalization are found in Tabor and Traugott (1998) for the English s-genitive, and Askedal (2000, 2003, 2008) and Börjars (2003) for the mainland Scandinavian (Swedish) s-genitive. Both Tabor and Traugott and Askedal assert that the history of the s-genitive is actually a case of *grammaticalization.* They both point out that the number of semantic relations expressed by the s-genitive has become smaller, but this is not really bleaching in the sense of generalization of meaning (characteristic of grammaticalization), but rather in the sense of polysemy reduction. The meanings that have disappeared, such as defining genitives (*Dublin's fair city*), were marginal to begin with. In the case of partitive genitives, loss is due to the fact that they were invariably postpositive (Norde 1997: 229). Askedal furthermore claims that since the number of grammatical functions has been reduced (the s-genitive is no longer found with prepositions, verbs, or adjectives that used to govern the genitive in Older Scandinavian), the s-genitive has become subject to 'increasing grammaticalization' (Askedal 2003: 29). Askedal thus seems to equate context reduction with semantic bleaching, a view which is incompatible with the now commonly accepted observation that linguistics items do not (de)grammaticalize in isolation, but in context (see section 1.5). The fact that the s-genitive is no longer found as a productive pattern with prepositions, verbs, and adjectives is a result of the loss of the category of case as a whole (see Norde 1997: 145ff.).

Another argument why the s-genitive should be considered an example of grammaticalization put forward by Tabor and Traugott is that its syntactic scope has increased. This presupposes the assumption (*contra* Lehmann 1995) that scope increases in grammaticalization, which is by no means an unproblematic position (see section 3.5.2).

Finally, both Askedal (2003, 2008) and Börjars (2003) call into question the clitic status of the s-genitive. Using different arguments, they claim that instead it is an 'agglutinative, non-fusional inflection' (Askedal 2003: 24),[28] or a 'phrasal affix' (Börjars 2003: 140), respectively. For example, Askedal is

[28] Askedal's suggestion that *-s* is agglutinative is problematic however, since Swedish suffixes (e.g. for number and definiteness) are generally best characterized as inflectional, not agglutinative (Norde 2006a: 224f.).

reluctant to regard the s-genitive as a clitic because it does not have a stressed counterpart, as do 'normal' clitics (e.g. *is* as the full form of enclitic verbal *'s*). There are, however, good reasons for analysing the s-genitive as a special clitic (see section 5.2.2).

To a large extent, discussions about the morphological status of the s-genitive are definitional quibbles. As we have seen above, affixes and clitics form a continuum, and if this continuum is subdivided *ad infinitum* we may very well reach the point where one linguist's clitic has become another linguist's affix.[29] Crucially, however, this has no bearing on the direction of the change. In other words, a shift from word-marking affix to phrasal affix could still qualify as a degrammaticalization.

A final alternative comes from construction grammar approaches to grammaticalization (see section 1.5 for a brief introduction). In construction grammar, different constructional levels can be distinguished (Traugott 2008: 236):

(i) 'macro-constructions: meaning–form pairings that are defined by structure and function'
(ii) 'meso-constructions: sets of similarly-behaving specific constructions'
(iii) 'micro-constructions: individual construction-types'
(iv) 'constructs: the empirically attested tokens, which are the locus of change'

In his discussion of English possessives, Trousdale (2008b) suggests that the history of the English s-genitive is an instance of grammaticalization from a construction grammar point of view. In terms of the hierarchy above, he argues that particular tokens involving an s-genitive, such as *Uncle Tom's cabin*, are

[29] Börjars presents an extensive line of reasoning for why she feels that *-s* is not a clitic and (hence) not an instance of degrammaticalization, the details of which cannot be discussed here (see Norde 2006a for discussion). Her main point is that group genitives of the type exemplified in (17) are very rare in Swedish and that, even in group genitives, *-s* seems to have a preference for nouns. However, she does admit that group genitives are possible in colloquial Swedish. The empirical evidence for her claim that group genitives are avoided is weak, moreover. Although she produces a number of constructions of (the Swedish equivalents of) the type *the queen's power of England*, no statistics are provided which show that this type is indeed more common than the *the queen of England's* type. Indeed, with the exception of prescriptive grammars, most grammars recommend avoiding constructions such as *the queen's of England*, which they regard as bookish and unnatural. Also, group genitives in which *-s* attaches to non-nouns are not 'difficult to come by' (p. 146) at all – a simple Google search yields scores of examples in which *-s* is attached to adverbs, inflected pronouns, prepositions, or verb forms. Even regardless of statistics, she misses an important generalization in grammaticalization theory, which is the observation that, in grammaticalization, the old and the new construction may coexist for considerable periods of time ('layering'; see Hopper and Traugott 2003: 124ff.). Of course this is true for degrammaticalization as well. In other words, the observation that one may still use the *the queen's of England* type in formal written Swedish is as significant to the claim that the s-genitive is a case of degrammaticalization as the observation that *considering* may still be used as a participle is relevant to the claim that *considering* has grammaticalized into a preposition.

constructs. But they are also an instance of a more general construction type on the micro-level, namely *Uncle Tom's* [NP]. Trousdale goes on to argue that there are two meso-levels for the s-genitive: the prenominal s-genitive (the *of*-genitive is another construction type at this level), and, one level up, the possessive construction. The macro-level, finally, is the determiner construction. Since grammaticalization generally involves upward movement along the hierarchy above (towards increasing schematicity), the development of the s-genitive, Trousdale claims, must be an instance of grammaticalization, because it shifted from a construction at the meso-level (possessive) to a construction on the macro-level (determiner). The construction grammar approach offers an interesting perspective on the history of the s-genitive, but more research is required to account for the apparently contradictory results of a morpheme-based approach to (de)grammaticalization, as adopted in this work, and a construction-based approach, as proposed by Trousdale.

## 5.4 Swedish *-er*: from case suffix to nominalization suffix

In section 5.2.1, I have argued that a shift from inflectional affix to derivational affix may be considered a valid case of deinflectionalization. In this section and the following two, I will discuss three cases in some detail. The first example concerns the shift of Old Swedish inflectional MASC.SG.NOM *-er* to a derivational suffix to form nouns from adjectives (mostly derogatory ones). An example of *-er* as a case suffix is given in (36):[30]

(36) mykilhughæþ***ær*** maðþ***ær*** oc
proud-MASC.SG.NOM man-MASC.SG.NOM and
girugh***ær*** (Vidh 14)
avaricious-MASC.SG.NOM
'a proud and avaricious man'

The suffix *-er* was used as a MASC.SG.NOM suffix in both nouns (virtually all masculine declensions) and adjectives. With nouns, the suffix was largely lost as a case suffix in the Middle Swedish period (Wessén 1968: 138), but with adjectives, *-er* was generally better preserved. According to Ejder (1945: 246), adjectival *-er* may even be considered a productive suffix until the first half of the eighteenth century. However, there is evidence that, even as a productive suffix, adjectival *-er* did not retain its original function. For example, in the

[30] Old Swedish spelling was not standardized, and <-ær> is a spelling variant of <-er>.

writings of the eighteenth-century Swedish poet Carl Michael Bellman, *-er* is evidently no longer associated with either nominative or masculine,[31] as can be seen in the examples in (37). In (37a), the noun phrase is not nominative but accusative, and in example (37b), the noun phrase is not masculine but feminine.

(37) a. Hyrde sig en svart*er* rock
hired him a black cloak
'he hired himself a black cloak'

b. Judith var en rik**er** änka
Judith was a rich widow

In Bellman's poetry, adjectives in *-er* evidently form a mere alternative form of adjectives without *-er*, and the longer variants could be used when metre or rhyme required it. It seems unlikely that *-er* degrammaticalized in these constructions.

The probable source context of degrammaticalization of *-er* was the adjectival noun construction. Until the eighteenth century, *-er* did not have exclusively derogatory meaning: it could also be used in such constructions as *en blinder* 'a blind person' (MoSw plainly *en blind*). It is likely that in these constructions, too, *-er* was no longer perceived as strictly MASC.SG.NOM and in Modern Swedish, *-er* has clearly been reanalysed as a derivational suffix, for example in nominalizations such as *en dummer* 'a stupid one' (Wessén 1968: 40; Söderberg 1971: 106). From there it developed into a derogatory suffix used with nouns expressing disgraceful activities, such as *en fjäsker* 'a fawning one' (< *fjäsk* 'fawning behaviour') or *en slarver* 'a messy one' (< *slarv* 'mess').

A related phenomenon is the use of *-er* to form nicknames (not necessarily deprecatory ones), but this usage is largely confined to fairy-tale style. Consider, for instance, the name of the seven dwarfs in the tale of Snow White (Disney's version):

(38) Trött*er*, Prosit, Butt*er*, Blyg*er*, Glad*er*, Tok*er*, Klok*er*
'Sleepy, Sneezy, Grumpy, Bashful, Happy, Dopey, Doc'

With the exception of *Prosit* 'bless you', all names contain derivational *-er*. Four are derived from adjectives: *trött* 'tired', *blyg* 'bashful', *glad* 'happy', *klok* 'wise'. *Butter*, though synchronically a simplex adjective, likewise derives from an adjective without *-er*: *butt* 'grumpy'. *Toker*, finally, derives from a noun: *tok* 'idiot, fool'.[32]

[31] The dissociation of *-er* from the nominative case is not surprising in view of the fact that the four-case system had already become obsolete in most varieties of Swedish in Bellman's day.

[32] In contemporary Swedish, *-er* is even used with masculine nouns in similar contexts, e.g. *fnasker*, *puttefnasker* 'lad' (< *putte* 'little boy' and *fnask* 'crumb'; Pettersson 2005: 171).

TABLE 5.4. Parameter analysis of Swedish *-er*

| Parameter | Primitive change(s) |
|---|---|
| **Integrity** | *resemanticization:* ☑; as a nominalizing suffix, it adds the meaning of 'person who is X', where X is an adjective, or 'person who is associated with X', where X is a noun.<br>*phonological 'strengthening':* ☐; there is no change at the phonological level.<br>*recategorialization:* not relevant in deinflectionalization. |
| **Paradigmaticity** | *deparadigmaticization:* ☑; *-er* no longer forms part of an inflectional paradigm (adjective or noun declensions). |
| **Paradigmatic variability** | *deobligatorification:* ☑; derivational suffixes are generally not obligatory (cf. 5.2.1); instead of adding the suffix *-er* to an adjective like *dum* 'stupid', other expressions can be used, e.g. *en dum person* 'a stupid person', or compounds such as *ett dumhuvud, en dummerjöns* 'a dickhead'. |
| **Structural scope** | *scope expansion:* ☐; there is no change in scope – both as a case suffix and as a derivational suffix *-er* only takes scope over the noun to which it is attached. |
| **Bondedness** | *severance:* ☐; *-er* remains bound to a noun or adjective. |
| **Syntagmatic variability** | not relevant in deinflectionalization. |

An interesting parallel to the development of Swedish *-er* is the Modern Greek suffix *-s* (Katerina Stathi, p.c.). Like Swedish *-er*, Greek *-s* is a MASC.SG.NOM suffix which can be used as a derivational nominalization suffix. The suffix *-s* can be attached to a feminine or neuter noun X, to derive a masculine noun meaning '(male) person who is in some respect X', e.g. *xália-s* 'a (male) person who produces a lot of mess' (from *xália* (NEUT.PL) 'mess') or *mápa-s* 'idiot' (from *mápa* (FEM.SG) 'cabbage; head (colloquial)').

## 5.5 Swedish *-on*: from number suffix to 'berry-name suffix'

The development of the Old Swedish plural suffix *-on* into a derivational marker is different from the example discussed in the previous section, because the suffix retained its original function along with the new one. It is hence an example of 'non-junk exaptation' (see section 3.3.5). In Old Swedish, *-on* was

TABLE 5.5. Parameter analysis of Swedish *-on*

| Parameter | Primitive change(s) |
|---|---|
| **Integrity** | *resemanticization:* ☑; *-on* gained the meaning of 'berry'. *phonological 'strengthening':* ☐; there has been no change at the phonological level. *recategorialization:* not relevant in deinflectionalization. |
| **Paradigmaticity** | *deparadigmaticization:* ☑; as a derivational suffix, *-on* does not form part of an inflectional paradigm. |
| **Paradigmatic variability** | *deobligatorification:* ☑; / ☐; derivational suffixes are generally not obligatory, but since the berry-nouns and other fruit names are now lexicalized into monomorphemic nouns, they cannot – obviously – be left out. |
| **Structural scope** | *scope expansion:* ☐; there has been no scope change, derivational *-on* attaches to nouns only. |
| **Bondedness** | *severance:* ☐; there is no evidence that *-on* has become 'less bound' in some way. |
| **Syntagmatic variability** | not relevant in deinflectionalization. |

the PL.NOM/ACC marker of weak neuter nouns ending in *-a*. In Modern Swedish, it is still found in the plural forms of *öga* 'eye' (PL *ögon*) and *öra* 'ear' (PL *öron*). In Old Swedish, original plural forms such as *hiūpon* 'rosehip(s)' (Modern Swedish *nypon*) and *smultron* 'wild strawberries' may have given rise to the reinterpration of *-on* as a 'berry-suffix', and as such it became quite productive (Hellquist 1980: 731; Wessén 1971: 45f.). Two examples are *hallon* 'raspberry' (still *hallbär* in some Swedish dialects) < *hall* 'slope / stony ground' and *lingon* 'lingonberry' (still *lingbär* in some Swedish dialects) < Proto-Scandinavian **lingwa* (Modern Swedish *ljung* 'heather'). In other words, *hallon* originally meant 'slope-berry', and *lingon* originally meant 'heather-berry'. By present-day speakers however, *hallon* and *lingon* are perceived of as monomorphemic.

Interestingly, the suffix *-on* underwent a further shift. *Hallon, lingon*, etc. usually refer to a substance and are hardly ever used in the singular (Wessén 1971: 45). At a later stage, however, the meaning of *-on* was generalized even further and suffixed to other fruit-names as well, e.g. *fikon* 'fig' (ultimately < Lat. *ficus* 'fig tree, fig'), *plommon* 'plum' (ultimately < Lat. *prunum* 'plum') and *päron* 'pear' (ultimately < Lat. *pirum* 'pear'). Unlike the berry-nouns, these nouns are clearly count nouns, that is, they are used both in the singular and the plural (they belong to the class of neuter nouns with a so-called 'zero plural'). The suffix *-on* thus evolved from a plural suffix to a derivational suffix in berry-names (with predominantly plural usage) to a derivational suffix in count nouns (as in the last three examples).

## 5.6 From inflection to derivation in Kwaza quotative constructions

Very little is known about (de)grammaticalization in polysynthetic languages, so it is not possible to say whether the parameters of (de)grammaticalization work in the same way in these languages as in the more familiar inflectional type.[33] If establishing the morphological status of morphemes in languages such as English or Swedish is complicated enough, this must be true *a fortiori* for languages in which entire sentences can be expressed by long sequences of morphemes. And the fact that most of these languages lack historical documentation makes diachronic claims even more complicated. In this section however, I will discuss one study which aims to show that degrammaticalization from inflection to derivation has occurred in a polysynthetic language.[34]

This study concerns degrammaticalization of mood inflections in quotative constructions in Kwaza, an isolated language spoken in Rondônia, Brazil (van der Voort 2004). In this language, a quotative construction is formed by embedding the quoted utterance in a layer of person and mood inflections. These inflections are identical to person and mood markers used in non-quotative contexts – it is the extra layer that makes the construction quotative. Thus, example (39a) is a 'simple' declarative sentence for the first person singular. In example (39b), the second *-da-ki* sequence refers to the quoting subject (also first person singular). Examples involving the third person singular are given in (39c–d). The quotative construction is fully productive and occurs with all persons and moods (van der Voort 2002: 312ff.).[35]

(39) a. kukui'hỹ-da-ki[36]
ill-1SG-DEC
'I am ill'

[33] The same goes for isolating languages, see section 1.6.4.

[34] This case, as well as the deaffixation in Hup case discussed in section 6.8, has been examined by a single author, and the evidence rests on reconstruction alone (and must hence be treated with care), but the argumentation seems sound enough.

[35] The origin of the quotative construction is unclear. It may derive from a construction containing another root, of a verb meaning 'to say', but this is uncertain (van der Voort 2002: 315).

[36] <'> indicates main stress.

b. kukuihỹ-da-'ki-da-ki
ill-1SG-DEC-1SG-DEC
'I said I am ill'

c. kukuihỹ-da-'ki-Ø-tsɛ
ill-1SG-DEC-3-DEC
'she$_i$ says she$_i$ is ill'

d. kukuihỹ-Ø-'ki-Ø-tsɛ
ill-3-DEC-3-DEC
'she$_i$ says she$_j$ is ill'

The kind of quotative construction where, according to van der Voort, degrammaticalization may have occurred is exemplified in (40). The degrammaticalized gram, in this example, is -*nĩ*. According to van der Voort, this (derivational) modality marker ((40a′)) developed out of an (inflectional) exhortative marker -*ni* (example (40a)), since the two differ only minimally from one another (the only difference between -*ni* and -*nĩ* is nasalization of the vowel in the latter). In example (40a), the sequence -*da-ki* signals a quotative, and -*ni* is an exhortative morpheme. The reason why (40a) may easily have given rise to (40a′) is that the third person is marked by a zero morpheme. As a consequence, the sequence -*da-ki* could also be interpreted as 'regular' (i.e. non-quotative) morphemes referring to the subject. Then, instead of quoting an exhortative utterance ('Let him drink!'), the construction can be interpreted as a causative ('I made him drink'). That this is the most plausible interpretation of expressions involving -*nĩ* is demonstrated by example (40b), because one cannot 'exhort' or 'tell' chickens to go to sleep, one can only make them sleep by feeding them.

(40) a. 'ja kui-Ø-'**ni**-da-ki (quotative)
already drink-3-EXH-1SG-DEC
'I already said: "Let him drink"'

a′. 'ja kui-'**nĩ**-da-ki (non-quotative)
already drink-CAUS-1SG-DEC
'I already let (him) drink'

b. kuraku'ra ja-dy-da-ki ũi-'**nĩ**-da-ta
chicken eat-CAU-1SG-DEC lie-CAUS-1SG-CSO[37]
'I feed the chickens so that they can go to sleep'

As van der Voort himself concedes (2002: 320), it cannot be ruled out that the near-homophony of -*ni* and -*nĩ* is purely accidental, but since Kwaza has

[37] Note that there is a difference between the causative morpheme -*dy*- (which is valency-increasing) and the causational element *nĩ*.

TABLE 5.6. Parameter analysis of Kwaza -*nĩ*

| Parameter | Primitive change(s) |
|---|---|
| **Integrity** | *resemanticization:* ☑; -*nĩ* has gained the function of marking causativity. *phonological 'strengthening':* (☑); there has been a slight change, in that a phonetic feature (nasality) has been added. *recategorialization:* not relevant in deinflectionalization. |
| **Paradigmaticity** | *deparadigmaticization:* ☑; exhortative -*ni* forms part of a 'persuasive' mood paradigm involving the imperative for the second person, the volitive for the first person and the exhortative for the third person and the first person inclusive (Hein van der Voort, p.c.). Derivational causational -*nĩ* does not form part of such a paradigm. |
| **Paradigmatic variability** | *deobligatorification:* ☑; mood is obligatory in the Kwaza verbal complex, but modality is not (Hein van der Voort, p.c.). |
| **Structural scope** | *scope expansion:* ☒; causational -*nĩ* only takes scope over the verb, whereas exhortative -*ni* takes scope over the whole proposition. |
| **Bondedness** | *severance:* ☐; there is no evidence that -*nĩ* is less bound than -*ni*. The primary reasons for analysing the suffix as derivational are not morphological, but paradigmatic (-*nĩ* does not belong to a paradigm and is optional). In addition, -*nĩ* can receive primary stress, which in Kwaza is always realized on the final syllable of the (derived) stem, before the inflectional affixes (Hein van der Voort, p.c.). |
| **Syntagmatic variability** | not relevant in deinflectionalization. |

several other morphemes that are either inflectional mood morphemes or derivational modality morphemes, and comparable developments have been observed in Ecuadorian Quechua (Muysken 1977: 105) and Kalaallisut (Kristoffersen 1991), as well as in other Inuit languages (de Reuse 1994), the shift from inflectional morpheme to derivational morpheme is not implausible.

# 6

# Debonding

## 6.1 Introduction

In this chapter, I will discuss examples of debonding, the type of degrammaticalization that is most frequently attested. It will be defined as follows:

(1) Debonding is a composite change whereby a bound morpheme in a specific linguistic context becomes a free morpheme.

As in previous definitions of degrammaticalization types (degrammation and deinflectionalization), the addition 'in a specific linguistic context' is crucial – grams that undergo debonding become reanalysed within the context of their own construction, and they continue their previous function.[1] Once they have become free morphemes, however, they may naturally start to appear in other constructions as well (following the parameter of syntagmatic variability). For instance, the Northern Saami abessive suffix *haga* first degrammaticalized into a postposition meaning 'behind', and subsequently started to appear independently as an adverb, and even as a preposition (see section 6.7). The principal difference between debonding and deinflectionalization is that in debonding bound morphemes become free morphemes, whereas in deinflectionalization bound morphemes remain bound. Another difference is that although debonding is a composite change, the primitive changes involved may be confined to the levels of morphology and syntax (in the case of inflectional affixes and clitics), whereas in deinflectionalization there is always a change in function or meaning. I will return to this issue below.

In this chapter, I will discuss cases of debonding involving clitics, inflectional affixes, or derivational affixes. Examples of debonding of clitics will be given in sections 6.3–5, of debonding of inflectional affixes in 6.6–8, and of debonding of derivational affixes in 6.9–12. It will be seen that they are

[1] This implies that affixes used metalinguistically, as in *the third person singular is formed by adding an s to the verb stem*, do not count as debonding. Anything can be named, including affixes, but this does not involve reanalysis of any kind.

slightly different: inflectional affixes generally have more positive scores than do clitics. This is not surprising – since inflections are further to the right on the cline of grammaticality than clitics, they have 'more to gain' when they become free morphemes. But neither inflectional affixes nor clitics gain new functions or meanings when they debond. On the other hand, this likewise sets them apart from debonding derivational affixes, because these all become semantically enriched in some way, *and* they may acquire morphosyntactic properties such as inflection. Deparadigmaticization, however, is not relevant to derivational affixes, because they do not form part of inflectional paradigms. For these reasons, debonding is more heterogeneous than degrammation and deinflectionalization.

Debonding is the type of degrammaticalization which has been discussed the most. Indeed, as we have seen in section 3.2, seven out of Haspelmath's (2004: 29) notorious 'eight cases of antigrammaticalization' (repeated here as (2)) involve debonding (the only exception is the s-genitive):

(2) a. English and Mainland Scandinavian genitive suffix -*s* > clitic =*s* (cf. 5.3)
   b. Irish 1st person plural suffix -*muid* > independent pronoun *muid* (cf. 6.6)
   c. Japanese adverbial subordinator -*ga* 'although' > free linker *ga* 'but' (cf. 6.4)
   d. Saami abessive suffix *-*ptaken* > clitic =*taga* > free postposition *taga* (cf. 6.7)
   e. Estonian question marker -*s* > =*es* > free particle *es*[2] (cf. 6.5)
   f. English infinitive prefix *to-* > proclitic *to* (cf. 6.3.1)
   g. Modern Greek prefix *ksana-* 'again' > free adverb *ksana* 'again'[3]
   h. Latin rigid prefix *re-* 'again' > Italian flexible prefix *ri-* (e.g. *ridevo fare* 'I must do again')[4]

[2] It is unclear why Haspelmath mentions the Estonian question particle *es*, but not the emphatic marker *ep*, from the same paper by Campbell (2001), which underwent a similar development.

[3] *Ksana* (Mendez-Dosuna 1997) is in fact a problematic example. Although it is true that it occurs both fused to the verb and as an independent adverb which always follows the verb (compare *ksanamolíno* / *molíno ksaná* 'pollute again'; Smirniotopoulos and Joseph 1998: 456), it is not quite clear whether *ksana*-V is a compound or a prefixed verb (ibid.: 482; Ralli 2003: 98). I have therefore chosen to disregard this example in the remainder of this work.

[4] The 'flexible' prefix *re-*/*-ri* (see McMillan 1970 for a similar development in French) is unlikely to be a case of degrammaticalization, as correctly pointed out by Idiatov (2008), because it is questionable whether *ridevo fare* and *devo rifare* really mean the same thing. They can be paraphrased differently as 'Again, I am obliged to do it' and 'I am obliged to do it for a second time', respectively. In both cases, the prefix only takes scope over the verb to which it attaches.

In a critical review of Haspelmath's eight cases, Askedal (2008: 71)[5] concludes that it makes little sense to characterize them as 'degrammaticalization'. About the first six cases (all involving inflectional affixes) he writes:

> It appears equally inappropriate to refer to 'degrammaticalization' when a grammatical element in the shape of a bound morpheme attains syntagmatic independence as a result of typological and/or syntactic restructuring, while retaining its grammatical function in the sense of membership in a 'closed' class or a class of elements of an 'abstract' functional or semantic nature, as seems to be the case in the other examples of, according to Haspelmath (2004), 'attested antigrammaticalization'.

Askedal's main objection is that all cases can be seen as resulting from typological restructurings (e.g. from inflectional to more agglutinative morphology). This is essentially correct, since obsolescent affixes are more prone to degrammaticalization than affixes that function within vital and fully productive inflectional systems.[6] The reason for Askedal's objection appears to be that degrammaticalization is not a 'process' or 'independent dynamic force', an argument that I will return to in Chapter 7.

## 6.2 Replacement and retraction

As with other types of degrammaticalization, it is important to separate examples of debonding from changes that are superficially similar, but which upon closer inspection involve replacement (section 3.3.6), retraction (3.4), or both. Before turning to what I consider valid examples of debonding, I will discuss a case of decliticization which I do not regard as an example of debonding. This case concerns decliticization of subject pronouns in Southern Dutch dialects, which have been studied in great detail by de Vogelaer (2005, forthcoming).

Many Dutch dialects in the south of the Netherlands (primarily Brabant) and most of Flanders (Belgium) have various ways of subject doubling, as exemplified in (3a–b) (de Vogelaer, forthcoming). In (3a), an enclitic (or possibly inflectional)[7] pronoun is combined with a strong pronoun[8] in sentences with inverted word order; in (3b), with regular word order, a proclitic pronoun is combined with a strong pronoun, and in (3c), the proclitic has detached itself from the verb to become a free morpheme.

[5] See Idiatov (2008) for a similar argument.

[6] An exception is Saami *haga*, discussed in section 6.7.

[7] See van Haeringen (1962 [1950]: 55).

[8] De Vogelaer distinguishes between three types of subject pronouns: enclitic pronouns, 'strong' pronouns which can be stressed, and 'weak' pronouns, which can never be stressed and are sometimes reduced variants of the strong pronouns.

(3a–c) represent the historical development of subject doubling, and it is the final stage which is of most interest to us.

(3) a.

| | | | |
|---|---|---|---|
| Ga-**de** | (**gij**) | naar | Brussel? |
| go-2SG=you | you$_{strong}$ | to | Brussels |

'Are you going to Brussels?'

b.

| | | | |
|---|---|---|---|
| **Ge**-gaat | (**gij**) | naar | Brussel. |
| you=go-2SG | you$_{strong}$ | to | Brussels |

'You are going to Brussels'

c.

| | | | | |
|---|---|---|---|---|
| **Gij** | gaat | **gij** | naar | Brussel. |
| you$_{strong}$ | go-2SG | you$_{strong}$ | to | Brussels |

'You are going to Brussels'

Subject doubling dates back to Middle Dutch, where it was first attested in sentences with inverted word order and the second person singular, as in (4a). This pattern then spread to the first person singular ((4b)) and the second person plural, with the other persons attested first in the eighteenth and nineteenth centuries, as in (4c):[9]

(4) a.

| | | | | | | | |
|---|---|---|---|---|---|---|---|
| wil-**de** | **ghy** | zulcke | zaken | doen | als | ... | (1496) |
| want=you | you$_{strong}$ | such | things | do | as | ... | |

'If you want to do things like...'

b.

| | | | | | |
|---|---|---|---|---|---|
| Sou'**ck** | **ick** | da | niet | wete | (17th century) |
| should=I | I$_{strong}$ | that | not | know | |

'Should I not know that?'

c.

| | | | | | | |
|---|---|---|---|---|---|---|
| En | **ze** zit | **zou** | daar | thuis | ... | (*c.* 1899) |
| and | she=sits | she$_{strong}$ | there | at.home | | |

'And she's sitting there at home...'

Even in present-day dialects, the second person is still the most widely used in this construction (de Vogelaer, forthcoming). In sentences with regular word order, constructions with a proclitic pronoun are geographically more widespread than constructions with two strong pronouns, which suggests that (3b) is the older construction. According to de Vogelaer, the existence of constructions such as (3c) suggests that *ge* in (3b) is no longer perceived as a clitic.

[9] Many examples are from plays figuring Brabantic immigrants to the Northern Netherlands. This is interesting, because it shows that the construction had approximately the same geographic distribution as today. The construction was even exaggerated to mock the speech of the Brabantic people, as the following example illustrates: ***Ik*** *ben* ***ik ik*** *noch vechterken noch smijterken, zey den braber* (no date; lit. 'I$_{strong}$ am I$_{strong}$ I$_{strong}$ neither a fighter nor a thrower, said the Brabantic man'; de Vogelaer, forthcoming)

It is not quite clear what motivated decliticization of the subject pronouns. The development forms part of a general trend in Brabantic from a clitic-based person-marking system to a (free) pronoun-based person-marking system, which may be due in part to convergence with the standard language, but it may also result from changes in Brabantic word order (de Vogelaer 2005: 282–4, 296–300; forthcoming). In sum, although there is evidence for decliticization, it is difficult to separate this change from the rise of constructions such as (3c), and therefore it cannot be ruled out that this is a case of replacement.

Note that the example of Southern Dutch decliticization is essentially different from a superficially similar case in the history of English, quoted as an example of degrammaticalization in Newmeyer (1998: 270f.). This concerns the replacement of forms such as *hastow* (<*hast thou* 'have you') by constructions involving full pronouns. The crucial difference is that the cliticized forms were always optional (unlike the Brabantic subject clitics), and largely confined to a relatively small group of verbs (including, among others, *be*, *have*, and modal auxiliaries). They are mostly found in questions and other constructions with subject-verb inversion, and hardly ever in preterite forms (Brinton 2004: 232). They are thus much more selective in their choice of 'hosts' than is usual for clitics (cf. section 5.2.2), from which Brinton (p. 244) concludes that they are 'not true clitics but merely reduced or contracted forms'.[10] But even if they were clitics, their decliticization would not be a case of degrammaticalization, because the enclitic pronouns alternated with free pronouns in the same construction. As a consequence, the loss of the enclitic variant would simply be a case of retraction (see section 3.4).

## 6.3 Infinitival markers

### 6.3.1 *English*

It is no exaggeration to say that infinitival *to* is one of the favourite hobby-horses of normative grammarians. Its decreasing bondedness, as evidenced by so-called 'split infinitives', has caused great vexation for centuries. The most famous example of a split infinitive in English is probably *To boldly go where no man has gone before...*, from the introductory text to many *Star Trek* episodes.

The split infinitive construction dates back to the thirteenth century (Visser 1966: 1035). From the beginning of the sixteenth century to the end

[10] According to Brinton (ibid.) the change from *thou* to *-tou* was motivated by a sandhi rule, not the result of cliticization.

of the eighteenth century split infinitives are hardly attested at all, but by the nineteenth century, the construction had become so frequent again that it raised much controversy among grammarians, and has continued to do so to the present day, with the interesting exception of co-ordinated infinitives of the type *We pray you to proceed and justly and religiously unfold* (Thackeray, 1852; quoted in Visser 1966: 1039). Split infinitives come in several types (see Visser 1966: 1039ff. for extensive treatment). The infinitival marker can be separated from the verb by *not*, as in (5a), by different kinds of adverbs, as in (5b–c), and by longer phrases as in (5d). In Middle English, the construction exemplified in (5e) was still quite common, but has now become obsolete because the direct object generally follows the verb.

(5) a. I've worked out here too long **to** not **know** how to protect myself
b. **to** always **keep** a mare for her
c. now he was only beginning **to** fully **realize** what a chump he'd been
d. she wants **to** honestly and legally **marry** that man
e. he sal þe send Angels **for to** þe **defend**
he will you send Angels for to you defend
'he will send angels to defend you'

Originally, *to* was a preposition with purposive meaning governing the dative, as in *an wulf wearð asend* ***to bewerigenne*** *þæt heafod* 'a wolf was sent to guard the head'. According to Fischer (2000), *to* started to grammaticalize into an infinitival marker in Old and (early) Middle English, which was reflected by strengthening of *to* by *for*, phonetic reduction (*to* > *te*), generalization of meaning (*to* started to appear in non-purposive constructions), and the occurrence of *to* after prepositions other than *for*. However, *to* appears to have retraced its steps by the end of the Middle English period – it ceases to be strengthened by *for*, the reduced variant *te* disappears, it can take scope over two co-ordinated verbs,[11] and the purposive meaning becomes once more predominant. While these developments can still be seen as retraction, the rise of split infinitives is not. Haspelmath (2004: 29) characterizes the change as one from prefix to proclitic, but note that Fischer does not make this claim. Her main point is that grammaticalization is not deterministic, that is, a linguistic item need not follow a grammaticalization pathway once it has set out on it. If Old and Middle English *to/te* was indeed inseparable from the infinitive, then the split infinitive and the co-ordination reduction are

[11] Fischer illustrates co-ordination reduction with the ModE example *you can use this shampoo* ***to wash*** *your hair and clean your clothes*, and notes that this is not possible with Dutch infinitival *te* (which according to her has grammaticalized further): *je kunt deze shampoo gebruiken om je haar* ***te wassen*** *en je kleren *(****te****)* ***reinigen***.

indicative of debonding. Unlike Haspelmath, however, I will not characterize this development as a shift from affix to clitic, since 'clitic' does not seem an appropriate term for the ModE infinitival marker (because adverbs and negation markers can separate it from the infinitive). I will therefore take this to be a shift from clitic to free morpheme, which is also more in line with Faarlund's (2007) analysis of the (similar) history of the Norwegian infinitival marker.

Fitzmaurice (2000) argues that degrammaticalization of *to* is continuing in American English, where split infinitives are also increasingly found with semi-auxiliaries such as *have to*, *going to*, and *want to*, as in the examples in (6) (p.171, 183): (6a–b) are typical of child language, (6c) is an overheard example uttered by a female adult.

(6) a. You have **to not say** that word. (instead of: 'You do not / don't have to say that word.')
b. I'm going **to not eat** strawberries. (instead of: 'I'm not going to eat strawberries.')
c. You want **to not be** confused about whose mother is who at kids' birthday parties.

TABLE 6.1. Parameter analysis of English infinitival *to*

| Parameter | Primitive change(s) |
|---|---|
| **Integrity** | *resemanticization:* ☐; there is no difference in meaning between e.g. *to boldly go* and *to go boldly.* *phonological 'strengthening':* (☐;); the reduced variant *te* has disappeared, but since the full form *to* had always been around, this is not a case of strengthening but of retraction. *recategorialization:* ☐; *to* does not join a major (inflected) word class. |
| **Paradigmaticity** | *deparadigmaticization:* not relevant for clitics. |
| **Paradigmatic variability** | *deobligatorification:* ☐; *to* is still obligatory with infinitives. |
| **Structural scope** | *scope expansion:* ☑; expanded scope is reflected by coordination reduction (*to serve and protect*) and split infinitives, where *to* does not just take scope over the infinitive, but over all kinds of adverbials as well (cf. the examples in (5)) |
| **Bondedness** | *severance:* ☑; *to* is a free morpheme. |
| **Syntagmatic variability** | *flexibilization:* ☑; *to* may or may not occur adjacent to the infinitive. |

According to Fitzmaurice (2000: 180) the emergence of the construction illustrated in (6) is pragmatically motivated: when the negator *not* is adjacent to the verb, it has the rhetorical effect of putting extra emphasis on the verb.

### 6.3.2 *Scandinavian*

The Scandinavian (standard) languages Swedish, Norwegian, Danish, Icelandic, and Faroese differ considerably as regards the syntactic freedom of the infinitival marker.

In Swedish (Teleman, Hellberg, and Andersson 1999b: 563f., 1999c: 176), negators obligatorily precede the infinitive ((7a)), and some other adverbials may be inserted too ((7b)):

(7) a. Ingen försökte ens övertala mig **att** **inte** resa
Nobody tried even persuade me to not leave
'Nobody even tried to persuade me not to leave'

b. (Hon njöt av) **att** **efter** **många** **år** **åter** känna
(She enjoyed) to after many years again feel
fast mark under fötterna
solid ground under feet-DEF
'She enjoyed feeling solid ground under her feet again, after many years'

Also in the two Norwegian standard languages, *Bokmål* and *Nynorsk* (Christensen 2007: 152), both an adverb and the negator can separate the infinitival marker from the verb:

*Bokmål*[12]

(8) a. Det å være mor, er ***å*** **alltid** komme for sent til avtaler
That to be mother is to always come too late to appoinments
'To be a mother, is to always be late for appointments'

b. men vi lovet å **ikke** avsløre deres synspunkter
but we promised to not reveal their viewpoints
'but we promised to not reveal their viewpoints'

*Nynorsk*

(9) a. Det er viktig å **framleis** gjere det vi kan
It is important to continuously do that we can
'It is important to keep doing what we can'

[12] Since Christensen only discusses *Nynorsk* Norwegian, I have excerpted the *Bokmål* examples myself, as well as the *Nynorsk* example in (9b), because it was shorter than Christensen's examples. The examples were taken from the Oslo corpus of tagged Norwegian texts at www.tekstlab.uio.no/norsk/bokmaal/ and www.tekstlab.uio.no/norsk/nynorsk/.

b. No var det min tur til å ikkje flire
Now was it my turn for to not sneer
'Now it was my turn not to sneer'

In Danish (Christensen 2007: 151), example (10a), with the infinitival marker directly preceding the verb, represents the unmarked order, but an adverb may be inserted between the two, as in (10b). The infinitival marker preceding a negator, as in (10c), is on the verge of being ungrammatical.

(10) Vi overtalte dem til...
We persuaded them to...

a. **ikke** **ofte** **at** prøve igen
not often to try again

b. **ikke** **at** **ofte** prøve igen
not to often try again

c. ??**at** **ikke** **ofte** prøve igen
to not often try again

In Icelandic (Christensen 2007: 153ff.; Jóhanna Barðdal, p.c.), splitting infinitives is only marginally possible. For some speakers, the infinitival marker may precede a negator, as in (11a), except when the negator is followed by a sentence adverb, as in (11b). When both a negator and a sentence adverb are present, a split infinitive is only possible when the sentence adverb is phrase-final, as in (11c).

(11) það væri vitlaust...
it were stupid...

a. ?að ekki lesa þessa bók
to not read this book
'It would be stupid not to read this book'

b. *að ekki strax lesa þessa bók.
to not immediately read this book
'It would be stupid not to read this book immediately'

c. að ekki lesa þessa bók strax.[13]
to not read this book immediately
'It would be stupid not to read this book immediately'

[13] This construction is not acceptable to all Icelanders, however. According to Jóhanna Barðdal (p.c.) it would be more natural to say *það væri ekki vitlaust að lesa þessa bók strax* 'It would not be unreasonable to read this book immediately.'

In Faroese, finally, the infinitival marker cannot be separated from the verb (Christensen 2007: 152f.):

(12) a. Hon hevur lovað ***ikki at*** gera tað aftur
she has promised not to do that again

b. *Hon hevur lovað **at ikki** gera tað aftur
she has promised to not do that again
'She has promised to not do that again'

It would be interesting to know how the differences in the Scandinavian languages reflect diachronic developments, but at present too few details are known about their respective histories. I will therefore confine myself to a discussion of the history of the infinitival marker in Norwegian, which has been argued to be a case of degrammaticalization.

Throughout the history of Norwegian,[14] the infinitival marker is generally immediately adjacent to the infinitive, as the following examples show (Faarlund 2007: 59):

(13) a. þeir ætluðu **at** hengja hann (Old Norse)
they intended to hang him

b. ko leidt aa dauvlegt dæ va **aa** vera so eisemadde (EMoNw)
how sad and boring it was to be so lonely

c. Dei prøvde å finna han (MoNw)
They tried to find him

However, when the infinitive clause contains a negation, word order differs in all three stages of Norwegian, with three different positions for the adverb – in Old Norse it immediately follows the verb, in Early Modern Norwegian it immediately precedes the verb, and in Modern Norwegian it may be inserted between the infinitival marker and the verb:

(14) a. **at** lata eigi skera hár sitt (Old Norse)
to let not cut hair his
'not to have his hair cut'

[14] Faarlund distinguishes three periods in the history of Norwegian: Old Norse, spoken in medieval Norway and Iceland and recorded in texts from the twelfth to the fourteenth century; Early Modern Norwegian (EMoNw), spoken from the fifteenth to the late nineteenth century, mostly recorded in dialect, because Norway had no written standard before the middle of the nineteenth century; and Modern Norwegian (MoNw), spoken from the end of the nineteenth century onwards.

b. Intje **aa** faa Qvile tyktes ham for leit (EMoNw)
Not to get rest seemed him too hard
'He found it too hard not to get a rest'

c. eg skal lova å ikkje seia noko (MoNw)
I shall promise to not say anything
'I promise not to say anything'

Adopting a generative point of view, Faarlund (2007: 62) assumes a similar structure for Old Norse infinitival clauses and subordinate clauses, with both the infinitival marker and the complementizer (which is also *at*)[15] occupying C. Faarlund provides several arguments why Old Norse *at* is not proclitic or prefixed to the verb: (i) *at* and the infinitive are never written as one word, (ii) *at* takes scope over co-ordinated infinitival phrases, and (iii) it is usually dropped after other complementizers such as *en* 'than' and *nema* 'unless'. The fact that the infinitival marker and the infinitive are always adjacent in Old Norse may be the result of other circumstances, according to Faarlund (2007: 64). In his syntactic representation of the infinitival clause, *at* is followed by the subject, but since the subject of infinitives is PRO, it is 'invisible'. Sentential adverbs (including negators) could, in principle, come in between, but they always follow the verb, suggesting that there is also V to I movement in infinitives. In this respect, too, infinitival clauses correspond to subordinate clauses, as in the example below:

(15) ef konunger bannaði **eigi** (Old Norse)
if king forbade not
'if the King did not forbid it'

In Early Modern Norwegian, V to I movement was lost, according to Faarlund, which is evidenced by the order adverb–finite verb in subordinate clauses:

(16) at han **icke** kendhe sseg mectig (EMoNw)
that he not felt himself powerful
'that he did not feel powerful'

Infinitival clauses, however, no longer pattern with subordinate clauses, in that the negator obligatorily precedes infinitival *at*, as we have seen in example (14b).[16] According to Faarlund, this implies that the infinitival

[15] Incidentally, the subordinator *at* developed out of infinitival *at*, which in turn grammaticalized from the local preposition *at*. See Heltoft (1995: 130ff.) for a detailed and convincing account of this development.

[16] Indeed, it is stated in Falk and Torp's (1900: 299) syntax of nineteenth-century Dano-Norwegian (the earlier name of Bokmål) that adverbials always precede the infinitival marker.

marker has now been reanalysed as a proclitic on the verb. As a consequence, *at* is no longer found in C, which should mean that it also appears in other constructions, e.g. as a complement of 'raising' verbs like 'seem' which do not take CPs as their complement, but IPs. Indeed we find examples of raised infinitives as in (17a), and compare a similar construction from Old Norse ((17b)), where *at* does not appear:

(17) a.

| | | | | | | |
|---|---|---|---|---|---|---|
| Jtem | kiændes | oc | for[de] | Anund | oc | |
| thus | know-PASS | also | above-mentioned | Anund | and | |
| gudri | **att** | hafue | opboret | xv | kiørlagh | (EMoNw) |
| Gudri | to | have | received | 15 | cow.values | |

'Thus the above-mentioned Anund and Gudri are known to have received the value of 15 cows'

b.

| | | | | | | |
|---|---|---|---|---|---|---|
| þótti | honum | hon | vel | hafa | gert | Old Norse |
| seemed | him-DAT | she-NOM | well | have | done | |

'She seemed to him to have done well'

A similar pattern is found in small clauses, where the infinitival marker does appear in Early Modern Norwegian ((18a)), but not in Old Norse ((18b)):

(18) a.

| | | | | | | | |
|---|---|---|---|---|---|---|---|
| oc | bekende | det | **at** | vere | en | velgerning | (EMoNw) |
| and | admit | that | to | be | a | good.deed | |

'and admit that it is a good deed'

b.

| | | | | | | | |
|---|---|---|---|---|---|---|---|
| ok | kenni | sik | sva | hafa | ast | guðs | (Old Norse) |
| and | know | himself-ACC | so | have | love | god-GEN | |

'and know that he thus has the love of God'

Two additional arguments in favour of the analysis of the Early Modern Norwegian infinitival marker as a proclitic are phonological reduction from *at* to *å* in the spoken language, as evidenced in text written in dialects (cf. example (14b)), and the fact that the infinitival marker and the infinitive may be written as one word, as in (19) (Faarlund 2007: 71):

(19)

| | | | |
|---|---|---|---|
| Traust | och | bescherming | **at**forswara |
| trust | and | safety | to.defend |

'to defend trust and safety'

To my mind, Faarlund has provided sufficient evidence to show that the Early Modern Norwegian infinitival marker was proclitic to the infinitive. So let us now move on to Modern Norwegian. As we have already seen in example (14c), split infinitives do occur at this stage, suggesting that the infinitival marker has decliticized, and moved 'back' to C.

As in Old Norse, the infinitival phrase is structurally identical to subordinate clauses, as is illustrated in (20a–b). Note however that the older structure with the negator preceding *å*, illustrated in (20b′), is still possible in present-day Norwegian (Faarlund 2007: 72):

(20) a. Det var best **at** du ikke tenkte på det (subordinate)
It was best [that you not thought of it]
'It was better that you did not think about it'

b. Det var best å PRO ikke tenke på det (infinitival)
It was best to PRO not think of it

b′. det var best ikke å tenke på det
it was best not to think of it
'It was better not to think about it'

There are no semantic or pragmatic differences between (20b) and (20b′). However, for some (especially younger) speakers, there is a stylistic difference: (20b′) is perceived as slightly more literal or formal. Decliticization of *å* thus bears all the hallmarks of a change in progress.

TABLE 6.2. Parameter analysis of Norwegian infinitival *å*

| Parameter | Primitive change(s) |
|---|---|
| **Integrity** | *resemanticization:* □; there is no change in function, nor does *å* acquire (lexical) meaning. *phonological 'strengthening':* □; there is no change at the phonological level. *recategorialization:* □; *å* does not join a major (inflected) word class. |
| **Paradigmaticity** | *deparadigmaticization:* not relevant for clitics. |
| **Paradigmatic variability** | *deobligatorification:* □; the infinitival marker remains obligatory in infinitival constructions. |
| **Structural scope** | *scope expansion:* ☑; that scope of *å* has expanded is evidenced by split infinitives (examples (8a–b)) and co-ordination reduction (example (21)). |
| **Bondedness** | *severance:* ☑; that *å* is no longer enclitic is likewise reflected by split infinitives and coordination reduction. |
| **Syntagmatic variability** | *flexibilization:* ☑; *å* need no longer be adjacent to the infinitive. |

A final characteristic that is relevant to the analysis of *å* is that it can be deleted before the second of two co-ordinated infinitival phrases:[17]

(21) [lesere], som så inviteres til å **se** **filmene** **og**
[readers] who then invited-PASS to to see movies-DEF and
**velge** **sin** **favoritt**
choose their favourite
'...who are then invited to see the films and choose their favourite'

The occurrence of split infinitives and co-ordination reduction make this change a valid example of debonding.

## 6.4 Japanese connectives

Modern Japanese possesses several devices for connecting two or more constituents, among them free connectives, illustrated in (22a), and enclitic 'connective particles', illustrated in (22b) (Matsumoto 1988: 340):

(22) a. Taroo-wa wakai(-yo). *Ga*, yoku yar-u-(-yo)
Taroo-TOP young(-PART). But well do-PRES(-PART)
'Taroo is young. But he does a good job'
b. Taroo-wa wakai(*-yo)-**ga**, yoku yar-u(-yo)
Taroo-TOP young(-*PART)-but well do-PRES(-PART)
'Taroo is young, but he does a good job'

The connective particles (apart from *-ga*, Matsumoto lists a handful of others) are clearly different from their non-bound counterparts. They are bound to free morphemes with which they usually form a prosodic unit. Free connectives such as *ga* on the other hand can be used independently and are preceded by a clear pause. Furthermore, a sentence-final particle such as *-yo* can occur before free connectives, but not before enclitic connectives, indicating that a free connective can start a new sentence. Finally, free connectives can start a new turn in discourse.

Similar pairs are found with (-)*dakara* 'because', in which a connective particle is attached to the enclitic copula *-da* (Matsumoto 1988: 341f.). This connective, too, appears as a free form, as in (23a), or as an enclitic connective, as in (23b). *Dakara* is even used 'to introduce an utterance in which the speaker insists on his/her opinion, in the face of a failure to understand on the part of the hearer' (Matsumoto 1988: 345f.). In such constructions (see

[17] This example was excerpted from the Oslo corpus of tagged Norwegian texts at www.tekstlab.uio.no/norsk/bokmaal/.

(23c)), the meaning 'because' has disappeared altogether and *dakara* is often followed by a clear pause. An interjection particle can be suffixed to it.

(23) a. Taroo-wa mada kodomo-da. ***Da-kara*** sore-wa
Taroo-TOP still child-COP. Therefore that-TOP
muri-da
unreasonable. request-COP
'Since Taroo is still a child, he is not up to that task'

b. Taroo-wa mada kodomo-**da-kara** sore-wa
Taroo-TOP still child-COP-because that-TOP
muri-da
unreasonable. request-COP
'Since Taroo is still a child, he is not up to that task'

c. **Dakara**(-ne), Ken-wa usotsuki-na-n-da-yo
'dakara'(-PART), Ken-TOP liar-COP-NOML-COP-PART
'I'm telling you that Ken is a liar!'

Since grammaticalization across clauses usually involves a transition from parataxis to hypotaxis (Hopper and Traugott 2003: 175ff.), unidirectionality claims would imply that the enclitic connective particles developed from the free connectives, but historical evidence clearly shows that the particles are older (Matsumoto 1988: 342f.). The connective particle *-ga* in (22a), for example, started as a genitive marker and a subject marker in Old Japanese and developed into a connective particle around the end of the eleventh century. The free form *ga* did not appear until the seventeenth century. Hopper and Traugott (2003: 210) therefore accept the Japanese case as a true counterexample to unidirectionality in clause combining.

A crucial aspect of the detachment of the enclitic connectives is, however, that it was not accompanied by an increase in semantic content. Quite the reverse: the free connective *ga* 'but' always has adversative meaning, whereas enclitic *-ga* can also have non-adversative meaning (Matsumoto 1988: 347f.). In other words, the development of independent *ga* goes hand in hand with increasing subjectivity (Hopper and Traugott 2003: 211), a change typically found in grammaticalization. *Dakara* in (23c) has developed into a discourse marker and thus follows a well-trodden semantic-pragmatic path. The other connectives discussed by Matsumoto also display pragmaticalization of meaning and are hence in accordance with predominant directions in semantic change.

According to Matsumoto (1988: 344), a possible explanation for the detachment of the enclitic connectives is that they appear clause-finally, the typical position of connective morphemes in OV languages. This position

TABLE 6.3. Parameter analysis of Japanese connectives

| Parameter | Primitive change(s) |
|---|---|
| **Integrity** | *resemanticization:* ☒; non-adversative meaning is lost. *phonological 'strengthening':* (☑); there is no change at the phonological level, but unlike the enclitic particles, the free particles can be stressed. *recategorialization:* ☐; the free connectives do not join a major (inflected) word class. |
| **Paradigmaticity** | *deparadigmaticization:* not relevant for clitics. |
| **Paradigmatic variability** | *deobligatorification:* ☑; subordinate clauses without an enclitic connective are not grammatical, whereas main clauses without a free connective are (Heiko Narrog, p.c.). |
| **Structural scope** | *scope expansion:* ☑; the enclitic connective only takes scope over a subordinate clause, whereas free connectives may take scope over the entire proposition (Heiko Narrog, p.c.). |
| **Bondedness** | *severance:* ☑; the connectives are no longer bound morphemes. |
| **Syntagmatic variability** | *flexibilization:* ☐; both are fixed: the enclitic connective at the end of a subordinate clause, the free connective at the beginning of a sentence. |

facilitates the movement from clause-final position to the initial position of the following clause, when two clauses are combined, a case of rebracketing which is also commonly found in grammaticalization.

## 6.5 Old Estonian emphatic *ep* and interrogative *es*: from clitic to free particle[18]

Old Estonian (sixteenth to eighteenth centuries) had two free particles: emphatic *ep* and interrogative *es*,[19] which correspond to clitics in cognate

[18] Shortly before I was to submit the final version of this book, I was informed of an alternative analysis by Metslang, Pajusalu, and Habicht (2008), which implies that *es* was not a case of decliticization, but of grammaticalization. According to Metslang et al., *es* developed out of *e*-stem negative verb forms, to which an interrogative suffix *-ko* and a confirmative particle *-s* had been added, and the rise of *ep* may have been an analogous development. At the time of writing the details of this argument were not known to me, but if it is correct, the Estonian examples discussed in this section are not a case of degrammaticalization.

[19] *Ep* is still found in Modern Estonian, but is extremely archaic, and *es* is now extinct (Cornelius Hasselblatt, p.c.).

languages such as Finnish or Karelian. According to Nevis (1986b) and Campbell (1991) the enclitic markers represent an older stage, and Old Estonian *ep* and *es* would hence be the result of decliticization.[20] The emphasis marker *ep* is regarded as the direct continuation of Proto-Finnic[21] **pa* (see Nevis 1986b: 13ff. and references there). Estonian *ep* occurs mostly in the same position and has the same meaning as the enclitic markers of emphasis in related languages (e.g. *=pa/=pä* in Finnish). *Ep* is usually found after the first constituent in a sentence, corresponding to the Wackernagel (i.e. second) position in which the enclitic cognates occur (example (24a)), but other positions are possible as well ((24b); Nevis 1986b: 13f.):

(24) a. selle kivi peal **ep** kolgitigi neid riideid
this rock on EMP pounded these clothes
'on *this* stone one pounded the clothes'

b. ... ja temale ta **ep** lilled viibki
... and her-ALLATIVE he EMP flowers brings-EMP
'and to her he brings flowers'

In other words, *ep* is not only prosodically independent, its position has become less fixed as well.

Interrogative *es*,[22] too, is largely, but not exclusively, a second-position word. In example (25a), from the 1686 translation of the New Testament, it is found after the first constituent, but in example (25b) (Southern Estonian, archaic) it occurs in third position. In the 1686 translation, the enclitic interrogative marker *=s*, as in (25c), can still be found as well (Nevis 1986b: 15f.):

(25) a. Kelt *es* Se Proweet Seddä ütlep
whom-ABL INT the prophet that says
'About whom does the prophet say that?'

b. Kellega teie **es** sin tahate kônelda
whom-COMIT you INT here want speak
'With whom here do you want to speak?'

[20] As Helle Metslang, Külli Habicht, and Karl Pajusalu informed me, Nevis was not the first to suggest a decliticization analysis for Estonian *es* and *ep*. For the record, it was discussed earlier in papers by Ariste (1973) and Alvre (1976).

[21] 'Finnic' is nowadays increasingly used as a term replacing the older 'Balto-Finnic', 'Baltic-Finnic', or 'Fennic' and includes (among others) Estonian, Finnish, and Karelian (Cornelius Hasselblatt, p.c.).

[22] Interrogative *es* is homophonous with, and possibly etymologically related to, a few other function words, but these bear no relevance to the decliticization analysis. See Nevis (1986b: 16ff.) for details.

c. Kustas meije Lanen ni paljo Leiba Same
whence-INT our kind so much bread get
'From where does our kind get so much bread?'

According to Nevis (1986b), emphatic *ep* and interrogative *es* both derive from Wackernagel-type clitics, **=pa* and **=(ko)s* respectively. Evidence for these reconstructed forms is found in quite a number of relic forms containing these clitics, both in Estonian and in other Finnic languages. Enclitic **=pa* is found for example in Estonian *juba* 'already', Finnish *jopa* 'even'[23] (from *ju/jo* 'already' + emphatic *=pa*), or Estonian *küllap* 'sure, probably'. Enclitic **=s* was originally an 'informal marker' (signalling casualness), which often co-occurred with interrogative **=ko* (which is now lost in Estonian). Relics of this sequence of clitics are, for example, Finnish *en=kö=s* 'don't I?', *et=kö=s* 'don't you?', etc. (negative verb + interrogative + informal marker). Estonian also has a number of interrogatives in which *=s* continues the interrogative **=(ko)s*, as in *kunas* 'when?' (cf. also example (25c)). They even co-occur in some Estonian relics, e.g. *eps*

TABLE 6.4. Parameter analysis of Estonian *ep* and *es*

| Parameter | Primitive change(s) |
|---|---|
| **Integrity** | *resemanticization:* ☐; *ep* and *es* do not gain a new function, nor do they acquire (lexical) meaning.<br>*phonological 'strengthening':* (☑); *ep* and *es* developed out of *=p* and *=s*, but the longer forms are the result of reanalysis of the final vowel of their host as part of the clitic.<br>*recategorialization:* ☐; *es* and *ep* do not join a major (inflected) word class. |
| **Paradigmaticity** | *deparadigmaticization:* not relevant for clitics. |
| **Paradigmatic variability** | *deobligatorification:* ☐; *ep* and *es* do not appear to have become either more or less obligatory. |
| **Structural scope** | *scope expansion:* ☐; there is no apparent change in scope; judging from the translations of the sentences in (24) and (25), *ep* and *es* continue to emphasize or interrogate one constituent. |
| **Bondedness** | *severance:* ☑; both *ep* and *es* have become free morphemes. |
| **Syntagmatic variability** | *flexibilization:* ☑; as free morphemes, *ep* and *es* are no longer restricted to Wackernagel position. |

[23] Nevis translates Estonian *juba* as 'even' as well, but according to Cornelius Hasselblatt (p.c.) this is incorrect.

(negative *e* + emphatic *pa* + interrogative *s*), as in *eps ta tule* 's/he'll come, won't s/he?' (Cornelius Hasselblatt, p.c.).

In Old Estonian, clitics such as =*s* and =*p* prevented the general apocope of final vowels (compare e.g. *veela*=*ks* 'still?' with *veel* 'still'). The non-apocopated vowel (often *ä*, which became *e* in non-initial position) was subsequently reanalysed as part of the clitic, which accounts for the free forms *ep* and *es*.

## 6.6 Irish *muid*: from verb suffix to pronoun

The development of the Irish 1PL pronoun *muid* from a 1PL verbal suffix is one of the stock examples in the degrammaticalization literature. The two stages in the development of this morpheme are illustrated in (26):[24]

(26) a. molfa-**maid** (Early Modern Irish)
praise-FUT.1PL

b. molfaid **muid** (Contemporary Connemara Irish)
praise-FUT we
'we will praise'

In Old Irish (*c.* 600–900), person marking was exclusively inflectional, but in the Middle Irish period (*c.* 900–1200) a parallel system was developed, consisting of the 3SG form of the verb + an enclitic personal pronoun. By the Early Modern Irish period (*c.* 1200–1600) verbs had two paradigms, a 'synthetic' and an 'analytic' one, illustrated in Table 6.5 by the future inflection of the verb *mol* 'to praise' (Doyle 2002: 68). In present-day Irish, the analytic forms are more common than the synthetic ones, increasingly more

TABLE 6.5. Synthetic and analytic verbal paradigms in Early Modern Irish

| | | Synthetic | Analytic |
|---|---|---|---|
| SG | 1 | *molfad* | *molfaidh mé* |
| | 2 | *molfair* | *molfaidh tú* |
| | 3 | *molfaidh* | *molfaidh sé / sí* |
| PL | 1 | *molfamaid* | *molfaidh sinn* |
| | 2 | *molfaidhe* | *molfaidh sibh* |
| | 3 | *molfaid* | *molfaidh siad* |

[24] The difference between -*maid* and *muid* is merely one of spelling and has no morphological significance (Aidan Doyle, p.c.).

so the further one proceeds northwards (Mac Congáil 2004: 117). According to Doyle (2002: 68f.) the 1PL suffix was first reanalysed as an independent pronoun in the future paradigms, because this form happened to be prosodically similar to the analytic forms in the right-hand column in Table 6.5. At a later stage, it spread to the other verbal paradigms and eventually replaced the pronoun *sinn* in the analytic paradigm.

Doyle (2002: 71ff.) discusses two factors which according to him facilitated the rise of independent *muid*. First, Irish ceased to be a PRO-drop language, which meant that subject–verb agreement came to be obligatorily marked by an overt personal pronoun. Secondly, the originally affixal verbal endings started to behave like clitics phonologically. Thus, Doyle (2002: 77) concludes, the development of *muid* into an independent pronoun was 'a conspiracy of syntactic and phonological factors', resulting from a combination of a 'parameter resetting' in Early Modern Irish (subject–verb agreement came to be expressed by a pronoun instead of an inflected verb) and the reanalysis of affixes as clitics in Middle Irish.

An alternative analysis is presented in Bybee, Perkins, and Pagliuca (1994: 13ff.). They claim that when the synthetic forms started to be substituted by analytic forms, only the 1PL suffix had been retained resulting in the following present tense paradigm (ibid.: 14):

(27) Irish *mol* 'praise', present tense

| | | | |
|---|---|---|---|
| 1SG | molann mé | 1PL | molaimid |
| 2SG | molann tú | 2PL | molann sibh |
| 3SG | molann sé/sí | 3PL | molann siad |

In its non-palatalized variant *muid*, the suffix may occur as an independent pronoun instead of the original 1PL pronoun *sinn*, as in examples (28a–b) (with an additional emphatic suffix *-e*):

(28) a. osclaíonn tusa an geata agus imríonn ***muide*** cluifí
open-PRES 2SG-EMP the gate and play-PRES 1PL.EMP games
'**You** open the gate and **we** play games'

b. Is **muide** a rinne é
Be 1PL.EMP who do-PAST it
'It is **we** who did it'

Bybee, Perkins, and Pagliuca (1994: 13) regard the demorphologization of *muid* as a case of 'paradigm pressure', because all other person forms were already expressed analytically.

Bybee et al.'s analysis is problematic, however (Aidan Doyle, p.c.), because there is no evidence for the paradigm in (27). In two out of three of the modern dialects, the first person singular is still synthetic as well (*molaim*; cf. also Mac Congáil 2004: 120), hence the 1PL was not the only suffix to be retained. In other words, if debonding of the 1PL suffix had been motivated by paradigm pressure, it is not clear why this did not happen to the 1SG suffix as well.

Askedal (2008: 54ff.), too, points out that the 1PL was not the only remaining synthetic form. In addition, Askedal claims that the history of *muid* is not a case of degrammaticalization because it formed part of a larger development towards 'analytic verb morphology with agglutinating traits'. In view of the general typological shift towards analyticity, Askedal claims, it would be 'structurally misleading' to speak of degrammaticalization in this case. Askedal thus appears to regard typological developments and degrammaticalization as competing changes. In my view, however, the two go perfectly well together because they are changes on entirely different levels.[25] The loss of inflections is a change on the level of grammatical categories, and it is observed in the history of many languages. The particular demorpholo-

TABLE 6.6. Parameter analysis of Irish *muid*

| Parameter | Primitive change(s) |
|---|---|
| **Integrity** | *resemanticization:* ☑; a pronoun is less abstract in meaning than a verbal suffix.<br>*phonological 'strengthening':* ☐; there has been no change at the phonological level.<br>*recategorialization:* ☑; although Irish pronouns are not inflected as such, they do form (partly suppletive) paradigms (including, among other things, emphatic forms as in (28)). |
| **Paradigmaticity** | *deparadigmaticization:* ☑; *muid* has left the paradigm of person inflections on the verb. |
| **Paradigmatic variability** | *deobligatorification:* ☐; both as a 1PL suffix, and as a pronoun (-)*muid* is obligatory to express 1PL. |
| **Structural scope** | *scope expansion:* ☑; a suffix only takes scope over its stem, but a pronoun can take scope over the entire predicate. |
| **Bondedness** | *severance:* ☑; *muid* has become a free morpheme. |
| **Syntagmatic variability** | *flexibilization:* ☑; *muid* need no longer be adjacent to the verb, but can also appear in other construction types, e.g. (28b). |

[25] In addition, agglutination appears not to be an accurate description of Irish verb morphology. According to Doyle (p.c.), it is still inflectional.

gization of *muid*, on the other hand, is a 'micro change' which only affected a particular morpheme. In Norde (2001a), I have argued that massive deflexion may result in the exaptation (see section 3.3.5) of obsolescent inflections, and this may be argued for Irish *muid* as well. In other words, Irish verbal deflexion facilitated degrammaticalization of *muid*, so the two are complementary rather than mutually exclusive, as Askedal appears to claim.

## 6.7 Northern Saami *haga*: from case suffix to postposition

Most Finno-Ugric languages possess an abessive case suffix, meaning 'without', e.g. Finnish *-tta*. In Northern Saami, however, the abessive morpheme *haga*[26] has the morphosyntactic characteristics of a postposition (Nielsen 1926: 65; Nevis 1986a).[27] Like postpositions (but unlike affixes), it governs the genitive case, it can be stressed, and it can occur independently. When the abessive is contrasted with similar constructions with different case marking, other differences become apparent as well. For example, the abessive prefers conjunction reduction as in (29a), which is not possible with case suffixes (cf. (29b)):

(29) a. áhči ja Issáh-a **haga** (ABESSIVE)
father.SG.GEN and Issát-SG.GEN without
'without father and (without) Issát'

b. áhči-in ja Issáhi-in / *Áhči- ja
father-COMIT and Issát-COMIT / father- and
Issáhi-in (CASE SUFFIX)
Issat-COMIT
'with father and Issát'

In addition, it follows the enclitic possessive morpheme as in (30a), whereas case suffixes precede the possessive, as in (30b):

(30) a. bárdná-n **haga** (ABESSIVE)
son-POSS.1SG without
'without my son'

[26] In Nevis (1986a) and literature based on that paper, this morpheme is usually spelled *taga*, but actually this is an older spelling which was only used in the Eastern Finnmark dialect group. The Western Finnmark dialects, on which the Saami literary language is based, underwent a regular sound change *ht > *h on the border of the second and the third syllable.

[27] Although Nevis's analysis of the historical events is generally correct, Ante Aikio (p.c.) has pointed out to me that his examples should be treated with care. First, examples are contrasted that are taken from different Saami languages (there are ten official Saami languages, six of which have their own written form). Secondly, the examples contain quite a few errors in morphological analyses and translations. Hence, the examples given here have either been rewritten or provided by Aikio, who is a native speaker.

b. áhku-i-dasa-n (CASE SUFFIX)
grandmother-PL-ILLATIVE-POSS.1SG
'to my grandmothers'

Even though *haga* is usually written separately in modern spelling,[28] in speech it is often cliticized. But since there is no phonological interaction with the host (which does not make it a true Saami clitic) Nevis characterizes the abessive as a 'semi-clitic postposition'.

In most Northern Saami dialects, the development of *haga* has gone even further towards complete phonological independence. In these dialects, *haga* functions as a phonologically independent adverb:

(31) mun báhcen **haga**
I remain-PRET.1SG without
'I was left ("remained") without'

In Northern Saami varieties in Norway, *haga* even occurs as a preposition. This usage is condemned by normative grammarians, and is probably due to the influence of Norwegian (a prepositional language):[29]

(32) **haga** skuova-id
without shoe-PL.GEN/ACC
'without shoes'

The early history of the Saami abessive is not documented, but judging from both language-internal and comparative evidence, the abessive must have been a suffix in Proto-Finno-Ugric, and not a full word which underwent cliticization and subsequent affixation in all Finno-Ugric languages but Saami. For Proto-Finno-Ugric a sequence of affixes can be reconstructed, namely **-pta-k-e/i-k/n* [CARITIVE-LATIVE-e[30]-('pleonastic') LATIVE], which in Proto-Saami would have become **-ptā-k-ë-k/n* (where <*ë*> represents a central unrounded vowel). The first element, **-pta* could never have been a free morpheme in Finno-Ugric, because Finno-Ugric originally allowed no initial consonant clusters at all; all instances of initial clusters in the present-day languages are of secondary origin. That this sequence of affixes developed into an abessive suffix is evidenced by the existence of suffixal *-httá*, which

[28] According to Jussi Ylikoski (p.c.), *haga* has been written as a separate word in most varieties since the nineteenth century. In frequent collocations, however, *haga* and its preceding noun may be written as one word, as in *lobihaga* 'without permission', but this is non-standard.

[29] I owe this example to Jussi Ylikoski.

[30] In the reconstructed form, the epenthetic vowel was added by Ante Aikio to Nevis's reconstruction.

TABLE 6.7. Parameter analysis of Northern Saami *haga*

| Parameter | Primitive change(s) |
|---|---|
| **Integrity** | *resemanticization:* ☑; *haga* can function as an independent adverb meaning 'without' (example (31)), which means that it no longer only modifies a noun phrase (as an abessive).<br>*phonological 'strengthening':* ☐; there has been no change at the phonological level.<br>*recategorialization:* ☐; *haga* does not join a major (inflected) word class. |
| **Paradigmaticity** | *deparadigmaticization:* ☑; *haga* no longer forms part of the paradigm of Northern Saami nominal case inflections. |
| **Paradigmatic variability** | *deobligatorification:* (☑); as a postposition, *haga* is still in opposition with the inflectional case markers, but in some varieties of Northern Saami, it may be substituted by other abessive elements (Ylikoski 2008: 106f.). |
| **Structural scope** | *scope expansion:* ☑; expanded scope of *haga* is reflected by co-ordination reduction in (29a) and the ability to follow the possessive in (30a). |
| **Bondedness** | *severance:* ☑; *haga* has become a free morpheme. |
| **Syntagmatic variability** | *flexibilization:* ☑; *haga* can occur independently (example (31)), and even as a preposition (example (32)). |

is no longer productive (as Nielsen already noted in his grammar from 1926, p. 65).

Kiparsky (2005) suggests that the changes to the abessive are due to analogy with the comitative plural *-guim*, which is a grammaticalized clitic (from *guoibme* 'fellow')[31] and likewise follows the possessive (cf. example (30a)), but this seems open to some debate. First, it is not immediately evident why the singular abessive, and the singular abessive alone, should pattern with the comitative plural. Secondly, the comitative plural is becoming increasingly suffixal – for instance, conjunction reduction is becoming very rare in modern usage (Aikio, p.c.). In other words, it is hard to see how a clitic which is grammaticalizing into a suffix should provide a pattern for a suffix degrammaticalizing into a clitic and hence into a postposition.

[31] In modern Northern Saami orthography, these morphemes are actually spelled *-guin* and *guoibmi*, respectively (Jussi Ylikoski, p.c.).

## 6.8 Deaffixation in the Hup verbal compound

As we have seen in section 5.6, very little is known about degrammaticalization in polysynthetic languages, and in this section I will discuss another one of those rare examples. This study deals with deaffixation in the verb compound in Hup (Epps 2008), a language spoken in north-west Amazonia, belonging to the Nadahup family. The Hup verb has multiple slots for grammatical formatives, as illustrated by the following template (Epps, in prep):

(33)

| Core | | | | | Periphery | |
|---|---|---|---|---|---|---|
| (Prefix) | - Stem | - (Inner Suffix) | - Boundary Suffix | = | (Enclitic) | (Particle) |
| hup | -yəd | -cɨ̃w | - ɨ̃y | = | cud | yæ̃h |
| REFLEXIVE | - hide | - COMPLETIVE | - DYNM | = | INFR | FRUST |

'had already hid himself, apparently, in vain'

In addition, verb stems can be compounded. Some very frequent roots seem to have grammaticalized into 'auxiliary-like' verb forms. For example, the stem *j'ap-* 'to break' is the conceivable source of a modifying verb root *j'ap-* 'to stop doing V':

(34) nupm'ǽ ʔãh ʔəg-j'ap-yiʔ-ɨy
at.this.time 1SG drink-snap-TEL-DYNM
'I quit drinking at about this time (of day)'

Modifying verb roots may develop further into inner suffixes, which have grammatical rather than lexical meaning. For example, the frustrative suffix *yæ̃h-* in (33) above also occurs as an independent verb meaning 'to request, order'. Such inner suffixes may be phonologically reduced (usually by the loss of a final consonant).

Apart from inner suffixes originating in verbal compounds, there also exist inner suffixes that derive from function words or clitics outside the verb. Again, the diachronic analysis is based on synchronic polyfunctionality, but since these patterns are found in groups of words rather than in isolated grams, it is likely that these are cases of grammaticalization. This is corroborated by the observation that if reduction occurs, it is always found in the more grammatical variant.

But according to Epps (in prep.), degrammaticalization can be observed as well, in at least four morphemes, and what follows is a description of two of them. The first is the polyfunctional morpheme *hɔ̃h-/-hɔ̃*. As a main verb (example (35a)), this root means 'make noise, produce sound'. Additionally, it appears as a modifying verb meaning 'make noise doing V' (example (35b)). And finally, it occurs as an inner suffix, where it functions as a nonvisual evidential (example (35c)):

(35) a. tɨh **hɔ̃́h**-ɔ̃p, nukán-ay tán yúw-úh
3SG make.sound-DEP over.here-INCH FUT.CNTR that.DEC
'When it (first becomes) audible, (the boat) is still over here in this direction.'

b. yam-**hɔ̃h**-nɨ́h=yɨʔ níh!
sing-make.sound-NEG=TEL be.IMP
'Don't make (so much) noise singing!'

c. yɨ́t-ɨʔ nɨŋ hipãh-nɨ́h-hɔ̃́-ʔ ?
thus-INT 2PL know-NEG-NONVIS-INT
'Don't you all know that it is thus?'

These three examples probably represent three successive stages in a grammaticalization chain (note that *hɔ̃* in example (35c) is phonologically reduced, and is also the most grammaticalized one). However, the nonvisual evidential can also occur as a clitic (i.e. outside the verb core, cf. the template in (33)), as in (36a). Moreover, it can be attached to non-verbal predicates, as in (36b).

(36) a. náciya pǽ-ǽy=**hɔ̃**
boat go.upriver-DYNM=NONVIS
'The boat is going upriver (I can hear it).'

b. pæ̌j=**hɔ̃**
umari=NONVIS
'It's umari fruit.' (speaker is smelling mess on baby's foot)

Of course, it is possible that the clitic developed independently from the same source as the inner suffix (i.e. from the verb root *hɔ̃-*), but Epps presents a careful argument for why this is likely to be a case of degrammaticalization. For example, the clitic always appears in the reduced form *hɔ̃*, which is the form of the inner suffix. The inner suffix lost its final consonant because it was followed by a vowel-initial boundary suffix, following a general Hup phonological rule. In other words, this form could only have arisen in an inner suffix, which means that the reduced clitic must derive from the reduced suffix.

A second morpheme discussed by Epps has even gone one step further. This is the morpheme *yæ̃h*, which as a main or auxiliary verb means 'request' or 'order'. An example of *yæ̃h* as an auxiliary is given in (37):

(37) deh cǎ̃y-ǎn tɨh hop-**yǣ́h**-ǣ́h
water beetle-OBJ 3SG immerse-request-DEC
'He sent the water-beetle down into the water.'

As an inner suffix, *yǣh* functions as a 'frustrative', indicating that the expected or desired outcome has not occurred – as such, *yǣh* may even co-occur with the verbal stem *yǣh* within one and the same verb phrase:

(38) ʔɨ́n-ǎn b'ɨ́yɨʔ tɨh d'ob-**yǣ́h**-cud-**yǣ́h**-ǣ́h
1pl.OBJ only 3SG go.to.river-request-INFR-FRUST-DEC
'He told only us to come down (in vain – others came as well).'

Like *hɔ̃* above, *yǣh* can also occur enclitically, both to verb phrases ((39a)) and non-verbal phrases ((39b)). But unlike *hɔ̃*, *yǣh* can be stressed, which makes it slightly less bound (according to Epps, it can also be analysed as a particle).

(39) a. ʔãh j'ɔm-tú-y=hɔ̃ **yǣ́h**
1SG bathe-want-DYNM=NONVIS FRUST
'I'd like to take a bath (in vain)' (i.e. I won't because it is too cold)

b. [hɔ̃p tǣ́h yǒ pay-nɨ́h mún] **yǣ́h** yúw-úh
fish small dangle bad-NEG INTS2 FRUST that.ITG-DEC
'It would make a not-bad minnow-fishing-line (in vain).'

What the degrammaticalizing grams have in common is that they all function as kinds of discourse markers, indicating evidentiality, frustration or failure to realize a goal, or topicality. In other words, this particular type of deaffixation occurs in precisely those contexts where scope usually increases (see section 1.4.2).

Epps hypothesizes that as the verb roots grammaticalized into inner suffixes and developed discourse-related functions, their syntactic and semantic scope was widened from the level of verb stem to that of predicate. They subsequently spread to other predicates, but since these have a very different morphological structure (most notably, they lack the boundary suffix found in verbs), they were interpreted as clitics, because non-verbal predicates do not have inner suffixes. They then came to be inserted in the periphery of the verbal predicate as well.

The Hup case is the only example of debonding where the gram does not become a free morpheme that I am aware of.[32] But it is not inconceivable that

[32] The reason why this case has not been analysed as a case of deinflectionalization is that there is no change in function.

TABLE 6.8. Parameter analysis of Hup *hɔ̃* and *yæ̃h*

| Parameter | Primitive change(s) |
|---|---|
| **Integrity** | *resemanticization:* ☐; there is no change in meaning or function between the inner suffix and the clitic. *phonological 'strengthening':* ☐; there is no change at the level of phonology. *recategorialization:* ☐; *hɔ̃* and *yæ̃h* do not join a major (inflected) word class. |
| **Paradigmaticity** | *deparadigmaticization:* ☑; *hɔ̃*, and *yæ̃h* no longer strictly function as verbal affixes, because they can also be attached to non-verbal phrases (examples (36b) and (39b)). |
| **Paradigmatic variability** | *deobligatorification:* ☐; there is no apparent change in obligatoriness. |
| **Structural scope** | *scope expansion:* ☑; as inner suffixes, *hɔ̃* and *yæ̃h* only take scope over the verb stem, but in (36b) and (39b) they take scope over larger units. |
| **Bondedness** | *severance:* ☑; *yæ̃h* more so than *hɔ̃*. |
| **Syntagmatic variability** | *flexibilization:* ☑; *yæ̃h* more so than *hɔ̃*. |

this is because Hup is polysynthetic, and it will be interesting to find out whether this holds for other polysynthetic languages as well.

## 6.9 Dutch/Frisian/German *tig/tich/zig*: from suffix to quantifier

In Dutch, Frisian, and German,[33] the cognates of the English numeral suffix *-ty* (as in *twenty*) can be used independently as a quantifier meaning 'umpteen, dozens' (see e.g. van Marle 1985 for Dutch and Drosdowski et al. 1984: 281 for German), as in the examples in (40a). The ordinal equivalents are illustrated in (40b).

(40) a. Die kerel heeft al tig vriendinnen gehad (Dutch)
Dy keardel hat al tich freondinnen hân (Frisian)
Der Kerl hat schon zig Freundinnen gehabt (German)
That guy has already dozens girlfriends had
'That guy has already had dozens of girlfriends'

b. Je vraagt dat nu al voor de tigste keer! (Dutch)
Do fregest da no al foar de tichste kear! (Frisian)

[33] Thanks to Liefke Reitsma and Heike Behrens for providing me with the Frisian and German equivalents respectively.

Du fragst das jetzt schon zum zigsten Mal! (German)
You ask that now already for the dozenth time
'Now you are asking that for the dozenth time already!'

What makes the case of *tig* particularly intriguing is that it is the only example, as far as I know, of a degrammaticalized item that has embarked upon a totally new grammaticalization pathway. This development, illustrated in (41), is so recent that no native speakers of Dutch I consulted (including myself) were familiar with it. Yet it occurs frequently in (informal) internet sources, as well as in newspapers (if sporadically), and it was even noted as early as 1985 by van Marle.

(41) maar tig leuk dat die in Portugal gaat voetballuh (Dutch)
but very nice that he in Portugal goes play.soccer[34]
'But how very nice that he is going to play soccer in Portugal!'

In this section, I will be primarily concerned with Dutch *tig*.[35] I will argue (following Norde 2006b) that Dutch *tig* was first degrammaticalized from a suffix to an independent quantifier, and was subsequently (re)grammaticalized into an adverb of degree. Including the pre-suffixal stages, the changes can be summarized as follows:

(42) PIE 'ten' > PGmc 'unit of ten' > PGmc 'x10' > Du 'many' > Du 'very'
free > free > bound > free > free

The etymological predecessor of the numeral suffix -*tig* was the PGmc u-stem **texu-*/**teʒu* which in turn derives from PIE **dékm̥* 'ten'. The original meaning of a numeral such as *veertig* 'forty' was thus 'four units of ten'.[36] The development from **texu-* to -*tig* is a copybook example of grammaticalization, featuring semantic bleaching, decategorialization, morphologization, and phonological reduction.

The subsequent development into a quantifier, conversely, bears all the hallmarks of degrammaticalization. *Tig* has gained semantic substance, in

[34] This quote was taken from a forum of soccer enthusiasts (www.voetbalzone.nl/doc.asp?id=6426), which, like many internet fora, is characterized by colloquial constructions and spellings, such as *voetballuh* for *voetballen* 'to play soccer'.

[35] It is possible that the independent quantifier did not arise in all three languages independently, but according to van Marle (1985: 147), German influence on Dutch is unlikely since the *tig* construction is typically found in colloquial speech, and none of his informants were familiar with the German *zig* construction (but of course the construction could have been borrowed by an earlier generation). Dutch influence on Frisian is somewhat more plausible, since all speakers of Frisian are bilingual.

[36] The origin of Germanic decades and the other numerals is notoriously complex. For details, which need not concern us here, see Ross and Berns (1992).

that it has an independent meaning (ranging from 'a few' to 'billions', see below), whereas the suffix only serves to multiply the numeral to which it is attached by ten – it has little meaning of its own (like all derivational suffixes). Secondly, it has recategorialized to some degree, because it has an ordinal form *tigste* (see example (40b)). Thirdly, it has demorphologized, obviously, and finally, it has gained phonetic substance, since there is a clear difference in pronunciation between the suffix, [təx], and the quantifier, [tɪx].[37] Unlike cardinal numerals, which can be either stressed or unstressed, *tig* is invariably stressed.

In the vast majority of cases, *tig* functions as a modifier of count nouns (example (43a)), the most frequent collocation being *tig keer* 'dozens of times'.[38] *Tig* modifying a mass noun, as in (43b), is also attested, but far less common.

(43) a. Die Scholten woont nu al **tig** jaar in Bloemendaal[39]
That Scholten lives now already dozens year in Bloemendaal
'That Scholten guy has been living in Bloemendaal for dozens of years now'

b. Maar ze verlangen ook **tig** ervaring
But they require also dozens experience
'But they also require a lot of experience'

*Tig* is not merely used as a quantifier in attributive position, but also appears in all kinds of quantifying expressions where it is used independently, as in (44a–c), or as part of a compound, as in (44d–e):

(44) a. Er lopen bij Daimler-Benz **tig** van dit soort projecten
There run at Daimler-Benz dozens of this kind projects
'DB has dozens of these kinds of projects running'

b. Suikerklontjes krijgen ze elke dag, een stuk of **tig**
Sugar cubes get they every day, a piece or dozens
'They get sugar cubes every day, dozens or so'

c. een **tig** of wat pilsjes
a dozen or what beers
'a dozen or so beers'

d. een Dior-rok van **tig-duizend** gulden
a Dior-skirt of umpteen-thousand guilders
'an umpteen-thousand-guilders Dior skirt'

[37] The same difference is found in Frisian, but in German, they are pronounced the same.

[38] The data were drawn from the Dutch *LexisNexis* corpus of newspapers. Three newspapers were searched, covering the period between 1992 and 2005. See further Norde (2006b: 39).

[39] In Dutch, nouns denoting measure, weight, time, etc. usually remain in the singular form after numerals and quantifiers, hence *tig jaar, twintig jaar* 'dozens of years, twenty years', not **tig jaren*.

e. **tig**-maal ingewikkelder
dozens-times more.complicated
'dozens of times more complicated'

It is furthermore important to observe that *tig* is not a hypernym (unlike lexicalized affixes such as *isms*), that is, it does not mean 'any amount between twenty and ninety'. In the examples in (44), *tig* will hardly denote more than twenty, and in (45a–b), by contrast, it refers to much larger quantities. It thus covers any amount between a few and billions, depending on the context.

(45) a. met... **tig** gigabyte harde schijf
with... dozens gigabyte hard disk
'with a hard disk with dozens (~hundreds) of gigabytes'

b. Ons lichaam bestaat uit **tig** cellen
Our body consists of dozens cells
'Our body is made up of dozens (~billions) of cells'

Language-users often appear to reconstruct *tig* as originating in the suffix -*tig*, since they frequently spell it as -*tig*, sometimes adding quotation marks:

(46) a. Dat geldt ook voor de **-tig** andere instanties
That counts also for the dozens other authorities
'That also holds for the dozens of other authorities'

b. Van Persie heeft **'tig'** begeleiders
Van Persie has dozens coaches
'Van Persie has dozens of coaches'

Why -*tig* became detached is not entirely clear. According to Hamans (1993) the Dutch suffix -*tig*, used in all multiples of ten between twenty and ninety, is a 'confusivum' with a meaning of its own, less exact than 'times ten'. It is precisely this connotation of vagueness which makes it a suitable candidate for an independent quantifier. Van Marle (1985: 147) suggests that the independent use of Dutch *tig* was originally meant to be humorous. This has also been suggested in *Deutsches Wörterbuch* (J. and W. Grimm) for German *zig*.

While the use of *tig* as an independent quantifier is well-established in the sense that it is known to, albeit not accepted by, all speakers of Dutch, this is certainly not true for the second stage in the development of *tig* (i.e. from quantifier to intensifier), as I already noted above. Nevertheless, the development from quantifier to intensifier is not unusual, even if quantifiers are not the most common source of intensifiers (Klein 1998: 25ff.; González-Diaz 2005). Other examples are English *much*, Dutch *veel*, Italian *molto*, and

Swedish *mycket*, which have a slightly dissimilar distribution (Swedish *mycket* can be used to intensify both adverbs and adjectives, whereas English *much* is nowadays restricted to the comparative forms of adjectives and adverbs). An important difference between these adverbs and *tig*, however, is that, as quantifiers, *much* etc. modify mass nouns (*much water*, **much tables*), whereas *tig* primarily modifies count nouns (?*tig water*, *tig tafels*).

Intensifying *tig* (here glossed as 'very') is found in several contexts: as the intensifier of adjectives ((47a)), of comparatives of adjectives and adverbs ((47b)), and of adverbs ((47c)):

(47) a.

| | | | | | | | | |
|---|---|---|---|---|---|---|---|---|
| die | telefoon | is | **-tig** | lelijk, | prolly | **-tig** | duur | en |
| that | phone | is | very | ugly | prolly | very | expensive | and |

| | | |
|---|---|---|
| duidelijk | **-tig** | overkill |
| clearly | very | overkill |

'That phone is very ugly, probably very expensive and clearly overkill'

b.

| | | | | | | |
|---|---|---|---|---|---|---|
| beetje | jammer, | middelburg | is | toch | **tig** | leuker |
| bit | pity | Middelburg | is | still | much | nicer |

'bit of a shame, (the city of) Middelburg is much nicer after all'

c.

| | | | | | | | | |
|---|---|---|---|---|---|---|---|---|
| Ik | heb | de | film | zelf | ook | **tig** | vaak | gezien |
| I | have | the | movie | myself | also | very | often | seen |

'I myself have seen the movie very often also'

In German, the corresponding construction with *zig* as an intensifier is as uncommon and controversial as it is in Dutch, yet examples are not difficult to come by:[40]

(48) a.

| | | | | | | |
|---|---|---|---|---|---|---|
| Ich | liebe | dich | seit | **zig** | viel | Jahren[41] |
| I | love | you | since | very | many | years |

'I have loved you for many years'

b.

| | | | | | | | |
|---|---|---|---|---|---|---|---|
| Ich | hab | mir | jedes | Detail | **zig** | oft | angehört |
| I | have | me | every | detail | very | often | listened.to |

'I have listened to every detail dozens of times'

Since the construction appears to be quite rare in both German and Dutch, and German influence on Dutch in general has decreased considerably during the past decades, it is not very likely that Dutch borrowed this usage of *tig* from German. But if the rise of intensifying *tig* is indeed a case of grammaticalization, as I will be arguing here, this is not necessarily a

[40] According to Hindrik Sijens (p.c.) *tich* cannot be used as an intensifier in Frisian – at least he had been unable to find examples of it in web pages (December 2007).

[41] The examples were excerpted from a Google-search on 22 January 2008.

problem, since similar grammaticalization processes have been observed to occur independently in different languages. In this case, it is not difficult to see how the reanalysis of *tig* as an intensifier could have come about. The most likely scenario, in my view, is one in which intensifying *tig* originates with comparatives, where *tig* could be interpreted as either a quantifier or an adverb. An example of such an ambiguous bridging context (see section 1.5) is (49), where *tig* can be either a quantifier, as in reading (a), or an adverb which intensifies the comparative adjective, as in reading (b).

| | | | | | | | | |
|---|---|---|---|---|---|---|---|---|
| (49) | Er | zijn | **tig** | betere | systemen | op | de | markt. |
| | a. There | are | dozens | better | systems | on | the | market. |
| | b. There | are | very | better | systems | on | the | market. |

'There are dozens of better systems / much better systems on the market'

Brinton and Traugott (2005: 136) consider degree adverbs as instances of grammaticalization because they show a transition from concrete meaning to abstract, grammatical meaning. They have little semantic substance of their own, but function primarily to intensify the meaning of the following adjective or adverb, in other words, they are 'synsemantic' in Heine, Claudi, and Hünnemeyer's (1991: 28) terms. To this observation we may add that (i) intensifier *tig* has decategorialized (unlike the quantifier *tig* it is indeclinable); (ii) it has become syntactically fixed, i.e. it can only appear in a slot preceding an adjective or adverb, whereas the quantifier *tig* could also be used independently (compare the examples in (44a–c)); (iii) its scope has decreased from the full NP to the adjective or adverb it modifies.

Thus far, *tig* is the only example of a gram that first degrammaticalizes and subsequently (re)grammaticalizes that I am aware of. The implications of this will be discussed in Chapter 7. For the remainder of this section, I will return to the stage where the suffix -*tig* debonded. That this is a case of degrammaticalization is not generally accepted. For instance, Haspelmath regards numerals such as Dutch *twintig* 'twenty' and *dertig* 'thirty' as compounds, and the independent use of *tig* as a case of back-formation. However, forms such as *twintig* and *dertig*, as well as their English equivalents, make it very clear that the numerals are not compounds consisting of a numeral and an element meaning 'tenfold', because *twin* 'twen' and *der* 'thir' do not exist as independent forms. This makes the back-formation analysis very implausible.

Lehmann (2004: 171ff.) criticizes the *tig* example for other reasons. According to him, *tig/zig* does not make a convincing case because it is based on synchronic observations, without proof of a historical stage which did have the suffix but not the independent quantifier. And it would never be possible to prove that such a stage ever existed because of the 'non-demonstrability of

TABLE 6.9. Parameter analysis of Dutch *tig*

| Parameter | Primitive change(s) |
|---|---|
| **Integrity** | *resemanticization:* ☑; the suffix -*tig* has modifying meaning, merely functions to multiply the preceding numeral by 10, but as a quantifier, *tig* has independent semantics.<br>*phonological 'strengthening':* ☑; the quantifier is pronounced with a full vowel ([tɪx]), whereas the suffix is pronounced with schwa ([təx]).<br>*recategorialization:* ☑; *tig* has an ordinal variant (*tigste*) and can be preceded by an article, as in example (44c). |
| **Paradigmaticity** | *deparadigmaticization:* not relevant for derivational affixes. |
| **Paradigmatic variability** | *deobligatorification:* (☑;) the suffix -*tig* is obligatory in the sense that it cannot be deleted in some numerals (*twintig* '20', *dertig* '30', *veertig* '40', and *tachtig* '80') because the '*tig*-less' forms are non-existent (**twin*, **tach*, etc.). The independent quantifier is not obligatory – it can be substituted by phrases such as *een boel, een hoop* 'a lot'. |
| **Structural scope** | *scope expansion:* ☑; the suffix -*tig* only takes scope over the numeral to which it attaches, but the quantifier *tig* can take scope over entire noun phrases. |
| **Bondedness** | *severance:* ☑; *tig* has become a free morpheme. |
| **Syntagmatic variability** | *flexibilization:* ☑; quantifier *tig* may occur in other construction types (cf. the examples in (44)). |

non-existence'. This, of course, is a position worth defending, but note the consequences for using grammaticalization in linguistic reconstruction. For it is equally impossible to prove that, say, there has been a stage in English where *to go* was only a verb of movement but not used as an auxiliary in constructions expressing future events. Certainly, we have texts from earlier periods where *to go* is only found as a lexical verb but, given the non-demonstrability of non-existence, how are we to know that auxiliary *go* did not exist at that time? Lehmann appears to be aware of this inconsistency, for he maintains that some languages are sufficiently documented for linguists to agree 'that whatever does not appear in the contemporary corpus before some date was not in the language before that date'. He goes on to argue that 'many examples of degrammaticalization concern much earlier stages of languages that are much worse documented', but this division between 'well-documented' and 'much worse documented' stages seems rather arbitrary.[42]

What is more, it is simply not true that 'many' examples of degrammaticalization, and certainly not *tig/zig*, date back to badly documented older stages. This is evidenced, for instance, by the absence of independent *tig* from the authoritative (forty-volume) Dutch dictionary *Woordenboek der Nederlandsche taal*, which suggests that the development must have been fairly recent (the volume in which *tig* should have been included appeared in 1941). It does appear in the 1957 volume of *Deutsches Wörterbuch*, where an example is given from a work written in 1935, but here it is stressed that *zig* can be used this way only '*in jüngster Zeit*'.

But this probably would not convince Lehmann either, for he also argues that, since *zig/tig* is typically colloquial, it is unlikely that it will be recorded in writing. Instead, Lehmann proposes a scenario in which Proto-Germanic **teguz* 'unit of ten' was reduced to a suffix in numerals denoting multiples of ten, and remained as an independent form, where it underwent a minor semantic change from 'unit of ten' to 'umpteen'. To me this seems a fantastically improbable development, not only because dictionaries suggest the change is quite recent, but also because I see no reason why the independent quantifier should have led a hidden life in abundantly documented languages, without occurring *a single time* in written sources from the first thousand-or-so years. It is not as if it refers to some terribly private body part or taboo-ridden action (and even those appear in writing).

## 6.10 Northern Swedish *bö-*: from prefix to lexical verb

Debonding of the Northern Swedish prefix *bö-* is exceptional in that it only occurs in one specific lexical context. But before I turn to the implications of this, I will first summarize the data (from Rosenkvist 2008).

In the Piteå dialect spoken in the North of Sweden, there are two verbs corresponding to standard Swedish *behöva* 'to need'.[43] These are the verbs *böhöv*, which is either used in a single form, as (50b), or with the prefix separated from it, as in (50c). The second verb is *bö*, exemplified in (50d):

(50) a. Det **behöver** han inte göra (Standard Swedish)
That need he not do

[42] To his credit however, Lehmann (2004: 156) is also critical of grammaticalization case studies that are largely or entirely based on reconstruction.

[43] The prefix *be-* is historically a transitivizing affix, and borrowed into Swedish from Middle Low German (Hellquist 1980: 58f.).

b. Hä **böhöv'n** it djära (Piteå Swedish)
That need=he not do

c. Hä **bö'n** it **höv** djära
That $\text{need}_1$=he not $\text{need}_2$ do

d. Hä **bö'n** it djära
That need=he not do
'He need not do that'

Rejecting an earlier analysis by Brännström (1933), according to whom *bö* is simply a phonologically reduced form of modal *böhöv*, Rosenkvist convincingly argues that the verb *bö* developed out of the prefix in *böhöv*.[44]

Rosenkvist points out several factors that may have facilitated the degrammaticalization of *bö*. First, the prefix *be-* only developed into *bö-* in the verb *böhöv*, and debonding of the prefix is not found in other verbs or in other varieties of Swedish. This unique development from *be-* to *bö-* may have dissociated *böhöv* from the other prefixed verbs. Secondly, the semantics of *bö* are more specific than of *böhöv*: the latter can be used both as a main verb, as in (51a), and as a modal auxiliary, as in (51b–c).[45] *Bö*, on the other hand, can only be used as a root modal – not as a full verb or an epistemic modal. This means that the number of contexts in which *bö* can appear decreased, which is exactly the opposite of context expansion typically observed in grammaticalization.

(51) a. I **böhövd** it öksa
I needed not axe
'I did not need the axe'

b. Kleda **böhöv** no twettes väsamma
clothes-DEF need probably wash-PASS immediately
'The clothes must probably be washed immediately'

c. Nöckeln **böhöv** it ha köme bort
key-DEF need not have come away
'The key need not have been lost'

More evidence for the independent status of *bö* comes from older speakers, who reportedly regard *höv* in constructions such as (50c) as an intensifier – for them, this sentence would translate as *he **really** did not need to do that.*

44 The main problem with Brännström's proposal is, obviously, that it does not explain the split construction in (50c).

45 As an epistemic modal, *böhöv* can only appear in negative clauses.

Contemporary younger speakers, however, have lost this connotation of *höv*, which may explain why *bö* can occur without *höv*.

Finally, *bö* may be stressed and is regularly inflected, following other weak verbs with their stem ending in a vowel; note that inflected *bö* occurs both independently, as in (52a), and with following *höv*, as in (52b).

(52) a. I **bödd** it fåra åt stan
I need-PAST not go to city-DEF
'I did not need to go to the city'

b. I **bödd** it **höv** öksa
I $need_1$-PAST not $need_2$ axe
'I did not need the axe'

This case of degrammaticalization is neither easy to explain nor easy to classify. Debonding of *bö* is not a case of replacement (see section 3.4), because there is no phonologically similar verb with which *bö* could have

TABLE 6.10. Parameter analysis of Northern Swedish *bö*

| Parameter | Primitive change(s) |
|---|---|
| **Integrity** | *resemanticization:* ☒: as a verb, *bö* is semantically more restricted than *böhöv*, because it can only be used as a root modal, where *böhöv* can also be used as a main verb or an epistemic modal. *phonological 'strengthening':* (☑); there is no phonological change, but unlike the prefix, independent *bö* can be stressed. *recategorialization:* ☑; *bö* has regular verb inflection (cf. example (52a)). |
| **Paradigmaticity** | *deparadigmaticization:* not relevant for derivational affixes. |
| **Paradigmatic variability** | *deobligatorification:* ☑; the prefix *bö* cannot be deleted, but independent *bö* is not obligatory. |
| **Structural scope** | *scope expansion:* ☑; the prefix only takes scope over the verb stem *höv*, but auxiliary *bö* can also take scope over the sentence adverbial. |
| **Bondedness** | *severance:* ☑; *bö* has become a free morpheme. |
| **Syntagmatic variability** | *flexibilization:* ☑; as an auxiliary, *bö* need not immediately precede the main verb (whereas the prefix naturally always preceded the verbal stem). |

become confused.[46] One factor that may have been involved is that there exists no such verb as **höv*, in contrast with other *be-* prefixed verbs: compare (standard Swedish) *röra* 'to touch' – *beröra* 'to touch', *söka* 'to search for' – *besöka* 'to visit', but **höva* – *behöva* 'to need' (Henrik Rosenkvist, p.c.). This may have facilitated the transfer of part of the semantics of *böhöv* to the prefix *bö*. Note however that independent *bö* can only be used, as we have seen above, as a root modal. In order to be used as a full verb meaning 'to need', *höv* must be added, as in example (52b). This implies that the development of *bö* was not a simple case of 'clipping' (see section 1.3.3), of the type *hood* (for *neighbourhood*).

I conclude that this is a unique case of degrammaticalization, because it is the only change in which a suffix becomes independent, retaining one function (i.e. of root modal) of the verb it used to be the prefix of.

## 6.11 English *-ish*: from suffix to free morpheme

The next example of a degrammaticalizing derivational suffix is different again. This example concerns the suffix *-ish* (see Kuzmack, in prep.). This suffix can be used (i) to derive adjectives from nouns referring to nations or ethnic groups (*English*, *Spanish*), (ii) to derive adjectives from a generic noun X meaning 'of the nature of X' (*boyish*), and (iii) as a suffix meaning 'somewhat like X', where X is mostly an adjective (*greenish*).[47] The second and third types of *-ish* are similar in meaning, but different in emphasis: 'Both involve a comparison, but comparative *ish* emphasizes the similarity, whereas qualifier *ish* emphasizes the lack of equivalence.' Another difference is prosodic: qualifier *ish* can be stressed (indicated by capitalization), but stressing comparative *ish* sounds very odd:

(53) a. That colour is greenish. [qualifier *ish*]
b. That colour is greenISH, but it's more of a blue shade.
c. John is boyish. [comparative *ish*]
d. ?? John is boyISH.

Kuzmack argues that both comparative *ish* and qualifier *ish* have degrammaticalized, but where comparative *ish* has become a clitic, qualifier *ish* has become a free morpheme. The reason why she analyses comparative *ish* as a clitic is that it can attach to entire phrases, as in (54):

[46] Standard Swedish has a modal verb *böra* (PRES *bör*), but according to Brännström (1933) there was no cognate verb in the Piteå dialect at the period when *bö* became an independent verb (Henrik Rosenkvist, p.c.).

[47] The third type of *-ish* can also be attached to adverbs (*soonish*) and numerals (*at sixish*).

(54) a. And the clothes could be old person-ish too.
b. Am I the only person that thinks this is pretty amateurish and all a bit duct-tape-and-superglue-ish?
c. This [book] took months to read. It's very long and generally not very 'can't put it down'-ish.

However, as we have seen in section 5.2.1, it is not uncommon for derivational affixes to attach to phrases, so I am not quite convinced that this is a case of deinflectionalization (from derivational suffix to clitic). The behaviour of comparative *ish* is reminiscent of Dutch derivational suffixes such as *-achtig* (with approximately the same meaning). This suffix, too, can be attached to phrases:

(55) klinkt beetje lief onschuldig kindje achtig[48]
sounds bit [sweet innocent child-DIM] like
'sounds a bit like a sweet, innocent little child'

Qualifier *ish*, on the other hand, is quite another matter, because it can occur as an independent word, which makes it a potential case of debonding:[49]

TABLE 6.11. Parameter analysis of *ish*

| Parameter | Primitive change(s) |
|---|---|
| **Integrity** | *resemanticization:* ☑; independent *ish* is no longer merely a modifying morpheme and must be paraphrased by a sentence. *phonological 'strengthening':* ☑; unlike 'ethnic' *ish* (as in *English*) and comparative *ish*, qualifier *ish* is always stressed when it occurs independently. *recategorialization:* ☐; *ish* does not join a major (inflected) word class. |
| **Paradigmaticity** | *deparadigmaticization:* not relevant for derivational affixes. |
| **Paradigmatic variability** | *deobligatorification:* not relevant, because derivational affixes are generally not obligatory in English. |
| **Structural scope** | *scope expansion:* ☑; *ish* can take scope over a predicate, as in (56d). |
| **Bondedness** | *severance:* ☑; *ish* has become a free morpheme. |
| **Syntagmatic variability** | *flexibilization*: ☑; *ish* can occur in various slots, as exemplified in (57). |

[48] The example is from www.weerwolvenvanwakkerdam.nl/forum/index.php?topic=1001.585.

[49] Note that this is not possible with comparative *ish*: *Sound a little [stop-and-smell-the roses]$_i$-ish?* *$t_i$ *ish*. (Yes, it does sound like that).

(56) a. They have a pleasantly happy$_i$ ending (well, $t_i$ ish)
b. Is everyone excited$_i$? I am – $t_i$ ish.
c. Can you swim well$_i$?: $t_i$ Ish.
d. If I [accept the premises]$_i$ (and from a maths viewpoint i sort of can – $t_i$ ish)

In addition, qualifier *ish* has become more flexible syntactically:[50]

(57) a. I have work but it should be an easyish day.
b. Tomorrow's an easy day (ish) – graduation audit, voice lesson, CS lab...

Debonding of *ish* is different from debonding of *bö-* discussed in the previous section, because *ish* as an independent word only continues its own semantics, and can be paraphrased as 'kind of, sort of'. In this sense, it is also clearly different from the lexicalization of affixes such as *ism*, which functions as a hypernym for all words ending in *-ism*.

Qualifier *ish* has even gone one step further, because it is also attested in constructions where it obviously does not modify an (elided) entity:

(58) Hobbies: painting, photography, documentary film, skating(ish)

In the above example, *ish* does not modify *skating*, but *hobbies* – it can be paraphrased as 'skating is kind of a hobby of mine, but not serious' (Kuzmack, in prep.).

## 6.12 Tura LÁ: from bound to free derivational marker

The final example I will discuss in this chapter is debonding of a derivational morpheme in Tura, an Eastern Mande (subbranch of Niger-Congo) language spoken in Ivory Coast (Idiatov 2008). This language possesses twenty-four verbs with a derivational suffix |-LÁ| 'somewhere, anywhere'. The notation |LÁ| stands for the suffix *-lɔ́* after ɔ, *-ná* after a nasal vowel, and *-lá* elsewhere. It is mainly attached to motion verbs, replacing an (obligatory) location adverbial. The suffix |-LÁ| can be separated from its verb by an adnominal modifier, as in (59):

(59)

| | | | | |
|---|---|---|---|---|
| òô | dɔ̂ | dɛ́ɛ̂ | kê | lɔ́ -'[51] |
| 3SG.SBJ.NEG.TAM | stand | new | a.certain | LÁ[=TR][52]\TAM-TAM |

'He did not stop again'

[50] Note that this is not possible with comparative *ish* either: *a clean-cravatish formality of manner*, but not **a clean-cravat formality ish of manner* or **a clean-cravat formality of manner ish.*

[51] The notation <’> represents a high or mid-high tone vowel identical in quality to the preceding one.

[52] TR is short for 'transposer', because TAM markers of the main verb are transferred to it.

This construction is equivalent to one in which the verb is placed in direct object position to an auxiliary *wô* 'accomplish, do':

(60) òô dɔ̂-lɔ́ dɛ́ɛ̂ kê **wô-'**
3SG.SBJ.NEG.TAM stand-LÁ new a.certain do[=TR]\TAM-TAM
'He did not stop again'

According to Idiatov, the constructions exemplified in (59) and (60) are functionally identical, except in one type of subordinate clause, where *wô*-transposition has a causal ('since') reading, as in (61a), whereas |-LÁ|-transposition of the same verb implies a temporal ('when') reading, as in (61b):

(61) a. é dɔ̂-lɔ́-' **wô-'** láà
3SG.SBJ.TAM stand-LÁ-FOC do[=TR]\TAM-TAM TM
'Since he stopped…'

b. é dɔ̂-' lɔ̂ -' láà
3SG.SBJ.TAM stand-FOC LÁ[or TR]\TAM-TAM TM
'When he stopped…'

In examples (59) and (61b), |-LÁ| is a derivational suffix which is separated from the verb. Even more remarkable, according to Idiatov, are examples such as (62), where |-LÁ| is an integral part of the verb (in this case *gbálá* 'to thunder, shout'), not a suffix (and comparative evidence suggests that it never was one), but can be transposed nevertheless:

(62) lâ-' gbá dɛ́ɛ̂ kê **lâ-'**
rain-PM thunder$_1$ new a.certain thunder$_2$[=Ø=TR]\TAM-TAM
'It thundered again'

The occurrence of examples such as (62) suggests that a possibility for an alternative structural analysis of |-LÁ| has become available even for verbs where it was not originally a separate morpheme. This reinterpretation was probably facilitated by semantic bleaching of the |-LÁ| morpheme, as a result of which verbs with |-LÁ|-derivation and their 'bare' equivalents were almost identical semantically.[53] And structurally, they were very similar to *wô*-transpositions, making a reanalysis from (63b) to (63c) plausible:

(63) a. òô gwɛɛ bân **wô-'** zúlú-lèè bhà
3SG.SBJ.NEG.TAM stone drop do[=TR]\TAM-TAM wash-place/L on
'He did not drop the stones in the washing place'

[53] Indeed, Tura speakers generally claim that they mean the same, even though often they cannot be substituted for one another.

TABLE 6.12. Parameter analysis of Tura LÁ

| Parameter | Primitive change(s) |
|---|---|
| **Integrity** | *resemanticization:* ☑; \|-LÁ\| gains the new function of focalizer (but it also retains its original function). *phonological 'strengthening':* ☐; there is no change on the phonological level. Note also that the phonological realization still depends on the verb – in example (59) it is still *lɔ́*, even though it no longer follows */dɔ́/*. *recategorialization:* ☑; independent \|-LÁ\| takes the same TAM-markers as auxiliary *wô*. |
| **Paradigmaticity** | *deparadigmaticization:* not relevant for derivational affixes. |
| **Paradigmatic variability** | *deobligatorification:* ☑; the derivational suffix is obligatory in the sense that we get a different verb when it is deleted; as a free morpheme, however, \|-LÁ\| can be said to be less obligatory because in many contexts it can be substituted by transposing *wô*. |
| **Structural scope** | *scope expansion:* ☑; as a transposer, \|-LÁ\| takes scope over the verb and its following modifiers (if it has any). |
| **Bondedness** | *severance:* (☑); \|-LÁ\| has become a free morpheme, but only in the transposer context. (For this reason. Idiatov speaks of 'partial antimorphologization'). |
| **Syntagmatic variability** | *flexibilization*: ☑; \|LÁ\| can be separated from the verb, as in example (59). |

b. òô gwɛɛ bân-**nâ**-' (sɛ́ɛ tà)
3SG.SBJ.NEG.TAM stone drop-LÁ\TAM-TAM ground on
'He did not drop the stones (on the ground)'

c. òô gwɛɛ bân **nâ**-' (sɛ́ɛ tà)
3SG.SBJ.NEG.TAM stone drop LÁ\TAM-TAM ground on
'He did not drop the stones (on the ground)'

That |-LÁ| was reinterpreted as a separate morpheme in (63c) becomes evident when it is separated from the verb by another constituent, as in (59). And once the construction in (63c) became entrenched in the language, it spread to verbs such as *gbálá* 'to thunder, shout', where |-LÁ| is not a suffix.

# 7

# Conclusions

## 7.1 Lehmann's parameters revisited

In this section, I will summarize the data discussed in Chapters 4–6, as well as reviewing Lehmann's parameters and their significance as a diagnostic to identify potential cases of degrammaticalization. In so doing, I will not only evaluate the case studies in the preceding chapters, but also the parameters themselves.

The parameter of **integrity** comprises three kinds of primitive changes: resemanticization, phonological strengthening, and recategorialization.

Resemanticization (an increase in semantic substance), as we will see below, is the defining characteristic of degrammation. For in all examples of degrammation, function words acquire lexical meaning. In deinflectionalization, resemanticization refers most often to the addition of a grammatical function, after which the original function may be (but need not be) lost. Thus, the s-genitive gained the function of determiner, Old Swedish MASC.SG.NOM *-er* gained the function of nominalizer, and Kwaza *nĩ* gained the function of causational marker. Only in the case of the Swedish 'berry-suffix' *-on* was the new meaning lexical rather than grammatical. In debonding changes, there is often no change in meaning. I will return to that issue in section 7.2.

Phonological change does not necessarily form part of a grammaticalization or degrammaticalization change. But although this means that phonological change cannot be used as a criterion, it is relevant to include it in the parameter analyses. For when it does occur in degrammaticalization it always comprises strengthening, as expected.

Recategorialization, finally, is a relevant criterion only in some types of degrammaticalization. In most cases of degrammation, it follows naturally from the transition from minor to major word class (see section 7.2). In deinflectionalization it is not relevant because grams remain bound. And in debonding, recategorialization is only attested in a handful of cases, namely Irish *muid* (1PL suffix > 'we'), which has an emphatic variant, Dutch *tig* ('*-ty*' > 'dozens'), which has an ordinal form *tigste*, Northern

Swedish *bö* (verbal prefix > full verb 'need'), which has regular verb inflection, and Tura |LÁ|, which can take TAM-markers of the main verb.

For the parameter of **paradigmaticity**, the relevant primitive change is deparadigmaticization.

I have been arguing that in primary degrammaticalization (degrammation), this implies a shift from a minor to a major word class. This can indeed be observed in all cases of degrammation discussed in Chapter 4: Pennsylvania German *wotte* 'would', Chinese *děi* 'should', and Welsh *yn ol* 'after' became lexical verbs, and Bulgarian *nešto* 'something' and Welsh *eiddo* 'his' became nouns.

In deinflectionalization and debonding of inflectional affixes, deparadigmaticization implies a discharge from an inflectional paradigm. In cases of debonding derivational affixes and clitics, however, it is hard to see the relevance of this parameter, because these grams did not form part of an inflectional paradigm in the first place, and they do not shift from a minor to a major word class either.

As regards the parameter of **paradigmatic variability**, the relevant primitive change in degrammaticalization is deobligatorification.

In degrammation, grams invariably become less obligatory, because they develop into lexical items, which are inherently optional from a grammatical point of view (as lexemes, they are only required by the lexical context).

In deinflectionalization also, deobligatorification can be observed to occur, because inflections are inherently obligatory. Hence, when they cease to be inflectional, they become less obligatory. This is most evident when they become derivational, because the non-obligatoriness of derivational affixes is one of the main properties that separates derivation from inflection (see section 5.2.1). But in the case of the s-genitive, too, it can be argued that the enclitic s-genitive is no longer obligatory, because there are other means of expressing possession, and because nouns need not have a clitic attached to them to be grammatical.

In debonding, the parameter of paradigmatic variability yields somewhat mixed results. In some cases, there is no change, because the debonded grams remain grammatically obligatory (e.g. the infinitival markers); in other cases, they do become less obligatory (Japanese connectives, Saami *haga*). In debonding of derivational affixes, this parameter is usually irrelevant, since derivational affixes (e.g. English *-ish*) are generally not grammatically obligatory. However, there appear to be a few exceptions to this. The Dutch suffix *-tig* '-ty' can be said to be obligatory at least in the numerals 20, 30, 40, and 80, because deletion of the suffix in these numerals results in nonce words (**twin*, **der*, **veer*, and **tach* respectively). Likewise, in the case of

Northern Swedish *böhöv* 'to need', the suffix cannot be deleted, because there exists no verb **höv*. However, this is a different kind of obligatoriness from that observed in inflectional affixes. What seems to be happening here is that increasing lexicalization (involving loss of compositionality) means that former component parts can no longer be used independently, because they have fused with another component part. More precisely, a numeral such as *twintig* 'twenty' has developed into an unanalysable whole, whereas in a numeral such as *zestig* 'sixty', the suffix can be still be separated from the preceding numeral *zes* 'six'.

The parameter of **structural scope** appears to be (almost as) problematic in degrammaticalization as it was in grammaticalization.

In the degrammation cases, the evidence is inconclusive. Only in the case of modals that become a lexical verb is there a clear increase in scope (which is expected, since scope decreases in grammaticalization, according to Lehmann at least). In the other cases (for instance in the shift from the Middle Welsh preposition *yn ol* 'after' to the Modern Welsh verb *nôl* 'to fetch') it is not evident that there has been increase in scope, because a PP has been reanalysed as a VP, which is a different type of phrase.

In deinflectionalization, scope appears to be an inconclusive parameter as well. Scope is clearly expanded in s-genitive constructions (as evidenced by group genitives), but in the case of Old Swedish MASC.SG.NOM *-er* and NEUT.PL.NOM/ACC *-on*, which both became derivational, there is no change in scope at all (both when inflectional and derivational, these suffixes only take scope over the word they attach to). In the Kwaza case, finally, where a (derivational) modality marker developed out of an (inflectional) exhortative marker, scope is not expanded but diminished.

Only in debonding is scope expansion generally attested (with the exception of Estonian *es* and *ep*), for instance in the rise of split infinitives and coordination reduction with the English and Norwegian infinitival markers. Another indication of scope increase is the ability to take scope over entire phrases, as with Dutch *tig* or English *ish*.

The parameter of **bondedness** only applies to secondary degrammaticalization (deinflectionalization and debonding), because grams that degrammaticalize in degrammation never were bound to begin with. Severance, the primitive change associated with bondedness, refers to slightly different changes in deinflectionalization and debonding. In the former, it implies a shift to a 'looser' morpheme boundary. For instance, a host–clitic boundary can be said to be less tight than a stem–affix boundary. But in debonding (of both inflectional and derivational affixes), severance implies a shift from bound morpheme to free morpheme which, as I will argue in section 7.2, is the defining characteristic of this type of degrammaticalization.

The parameter of **syntagmatic variability**, finally, has been shown to be irrelevant in deinflectionalization, because in this type of degrammaticalization grams remain bound, and hence they cannot be said to gain in syntactic freedom (flexibilization). In degrammation, flexibilization is generally observed, with the exception of Chinese *děi* (but this is primarily due to lack of data). In debonding, flexibilization always occurs, with the exception of the Japanese connectives, which always occupy a specific syntactic slot, albeit different ones for enclitic and free connectives, respectively.

## 7.2 Defining characteristics of the three types of degrammaticalization

In degrammation, the crucial parameter is integrity. In all cases (Pennsylvania German *wotte* 'would' > 'wish'; Chinese *děi* 'should' > 'need'; Bulgarian *nešto* 'something' > 'thing'; Welsh *eiddo* 'his' > 'property'; Welsh *yn ol* 'after' > *nôl* 'to fetch'), the grams gain in semantic substance (resemanticization) and morphosyntactic properties (recategorialization). Resemanticization will be taken to be the defining primitive change in degrammation – therefore, grams which only acquire new morphosyntactic properties (e.g. some of the modals discussed in 4.2) do not qualify as cases of degrammation.

In deinflectionalization, the crucial parameter is paradigmaticity, because what is most characteristic of these cases is that inflectional suffixes cease to form part of inflectional paradigms (deparadigmaticization). Thus they develop into a less bound type of morpheme (severance), and they gain a new function or new meaning (resemanticization). However, they are not being recategorialized, because they do not become members of a major word class.

In debonding, finally, the crucial parameter is bondedness, because in all cases, bound morphemes (inflectional, enclitic, or derivational) become free morphemes (severance). This sets them apart from cases of deinflectionalization, because in those cases grams remain bound. Resemanticization appears to be perfectly possible when derivational affixes debond, but when inflectional affixes and clitics debond, there is often no change in meaning or function at all. Incidentally, this reveals an interesting difference between inflectional and derivational affixes. Inflections are the most abstract of grams, and therefore debonding often does not result in new meanings or functions being added (with the exception of Irish *muid* 1PL > 'we').

Derivational affixes, on the other hand, are less bleached in meaning, which may offer a possibility of inferring a new meaning. This difference between inflections and derivations must be due to their different origins – as the clines of grammaticality and lexicality (see section 2.2.1) show, both inflectional and derivational affixes ultimately derive from lexical items, but it is the intermediate stages that set them apart. Along the cline of grammaticality, lexical items first develop into function words, which implies that these grams acquire grammatical meaning early on. Derivational affixes crucially lack this stage, since they typically develop out of (contentful) compound members.

The obvious follow-up question is *when* a change qualifies as a type of degrammaticalization. I have chosen to include all cases that had a positive score for the defining primitive change in the relevant type of degrammaticalization. Thus, for a change to qualify as degrammation, it had to have a positive score for resemanticization. In other words, degrammation is primarily a semantic change. Usually recategorialization was observed as well, with the exception of Chinese *děi* (but then it is questionable whether recategorialization is relevant in isolating languages anyhow; see section 7.4). As regards the other parameters, degrammation changes usually had positive scores as well, or blank scores (see Tables 4.1–4.6). One or two blank scores are no problem in my view, since grammaticalization changes often have some blank scores as well (notably for phonological attrition).

For a change to qualify as deinflectionalization it had to have a positive score for deparadigmaticization, but also for resemanticization, since the definition of deinflectionalization includes a gain in function. Thus, deinflectionalization is both a morphological and a semantic change. In the cases discussed in Chapter 5, there were generally positive scores for the other primitive changes as well. Only Kwaza *nĩ* had one negative score, for scope expansion, but given that scope is a controversial parameter, this single negative score did not suffice for me to reject the Kwaza case as a valid instance of deinflectionalization.

For a change to qualify as debonding, finally, a positive score for severance sufficed, provided the constructional identity of the debonding gram was preserved. Thus, debonding is primarily a morphological change, but it usually involves syntactic change as well because, as free morphemes, the debonded items gain in syntactic freedom. Indeed, in cases of debonding inflectional affixes or clitics, there is mostly no change in semantics at all. Also, there is usually no deobligatorification – as free grams, the debonded items simply continue the grammatical function they had when bound. Debonding derivational affixes however turned out to be different, because they often do become semantically enriched. The only case of debonding which I regard as problematic is the Japanese connectives, because these appear to be a case of degrammaticalization on the morphosyntactic level, but of grammaticalization on the semantic level. It is therefore not a prototypical example of degrammaticalization, but it isn't an example of grammaticalization either.

As a general requirement for all types of degrammaticalization, the change needed to be construction-internal. This means that metalinguistic usages of affixes or function words (*isms, ifs and buts*) did not qualify as cases of debonding or degrammation. A final, and crucial, observation is that there are virtually no negative scores – which implies that, on the whole, degrammaticalization is as consistent in the directionality of its primitive changes as is grammaticalization.

To conclude this section, I will briefly return to Andersen's levels of observation (section 3.5.4), and its relevance to the classification of degrammaticalization changes. Degrammation is primarily a change on the content level, deinflectionalization is primarily a change on the content-syntactic level, and debonding is primarily a change on the morphosyntactic level. When all cases are compared, it turns out that there exists an interesting implicational hierarchy between changes in content, changes in content syntax, and changes in morphosyntax in the following way:

(i) a change in content implies changes in content syntax and morphosyntax
(ii) a change in content syntax implies a change in morphosyntax, but not necessarily one in content
(iii) a change in morphosyntax does not imply a change in either content syntax or content

Changes in expression (in the case of degrammaticalization: phonetic strengthening) do not form part of this hierarchy – as in grammaticalization, they may or may not occur.

## 7.3 Mechanisms and motivating forces

As we have seen in section 1.3.6, analogy and reanalysis are seen as the main mechanisms in morphosyntactic change, but there is no general agreement on which mechanism is primary in grammaticalization. As far as degrammaticalization is concerned, both analogy and reanalysis can be observed as well, and deciding which one is primary is dependent on the case at hand. In degrammation, the primary mechanism is reanalysis: function words are reanalysed as content items in the appropriate (ambiguous) context. The subsequent context expansion can be seen as analogical, because the new lexical item starts to behave like other members of its word class, with corresponding inflection and syntactic properties. In deinflectionalization, reanalysis appears to be primary, too. For example, the Swedish s-genitive was first reanalysed as a phrase-marking affix. Subsequently, when a specific slot for determiners became available, the s-genitive started to pattern with other determiners (analogy) and became enclitic. In debonding, the picture is less clear. For Irish *muid*, it may be argued that the primary force was analogy, because most other persons in the verbal paradigm had analytic pronouns already. For Northern Saami *haga* on the other hand, it is unlikely that the change was analogical, since it is not clear what construction the analogy would be based on. Rather, it seems a case of reanalysis of morpheme boundary (from stem–affix boundary to word boundary). In any event, where it seems reasonable to invoke analogy in some cases of debonding, it is certainly not the case that degrammaticalization in general 'is ordinary exemplar-based analogical change' (Kiparsky 2005).

Reanalysis and analogy are mechanisms of change, but I do not regard them as motivating forces. What, then, motivates degrammaticalization? Such forces are not easy to identify, and in a sense these are always post-hoc observations, but I will make a few suggestions nevertheless.

In degrammation, the first stage always appears to involve pragmatic inferencing. In this sense, degrammation is similar to grammaticalization, but there are two crucial differences. First, there is of course the direction of the change – if pragmatic inferencing results in increasing abstraction (grammaticalization), subsequent stages will involve reduction on other linguistic levels as well. If, however, lexical meaning is inferred from a function word (degrammation), enrichment will follow on other levels as well. The second difference concerns frequency – grammaticalization is evidently far more common than degrammation. This is partly due to a universal inclination towards metaphorical abstraction in semantic change (see section 2.6.1). Another reason may be that, in inflectional languages at least, lexical items are usually morphologically more complex than grammatical items. This makes it easier to shift from lexical to grammatical item than vice versa (section 2.7.4).

In sum, what prompts degrammation is semantic contiguity between a grammatical and a lexical item, and the possibility of recategorialization. As regards Pennsylvania German *wotte*, euphemism (see section 3.3.4) may have been an additional factor, as a subjunctive modal can be seen as a euphemistic expression for the more direct concept of 'wishing'.

Returning to the process question raised in section 1.6.1, I conclude that degrammation is a process in much the same way as grammaticalization. Both start with a new meaning being inferred (more grammatical in grammaticalization, more lexical in degrammation), after which the word is reanalysed as the member of a minor (grammaticalization) or major (degrammation) word class, acquiring morphosyntactic properties typical of (a subgroup in) that word class.

Deinflectionalization may be triggered by different factors. In the case of the s-genitive and the change of Old Swedish MASC.SG.NOM *-er* to derivational nominalization suffix, the loss of the Old Scandinavian case system is likely to have been the prompting factor. When case was no longer realized inflectionally, many suffixes lost their function, which made them particularly prone to exaptation (see section 3.3.5). Former MASC.SG.GEN was lost in lexical genitive constructions, but it could be retained in attributive constructions, because the structure of the NP had been reorganized in such a way that a specific position for determiners had become available. The former suffix *-s* was reanalysed as an enclitic determiner, while continuing its possessive function too. In the case of former MASC.SG.NOM *-er*, deinflectionalization may furthermore have been facilitated by the fusion of masculine and feminine gender into a common gender. As a result, adjectival noun constructions such as Old Swedish *en blinder* (a blind-MASC.SG.NOM) 'a blind person', could be reinterpreted as nominalizations for both genders. And indeed, such constructions as *hon är en slarver* 'she is a messy person' are perfectly possible in present-day Swedish. In sum, deinflectionalization of MASC.SG.GEN *-(e)s* and MASC.SG.NOM *-er* was prompted by the loss of inflectional case in English and Mainland Scandinavian (Norde 2001a). For such cases Plank (1995) coined the apt term *Systemstörung* 'disruption of the system'. In these two cases of deinflectionalization, then, I would argue that they are results rather than processes, as they are essentially side-effects of a major structural change.

As regards the 'berry-suffix' *-on*, it is less evident that it arose as a result of the demise of the case system, because *-on* is still in use as a plural suffix. It is not inconceivable that some form of pragmatic inferencing has been at work here, because the suffix was used as a plural in such nouns as *smultron* 'wild strawberries' and *hiūpon* 'rosehips'. Presumably, these nouns were most frequently used in the plural, where they could easily have been reinterpreted as a mass noun, with *-on* as a derivational suffix meaning 'berry'. Also in the Kwaza case, pragmatic inferencing may have played a role. Here the inflectional exhortative affix *-ni* was reanalysed, probably in quotative constructions, as a derivational causational marker -*nĩ*. It is not difficult to see how a causational meaning (as in 'I made him drink') can be inferred from a quotative exhortative ('I said "Let him drink"').

As far as debonding is concerned, it is often difficult to assess what the motivating factors are. Split infinitives are a case in point (Fitzmaurice 2000, Faarlund 2007). For example, is the separation of English infinitival *to* from the verb in such present-day American English expressions as *I am going to not eat strawberries* indicative of debonding of the infinitival marker or of changes in the position of the negator? Likewise, in the case of debonding of the Norwegian infinitival *å* it is not possible to separate this development from ongoing syntactic restructurings in Norwegian. These are issues that need to be investigated further.

As regards Old Estonian *es* and *ep*, debonding was a result not of syntactic but of phonological change, according to Campbell (1991). At one point in the history of Estonian, all final vowels were apocopated and vowel harmony was lost. The clitics **-s* and **-pa* prevented the final vowel from being lost. Due to the frequency of apocopated stems, the morpheme boundary was subsequently reinterpreted in that the vowel became part of the clitic, and due to the loss of vowel harmony there was no longer evidence that *-es* and *-ep* (in which the final vowel had been apocopated as well) were phonologically dependent on their hosts. Hence, they could be reinterpreted as independent words.

In the case of Irish *muid*, finally, both phonological and syntactic changes may be held responsible for debonding of the 1PL verbal suffix (Doyle 2002), involving both 'parameter resetting' in Early Modern Irish (subject–verb agreement came to be expressed by a pronoun instead of an inflected verb) and the reanalysis of affixes as clitics in Middle Irish.

Debonding of Japanese connectives, on the other hand, does not appear to be the result of another change, but simply a reanalysis from a clause-final enclitic connective to a clause-initial free connective. The same appears to be true of Saami *haga* – there is no evidence of *Systemstörung* or syntactic restructuring which could have resulted in the abessive suffix becoming a free morpheme. And in the cases of deaffixation in the Hup verbal compound, it is not clear to me why some suffixes have been able to debond.

Summing up thus far, it seems that debonding of clitics and affixes is often the result of some major restructuring on the syntactic or phonological level, but in some cases a motivating force cannot be identified, at least not on the basis of the data available up to now. As far as derivational affixes are concerned, however, a different picture emerges, underlining once more that inflectional and derivational affixes are fundamentally dissimilar. In none of these cases has there been a major change in phonology, morphology, or syntax of which debonding can be said to be the result. As regards Dutch *tig* 'dozens' and English *ish*, the change appears to be essentially pragmatic – both are used as emphatic markers, strengthening the semantics of the suffix. Northern Swedish *bö* 'need' is an entirely unique case of a debonding prefix that continues only part of the semantics of the verb it used to form part of. Tura |LÁ| 'somewhere, anywhere', finally, appears to have been an analogical change – because its semantics had faded, it was reinterpreted as a gram similar to the (independent) auxiliary *wô*. |LÁ| started to appear in the same syntactic slot as *wô*, and could likewise take the TAM-markers of the main verb (as can *wô*).

It is therefore understandable that examples of debonding do not qualify as instances of degrammaticalization according to alternative definitions of degrammaticalization (e.g. Askedal 2008). The reason why they have been included in the present work nevertheless is that the criteria applied here were the primitive changes involved and their directionality, regardless of what prompted them. Since it is sometimes not possible to establish whether a degrammaticalization is a process or a result of other changes (notably in cases of debonding), the question of whether or not a change is a process is not a useful criterion.

## 7.4 Outlook

In this book, degrammaticalization has been treated as a composite change, comprising primitive changes on several linguistic levels. This approach to degrammaticalization is essentially morpheme-based, even though (initial) preservation of constructional identity forms part of the definitions of all three types of degrammaticalization. The advantage of a rigid set of criteria such as Lehmann's parameters is, in my view, that it can be made explicit what happens to a gram on the semantic, morphological, syntactic and/or phonological level. I have also tried to explain how I interpreted the parameter analyses of the individual case studies, but this does not mean that they cannot be interpreted otherwise. For example, those who only accept primary grammaticalization as grammaticalization will probably only accept degrammation as 'true' degrammaticalization. I hope that the data discussed in this book, as well as the theoretical discussions in the first three chapters, will provide guidance for further research.

More specifically, research questions that require further study are both of an empirical and a theoretical nature. As regards the former, it should be noted that most current theorizing is based on work from inflectional languages (primarily from the Indo-European family). In such languages, categories that are expressed by suffixes are for the most part on the highest level of abstraction (e.g. grammatical gender or case), whereas in polysynthetic languages, suffixes cover a much larger array of functions and meanings. This might imply (but this is purely hypothetical) that it is easier for (some) suffixes in polysynthetic languages to degrammaticalize, simply because they are more contentful (and hence it might be easier to infer new meanings). In isolating languages, on the other hand, debonding and deparadigmaticization seem unlikely events, since such languages hardly possess any morphemes that are bound in some way. Again, this is speculative because so little is known about (de)grammaticalization in this type of language, and empirically based research is badly needed.

As far as the theoretical agenda is concerned, I think that the most promising approaches at present are priming research, which may yield a cognitive explanation of directional tendencies (see section 2.7.2), the construction grammar approach to (de)grammaticalization and lexicalization (section 1.5), and research into the role of analogy in morphosyntactic change (see e.g. Fischer 2007).

On a concluding note, I wish to quote the German saying, commonly attributed to Kafka (but unsourced) that *Wege entstehen dadurch, dass man sie geht* ('Paths are made by walking'). Although there is quite a bit of regularity in both semantic and morphosyntactic change, pathways cannot be predicted. Every now and again, a gram may take an entirely different and unexpected course, and it often remains obscure why this happens to this particular gram. There is no determinism in change, and this seems even more true for degrammaticalization than for grammaticalization. Where primary grammaticalization may be followed by secondary grammaticalization, secondary degrammaticalization is never followed by primary degrammaticalization. I have retained the term 'degrammaticalization' as a hypernym for all changes subsumed under the labels of degrammation, deinflectionalization, and debonding, but I wish to stress once more that there exist no diachronic links between these three types. Finally, the history of Dutch *tig* teaches us that grams may even take u-turns more than once – *tig* had first grammaticalized from a noun meaning 'ten' to a numeral suffix '-ty', then degrammaticalized into an independent quantifier 'dozens', only to grammaticalize once more into an intensifying adverb. To me, it is precisely this unpredictability of change, rather than attested regularities, that makes degrammaticalization such a fascinating object of study.

# *References*


Abney, Steven Paul. 1987. *The English Noun Phrase in its Sentential Aspect.* PhD dissertation, MIT.

Aijmer, Karin. 1997. *I think* – an English modal particle. In Toril Swan and Olaf Jansen Westvik (eds.) *Modality in Germanic Languages: Historical and Comparative Perspectives*, 1–47. Berlin/New York: Mouton de Gruyter.

Allen, Andrew S. 1995. Regrammaticalization and degrammaticalization of the inchoative suffix. In Henning Andersen (ed.) *Historical Linguistics 1993. Selected Papers from the 11th International Conference on Historical Linguistics*, 1–8. Amsterdam/Philadelphia: John Benjamins.

Allen, Cynthia L. 1997. The origins of the 'group genitive' in English. *Transactions of the Philological Society* 95:1, 111–31.

—— 2003. Deflexion and the development of the genitive in English. *English Language and Linguistics* 7:1, 1–28.

Alvre, Paul. 1976. Vana kirjakeele küsisõnu. *Keel ja Kirjandus* 19, 343–50.

Amis, Martin. 1991. *Time's Arrow.* London: Penguin.

Andersen, Henning. 1987. From auxiliary to desinence. In Martin Harris and Paolo Ramat (eds.) *Historical Development of Auxiliaries*, 21–51. Berlin/New York/Amsterdam: Mouton de Gruyter.

—— 2001. Actualization and the (uni)directionality of change. In Henning Andersen (ed.) *Actualization: Linguistic Change in Progress*, 225–48. Amsterdam/Philadelphia: John Benjamins.

—— 2005. Review of Joseph and Janda 2003. *Diachronica* 22:1, 155–176.

—— 2006. Grammation, regrammation and degrammation: Tense loss in Russian. *Diachronica* 23:2, 231–58.

—— 2008. Grammaticalization in a speaker-oriented theory of change. In Thórhallur Eythórsson (ed.) *Grammatical Change and Linguistic Theory: The Rosendal Papers*, 11–44. Amsterdam/Philadelphia: John Benjamins.

Anderson, Stephen R. 1992. *A-morphous Morphology.* Cambridge: Cambridge University Press.

—— 2005. *Aspects of the Theory of Clitics.* Oxford: Oxford University Press.

—— 2008. The English 'Group Genitive' is a special clitic. To appear in *English Linguistics.* http://bloch.ling.yale.edu/Files/ELSJ.pdf

Andersson, Peter. 2007. *Modalitet och Förändring: En Studie av* må *och* kunna *i Fornsvenska.* Gothenburg: Institutionen för Svenska Språket.

Ansaldo, Umberto and Lisa Lim. 2004. Phonetic absence as syntactic prominence: Grammaticalization in isolating tonal languages. In Olga Fischer, Muriel Norde, and Harry Perridon (eds.) *Up and Down the Cline: The Nature of Grammaticalization*, 345–62. Amsterdam/Philadelphia: John Benjamins.

Anttila, Raimo. 1989. *Historical and Comparative Linguistics.* Amsterdam/Philadelphia: John Benjamins.

Ariste, Paul. 1973. Eesti rõhumäärsõna *ep. Journal de la Société Finno-ougrienne* 72, 33–7.

Askedal, John Ole. 2000. Nordisk *s*-genitiv: 'degrammatikalisering' eller 'regrammatikalisering' eller ingen av delene? *Norsk Lingvistisk Tidsskrift* 18:2, 203–10.

—— 2003. Grammaticalization and the historical development of the genitive in Mainland Scandinavian. In Barry J. Blake and Kate Burridge (eds.) *Papers from the 15th International Conference on Historical Linguistics*, 21–32. Amsterdam/Philadelphia: John Benjamins.

—— 2008. 'Degrammaticalization' versus typology: Reflections on a strained relationship. In Thórhallur Eythórsson (ed.) *Grammatical Change and Linguistic Theory: The Rosendal Papers*, 45–77. Amsterdam/Philadelphia: John Benjamins.

Auwera, Johan van der. 2002. More thoughts on degrammaticalization. In Ilse Wischer and Gabriela Diewald (eds.) *New Reflections on Grammaticalization*, 19–29. Amsterdam/Philadelphia: John Benjamins.

—— and Vladimir A. Plungian. 1998. Modality's semantic map. *Linguistic Typology* 2, 79–124.

Battye, Adrian and Ian Roberts. 1995. Introduction. In Adrian Battye and Ian Roberts (eds.) *Clause Structure and Language Change*, 3–28. Oxford: Oxford University Press.

Bauer, Brigitte L. M. 2003. The adverbial formation in *mente* in vulgar and late Latin: A problem in grammaticalization. In Heikki Solin, Martti Leiwo, and Hilla Halla-aho (eds.) *Latin vulgaire: latin tardif VI.* Hildesheim, Zürich and New York: Olms-Weidmann.

Bauer, Laurie. 1983. *English Word-formation.* Cambridge: Cambridge University Press.

Beard, Robert. 1998. Derivation. In Andrew Spencer and Arnold M. Zwicky (eds.) *The Handbook of Morphology*, 44–65. Oxford: Blackwell.

Beths, Frank. 1999. The history of *dare* and the status of unidirectionality. *Linguistics* 37:6, 1069–1110.

Blake, Barry J. 1994. *Case.* Cambridge: Cambridge University Press.

—— 2001. *Case*, 2nd edn. Cambridge: Cambridge University Press.

Boer, R. C. 1918. *Oergermaansch handboek.* Haarlem: H.D. Tjeenk Willink and Zoon.

—— 1920. *Oudnoorsch handboek.* Haarlem: H.D. Tjeenk Willink and Zoon.

Booij, Geert. 2002. *The Morphology of Dutch.* Oxford: Oxford University Press.

Bopp, Franz. 1816. *Über das Conjugationssystem der Sanskritsprache, in Vergleichung mit jenem der griechischen, lateinschen, persischen und germanischen Sprache.* Frankfurt am Main: in der Andreäischen Buchhandlung. Reprinted in Chris Hutton (ed.) 1995. *18th and 19th Century German Linguistics* IV. London: Routledge/Thoemmes Press.

Börjars, Kersti. 2003. Morphological status and (de)grammaticalisation: The Swedish possessive. *Nordic Journal of Linguistics* 26:2, 133–63.

Boroditsky, Lera. 2000. Metaphoric structuring: Understanding time through spatial metaphors. *Cognition* 71:1, 1–28.

Brännström, Edvin. 1933. En syntaktisk egendomlighet i norrländska dialekter. *Nysvenska Studier* 13, 112–27.

Braunmüller, Kurt. 1978. Remarks on the formation of conjunctions in Germanic languages. *Nordic Journal of Linguistics* 1, 99–120.

Bree, Cor van. 2004 [1990]. *Historische taalkunde*. Leuven/Amersfoort: Acco. Revised electronic edition at http://www.dbnl.org/tekst/bree001hist01/.

Brinton, Laurel J. 1996. *Pragmatic Markers in English: Grammaticalization and Discourse Functions*. Berlin/New York: Mouton de Gruyter.

—— 2001. From matrix clause to pragmatic marker: The history of *look*-forms. *Journal of Historical Pragmatics* 2, 177–99.

—— 2004. Subject clitics in English: A case of degrammaticalization? In Hans Lindquist and Christian Mair (eds.) *Corpus Approaches to Grammaticalization in English*, 227–56. Amsterdam/Philadelphia: John Benjamins.

—— and Dieter Stein. 1995. Functional renewal. In Henning Andersen (ed.) *Selected Papers from the 11th International Conference on Historical Linguistics*, 33–47. Amsterdam/Philadelphia: John Benjamins.

—— and Elizabeth Closs Traugott. 2005. *Lexicalization and Language Change*. Cambridge: Cambridge University Press.

Burridge, Kate. 1995. On the trail of the Conestoga Modal: Recent movements of modal auxiliaries in Pennsylvania German. La Trobe Working Papers in Linguistics 8. http://www.latrobe.edu.au/linguistics/LaTrobePapersinLinguistics/Vol%2008/2Burridge.pdf

—— 1998. From modal auxiliary to lexical verb: The curious case of Pennsylvania German *wotte*. In Richard M. Hogg and Linda van Bergen (eds.) *Historical Linguistics 1995*, Vol. II: *Germanic Linguistics*, 19–33. Amsterdam/Philadelphia: Benjamins.

Bybee, Joan. 1985a. Diagrammatic iconicity in stem-inflection relations. In John Haiman (ed.) *Iconicity in Syntax*, 11–47. Amsterdam/Philadelphia: John Benjamins.

—— 1985b. *Morphology: A Study of the Relation between Meaning and Form*. Amsterdam/Philadelphia: John Benjamins.

—— 2003. Mechanisms of change in grammaticization: The role of frequency. In Brian D. Joseph and Richard D. Janda (eds.) *The Handbook of Historical Linguistics*, 601–23. Oxford: Blackwell.

——, Revere Perkins, and William Pagliuca. 1994. *The Evolution of Grammar: Tense, Aspect and Modality in the Languages of the World*. Chicago and London: The University of Chicago Press.

Campbell, Lyle. 1991. Some grammaticalization changes in Estonian and their implications. In Elizabeth Closs Traugott and Bernd Heine (eds.) *Approaches to Grammaticalization I*, 285–99. Amsterdam/Philadelphia: John Benjamins.

Campbell, Lyle. 2001. What's wrong with grammaticalization? *Language Sciences* 23, 2–3: 113–61.

Carey, Kathleen. 1995. Subjectification and the English perfect. In Dieter Stein and Susan Wright (eds.) *Subjectivity and Subjectivisation*, 83–102. Cambridge: Cambridge University Press.

Carstairs, Andrew. 1987. Diachronic evidence and the affix–clitic distinction. In Anna Giacalone Ramat, Onofrio Carruba, and Giuliano Bernini (eds.) *Papers from the 7th International Conference on Historical Linguistics*, 151–62. Amsterdam/Philadelphia: John Benjamins.

Christensen, Ken Ramshøy. 2007. The infinitive marker across Scandinavian. *Nordlyd* 34, 147–65.

Comrie, Bernard. 1980. Morphology and word order reconstruction: Problems and prospects. In Jacek Fisiak (ed.) *Historical Morphology*. The Hague: Mouton.

Cristofaro, Sonia. 1998. Grammaticalization and clause linkage strategies: A typological approach with particular reference to Ancient Greek. In Anna Giacalone Ramat and Paul J. Hopper (eds.) *The Limits of Grammaticalization*, 59–88. Amsterdam/Philadelphia: John Benjamins.

Croft, William. 2000. *Explaining Language Change: An Evolutionary Approach*. Harlow: Pearson Education.

Dahl, Östen. 1996. Discussion of grammaticalization at LINGUIST 7.1170.

—— 2003. *Grammatik*. Lund: Studentlitteratur.

—— 2007. Grammaticalization in the north: Noun phrase morphosyntax in Scandinavian vernaculars. Ms., University of Stockholm. http://www.ling.su.se/staff/oesten/downloads/Gram_north.pdf

Dalton-Puffer, Christiane. 1996. The French influence on Middle English morphology: A corpus-based study of derivation. Berlin/New York: Mouton de Gruyter.

Daniliuc, Laura and Radu Daniliuc. 2000. *Descriptive Romanian Grammar: An Outline*. Lincom Studies in Romance Linguistics 14. Munich: Lincom Europa.

Davidsen-Nielsen, Niels. 1990. *Tense and Mood in English: A Comparison with Danish*. Berlin: Mouton de Gruyter.

DeLancey, Scott. 1994. Grammaticalization and linguistic theory. In Jule Gomez de Garcia and David S. Rood (eds.) *Proceedings of the 1993 Mid-America Linguistics Conference and Conference on Siouan/Caddoan Languages*, 1–22. Boulder: University of Colorado.

Delsing, Lars-Olof. 1991. Om genitivens utveckling i fornsvenskan. In Sven Göran Malmgren and Bo Ralph (eds.) *Studier i Svensk Språkhistoria* 2, 12–30. Gothenburg: Institutionen för Nordiska Språk.

—— 1993. *The Internal Structure of Noun Phrases in the Scandinavian Languages: A Comparative Study*. Lund: Department of Scandinavian Languages.

—— 1999. Review of Norde (1997). *Nordic Journal of Linguistics* 22, 77–90.

—— 2001. The Swedish genitive: A reply to Norde. *Nordic Journal of Linguistics* 24, 119–20.

Detges, Ulrich. 1998. Echt die Wahrheit sagen: Überlegungen zur Grammatikalisierung von Adverbmarkern. *Philologie im Netz* 4, 1–29. http://web.fu-berlin.de/phin/phin4/p4t1.htm

—— 2004. How cognitive is grammaticalization? The history of the Catalan *Perfet Perifràstic.* In Olga Fischer, Muriel Norde, and Harry Perridon (eds.) *Up and Down the Cline: The Nature of Grammaticalization*, 211–27. Amsterdam/Philadelphia: John Benjamins.

—— and Richard Waltereit. 2002. Grammaticalization vs. reanalysis: A semantic-pragmatic account of functional change in grammar. *Zeitschrift für Sprachwissenschaft* 21, 151–95.

Deutscher, Guy. 2005. *The Unfolding of Language: An Evolutionary Tour of mankind's Greatest Invention.* New York: Metropolitan Books.

Diewald, Gabriele. 1997. *Grammatikalisierung: Eine Einführung in Sein und Werden grammatischer Formen.* Tübingen: Max Niemeyer Verlag.

—— 2002. A model for relevant types of context in grammaticalization. In Ilse Wischer and Gabriela Diewald (eds.) *New Reflections on Grammaticalization*, 103–20. Amsterdam/Philadelphia: John Benjamins.

—— 2006. Context types in grammaticalization as constructions. *Constructions* SV1-9. www.constructions-online.de.

Doyle, Aidan. 2002. Yesterday's affixes as today's clitics: A case-study in degrammaticalization. In Ilse Wischer and Gabriela Diewald (eds.) *New Reflections on Grammaticalization*, 67–81. Amsterdam/Philadelphia: John Benjamins.

Drosdowski, Günter et al. 1984. *Duden Grammatik der deutschen Gegenwartssprache*, 4th edn. Mannheim/Wien/Zürich: Dudenverlag.

Ejder, Bertil. 1945. *Adjektivändelsen* -er *i de Nordiska Språken, särskilt i Svenskan.* Lund: Gleerupska Universitetsbokhandeln.

Elcock, W. D. 1960. *The Romance Languages.* London: Faber and Faber Ltd.

Enger, Hans-Olav. 2002. The story of Scandinavian –*s*(*t*) retold: Grammaticalising a clitic to a derivational affix. *Folia Linguistica Historica* 23:1–2, 79–105.

—— 2003. Skandinavisk -*s(t)* en gang til: Grammatikalisering fra klitikon til avledningsaffiks. In Jan Terje Faarlund (ed.) *Språk i Endring: Indre Norsk Språkhistorie*, 29–56. Oslo: Novus Forlag.

Enrique-Arias, Andrés. 2005. When clitics become affixes, where do they come to rest? In Wolfgang U. Dressler, Dieter Kastovsky, Oskar E. Pfeiffer, and Franz Rainer (eds.) *Morphology and its Demarcations: Selected Papers from the 11th Morphology Meeting*, 67–79. Amsterdam/Philadelphia: John Benjamins.

Epps, Patience. 2008. *A Grammar of Hup.* Berlin/New York: Mouton de Gruyter.

—— In prep. On directionality in language change: The case of productive deaffixation in Hup.

Faarlund, Jan Terje. 2005. From clitic to affix: On the history of Scandinavian reflexive verbs. *Nowele* 46–47, 53–72.

—— 2007. Parameterization and change in non-finite complementation. *Diachronica* 24:1, 57–80.

Falk, Hjalmar and Alf Torp. 1900. *Dansk-norskens syntax.* Kristiania: Aschehoug and Co.

Fanego, Teresa. 2004. Some strategies for coding sentential subjects in English. *Studies in Language* 28:2, 321–61.

Fischer, Olga. 2000. Grammaticalisation: Unidirectional, non-reversable? The case of *to* before the infinitive in English. In Olga Fischer, Anette Rosenbach, and Dieter Stein (eds.) *Pathways of Change: Grammaticalization in English*, 149–69. Amsterdam/Philadelphia: John Benjamins.

—— 2004. What counts as evidence in historical linguistics? *Studies in Language* 28:3, 710–40.

—— 2007. *Morphosyntactic Change: Functional and Formal Perspectives.* Oxford: Oxford University Press.

—— 2008. On analogy as the motivation for grammaticalization. *Studies in Language* 32:2, 336–82.

—— in prep. An analogical approach to grammaticalization. Submitted to Ekkehard König, Elke Gehweiler, and Katerina Stathi (eds.) *What's New in Grammaticalization?* Amsterdam/Philadelphia: John Benjamins.

—— and Anette Rosenbach. 2000. Introduction. In Olga Fischer, Anette Rosenbach, and Dieter Stein (eds.) *Pathways of Change: Grammaticalization in English*, 1–37. Amsterdam/Philadelphia: John Benjamins.

—— , Muriel Norde, and Harry Perridon. 2004. Introduction: In search of grammaticalization. In Olga Fischer, Muriel Norde, and Harry Perridon (eds.) *Up and Down the Cline: The Nature of Grammaticalization*, 1–16. Amsterdam/Philadelphia: John Benjamins.

Fitzmaurice, Susan. 2000. Remarks on de-grammaticalization of infinitival *to* in present-day American English. In Olga Fischer, Anette Rosenbach, and Dieter Stein (eds.) *Pathways of Change: Grammaticalization in English*, 171–86. Amsterdam/Philadelphia: John Benjamins.

Fiva, Toril. 1987. *Possessor Chains in Norwegian* (= Tromsø studier i språkvitenskap 9). Oslo: Novus Forlag.

Fleischman, Suzanne. 1982. *The Future in Thought and Language: Diachronic Evidence from Romance.* Cambridge: Cambridge University Press.

Fortson, Benjamin W. 2003. Semantic change. In Brian D. Joseph and Richard D. Janda (eds.) *The Handbook of Historical Linguistics*, 648–66. Oxford: Blackwell.

Gabelentz, Georg von der. 1901. *Die Sprachwissenschaft, ihre Aufgaben, Methoden und bisherigen Ergebnisse*, 2nd enlarged and improved edn. Leipzig: Chr. Herm. Tauchnitz. Reprinted in Chris Hutton (ed.) 1995. *18th and 19th Century German Linguistics* VII. London: Routledge/Thoemmes Press.

Gelderen, Elly van. 2004. *Grammaticalization as Economy.* Amsterdam/Philadelphia: John Benjamins.

Giacalone Ramat, Anna. 1998. Testing the boundaries of grammaticalization. In Anna Giacalone Ramat and Paul J. Hopper (eds.) *The Limits of Grammaticalization*, 107–27. Amsterdam/Philadelphia: John Benjamins.

Giacalone Ramat, Anna. and Paul J. Hopper. 1998. Introduction. In Anna Giacalone Ramat and Paul J. Hopper (eds.) *The Limits of Grammaticalization*, 1–11. Amsterdam/Philadelphia: John Benjamins.

Givón, Talmy. 1971. Historical syntax and synchronic morphology: An archaeologist's field trip. *Papers from the 7th Regional Meeting, Chicago Linguistic Society*, 394–415. Chicago: Chicago Linguistic Society.

—— 1975. Serial verbs and syntactic change: Niger-Congo. In Charles Li (ed.) *Word Order and Word Order Change*, 47–112. Austin/London: University of Texas Press.

—— 1979. *On Understanding Grammar.* New York/San Francisco/London: Academic Press.

—— 1991. The evolution of dependent clause morpho-syntax in Biblical Hebrew. In Elizabeth Closs Traugott and Bernd Heine (eds.) *Approaches to Grammaticalization*, vol. II: 257–310. Amsterdam/Philadelphia: John Benjamins.

Goldberg, Adele. 1995. *Constructions: A Construction Grammar Approach to Argument Structure.* Chicago: University of Chicago Press.

—— 2006. *Constructions at Work: The Nature of Generalization in Language.* Oxford: Oxford University Press.

González-Diaz, Victorina. 2005. *Very* and *much: very much* the same thing? Paper presented at *New Reflections on Grammaticalization 3*, Santiago de Compostela, 17–20 July 2005.

Gould, Stephen Jay and Elisabeth S. Vrba. 1982. Exaptation: a missing term in the science of form. *Paleobiology* 8:1, 4–15.

Greenberg, Joseph. 1991. The last stages of grammatical elements: Contractive and expansive desemanticization. In Elizabeth Closs Traugott and Bernd Heine (eds.) *Approaches to Grammaticalization I*, 301–14. Amsterdam/Philadelphia: John Benjamins.

Haeringen, C. B. van. 1962. Nieuwe synthese. In Smit, W. A. P et al. (eds.) *Gramarie*, 45–67. [Reprinted 1979: HES Publishers]

Halpern, Aaron. 1995. *On the Placement and Morphology of Clitics.* Stanford: CSLI Publications.

Hamans, Camiel. 1993. Van epicentrum tot episch centrum: enige notities over distinctieve morfologie. *Tabu* 1993, 63–73.

Hamel, A. G. van. 1923. *Gotisch Handboek.* Haarlem: H.D. Tjeenk Willink and Zoon.

Hansen, Erik. 1977. Behøver vi *at*? *Nyt fra Sprognævnet* 19, 1–4.

Harris, Alice C. and Lyle Campbell. 1995. *Historical Syntax in Cross-linguistic Perspective.* Cambridge: Cambridge University Press.

—— and Jan Terje Faarlund. 2006. Trapped morphology. *Journal of Linguistics* 42, 289–315.

Haspelmath, Martin. 1993. The diachronic externalization of inflection. *Linguistics* 31:2, 279–309.

—— 1995. The growth of affixes in morphological reanalysis. In Geert Booij and Jaap van Marle (eds.) *Yearbook of Morphology 1994*, 1–29. Dordrecht/Boston/London: Kluwer Academic Publishers.

Haspelmath, Martin. 1996. Word-class-changing inflection and morphological theory. In Geert Booij and Jaap van Marle (eds.) *Yearbook of Morphology 1995*, 43–66. Dordrecht/Boston/London: Kluwer Academic Publishers.

—— 1997a. *Indefinite Pronouns.* Oxford: Oxford University Press.

—— 1997b. *From Space to Time: Temporal Adverbials in the World's Languages.* Munich/Newcastle: Lincom Europa.

—— 1998. Does grammaticalization need reanalysis? *Studies in Language* 22:2, 315–51.

—— 1999a. Why is grammaticalization irreversible? *Linguistics* 37:6, 1043–68.

—— 1999b. Are there principles of grammatical change? *Journal of Linguistics* 35, 579–95.

—— 1999c. Optimality and diachronic adaptation. *Zeitschrift für Sprachwissenschaft* 18:2, 180–205.

—— 2004. On directionality in language change with particular reference to grammaticalization. In Olga Fischer, Muriel Norde, and Harry Perridon (eds.) *Up and Down the Cline: The Nature of Grammaticalization*, 17–44. Amsterdam/Philadelphia: John Benjamins.

Hawking, Stephen. 1996 [1988]. *A Brief History of Time. From the Big Bang to Black Holes.* London: Bantam Books.

Heath, Jeffrey. 1998. Hermit crabs: Formal renewal of morphology by phonologically mediated affix substitution. *Language* 74:4, 728–59.

Heine, Bernd. 1994. Grammaticalization as an explanatory parameter. In William Pagliuca (ed.) *Perspectives on Grammaticalization*, 255–87. Amsterdam/Philadelphia: John Benjamins.

—— 1997. *Cognitive Foundations of Grammar.* Oxford/New York: Oxford University Press.

—— 2002. On the role of context in grammaticalization. In Ilse Wischer and Gabriela Diewald (eds.) *New Reflections on Grammaticalization*, 83–101. Amsterdam/Philadelphia: John Benjamins.

—— 2003a. On degrammaticalization. In Barry J. Blake and Kate Burridge (eds.) *Historical Linguistics 2001*, 163–79. Amsterdam/Philadelphia: John Benjamins.

—— 2003b. Grammaticalization. In Brian D. Joseph and Richard D. Janda (eds.) *The Handbook of Historical Linguistics*, 575–601. Oxford: Blackwell.

——, Ulrike Claudi, and Friederike Hünnemeyer. 1991. *Grammaticalization: A Conceptual Framework.* Chicago: University of Chicago Press.

—— and Tania Kuteva. 2002. *World Lexicon of Grammaticalization.* Cambridge: Cambridge University Press.

—— and Mechtild Reh. 1984. *Grammaticalization and Reanalysis in African Languages.* Hamburg: Buske.

Hellquist, Elof. 1980 [1922]. *Svensk Etymologisk Ordbok.* Tredje upplagan. Malmö: Liber.

Heltoft, Lars. 1995. Grammatikaliseringsprocesser i dansk syntakshistorie. In Bente Holmberg (ed.) *Sproghistorie i 90'erne*, 125–68. Copenhagen: Selskab for Nordisk Filologi.

Herlin, Ilona and Lari Kotilainen. 2004. External factors behind cross-linguistic similarities. In Olga Fischer, Muriel Norde, and Harry Perridon (eds.) *Up and Down the Cline: The Nature of Grammaticalization*, 263–79. Amsterdam/Philadelphia: John Benjamins.

Herslund, Michael. 2001. The Danish s-genitive: From affix to clitic. *Acta Linguistica Hafniensia* 33, 7–18.

Himmelmann, Nikolaus P. 2004. Lexicalization and grammaticalization: Opposite or orthogonal? In Walter Bisang, Nikolaus P. Himmelmann, and Björn Wiemer (eds.) *What Makes Grammaticalization? A Look from its Fringes and Components*, 21–42. Berlin/New York: Mouton de Gruyter.

Hock, Hans Henrich and Brian D. Joseph. 1996. *Language History, Language Change and Language Relationship: An Introduction to Historical and Comparative Linguistics.* Berlin/New York: Mouton de Gruyter.

Hoenigswald, Henry M. 1966. Are there universals of linguistic change? In Joseph H. Greenberg (ed.) *Universals of Language*, 2nd edn. Cambridge, MA: MIT Press.

Hopper, Paul J. 1987. Emergent grammar. In *Proceedings of the 13th Annual Meeting of the Berkeley Linguistics Society*, 139–57.

—— 1991. On some principles of grammaticization. In Elizabeth C. Traugott and Bernd Heine (eds.) *Approaches to Grammaticalization*, vol. 1: 17–35. Amsterdam/Philadelphia: John Benjamins.

—— 1994. Phonogenesis. In William Pagliuca (ed.) *Perspectives on Grammaticalization*, 29–45. Amsterdam/Philadelphia: John Benjamins.

——1998. The paradigm at the end of the universe. In Anna Giacalone Ramat and Paul J. Hopper (eds.) *The Limits of Grammaticalization*, 147–58. Amsterdam/Philadelphia: John Benjamins.

—— and Elizabeth Closs Traugott. 1993. *Grammaticalization.* Cambridge: Cambridge University Press.

—— —— 2003. *Grammaticalization*, 2nd edn. Cambridge: Cambridge University Press.

Horst, Joop van der and Freek van de Velde. 2007. A second look at so odd a noun phrase. Ms., Leuven University.

Hultman, Tor G. 2003. *Svenska Akademiens Språklära.* Stockholm: Norstedts.

Hummel, Martin. 2000. *Adverbale und adverbialisierte Adjektive im Spanischen: Konstruktionen des Typs* Los niños duermen tranquillos *und* María corre rápido. Tübingen: Gunter Narr Verlag.

Idiatov, Dmitry. 2008. Antigrammaticalization, antimorphologization and the case of Tura. In Elena Seoane and María José López-Couso, in collaboration with Teresa Fanego (eds.) *Theoretical and Empirical Issues in Grammaticalization*, 151–69. Amsterdam/Philadelphia: John Benjamins.

Jacobsen, Henrik Galberg and Peter Stray Jørgensen. 2005. *Politikens håndbog i nudansk*, 5th edn. Copenhagen: Politikens Forlagshus.

Janda, Richard D. 1980. On the decline of declensional systems: The overall loss of OE nominal case inflections and the ME reanalysis of *-es* as *his.* In Elizabeth

C. Traugott, Rebecca Labrum, and Susan Shepherd (eds.) *Papers from the 4th International Conference on Historical Linguistics*, 243–52. Amsterdam/Philadelphia: John Benjamins.

Janda, Richard D. 1995. From agreement affix to subject 'clitic' – and bound root: *-mos* > *-nos* vs. (-)*nos*(-) and *nos-otros* in New Mexican and other regional Spanish dialects. In Audra Dainora et al. (eds.) *Papers from the 31st Regional Meeting of the Chicago Linguistic Society*, vol. II: *The Parasession on Clitics*, 118–39. Chicago: The Chicago Linguistic Society.

—— 2001. Beyond 'pathways' and 'unidirectionality': On the discontinuity of transmission and the counterability of grammaticalization. *Language Sciences* 23:2–3, 265–340.

—— 2005. Morphemes grammatizing gradually vs. theories scientizing glacially: On pushing grammaticalization studies along the path towards science. *Logos and Language* 6:2, 45–65.

—— and Brian D. Joseph. 2003. On language, change, and language change – Or, of history, linguistics, and historical linguistics. In Brian D. Joseph and Richard D. Janda (eds.) *The Handbook of Historical Linguistics*, 3–180. Oxford: Blackwell.

Jespersen, Otto. 1894. *Progress in Language: With Special Reference to English.* London: Swan Sonnenschein and Co.

—— 1917. *Negation in English and Other Languages.* Copenhagen: Andr. Fred. Høst and Søn.

—— 1918. *Chapters on English.* London: George Allen and Unwin Ltd.

—— 1921. *Language: Its Nature, Development and Origin.* London: George Allen and Unwin Ltd.

—— 1924. *The Philosophy of Grammar.* London: George Allen and Unwin Ltd.

Joseph, Brian D. 2001. Is there such a thing as grammaticalization? *Language Sciences* 23:2–3, 163–86.

—— 2003. Morphologization from syntax. In Brian D. Joseph and Richard D. Janda (eds.) *The Handbook of Historical Linguistics*, 472–92. Oxford: Blackwell.

—— 2004. Rescuing traditional (historical) linguistics from grammaticalization theory. In Olga Fischer, Muriel Norde, and Harry Perridon (eds.) *Up and Down the Cline: The Nature of Grammaticalization*, 45–71. Amsterdam/Philadelphia: John Benjamins.

—— 2005. How accomodating of change is grammaticalization? The case of 'lateral shifts'. *Logos and language* 6:2, 1–7.

—— and Richard D. Janda. 1988. The how and why of diachronic morphologization and demorphologization. In Michael Hammond and Michael Noonan (eds.) *Theoretical Morphology: Approaches in Modern Linguistics*, 193–210. San Diego: Academic Press.

—— and Richard D. Janda (eds.). 2003. *The Handbook of Historical Linguistics.* Oxford: Blackwell.

Karlsson, Keith E. 1981. *Syntax and Affixation: The Evolution of MENTE in Latin and Romance.* Tübingen: Max Niemeyer Verlag.

Keller, Rudi. 1994 [1990]. *Sprachwandel: Von der unsichtbaren Hand in der Sprache*, 2nd edn. Tübingen and Basel: Francke Verlag.

Kemenade, Ans van. 1999. Functional categories, morphosyntactic change, grammaticalization. *Linguistics* 37:6, 997–1010.

Kiparsky, Paul. 2003. *The Germanic Weak Preterite.* www.stanford.edu/~kiparsky/Papers/lahiri_weakpreterite.pdf

—— 2005. *Grammaticalization as Optimization.* www.stanford.edu/~kiparsky/Papers/yalegrammaticalization.pdf.

Klausenburger, Jurgen. 2000. *Grammaticalization: Studies in Latin and Romance Morphosyntax.* Amsterdam/Philadelphia: John Benjamins.

—— 2002. Grammaticalization within a theory of morphocentricity. In Ilse Wischer and Gabriela Diewald (eds.) *New Reflections on Grammaticalization*, 31–43. Amsterdam/Philadelphia: John Benjamins.

Klein, Henny. 1998. *Adverbs of Degree in Dutch and Related Languages.* Amsterdam/Philadelphia: John Benjamins.

Koch, Harold. 1996. Reconstruction in morphology. In Mark Durie and Malcolm Ross (eds.) *The Comparative Method Reviewed: Regularity and Irregularity in Language Change*, 218–63. Oxford: Oxford University Press.

Krahe, Hans and Wolfgang Meid. 1969. *Germanische Sprachwissenschaft*, II: *Formenlehre*, 7th edn., revised by Wolfgang Meid. Berlin: Walter de Gruyter and Co.

Kranich, Svenja. 2008. Subjective progressives in seventeenth and eighteenth century English: Secondary grammaticalization as a process of objectification. In Maurizio Gotti, Marina Dossena, and Richard Dury (eds.) *English Historical Linguistics 2006*, vol. I: *Syntax and Morphology*, 241–56. Amsterdam/Philadelphia: John Benjamins.

—— in prep. Grammaticalization, subjectification and objectification. Submitted for review to Ekkehard König, Elke Gehweiler, and Katerina Stathi (eds.) *What's New in Grammaticalization?* Amsterdam/Philadelphia: John Benjamins.

Kreidler, Charles W. 1989. *The Pronunciation of English: A Course Book in Phonology.* Oxford/New York: Basil Blackwell.

Kristoffersen, Lars. 1991. *Verbal Derivation and Inflection in a Functional Grammar of West Greenlandic.* MA thesis, University of Copenhagen.

Krug, Manfred G. 2000. *Emerging English Modals: A Corpus-based Study of Grammaticalization.* Berlin/New York: Mouton de Gruyter.

Kruisinga, Etsko. 1932. *A Handbook of Present-day English*, II: *English Accidence and Syntax.* Oxford/New York: Basil Blackwell.

Kuryłowicz, Jerzy. 1966 [1945–9]. La nature des procès dits 'analogiques'. *Acta Linguistica* 5, 121–38. Reprinted in E. P. Hamp et al. 1966. *Readings in Linguistics*, vol. II: 158–74. Chicago: University of Chicago Press.

—— 1975 [1965]. The evolution of grammatical categories. In *Esquisses Linguistiques II*, J. Kuryłowicz, 38–54. Munich: Wilhelm Fink Verlag.

Kuteva, Tania. 2001. *Auxiliation: An Enquiry into the Nature of Grammaticalization.* Oxford: Oxford University Press.

Kuzmack, Stefanie. in prep. *Ish*: A new case of antigrammaticalization. Ms., University of Chicago.

Lahiri, Aditi. 2003 [2000]. Hierarchical restructuring in the creation of verbal morphology in Bengali and Germanic: Evidence from phonology. In Aditi Lahiri (ed.) *Analogy, Levelling, Markedness*, 71–123. Berlin: Mouton de Gruyter.

Lakoff, George. 1974. Syntactic amalgams. *Papers from the Tenth Regional Meeting of the Chicago Linguistic Society*, 321–44.

Langacker, Ronald W. 1977. Syntactic reanalysis. In Charles N. Li (ed.) *Mechanisms of Syntactic Change*, 57–139. Austin, TX/London: University of Texas Press.

—— 1990. Subjectification. *Cognitive Linguistics* 1:1, 5–38.

Lass, Roger. 1990. How to do things with junk: Exaptation in language evolution. *Journal of Linguistics* 26, 79–102.

—— 1997. *Historical Linguistics and Language Change*. Cambridge: Cambridge University Press.

—— 2000. Remarks on (uni)directionality. In Olga Fischer, Anette Rosenbach, and Dieter Stein (eds.) *Pathways of Change: Grammaticalization in English*, 207–27. Amsterdam/Philadelphia: John Benjamins.

Lausberg, Heinrich. 1972. *Romanische Sprachwissenschaft*, III: *Formenlehre*. Berlin/New York: Walter de Gruyter.

Lehmann, Christian. 1985. Grammaticalization: Synchronic variation and diachronic change. *Lingua e stile* 20:3, 303–18.

—— 1989. Grammatikalisierung und Lexikalisierung. *Zeitschrift für Phonetik, Sprachwissenschaft und Kommunikationsforschung* 42, 11–19.

—— 1995 [1982]. *Thoughts on Grammaticalization*. Munich/Newcastle: Lincom Europa.

—— 2002. New reflections on lexicalization and grammaticalization. In Ilse Wischer and Gabriela Diewald (eds.) *New Reflections on Grammaticalization*, 1–18. Amsterdam/Philadelphia: John Benjamins.

—— 2004. Theory and method in grammaticalization. *Zeitschrift für Germanistische Linguistik* 32:2, 152–87.

Levander, Lars. 1909. *Älvdalsmålet i Dalarna. Ordböjning och Syntax*. Stockholm: P.A. Norstedt and Söner.

Lightfoot, David W. 1979. *Principles of Diachronic Syntax*. Cambridge: Cambridge University Press.

—— 1999. *The Development of Language: Acquisition, Change and Evolution*. Oxford: Blackwell.

—— 2002. Myths and the prehistory of grammars. *Journal of Linguistics* 38, 113–36.

Lightfoot, Douglas J. 2005. Can the lexicalization/grammaticalization distinction be reconciled? *Studies in Language* 29:3, 583–615.

Lindström, Therese. 2004. Lexicalised grammaticalization? In Gerda Haßler and Gesina Volkmann (eds.) *History of Linguistics in Texts and Concepts*, vol. II: 835–51. Münster: Nodus Publikationen.

Lødrup, Helge. 1989. *Norske Hypotagmer. En LFG-beskrivelse av Ikke-verbale Hypotagmer.* (= Oslo-studier i språkvitenskap 4). Oslo: Novus Forlag.

Lorenz, Gunter. 2002. Really worthwhile or not really significant? A corpus-based approach to the delexicalization and grammaticalization of intensifiers in Modern English. In Ilse Wischer and Gabriela Diewald (eds.) *New Reflections on Grammaticalization*, 143–61. Amsterdam/Philadelphia: John Benjamins.

Luraghi, Silvia. 2005. Does a theory of language change need unidirectionality? *Logos and Language* 6:2, 9–17.

Lyons, John. 1977. *Semantics*, vol. II. Cambridge: Cambridge University Press.

Mac Congáil, Nollaig. 2004. *Irish Grammar Book.* Indreabhán: Cló Iar-Chonnachta.

Marle, Jaap van. 1985. Bij de woordvorming van *tig. De nieuwe taalgids* 78, 145–8.

—— 1996. The unity of morphology: On the interwovenness of the derivational and inflectional dimension of the word. In Geert Booij and Jaap van Marle (eds.) *Yearbook of Morphology 1995*, 67–82. Dordrecht/Boston/London: Kluwer Academic Publishers.

Matsumoto, Yo. 1988. From bound grammatical markers to free discourse markers: History of some Japanese connectives. *Proceedings of the Fourteenth Annual Meeting of the Berkeley Linguistics Society*, 340–351.

McMillan, D. 1970. Note de syntaxe médiévale: La particule *re-* en ancien français. *Revue de Linguistique Romane* 34, 1–15.

Meillet, Antoine. 1926 [1912]. L'évolution des formes grammaticales. In Antoine Meillet, *Linguistique Historique et Linguistique Générale*, I: 130–48. Paris: Edouard Champion.

Mendez-Dosuna, Julian. 1997. Fusion, fission, and relevance in language change: De-univerbation in Greek verb morphology. *Studies in Language* 21:3, 577–612.

Mengden, Ferdinand von. 2008. The modules of grammatical change. Paper presented at *New Reflections on Grammaticalization* 4, Leuven, 16–19 July 2008.

Metslang, Helle, Karl Pajusalu, and Külli Habicht. 2008. Developmental paths of Estonian question particles. Paper presented at the *41st Annual Meeting of the Societas Linguistica Europaea*, Forly (Italy), September 2008.

Mithun, Marianne. 1988. The grammaticization of coordination. In John Haiman and Sandra A. Thompson (eds.) *Clause Combining in Grammar and Discourse*, 331–59. Amsterdam/Philadelphia: John Benjamins.

Moreno Cabrera, Juan C. 1998. On the relationships between grammaticalization and lexicalization. In Anna Giacalone Ramat and Paul J. Hopper (eds.) *The Limits of Grammaticalization*, 211–27. Amsterdam/Philadelphia: John Benjamins.

Muysken, Pieter. 1977. *Syntactic Developments in the Verb Phrase of Ecuadorian Quechua.* Lisse: Peter de Ridder Press.

Narrog, Heiko. 2007. Exaptation, grammaticalization and reanalysis. *California Linguistic Notes* 23:1. http://hss.fullerton.edu/linguistics/cln/pdf/Exaptation_Narrog.pdf.

Nesse, Agnete. 2002. *Språkkontakt mellom Norsk og Tysk i Hansatidens Bergen.* Oslo: Novus Forlag.

Nevis, Joel A. 1986a. Decliticization and deaffixation in Saame: Abessive *taga.* In Brian D. Joseph (ed.) *Studies on Language Change* (= The Ohio State University Working Papers in Linguistics 34), 1–9.

—— 1986b. Decliticization in Old Estonian. In Brian D. Joseph (ed.) *Studies on Language Change* (= The Ohio State University Working Papers in Linguistics 34), 10–27.

Newmeyer, Frederick J. 1998. *Language Form and Language Function.* Cambridge, MA: MIT Press.

—— 2001. Deconstructing grammaticalization. *Language Sciences* 23:2–3, 187–229.

Nielsen, Konrad. 1926. *Lærebok i Lappisk*, I: *Grammatik.* Oslo: A.W. Brøggers Boktrykkeris Forlag.

Norde, Muriel. 1997. *The History of the Genitive in Swedish: A Case Study in Degrammaticalization.* PhD thesis, University of Amsterdam.

—— 2000. The grammaticalization of adpositions in the history of Swedish. In Guðrún Þórhallsdóttir (ed.) *Proceedings of The 10th Conference of Nordic and General Linguistics*, 177–87. Reykjavik: Institute of Linguistics.

—— 2001a. Deflexion as a counterdirectional factor in grammatical change. *Language Sciences* 23: 2–3, 231–64.

—— 2001b. The loss of lexical case in Swedish. In Jan Terje (ed.) *Grammatical Relations in Change*, 241–72. Amsterdam/Philadelphia: John Benjamins.

—— 2002. The final stages of grammaticalization: Affixhood and beyond. In Ilse Wischer and Gabriela Diewald (eds.) *New Reflections on Grammaticalization.* Amsterdam/Philadelphia: John Benjamins, 45–65.

—— 2005. Adverb och adjektiv på *-vis* i svenskan. *Svenskans Beskrivning* 27, 233–45. Växjö: Växjö University Press.

—— 2006a. Demarcating degrammaticalization: The Swedish s-genitive revisited. *Nordic Journal of Linguistics* 29:2, 201–38.

—— 2006b. Van suffix tot telwoord tot bijwoord: Degrammaticalisering en (re) grammaticalisering van *tig.* TABU 35:1/2, 33–60.

—— 2007. Epistemic adverbs at the interface of lexicalization and grammaticalization. Paper presented at *TIN*-dag [Linguistics in the Netherlands Day], University of Utrecht, 3 February 2007. http://odur.let.rug.nl/~norde/TIN07%20epistemix.ppt.

—— 2008. East Scandinavian *på*: A preposition of the 'third kind'. In Kees Dekker, Alasdair MacDonald, and Hermann Niebaum (eds.) *Northern Voices: Essays on Old Germanic and Related Topics Offered to Professor Tette Hofstra* (= Germania Latina VI), 383–98. Leuven: Peeters.

—— Forthcoming. Review of Brinton and Traugott (2005). To appear in *Language.*

—— In prep. Degrammaticalization: Three common controversies. Submitted to Ekkehard König, Elke Gehweiler, and Katerina Stathi (eds.) *What's New in Grammaticalization?* Amsterdam/Philadelphia: John Benjamins.

Ocampo, Francisco. 2006. Movement towards discourse is not grammaticalization: The evolution of *claro* from adjective to discourse particle in spoken Spanish.

In Nuria Sagarra and Almeida Jacqueline Toribio (eds.) *Selected Proceedings of the 9th Hispanic Linguistics Symposium*, 308–19. Somerville, MA: Cascadilla Proceedings Project.

Perridon, Harry. 1989. *Reference, Definiteness and the Noun Phrase in Swedish*. PhD thesis, University of Amsterdam.

—— 1994. The Scandinavian article systems: Unity in diversity. In Jens Alwood, Bo Ralph, Paula Andersson, Dora Kós-Dienes, and Åsa Wengelin (eds.) *Proceedings of the XVIth Scandinavian Conference of Linguistics and the VIIIth Conference of Nordic and General Linguistics, General Session*, vol. II: 323–33. Gothenburg: Institutionen för Nordiska Språk.

Pettersson, Gertrud. 2005. *Svenska Språket under Sjuhundra År: En Studie om Svenskan och dess Utforskande*. Lund: Studentlitteratur.

Picard, Marc. 1990. More on the English genitive plural. *Folia Linguistica* 24:3–4, 373–6.

Pinkster, Harm. 1987. The strategy and chronology of the development of future and perfect tense auxiliaries in Latin. In Martin Harris and Paolo Ramat (eds.) *Historical Development of Auxiliaries*, 193–223. Berlin/New York/Amsterdam: Mouton de Gruyter.

Plank, Frans. 1985. The interpretation and development of form alternations conditioned across word boundaries: The case of *Wife's*, *Wives* and *Wives'*. In Roger Eaton, Olga Fischer, Willem Koopman, and Frederike van der Leek (eds.) *Papers from the 4th International Conference on English Historical Linguistics*, 205–33. Amsterdam/Philadelphia: John Benjamins.

—— 1992. From cases to adpositions. In Nicola Pantaleo (ed.) *Aspects of English Diachronic Linguistics: Papers Read at the Second National Conference of History of English*, 19–61. Fasano: Schena.

—— 1995. Entgrammatisierung: Spiegelbild der Grammatisierung? In Norbert Boretzky et al. (eds.) *Natürlichkeitstheorie und Sprachwandel*, 199–219. Bochum: Universitätsverlag Brockmeyer.

—— 2003 [2000]. Morphological re-activation and phonological alternations. In Aditi Lahiri (ed.) *Analogy, Levelling, Markedness*, 171–91. Berlin: Mouton de Gruyter.

Platzack, Christer. 1998. *Svenskans Inre Grammatik – det Minimalistiska Programmet: En Introduktion till Modern Generativ Grammatik*. Lund: Studentlitteratur.

Pottelberge, Jeroen van. 2005. Review of Fischer, Norde and Perridon 2004. *Logos and Language* 6:2, 37–44.

Prokosch, E. 1939. *A Comparative Germanic Grammar*. Philadelphia: Linguistic Society of America.

Ralli, Angela. 2003. Morphology in Greek linguistics: The state of the art. *Journal of Greek linguistics* 4:1, 77–129.

Ramat, Paolo. 1981. *Einführung in das Germanische*. Tübingen: Max Niemeyer Verlag.

—— 1992. Thoughts on degrammaticalization. *Linguistics* 30, 549–60.

Ramat, Paolo. 2001. Degrammaticalization or transcategorization? In Chris Schaner-Wolles, John Rennison, and Friedrich Neubarth (eds.) *Naturally! Linguistic Studies in Honour of Wolfgang Ulrich Dressler*, 393–401. Torino: Rosenberg and Sellier.

Reuse, Willem J. de. 1994. *Siberian Yupik Eskimo: The Language and its Contacts with Chukchi*. Salt Lake City: University of Utah Press.

Ricca, Davide. 2005. Cumulative exponence involving derivation: Some patterns for an uncommon phenomenon. Wolfgang U. Dressler, Dieter Kastovsky, Oskar E. Pfeiffer, and Franz Rainer (eds.) *Morphology and its Demarcations*, 197–213. Amsterdam/Philadelphia: John Benjamins.

Rietveld, Toni and Vincent van Heuven. 2001. *Algemene fonetiek: Tweede aangevulde druk*. Bussum: Uitgeverij Coutinho.

Ringmar, Martin. 2006. Älvdalska – en önordisk språkö på fastlandet? www.nordiska.uu.se/arkiv/konferenser/alvdalska/konferensbidrag/Ringmar.pdf.

Roberts, Ian and Anna Roussou. 1999. A formal approach to 'grammaticalization'. *Linguistics* 37:6, 1011–41.

—— —— 2003. *Syntactic Change: A Minimalist Approach to Grammaticalization*. Cambridge: Cambridge University Press.

Rosenbach, Anette. 2004. The English s-genitive: A case of degrammaticalization? In Olga Fischer, Muriel Norde, and Harry Perridon (eds.) *Up and Down the Cline: The Nature of Grammaticalization*, 73–96. Amsterdam/Philadelphia: John Benjamins.

—— and Gerhard Jäger. Forthcoming. Priming and unidirectional language change. *Theoretical Linguistics*.

Rosenkvist, Henrik. 2004. *The Emergence of Conditional Subordinators in Swedish: A Study in Grammaticalization*. (= *Lundastudier i nordisk språkvetenskap* A62).

—— 2008. A case of degrammaticalization in Northern Swedish. Paper presented at the *Continuity and Change in Grammar* workshop, University of Cambridge, March 2008.

Ross, Alan S. C. and Jan Berns. 1992. Germanic. In Jadranka Gvozdanović (ed.) *Indo-European Numerals*, 555–715. Berlin/New York: Mouton de Gruyter.

Rostila, Jouni. 2004. Lexicalization as a way to grammaticalization. In Fred Karlsson (ed.) *Proceedings of the 20th Scandinavian Conference of Linguistics*. www.ling.helsinki.fi/kielitiede/20scl/Rostila.pdf.

Seppänen, Aimo. 1997. The genitive and the category of case in the history of English. In Raymond Hickey and Stanisław Puppel (eds.) *Language History and Linguistic Modelling: A Festschrift for Jacek Fisiak on his 60th Birthday*, vol. 1: 193–214. Berlin/New York: Mouton de Gruyter.

Smirniotopoulos, Jane C. and Brian D. Joseph. 1998. Syntax versus the lexicon: Incorporation and compounding in Modern Greek. *Journal of Linguistics* 34:2, 447–88.

Söderberg, Ragnhild. 1971. *Svensk Ordbildning: Andra Upplagan*. Stockholm.

SRB = 2005. *Språkriktighetsboken: Utarbetad av Svenska Språknämnden*. Stockholm: Norstedts Akademiska Förlag.

Stein, Dieter. 1995. Subjective meanings and the history of inversions in English. In Dieter Stein and Susan Wright (eds.) *Subjectivity and Subjectivisation*, 129–50. Cambridge: Cambridge University Press.

Stoett, F. A. 1923. *Middelnederlandse Spraakkunst: Syntaxis*. 's-Gravenhage: Martinus Nijhoff.

Stump, Gregory T. 1998. Inflection. In Andrew Spencer and Arnold M. Zwicky (eds.) *The Handbook of Morphology*, 13–43. Oxford: Blackwell.

Tabor, Whitney and Elizabeth Closs Traugott. 1998. Structural scope expansion and grammaticalization. In Anna Giacalone Ramat and Paul J. Hopper (eds.) *The Limits of Grammaticalization*, 229–72. Amsterdam/Philadelphia: John Benjamins.

Taeymans, Martine. 2004. An investigation into the marginal modals DARE and NEED in British present-day English: A corpus-based approach. In Olga Fischer, Muriel Norde, and Harry Perridon (eds.) *Up and Down the Cline: The Nature of Grammaticalization*, 97–114. Amsterdam/Philadelphia: John Benjamins.

Teleman, Ulf, Staffan Hellberg, and Erik Andersson. 1999a. *Svenska Akademiens Grammatik*, II: *Ord*. Stockholm: Norstedts.

—— —— —— 1999b. *Svenska Akademiens Grammatik*, III: *Fraser*. Stockholm: Norstedts.

—— —— —— 1999c. *Svenska Akademiens Grammatik*, IV: *Satser och Meningar*. Stockholm: Norstedts.

Tomasello, Michael. 2003. *Constructing a Language: A Usage-based Theory of Language Acquisition*. Cambridge, MA: Harvard University Press.

Tops, Guy. 1974. *The Origin of the Germanic Dental Preterit*. Leiden: E.J. Brill.

—— 1978. The origin of the Germanic dental preterit: Von Friesen revisited. In Jacek Fisiak (ed.) *Historical Phonology*, 349–71. The Hague: Mouton Publishers.

Torner, Sergi. 2005. Spanish adverbs in *-mente*. *Probus* 17:1, 115–44.

Torp, Arne. 1992. Der sogenannte 'Garpegenitiv': Ursprung, Alter und Verbreitung im heutigen Norwegisch. In Lennart Elmevik and Kurt Erich Schöndorf (eds.) *Niederdeutsch in Skandinavien*, III: 151–66. (=*Beihefte zur Zeitschrift für deutsche Philologie* 6).

Traugott, Elizabeth Closs. 1982. From propositional to textual and expressive meanings: Some semantic-pragmatic aspects of grammaticalization. In Winfred P. Lehmann and Yakov Malkiel (eds.) *Perspectives on Historical Linguistics*, 245–71. Amsterdam/Philadelphia: John Benjamins.

—— 1989. On the rise of epistemic meanings in English: An example of subjectification in semantic change. *Language* 65:1, 31–55.

—— 1995. Subjectification in grammaticalisation. In Dieter Stein and Susan Wright (eds.) *Subjectivity and Subjectivisation*, 31–54. Cambridge: Cambridge University Press.

—— 1997a. The role of the development of discourse markers in a theory of grammaticalization. www.stanford.edu/~traugott/papers/discourse.pdf.

—— 1997b. Subjectification and the development of epistemic meaning: The case of *promise* and *threaten*. In Toril Swan and Olaf Jansen Westvik (eds.) *Modality in*

*Germanic Languages: Historical and Comparative Perspectives*, 185–210. Berlin/ New York: Mouton de Gruyter.

Traugott, Elizabeth Closs. 2001. Legitimate counterexamples to unidirectionality. Paper presented at Freiburg University, 17 October 2001. www.stanford.edu/~ traugott/ papers/Freiburg.Unidirect.pdf.

—— 2002. From etymology to historical pragmatics. In Donka Minkova and Robert Stockwell (eds.) *Studies in the History of the English Language*, 19–49. Berlin/ New York: Mouton de Gruyter.

—— 2003. Constructions in grammaticalization. In Brian D. Joseph, and Richard D. Janda (eds.) *The Handbook of Historical Linguistics*, 624–47. Oxford: Blackwell.

—— 2004. Exaptation and grammaticalization. www.stanford.edu/~traugott/ papers/Traugott.Exapt.pdf.

—— 2007. The concepts of constructional mismatch and type-shifting from the perspective of grammaticalization. *Cognitive Linguistics* 18:4, 523–57.

—— 2008. Grammaticalization, constructions and the incremental development of language: Suggestions from the development of degree modifiers in English. In Regine Eckardt, Gerhard Jäger, and Tonjes Veenstra (eds.) *Variation, Selection, Development: Probing the Evolutionary Model of Language Change*, 219–50. Berlin/ New York: Mouton de Gruyter.

—— and Richard B. Dasher. 2002. *Regularity in Semantic Change*. Cambridge: Cambridge University Press.

—— and Bernd Heine. 1991. Introduction. In Elizabeth C. Traugott and Bernd Heine (eds.) *Approaches to Grammaticalization*, vol. I: 1–14. Amsterdam/Philadelphia: John Benjamins.

—— and Ekkehard König. 1991. The semantics-pragmatics of grammaticalization revisited. In Elizabeth Closs Traugott and Bernd Heine (eds.) *Approaches to Grammaticalization*, vol. I: 189–218. Amsterdam/Philadelphia: John Benjamins.

—— and Graeme Trousdale. 2008. Gradience, gradualness and grammaticalization. Paper presented at *New Reflections on Grammaticalization 4*, University of Leuven, 16–19 July 2008.

Trosterud, Trond. 2001. The changes in Scandinavian morphology from 1100 to 1500. *Arkiv för Nordisk Filologi* 116, 153–91.

Trousdale, Graeme. 2008a. Constructions in grammaticalization and lexicalization: Evidence from the history of a composite predicate construction in English. In Graeme Trousdale and Nikolas Gisborne (eds.) *Constructional Approaches to English Grammar*, 33–67. Berlin/New York: Mouton de Gruyter.

—— 2008b. A constructional approach to lexicalization processes in the history of English: evidence from possessive constructions. *Word Structure* 1:2, 156–77.

—— In prep. Issues in constructional approaches to grammaticalization in English. Ms., University of Edinburgh.

Tsangalides, Anastasios. 2004. Unidirectionality in the grammaticalization of modality in Greek. In Olga Fischer, Muriel Norde, and Harry Perridon (eds.) *Up and*

*Down the Cline: The Nature of Grammaticalization*, 193–209. Amsterdam/ Philadelphia: John Benjamins.

Vangsnes, Øystein Alexander. 1998. Double definiteness and possessive constructions in an Eastern Swedish dialect. In Timo Haukioja (ed.) *Papers from the 16th Scandinavian Conference of Linguistics*, 425–39. Turku: Department of Finnish and General Linguistics.

Venås, Kjell. 1989. Review of Fiva 1987. *Norsk Lingvistik Tidsskrift* 1/1989, 90–109.

Verhagen, Arie. 1995. Subjectification, syntax, and communication. In Dieter Stein and Susan Wright (eds.) *Subjectivity and Subjectivisation*, 103–28. Cambridge: Cambridge University Press.

Vincent, Nigel. 1980. Iconic and symbolic aspects of syntax: Prospects for reconstruction. In Paolo Ramat (ed.) *Linguistic Reconstruction and Indo-European Syntax*, 49–68. Amsterdam: John Benjamins.

—— 1987. The interaction of periphrasis and inflection: Some Romance examples. In Martin Harris and Paolo Ramat (eds.) *Historical Development of Auxiliaries*, 237–56. Berlin/New York/Amsterdam: Mouton de Gruyter.

—— 1995. Exaptation and grammaticalization. In Henning Andersen (ed.) *Historical Linguistics 1993: Selected Papers from the 11th International Conference on Historical Linguistics*, 433–45. Amsterdam/Philadelphia: John Benjamins.

Visconti, Jacqueline. 2004. Conditionals and subjectification: Implications for a theory of semantic change. In Olga Fischer, Muriel Norde, and Harry Perridon (eds.) *Up and Down the Cline: The Nature of Grammaticalization*, 169–92. Amsterdam/ Philadelphia: John Benjamins.

Visser, F. T. 1966. *An Historical Syntax of the English Language*, vol. II: *Syntactical Units with One Verb (continued)*. Leiden: E.J. Brill.

Vogelaer, Gunther de. 2005. *Subjectsmarkering in de Nederlandse en Friese Dialecten.* PhD thesis, University of Ghent.

—— Forthcoming. (De)grammaticalisation as a source for new constructions: The case of subject doubling in Dutch. In Alexander Bergs and Gabriele Diewald (eds.) *Constructions and Language Change.* Berlin: Mouton de Gruyter.

Voort, Hein van der. 2002. The quotative construction in Kwaza and its (de-) grammaticalisation. In Mily Crevels, Simon van de Kerke, Sérgio Meira, and Hein van der Voort (eds.) *Selected Papers from the 50th International Congress of Americanists in Warsaw and the Spinoza Workshop on Amerindian Languages in Leiden*, 307–28. Leiden: Research School of Asian, African and Amerindian studies (CNWS).

—— 2004. *A Grammar of Kwaza.* Berlin/New York: Mouton de Gruyter.

Wessén, Elias. 1965. *Svensk Språkhistoria*, vol. III: *Grundlinjer till en Historisk Syntax.* Reprinted 1992. Edsbruk: Akademitryck.

—— 1968. *Svensk Språkhistoria*, vol. I: *Ljudlära och Ordböjningslära.* Reprinted 1992. Edsbruk: Akademitryck.

—— 1971. *Svensk språkhistoria*, vol. II: *Ordbildningslära.* Reprinted 1992. Edsbruk: Akademitryck.

Willis, David. 2007. Syntactic lexicalization as a new type of degrammaticalization. *Linguistics* 45:2, 271–310.

—— Forthcoming. Degrammaticalization and obsolescent morphology: Evidence from Slavonic. In Ekkehard König, Elke Gehweiler, and Katerina Stathi (eds.) *What's New in Grammaticalization?* Amsterdam/Philadelphia: John Benjamins.

Wischer, Ilse. 2000. Grammaticalization versus lexicalization: '*Methinks*' there is some confusion. In Olga Fischer, Anette Rosenbach, and Dieter Stein (eds.) *Pathways of Change: Grammaticalization in English*, 355–70. Amsterdam/Philadelphia: John Benjamins.

*WNT* = *Woordenboek der Nederlandsche Taal*. Available online at http://gtb.inl.nl/?owner=WNT.

Yap, Foong Ha, Stephen Matthews, and Kaoru Horie. 2004. From pronominalizer to pragmatic marker: Implications for unidirectionality from a crosslinguistic perspective. In Olga Fischer, Muriel Norde, and Harry Perridon (eds.) *Up and Down the Cline: The Nature of Grammaticalization*, 137–68. Amsterdam/Philadelphia: John Benjamins.

Ylikoski, Jussi. 2008. Non-finites in North Saami. Ms., University of Oulu. http://cc.oulu.fi/~jylikosk/080216.pdf.

Ziegeler, Debra. 2004. Redefining unidirectionality: Is there life after modality? In Olga Fischer, Muriel Norde, and Harry Perridon (eds.) *Up and Down the Cline: The Nature of Grammaticalization*, 115–35. Amsterdam/Philadelphia: John Benjamins.

Zola Christensen, Robert and Lisa Christensen. 2005. *Dansk grammatik*. Odense: Syddansk Universitetsforlag.

Zwicky, Arnold M. 1987. Suppressing the Zs. *Journal of Linguistics* 23, 133–48.

—— 1988. Direct reference to heads. *Folia Linguistica* 22:3–4, 397–404.

—— and G. K. Pullum. 1983. Cliticization vs inflection: English *n't*. *Language* 59:3, 502–51.

# Author Index


Abney, Steven Paul 162
Aijmer, Karin, 22
Allen, Andrew S. 110
Allen, Cynthia L. 158, 162, 176
Alvre, Paul 202 n. 20
Amis, Martin 48
Andersen, Henning 3, 35, 55, 55 n. 9, 77, 99, 107, 123, 132–4, 136–7, 233
Anderson, Stephen R. 153–5, 157, 158 n. 4, 162, 172
Andersson, Erik 137, 166 n. 21, 167 n. 22, 193
Andersson, Peter 137–8
Ansaldo, Umberto 38, 38 n. 37
Anttila, Raimo 14, 23, 112
Ariste, Paul 202 n. 20
Askedal, John Ole 51, 58–9, 177, 177 n. 28, 188, 206–7, 237
Auwera, Johan van der 3, 112, 136–8

Battye, Adrian 96
Bauer, Brigitte L. 41, 41 n. 42, 42–3, 44 n. 46, 45
Bauer, Laurie 135 n.1
Beard, Robert 113–14, 153
Berns, Jan 214 n. 46
Beths, Frank 121, 136
Blake, Barry J. 62–3, 163 n. 13
Boer, R.C. 77, 77 n. 40, 80
Booij, Geert 155, 159
Bopp, Franz 80
Börjars, Kersti 158, 169 n. 24, 177, 178 n. 29
Boroditsky, Lera 93
Brännström, Edvin 221, 221 n. 44, 223 n. 46
Braunmüller, Kurt 70
Bree, Cor van 77
Brinton, Laurel J. 9–12, 12 n. 7, 13–18, 21–2, 22 n. 21, 23, 26, 50, 67 n. 26, 73, 77 n. 38, 112–13, 115 n. 10, 128 n. a, 154, 190, 190 n. 10, 218
Burridge, Kate 75, 138–42
Bybee, Joan 6 n. 3, 17, 26, 31, 38–40, 40 n. 39, 55, 68, 102, 118 n. 14, 139, 153, 205

Campbell, Lyle 1, 2, 18, 31, 49, 160, 187 n. 2, 202, 236
Carey, Kathleen 86
Carstairs, Andrew 166 n. 20, 172–4, 176
Christensen, Ken Ramshøy 193, 193 n. 12, 194–5
Christensen, Lisa 137
Comrie, Bernard 36, 38
Cristofaro, Sonia 23 n. 23, 73
Croft, William 7, 26, 100 n. 68, 101, 115 n. 10

Dahl, Östen 31, 59, 111, 161 n. 7, 169 n. 24
Dalton-Puffer Christiane, 159, 159 n. 6
Daniliuc, Laura 79 n. 44
Daniliuc, Radu 79 n. 44
Dasher, Richard B. 21, 87, 90
Davidsen-Nielsen, Niels 137
DeLancey, Scott 72
Delsing, Lars-Olof 162, 164–5, 165 n. 18, 166 n. 20, 171
Detges, Ulrich 20–1, 33 n. 33, 42, 67 n. 26, 90, 90 n. 55, 124
Deutscher, Guy 48 n. 1, 68
Diewald, Gabriele 23, 26–7, 27 n. 27, 73
Doyle, Aidan 5, 204, 204 n. 24, 205, 206 n. 25, 236
Drosdowski, Günter 213

Ejder, Bertil 179
Elcock, W.D. 42, 44 n. 46, 58
Enger, Hans-Olav 21, 32, 160
Enrique-Arias, Andrés 38–9, 39 n. 38
Epps, Patience 210–12

Faarlund, Jan Terje 21, 40, 98–9, 160, 192, 195, 195 n. 14, 196–8, 236
Falk, Hjalmar 196 n. 16
Fanego, Teresa 116 n. 11
Fischer, Olga 7, 13, 19, 25–6, 29, 29 n. 29, 30, 30 n. 30, 33, 64, 66, 90 n. 54, 99, 100 n. 70, 106 n. 1, 107, 129–30, 161 n. 11, 191, 191 n.11, 238
Fitzmaurice, Susan 192–3, 236
Fiva, Toril 37–8

Fleischman, Suzanne 56, 78–9, 79 n. 42
Fortson, Benjamin W. 102

Gabelentz, Georg von der 5 n. 2, 57, 90
Gelderen, Elly van 94, 97 n. 64, 97 n. 65
Giacalone Ramat, Anna 14, 41, 61
Givón, Talmy 21 n. 20, 23, 38, 38 n. 36, 50, 55, 101, 113
Goldberg, Adele 28, 28 n. 28
González-Diaz, Victorina 216
Gould, Stephen Jay 115
Greenberg, Joseph 1, 107–8, 115 n. 10

Habicht, Külli 201 n. 18, 202 n. 20
Haeringen, C.B. van 80, 188 n. 7
Halpern, Aaron 158, 172, 174
Hamans, Camiel 216
Hamel, A.G. van 80
Hansen, Erik 137
Harris, Alice C. 18, 40, 160
Haspelmath, Martin 2, 6, 8, 9, 18 n. 14, 26, 30, 34, 40, 40 n. 40, 50–1, 51 n. 5, 52–3, 58–9, 64, 67 n. 26, 68–9, 77, 77 n. 40, 78, 78 n. 41, 90 n. 54, 91, 91 n. 56, 91 n. 57, 92, 96 n. 62, 99, 105–6, 108–9, 109 n. 4, 121–2, 143, 153–4, 156–7, 187, 187 n. 2, 188, 191–2, 218
Hawking, Stephen 48
Heath, Jeffrey 52, 65–6, 81 n. 45
Heine, Bernd 1, 5 n. 2, 6–8, 14, 20, 23, 26–7, 27 n. 27, 30–2, 34, 49–51, 55–6, 67, 67 n. 26, 70, 106, 108–11, 114, 114 n. 8, 115, 119, 125, 143, 149 n. 10, 156, 218
Hellberg, Staffan 137, 166 n. 21, 167 n. 22, 193
Hellquist, Elof 75 n. 34, 182, 220 n. 43
Heltoft, Lars 158 n. 5, 196 n. 15
Herlin, Ilona 32
Herslund, Michael 162
Heuven, Vincent van 84
Himmelmann, Nikolaus P. 12, 12 n. 8, 13, 14 n. 9, 15, 26, 112 n.6, 114
Hock, Hans Henrich 19
Hoenigswald, Henry M. 41
Hopper, Paul J. 2, 2 n.1, 6–8, 8 n. 4, 11, 14, 16–19, 24–6, 32, 36–7, 41–2, 44, 54, 54 n. 7, 55, 55 n. 8, 57–8, 61, 67, 67 n. 26, 70, 72, 72 n. 32, 78, 101, 101 n. 71, 105, 108, 112–13, 121, 124 n. 18, 133, 149, 159, 159 n. 6, 160, 178, 200
Horie, Kaoru 63, 64, 64 n. 19
Horst, Joop van der 119
Hultman, Tor G. 169 n. 24
Hummel, Martin 42–3, 43 n. 45

Idiatov, Dmitry 187 n. 4, 188 n. 5, 225–7

Jacobsen, Henrik Galberg 137
Jäger, Gerhard 93, 94, 95 n. 61
Janda, Richard D. 33, 33 n. 34, 34–5, 37–8, 49, 95 n. 61, 107, 115, 119, 119 n. 15, 119 n. 16, 133, 175–6
Jespersen, Otto 57–8, 90, 97 n. 65, 162, 166 n. 20, 175–6
Jørgensen, Peter Stray 137
Joseph, Brian D. 19, 29, 30, 33, 35–6, 46, 49, 52, 52 n. 6, 53, 61–2, 122, 133, 187 n.3

Karlsson, Keith E. 42, 42 n. 43, 44 n. 46, 45–6
Keller, Rudi 91, 91 n. 57
Kemenade, Ans van 95, 97
Kiparsky, Paul 19, 81, 209, 234
Klausenburger, Jurgen 78, 119
Klein, Henny 216
Koch, Harold 110
König, Ekkehard 32
Kotilainen, Lari 32
Krahe, Hans 80
Kranich, Svenja 21, 88, 88 n. 53, 89
Kreidler, Charles W. 175
Kristoffersen, Lars 185
Krug, Manfred G. 121
Kruisinga, Etsko 172
Kuryłowicz, Jerzy 6, 20–1, 32, 124, 156
Kuteva, Tania 1, 7, 8, 20, 23, 30–2, 67 n. 25, 70, 143, 149 n. 10
Kuzmack, Stefanie 223, 225

Lahiri, Aditi 81–2, 82 n. 49
Lakoff, George 78, 78 n. 41
Langacker, Ronald W. 18, 18 n. 15, 50, 50 n. 3, 56, 86 n. 52, 87, 101
Lass, Roger 32 n. 31, 35, 48 n. 1, 49 n. 2, 57, 57 n. 11, 62, 94, 102, 104–5, 110, 115–17, 118 n. 14, 122
Lausberg, Heinrich 43, 78–9, 79 n. 43, 79 n. 44
Lehmann, Christian 1, 3, 6, 7, 9, 11, 11 n. 5, 12, 14, 16, 20, 26, 37, 41, 50–1, 58, 61, 61 n. 18, 67, 67 n. 24, 77 n. 38, 91–2, 101, 107, 111–12, 118, 124, 124 n. 18, 125–6, 126 n. 20, 130 n. 21, 177, 218–20, 220 n. 42, 230
Levander, Lars 163 n. 15
Lightfoot, David W. 96, 96 n. 62, 99, 105
Lightfoot, Douglas J. 15, 16, 55, 112

Lim, Lisa 38, 38 n. 37
Lindström, Therese 112 n. 6
Lødrup, Helge 38
Lorenz, Gunter 44
Luraghi, Silvia 52–3, 91 n. 56, 122, 157
Lyons, John 64

Mac Congáil, Nollaig 205–6
McMillan, D. 187 n. 4
Marle, Jaap van 153, 213–14, 214 n. 35, 216
Matsumoto, Yo 199, 200
Matthews, Stephen 63, 64, 64 n. 19
Meid, Wolfgang 80
Meillet, Antoine 5, 5 n. 2, 6, 66
Mendez-Dosuna, Julian 187 n. 3
Mengden, Ferdinand von 20, 20 n. 17, 124–5
Metslang, Helle 201 n. 18, 202 n. 20
Mithun, Marianne 23
Moreno Cabrera, Juan C. 16, 104
Muysken, Pieter 185

Narrog, Heiko 118, 201
Nesse, Agnete 38
Nevis, Joel A. 202, 202 n. 20, 202 n. 22, 203, 203 n. 23, 207, 207 n. 26, 207 n. 27, 208, 208 n. 30
Newmeyer, Frederick J. 9, 29, 31, 33, 33 n. 34, 37, 51, 59, 91–2, 95, 107, 112, 119 n. 15, 122, 190
Nielsen, Konrad 207, 209
Norde, Muriel 4, 8, 8 n. 4, 12, 14, 32–3, 37, 51, 56 n. 10, 58, 64–5, 65 n. 23, 75, 75 n. 35, 76, 90, 102, 113, 118 n. 14, 161 n. 7, 162–3, 163 n. 14, 164 n. 17, 166, 166 n. 20, 167–8, 170–1, 176–7, 177 n. 28, 178 n. 29, 207, 214, 215 n. 38, 235

Ocampo, Francisco 22–3

Pagliuca, William 6 n. 3, 31, 38, 55, 68, 205
Pajusalu, Karl 201 n. 18, 202 n. 20
Perkins, Revere 6 n. 3, 31, 38, 55, 68, 205
Perridon, Harry 33, 64, 162
Pettersson, Gertrud 180 n. 32
Picard, Marc 174
Pinkster, Harm 42, 43 n. 44, 44, 78–9, 79 n. 43, 79 n. 44
Plank, Frans 59, 59 n. 14, 60 n. 17, 74, 102, 110, 166 n. 20, 172, 175, 235
Platzack, Christer 162
Pottelberge, Jeroen van 53, 103

Prokosch, E. 81 n. 45
Pullum, Geoffrey K. 157–8, 166, 170, 172

Ralli, Angela 187 n. 3
Ramat, Paolo 1, 14, 38 n. 36, 73, 76 n. 36, 80 n. a, 81, 110–13, 122
Reuse, Willem J. de 185
Ricca, Davide 154
Rietveld, Toni 84
Ringmar, Martin 163 n. 15
Roberts, Ian 78, 96–7, 97 n. 63, 98–9, 99 n. 66, 99 n. 67
Rosenbach, Anette 7, 66, 93–4, 95 n. 61, 107, 121 n. 17, 162, 176–7
Rosenkvist, Henrik 70–1, 98, 220–1, 223, 223 n. 46
Ross, Alan S.C. 214 n. 46
Rostila, Jouni 16 n. 13
Roussou, Anna 78, 96–7, 97 n. 63, 98–9, 99 n. 66, 99 n. 67

Seppänen, Aimo 165 n. 19
Smirniotopoulos, Jane C. 187 n. 3
Söderberg, Ragnhild 180
Stein, Dieter 86, 115 n. 10
Stoett, F.A. 92 n. 58
Stump, Gregory T. 153

Tabor, Whitney 21, 126, 177
Taeymans, Martine 136
Teleman, Ulf 137, 166 n. 21, 167 n. 22, 193
Tomasello, Michael 34
Tops, Guy 80, 81 n. 45, 81 n. 47
Torner, Sergi 44, 44 n. 47, 45–6
Torp, Alf 196 n. 16
Torp, Arne 37, 196 n. 16
Traugott, Elizabeth Closs 1, 2, 2 n. 1, 6, 8, 8 n. 4, 9–12, 12 n. 7, 13–19, 21, 21 n. 20, 22, 22 n. 21, 23–6, 28, 31–2, 32 n. 31, 33, 36–7, 41–2, 44, 49, 50, 54, 54 n. 7, 55, 55 n. 8, 57–8, 67, 67 n. 26, 70, 72–3, 77 n. 38, 78, 85–6, 86 n. 51, 87, 90–1, 99, 100, 105, 108, 112–13, 115, 118, 118 n. 13, 121–2, 124 n. 18, 126, 128 n. a, 149, 154, 159, 159 n. 6, 160, 177–8, 178 n. 29, 200, 218
Trosterud, Trond 38, 164 n. 16
Trousdale, Graeme 12, 16, 28, 28 n. 28, 29, 178–9
Tsangalides, Anastasios 33 n. 33

Vangsnes, Øystein Alexander 166
Velde, Freek van der 119

Venås, Kjell 37
Verhagen, Arie 86
Vincent, Nigel 50–1, 78, 103, 117
Visconti, Jacqueline 21, 86, 126
Visser, F.T. 190–1
Vogelaer, Gunther de 188, 188 n. 8, 189, 189 n. 9, 190
Voort, Hein van der 183, 183 n. 35, 184–5
Vrba, Elisabeth S. 115

Waltereit, Richard 20–1, 67 n. 26, 124
Wessén, Elias 65, 170, 179–80, 182
Willis, David 3, 51, 87, 102, 113, 115 n. 9, 117, 119, 123, 135 n. 1, 143, 143 n. 6, 144–6, 146 n. 8, 147–51
Wischer, Ilse 21–2

Yap, Foong Ha 63, 64, 64 n. 19
Ylikoski, Jussi 208 n. 28, 208 n. 29, 209, 209 n. 31

Ziegeler, Debra 60, 71, 71 n. 31, 142, 143 n. a
Zola Christensen, Robert 137
Zwicky, Arnold M. 157–8, 166, 170, 172–4

# Subject Index


abessive, degrammaticalization of 109, 186–7, 207–9, 236
ablaut 80
abruptness (of change) 16, 18, 74, 76, 95, 100
acronym 10, 112
adaptation 106, 110, 115
adjective 13, 42–5, 60–1, 74–7, 116–18, 143–4, 146, 148, 154–5, 168–9, 177, 179–81, 217–18, 223
  (zero) derivation of 14, 60, 75–6, 114, 154, 223
  inflection of 4, 16, 41, 60, 116–19, 154, 166, 177, 179–81
adposition 4, 7, 26, 52, 54, 67, 111, 125–6, 160 *see also* postposition, preposition
adverb 11, 13, 23, 57, 59, 60, 74–6, 109, 113–14, 125, 166, 178 n. 29, 186–7, 191–6, 208–9, 217–18, 223 n. 47
  (zero) derivation of 14, 41–6, 75, 154, 156, 159 n. 6
  epistemic 12, 130
  of degree 214, 217–18, 238 *see also* intensifier
adverbial 21, 24, 192–3, 222
  locative 154, 161 n. 9, 225
  temporal 24, 27–8, 88
affix *see* derivational affix, inflectional affix
Afrikaans 116 *see also* Germanic
agglutinative language 105
agglutinative marker 54, 177, 188
amalgam, syntactic 78
analogy 5, 18–20, 30, 46, 71, 138, 209, 233–4, 238
analytic phase 56–7
analytic structure 56, 204–6, 234
Andersen's levels of observation 3, 107, 123, 132–4, 233
antigrammaticalization 107–9, 134, 187–8
aphaeresis 84
apocope 84, 204, 236
Aragonese 46
article 26, 72, 74, 127, 219
  definite 13, 64–6, 73, 83–4, 116 n. 11, 144–8
  indefinite 7, 119
aspect 12, 21, 39, 62–3, 88
  inchoative, inflectional 110–11
  perfect auxiliary 81 n. 47, 86, 119, 128
  perfect, inflectional 82
  progressive auxiliary 86
  progressive, inflectional 82, 88, 153
attrition
  morphological 49, 104 *see also* decategorialization, morphologization, univerbation
  phonological 83–5, 89, 91 n. 56, 102, 104, 124–5, 127, 151, 232 *see also* erosion; reduction, phonological
  semantic 49, 104, 124 n. 18 *see also* bleaching, desemanticization
autonomy 6, 10, 12, 16, 72, 120, 124, 157, 159
auxiliary verb *see* aspect, modality, tense

back formation 10, 218
Bengali 82
*Bequemlichkeitstrieb* 90
bleaching 14, 21, 26, 30–1, 67, 89, 102, 104, 177, 214, 226 *see also* desemanticization; attrition, semantic
blending 10
body-part noun *see* noun
bondedness *see* Lehmann's parameters
bonding 47, 104 *see also* morphologization, univerbation
borrowing 38, 45–6, 155, 214 n. 35, 217, 220 n. 43 *see also* loan
bridging context *see* context
Bulgarian 77, 143–5, 229, 231 *see also* Slavonic
Buryat 36–8

case marking 21 n. 20, 40, 56, 62–3, 101, 116, 162–3, 171, 207, 209, 238
case system, demise of 65 n. 23, 144, 180, 235 *see also* deflexion
Catalan 41, 46 *see also* Romance

category
  category shift 10, 73, 76 *see also* conversion, derivation, lateral shift
  closed, *see* word class, closed
  functional 21, 91, 97 n. 63
  lexical 21, 91, 97 n. 63, 102–3
  open, *see* word class, open
Celtic 146 *see also* Irish, Welsh
chain
  degrammaticalization 8, 107, 111, 123
  grammaticalization 7, 8, 18, 21, 34, 47, 55, 59, 71, 78, 100, 109, 112, 123, 125, 132, 211
change
  composite 36, 47
  conceptualizations of 54–8
  mechanisms of 18, 19, 30–1, 67 n. 25, 94, 123, 134, 233–4
  morphological 72–83, 102, 104 *see also* decategorialization, morphologization, recategorialization, severance, univerbation; attrition, morphological
  motivating forces in 97 n. 65, 233–6
  phonological 83–8, 89, 91 n. 56, 102 *see also* attrition, phonological; reduction, phonological; strengthening, phonological / phonetic
  primitive 20 n. 17, 26, 36, 47
  reversibility of 1, 52, 58–61, 66–89, 91, 102–3, 112
  semantic 67–72, 101–4 *see also* bleaching, desemanticization, resemanticization; attrition, semantic; enrichment, semantic
Chibchan-Paezan 108
Chinese 38 n. 36, 63, 71, 142–3, 229, 231–2
  Old Chinese 142
clause combining 23–4, 26, 129, 200 *see also* clines
clines
  cline of clause combining 24–5, 54–5
  cline of grammaticality 2, 8, 32, 49, 51–2, 54–5, 59, 61, 78, 82, 103, 111–12, 118, 121, 123, 157, 159, 176–7, 187, 232
  cline of lexicality 46, 54–5, 159, 232
    clitic > inflection cline 160
  derivation > inflection cline 159–60
  discourse > zero cline 23, 55
  noun > affix cline 54–5
  PERSON > QUALITY cline 67–8
  verb > affix cline 54–5
clipping 10, 11, 223
clitic 2, 4, 5, 6 n. 3, 8, 17, 20, 32, 38–40, 45, 50, 52, 82, 103, 107–9, 118–19, 125, 127, 130–3, 152, 157–75, 177–8, 186–7, 191–2, 196, 205, 207–13, 223–4, 229–36
  degrammaticalization of 87, 99, 103, 109, 188–204
  position of 38–40, 157–8, 202–3
  simple clitic 157–8
  special clitic 157–8
  *see also* cline of grammaticality
cliticization 20–1, 38, 65, 98, 160, 190, 208
  versus inflection 152, 157–9, 166–70, 175, 187
coalescence 10, 12, 14 n. 10, 77 n. 38, 125, 128 *see also* univerbation
cohesion 124–5
complementizer 23–4, 26, 38, 63, 116 n. 11, 196
compositionality, loss of 10, 230
compounding 10, 14, 15, 44–5, 60, 77, 132, 135 n. 1, 152, 159–60, 187 n. 3, 210, 215 *see also* cline of lexicalization
condensation 125, 128
conformity 91
conjunction reduction *see* co-ordination reduction
constructional identity, preservation of 9, 232, 237 *see also* context-internal change
construction grammar 28–9, 178–9, 238
context
  context-internal change, degrammaticalization as 120, 135, 152, 186 *see also* constructional identity, preservation of
  bridging context 27–8, 218
  switch context 27
conventionalization 27, 69, 70, 115
conversion 10, 11, 43, 73, 113–14 *see also* category shift, derivation, lateral shift
co-ordination reduction 44, 191, 198–9, 207, 209
correspondence (versus change) 35–6, 46–7
cumulative exponence 153–4, 174 *see also* portmanteau morpheme

Danish 7, 136–7, 161–2, 193–4 *see also* Scandinavian, Germanic
deaffixation *see* derivational affix, degrammaticalization of; inflectional affix, degrammaticalization of
debonding 3, 8, 109 n. 4, 131–4, 186–234, 236–8
  definition of 186
  *see also* clitic, derivational affix, inflectional affix
decategorialization 14, 21, 26, 30–1, 59, 61, 72–4, 76, 89, 123–4, 127, 214 *see also* word-class, shift from major (open) to minor (closed)
decliticization *see* clitic, degrammaticalization of
deflexion 165, 207 *see also* case system, demise of
degrammaticalization *passim*
  definition of 120
  versus lexicalization 47, 110, 112–14, 120, 122, 134–5, 225
  *see also* debonding, degrammation, deinflectionalization
degrammation 3, 4, 8, 74, 132–3, 135–51, 187, 228–35, 237–8
  definition of 135
  *see also* modal auxiliary, possessive pronoun, preposition
deinflectionalization 3, 4, 8, 109 n. 4, 118, 131, 133, 152–87, 212 n. 32, 224, 228–35, 238
  definition of 152
  *see also* inflectional affix
demorphologization 133, 205, 215 *see also* severance
demotivation 12, 14 n. 10
deobligatorification 131, 141, 143, 145, 148, 150, 171, 181–2, 185, 192, 198, 201, 203, 206, 209, 213, 219, 222, 224, 227, 229, 232
deparadigmaticization 131, 141, 143, 145, 148, 150, 171, 181–2, 185, 187, 192, 198, 201, 203, 206, 209, 213, 219, 222, 224, 227, 229, 231–2, 238
derivation 10–15
  versus inflection 152–7, 159–60
  zero derivation 61, 113–14 *see also* conversion, category shift, lateral shift
derivational affix 5, 10, 12–17, 32, 40–1, 44–5, 50, 54–5, 102, 110–11, 113–14, 130–1, 152–4, 156–7, 159–60, 179–85, 230, 235
  degrammaticalization of 186–7, 213–227, 229–32, 236
  *see also* cline of lexicality
desemanticization 30, 61, 67, 89, 123–5, 127 *see also* bleaching; attrition, semantic
*Deutlichkeitstrieb* 90
discourse markers *see* pragmaticalization
divergence 21, 138, 149, 151
downgrading 91, 118 n. 14, 132
Dutch 7, 19 n. 16, 25 n. 25, 52, 77, 80–1, 83–6, 92 n. 58, 110, 113, 115, 116 n. 12, 119, 144 n. 7, 153, 155–6, 191 n. 11, 213–14, 215 n. 38, 215 n. 39, 216–20, 224, 228–30, 237–8
  Early Modern Dutch 116, 120
  Middle Dutch 92 n. 58, 120, 189
  Southern Dutch 188, 190
  *see also* Germanic

economy 56, 84, 90–1, 97 n. 65
elaboration 133
ellipsis 10
emancipation 10, 132
emergent grammar 17
English 4, 7, 9, 10, 12–14, 19, 21, 25–6, 59, 69, 72, 74, 80–1, 83–4, 86, 89, 97, 106, 109, 113–14, 116–17, 121, 126–30, 136, 154, 156–7, 159, 161–2, 165 n. 19, 166 n. 20, 166 n. 21, 172–8, 187, 190, 216–17, 219, 223–4, 229–30, 235–7
  American English 136, 175, 192, 236
  Early Modern English 88, 120
  Middle English 25, 119, 129–30, 191
  Old English 9, 10, 12–14, 19, 84, 119, 121, 127, 129–30, 156, 160–1, 175, 191
  *see also* Germanic
enrichment 234
  functional 171
  pragmatic 67
  semantic 50, 89, 101, 187, 233–4 *see also* resemanticization
epenthesis 74 n. 33, 84, 113 n. 7, 208 n. 30
erosion 30, 41, 50, 56, 84, 101 *see also* attrition, phonological; reduction, phonological

Estonian 203
Old Estonian 109, 187, 201–4, 230, 236
*see also* Finno-Ugric
euphemism 85, 106, 110, 114–15, 234 *see also* taboo
exaptation 62, 106, 110, 115–18, 181, 207, 235
extravagance 91

Faroese 193, 195 *see also* Scandinavian, Germanic
Finnic 202 n. 21, 203
Proto-Finnic
*see also* Estonian, Finnish, Finno-Ugric, Karelian
Finnish 23, 32–3, 33, 202–3, 207 *see also* Finno-Ugric
Finno-Ugric 207–8
Proto-Finno-Ugric 208
*see also* Estonian, Finnish, Finnic, Karelian, Saami
fixation 22, 125, 128
flexibilization 131, 141, 143, 145, 148, 150, 192, 198, 201, 203, 206, 209, 213, 219, 222, 224, 227, 231
fossilization 13, 40, 90 n. 55, 156 *see also* petrified expression
French 7, 8, 41, 43 n. 45, 46, 52, 58, 69, 78–9, 84, 87, 89, 110–14, 127–8, 154, 156, 159, 187 n. 4
Old French 45, 48
*see also* Romance
frequency 1, 2, 14, 16, 17, 28, 39, 49, 79, 91, 102, 121–2, 139, 234
functional linguistics 95
fusion 10–12, 14, 22, 128 n. a *see also* univerbation
fusional language *see* inflectional language
future *see* tense

gap (in paradigm) 155, 158, 168, 175 *see also* suppletion
gender 76, 116, 154, 235, 238
generative grammar 18, 29, 34–5, 93–100, 104, 196
genitive
degrammaticalization of 4, 160–179, 228–30, 234–5
morphological status of 166–70
German 9, 12, 15, 16, 19, 23, 27, 59, 60 n. 15, 60 n. 16, 70, 73–4, 92 n. 58, 110, 112–13, 115, 141, 154, 213–14, 215 n. 37, 216–17
Middle High German 15, 60, 77
Middle Low German 38, 176, 220 n. 43
Old High German 15, 60, 80
Pennsylvania German 74, 115, 138–41, 229, 231, 234
*see also* Germanic
Germanic 19, 66, 70, 77, 80–2, 117, 141, 214 n. 36
Proto-Germanic 77 n. 40, 80–1, 110, 220
*see also* Afrikaans, Danish, Dutch, English, Faroese, German, Gothic, Icelandic,Norwegian, Scandinavian, Swedish
Gothic 80–1
*see also* Germanic
gradience 16, 25, 85, 157, 160
gradualness (of change) 10, 11, 14, 16–18, 46, 54–7, 74–6, 79, 95, 100, 105, 108–9, 146, 162–3, 172
gram 6 n. 3
grammaticality *see* clines
grammaticalization
as a theory 33–5
definitions of 5–8
primary 21, 47, 56, 76, 78, 98, 125–8, 132, 237–8
secondary 20–1, 23 n. 22, 47, 55–6, 78, 82, 88–9, 98, 124–8, 131–2, 238
versus lexicalization 11–16, 46–7
grammation 132
Grimm's law 81 n. 47

hearer versus speaker strategies 56, 86, 90, 97 n. 65
hermit crab scenario 65–6, 81 n. 45
hierarchy
in Andersen's levels 233
of constructional levels 178–9
of markedness 98
of ontological entities 64
*his*-genitive 175–6
Hup 183 n. 34, 210–13, 236
hypernym 9, 113, 134, 216, 225
hypoanalysis 115 n. 10
hypotaxis 24–5, 200 *see also* cline of clause combining

Icelandic 193–4
Old Icelandic 80
*see also* Scandinavian, Germanic
inchoative *see* aspect
inferencing, pragmatic 3, 4, 7, 27, 67, 101, 135, 150–1, 234–5

infinitive
  infinitival marker, degrammaticalization of 190–199
  split infinitive 190–2, 194, 197–9, 230, 236
inflection 14, 19, 22 n. 21, 30, 39, 40, 60, 65, 74, 76, 97, 103, 105, 113, 116, 126–7, 131, 234
  externalization of 40–1
  internal inflection 65
  versus cliticization *see* cliticization
  versus derivation *see* derivation
inflectional affix 5, 8 n. 4, 12, 17, 20, 39, 40, 45, 54, 56, 59, 60, 65, 72, 75, 78–9, 82, 89, 97, 102–3, 113, 116–19, 125, 130–1, 135, 229–30, 232, 236
  degrammaticalization of 4, 38, 152–85, 204–13, 229–35, 238
  *see also* cline of grammaticality
inflectional language 105
integration 132
integrity *see* Lehmann's parameters
intensifier 217–8, 238 *see also* adverb of degree
Inuit 185
invisible-hand framework 91, 99
Irish 5, 20, 109, 119 n. 16, 187, 204–7, 228, 231, 234, 236
  Early Modern Irish 5, 204–5, 236
  Middle Irish 204–5, 236
  Old Irish 204
  *see also* Celtic
isolating language 38, 57 n. 12, 105, 143, 183 n. 33, 232, 238
Italian 41, 44 n. 46, 45–6, 58, 78–9, 86, 92 n. 58, 109, 111, 128, 154, 157, 187, 216 *see also* Romance

Japanese 63–4, 87, 109, 118, 187, 199–201, 229, 231, 233, 236
  Old Japanese 200
Jespersen's cycle *see* negation

Kala Lagau Ya 62
Karelian 202 *see also* Finno-Ugric
Kwaza 183–5, 228, 230, 232, 235

language acquisition 18, 30 n. 30, 38, 93, 95, 97, 99, 100
lateral shift 54, 61–2, 73, 76, 104, 108, 118, 134 *see also* category shift, conversion, derivation
Latin 8, 13, 16, 36, 38, 40–4, 46, 58, 78–9, 84, 86 n. 51, 109–10, 112, 127–8, 154, 158, 187
  Vulgar Latin 78
  *see also* Romance
layering 7, 21, 29, 178 n. 29
Lehmann's parameters
  general 3, 13, 20 n. 17, 23, 102, 107, 123–8, 130–1, 134, 183, 228–31
  parameter of bondedness 124–6, 128, 131, 230
  parameter of integrity 124, 127, 130–1, 228
  parameter of paradigmaticity 125, 127, 131, 229
  parameter of paradigmatic variability 125, 127, 131, 229
  parameter of structural scope 23, 26 n. 26, 51, 84, 125–8, 131, 230
  parameter of syntagmatic variability 125–6, 128, 131–2, 186, 231
levelling 19
lexicality *see* clines
lexicalization 9–17, 22 n. 21, 46, 92, 102, 107, 110, 112–14, 122, 134–5, 225, 230
  as fusion 10, 14, 22 n. 21
  as separation 10
  as word formation 10, 14
  definitions of 11
  directionality of 112
  of function words and affixes 11, 74, 92, 102, 112–14, 120, 122, 134–5, 225
  versus degrammaticalization *see* degrammaticalization
  versus grammaticalization *see* grammaticalization
loan 10, 46, 75 n. 43 *see also* borrowing

Malay 63–4
mechanisms of change *see* change
metalinguistic citation 10, 92, 186 n. 1, 233
metaphor 14 n. 10, 30, 63, 67–9, 87, 93, 94 n. 60, 101, 104, 234
  SPACE >TIME metaphor 63, 68–70, 93, 94 n. 60, 104
metonymy 14 n. 10, 30, 42, 67 n. 24, 67 n. 26, 69, 71, 150
modal auxiliary *see* modality
modality
  causational 184, 230
  deontic 129

modality (*cont.*)
epistemic 73, 85, 129
modal auxiliary, degrammaticalization of 74–5, 88, 115, 136–43, 229, 231, 234
mood 39, 40, 97, 116, 139, 183, 185
morphologization 14, 21, 26, 38–9, 78, 80–3, 98, 102, 159–60, 214 *see also* bonding, univerbation
motivating forces in change *see* change

negation 38, 57–8, 192, 195
Neogrammarians 51, 53, 104 n. 72
nominalization 11 n. 6, 61, 112–13, 143–8, 154, 179–81, 235
Norwegian 20, 37–8, 40, 99, 127, 161, 192–3, 195, 198, 199 n. 17, 208, 230, 236
Bokmål Norwegian 161, 193, 196 n. 16, 199 n. 17
Dano-Norwegian 196 n. 16
Early Modern Norwegian 195–7
Nynorsk Norwegian 161 n. 7, 161 n. 8, 193
*see also* Scandinavian, Germanic
noun 7, 9, 13, 15, 16, 18, 31–2, 36, 39, 41, 52, 54–5, 59–61, 64, 72, 75–6, 92 n. 58, 108, 114, 125, 127, 154, 223, 238
body-part noun 7, 30, 52, 114, 125, 220
(zero) derivation of *see* nominalization
inflection of 64–5, 135, 171
novelty 104, 107, 117, 120–1
number 36, 39, 127, 147, 154–5, 177 n. 28, 181–3

objectification 88–9
obligatorification 22, 118 n. 14, 125, 127
obsolescent morphology 56 n. 10, 66, 103, 117, 188, 207
Old Russian 119
Optimality Theory 54 n. 90

paradigmaticity *see* Lehmann's parameters
paradigmaticization 125–7
paradigmatic variability *see* Lehmann's parameters
paragoge 84
parameters (in the Chomskyan sense) 96–7, 99 n. 67, 100
parameters of grammaticalization *see* Lehmann's parameters
parataxis 24–5, 200 *see also* cline of clause combining
parenthetical 22
participle
past 75, 86 n. 51, 140
present 32, 126, 154, 178 n. 29
particle
conditional 119
connective 86
connective, degrammaticalization of 87, 199–201, 229, 231, 233, 236
emphatic 33
emphatic, degrammaticalization of 109, 187, 201–4, 230, 236
interrogative, degrammaticalization of 109, 187, 201–4, 230, 236
verbal 74, 167
passive marker 20, 32, 127, 160
perfect *see* aspect
periphrastic expression 17, 56–7, 79, 101, 103
person 36, 39, 40, 72, 82, 147, 155, 183, 190, 204
petrified expression 116, 168 *see also* fossilization
phonogenesis 134
phonological change *see* change
polysemy 177
polysynthetic language 183, 210, 213, 238
portmanteau morpheme 39 n. 39, 154 *see also* cumulative exponence
Portuguese 41, 45, 79 n. 44 *see also* Romance
possessive pronoun *see* pronoun
postposition 108–9, 123, 186–7, 207–9
pragmaticalization 21–3, 47, 200
predicate, composite 12
preposition 13, 16, 18, 21, 32, 50, 56, 58, 68–70, 72, 78, 87, 97 n. 63, 103, 112, 123, 125–6, 146–7, 167, 172, 175, 177, 186, 191, 208–9, 230
degrammaticalization of 148–51
preterite *see* tense
priming 93–4, 104, 238
process (versus result) 29–33
progressive *see* aspect
pronoun
demonstrative 13, 23, 25, 64, 66
emphatic 40
indefinite 7, 9, 77, 127
indefinite, degrammaticalization of 143–5
personal 5, 20, 38–9, 84–5, 92, 109, 113, 119, 166 n. 21, 187–90, 204–5, 234, 236

possessive, degrammaticalization of 145–8
reflexive 20, 32, 160
resumptive possessive 37–8
prothesis 84

quantifier 213–19
quotative 183–4, 235–6
Quechua 185

reanalysis 8, 18–20, 29, 30, 46, 64, 78, 97–9, 102, 107, 119, 132, 135, 144, 151, 165, 186 n. 1, 203, 205, 218, 226, 233–4, 236
recategorialization 60 n. 17, 61, 74–6, 89, 123, 131, 141, 143, 145, 148, 150, 171, 181–2, 185, 192, 198, 201, 203, 206, 209, 213, 219, 222, 224, 227–8, 231–2, 234 *see also* word-class, shift from minor (closed) to major (open)
reconstruction 34–40, 47, 49–52, 78, 106, 183 n. 34, 219, 220 n. 42
reduction, phonological 4, 14, 21, 26, 31–2, 47, 77–8, 81, 84–5, 123, 125, 128, 151, 191, 197, 210, 214 *see also* attrition, phonological; erosion
regrammaticalization 107–8, 115 n. 10, 134
regrammation 132
reinforcement 55, 57–8
replacement 110, 118, 120, 134, 188, 190, 222
resemanticization 61, 123, 130, 133, 141, 143, 145, 148, 150, 171, 181–2, 185, 192, 198, 201, 203, 206, 209, 213, 219, 222, 224, 227–8, 231–2 *see also* enrichment, semantic
retraction 9, 121, 136, 188, 190–2
reversal, mirror-image 59, 103, 110–12, 123
reversibility *see* change, reversibility of
Romance 13, 36, 41–6, 56, 66, 78–9, 98, 110, 158 n. 4 *see also* Aragonese, Catalan, French, Italian, Latin, Portuguese, Romanian, Spanish
Romanian 41, 45, 79 n. 44 *see also* Romance

Saami 207 n. 27, 208
Northern Saami 109, 123, 186–7, 188 n. 6, 207–9, 229, 234, 236
Proto-Saami 208
*see also* Finno-Ugric
Scandinavian 20, 64, 160, 176–7, 193, 195
Continental Scandinavian *see* Mainland Scandinavian
Mainland Scandinavian 4, 32, 40, 58, 109, 161 n. 7, 162, 177, 187, 235
Old Norse 32, 40, 77, 127–8, 160, 195–7
Proto-Norse *see* Proto-Scandinavian
Proto-Scandinavian 32, 65, 128, 160, 182
*see also* Danish, Faroese, Icelandic, Norwegian, Swedish
scope, parameter of *see* Lehmann's parameters
scope expansion 126, 130–1, 141, 143, 145, 148, 150, 171, 181–2, 185, 192, 198, 201, 203, 206, 209, 213, 219, 222, 224, 227, 230, 232
semantic change *see* change
severance 131, 134, 171, 181–2, 185, 192, 198, 201, 203, 206, 209, 213, 219, 222, 224, 227, 230–2 *see also* demorphologization
s-genitive *see* genitive
Slavonic 119
Old Church Slavonic 77, 143–4
*see also* Bulgarian, Old Russian
sound change *see* change
Spanish 16, 38–9, 41, 43–6, 119 n. 15, 159
New Mexican Spanish 119
Old Spanish 38, 41
*see also* Romance
speaker strategies *see* hearer versus speaker strategies
spelling pronunciation 84–5
split infinitive *see* infinitive
standardization 32
strengthening, phonological / phonetic 84–5, 123, 130, 141, 143, 145, 148, 150, 171, 181–2, 185, 191–2, 198, 201, 203, 206, 209, 213, 219, 222, 224, 227–8, 233
subjectification 14, 22, 85–9
subordination 24–5 *see also* cline of clause combining
suppletion 116, 155, 168, 206 *see also* gap (in paradigm)
Swedish 4, 12, 32–3, 64, 70–1, 75–6, 92 n. 58, 98, 110, 113, 136–8, 154, 160–6, 168–71, 175–7, 178 n. 29, 179–82, 193, 217, 220, 223, 228, 234
Early Modern Swedish 65, 71, 161 n. 10, 164, 180
Middle Swedish 161 n. 10, 163, 179

Swedish (*cont.*)
Old Swedish 4, 56 n. 10, 65, 70–1, 138, 161–3, 165, 166, 168, 171, 179, 181–2, 228, 230, 235
Runic Swedish 161 n. 10, 163 n. 14
Älvdalen dialect 163 n. 15
Lappträsk dialect 166
Piteå dialect 220–2, 229–30, 237
*see also* Scandinavian, Germanic
switch context *see* context
syncope 84
syntagmatic variability *see* Lehmann's parameters
synthetic phase 56–7
synthetic structure 56, 79 n. 42, 127, 139, 204–6
*Systemstörung* 102, 235–6

taboo 114, 220 *see also* euphemism
tense 21, 39, 40, 62–3, 82, 88, 113, 155
future auxiliary 7, 17, 22 n. 21, 29, 56, 67–8, 79 n. 44, 87, 89, 127
future, Romance inflectional 8, 56, 78–9, 89, 98, 112, 127
preterite, Germanic weak inflectional 59, 66, 80–2
transcategorization 73
Tura 225–7, 229, 237

unidirectionality
explanations of 90–105
hypothesis of 2, 49–51
principle of 2, 49, 51–3
uniformitarianism 94, 104–5
univerbation *see also* coalescence, fusion, morphologization 10, 12, 13, 22 n. 21, 77–8, 83, 89, 125, 128
universal grammar 34, 99
upgrading 9, 51, 92, 107, 110, 132

variability 124–5
verb 4, 7, 8, 12, 16–19, 29, 36, 38–40, 54–5, 59–62, 64, 71, 73, 79–81, 86–8, 97–8, 121, 126–7, 129–30, 135–43, 148–51, 155, 160, 167–8, 191, 193–7, 204–7, 210–13, 219, 220–3, 225–7
*see also* aspect, modality, mood, tense
(zero) derivation of 11, 61, 74, 76, 82, 112–15

Wackernagel position *see* clitic, position of
weight 124–5
Welsh 3, 20, 87, 145–8, 150, 229–31
Middle Welsh 146–9, 230
*see also* Celtic
word-class 113, 154, 175
closed 73, 103, 126, 131, 188 *see also* word-class, minor
major 9, 74, 114, 131, 135, 234–5 *see also* word-class, open
minor 74, 235 *see also* word-class, closed
open 126 *see also* word-class, major
shift from major (open) to minor (closed) 73–4, 124 n. 18, 125, 127 *see also* decategorialization
shift from minor (closed) to major (open) 74, 131, 141, 143, 145, 148, 150, 192, 198, 201, 203, 209, 213, 224, 228–9, 231 *see also* recategorialization
word formation 10–12, 14, 15, 112, 135 n. 1, 153 *see also* lexicalization
word order 39, 86, 100 n. 70, 144, 163, 188–90, 195
OV 25, 81, 200
VO 25
verb-second (V2) 97

zero derivation *see* derivation
Z-suffix 173–5

Lightning Source UK Ltd.
Milton Keynes UK
11 August 2010

158210UK00003B/3/P



9 780199 207930